REX V.
EDITH
THOMPSON

Laura Thompson is the award-winning author of *Agatha Christie: An English Mystery, Life in a Cold Climate: A Biography of Nancy Mitford, A Different Class of Murder: The Story of Lord Lucan* and *Take Six Girls: The Lives of the Mitford Sisters.*

REX V.
EDITH
THOMPSON

A TALE OF TWO MURDERS

LAURA THOMPSON

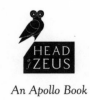

HEAD
&ZEUS

An Apollo Book

This is an Apollo book, first published in the UK in 2018 by Head of Zeus Ltd

Lines from *The Waste Land* by T. S. Eliot (© The Estate of T. S. Eliot)
reproduced with kind permission of Faber and Faber Ltd

9 7 5 3 1 2 4 6 8

A catalogue record for this book is available from the British Library.

ISBN (HB): 9781784082444
ISBN (E): 9781784976095

Printed and bound by CPI Group (UK) Ltd, Croydon, CR0 4YY

Head of Zeus Ltd
First Floor East
5–8 Hardwick Street
London EC1R 4RG
WWW.HEADOFZEUS.COM

Contents

' "Whoever invented love ought to be shot." '

As spoken in *Love in a Cold Climate* by Nancy Mitford

BEFORE

'Please don't let me fall.'

The last words of Mary Surratt, hanged in 1865

THERE WAS A double hanging at Holloway jail on the morning of 3 February 1903. As Edith Graydon was skip-hop-skipping her way to school, travelling without foreknowledge through the neat, self-respecting, know-your-place streets of suburban east London, two women were waiting in their death cells to experience the last seconds of life. They had conspired together in their crimes, and they died side by side, in the same jolting moments of the morning. These were the first of the five hangings that would take place at Holloway, which had become an exclusively female prison in 1902.

Some murderers permit empathy, but Annie Walters and Amelia Sach do not: they were baby farmers, taking in unwanted children (of whom there were many) for an 'adoption fee', then disposing of them with chlorodyne. Such crimes were impossible to forgive. Despite the usual mitigating circumstance of poverty there was never any chance of a reprieve for Walters and Sach.

Anyway there was only muted opposition to the death penalty in 1903. Abolitionists had been making their case since the 1830s, but they did not really hit their stride until the 1920s, and even then the authorities remained adamantine. As Sir John Anderson, Permanent Under-Secretary of State in the Home Department, said in 1923 to the prison reformer, Margery Fry, those who opposed the death penalty were all too often 'sentimentalists'.

So the public face of authority was obdurate, even as the stirrings of national queasiness were beginning to be felt (these came in waves, and were not felt by everybody). Throughout the eighteenth and early nineteenth centuries, hangings had been the rampageous stuff of fatalistic folklore, part of the terrible theatre of daily life. From 1868 they took place in private, and perversely this made their reality less tenable. One knew where one was, at least, with the condemned who drank their nerves down on the ride from Newgate to Tyburn, and made bravura speeches to the open skies. The spectacle was appalling, but it was honest. Behind closed doors everything was contained within brick and stone, institutional buff and grey. It was measured and mechanistic, catalogued in paperwork by civil servants who blotted their words with passionless care. But it was still what it was. The form signed by the sheriff, the under sheriff, the prison governor, to the effect that they had witnessed the event – how stately it looked, with its black flourishes and curlicues – but the question remained: what *had* they witnessed? The inquest upon the executed person, conducted almost immediately and with such conscientiousness, with evidence and a jury, as if enclosing the event within the jaws of legal righteousness – but still the words had to be written, in crabbed fountain pen, that the said person 'died from fractured dislocation of the cervical vertebrae'.

The bureaucracy was absolute, however; it could not be faulted or gainsaid. 'Gentlemen, As directed in Standing Order no.459, I have the honour to submit the annexed Record of the execution of the above-named Prisoner': so ran the printed words on a form sent to the Home Office from the prison governor. When opened out, the form requested 'Particulars of the Execution'. Rather like an examination paper in human biology, it asked for an 'Approximate statement of the character and amount of destruction to the soft and bony structures of the neck.' A typical reply recorded 'Bruising of neck from rope. Fracture of odontoid process and right half of arch of Axis.' Then came a request for 'The length of the drop as determined before the execution,' and a subsequent request for 'The length of the drop, as measured after the execution, from the level of the floor of the scaffold to the heels of the suspended culprit.' The answers to these two questions differed by a neatly inked two or three inches, nothing more.

There was also a Memorandum of Instructions for carrying out an Execution, drawn up in 1891 and amended three times, in reaction to events that did not quite go to plan. Again the attention to detail was irreproachable. The 'apparatus', meaning the drop, had to be tested a week before the hanging, first without any weight attached, then with a sandbag. 'As the gutta percha [rubber] round the noose end of the execution rope hardens in cold weather,' the memorandum continued, for all the world as if advising on the best outcome for a recipe, 'care should be taken to have it warmed and manipulated immediately before the bag is tested.' On the day before the hanging the apparatus was tested again, and the sandbag left in place overnight to 'take the stretch out of the rope'. Then the execution shed, with its makeshift aspect and its array of basic tools, was locked. The key was kept by the prison governor.

As with the appointment of hangmen who knew their job, and killed with the intention to inflict a minimum of extraneous suffering – men such as the Pierrepoints, whose family trade this was – so every trouble was taken to make judicial execution a series of coolly predictable processes. Some of these could not help but be dramatic – the piece of black cloth floating on the judge's wig; the chaplain reciting 'I am the Resurrection and the life' on the way to the scaffold – but the rolling gravitas of ritual was, after all, what the supreme penalty required. And these rituals had God on their side, albeit a Low Church kind of God. What was going on was functional, formulaic, a regrettable necessity. Death for those found guilty of a capital crime was 'the due course of the law': a phrase so deliberately impersonal as to imply that 'the law' had its own independent volition, and was not something created by mere people.

★

More accurately it was created by men. 'Gentlemen...' Not until 1919 did a sole female legislator enter the House of Commons, and in 1922 two women were called to the English Bar – 'I confess that at first I viewed the new step with alarm,' the distinguished barrister Travers Humphreys (born 1867) would later write. He came round eventually, although he worried that women spoke too quietly in court, and wished that they would stay away from criminal law: 'There must be so much that is repulsive to a young woman in criminal practice.'

Women, with their soft voices and soft bodies, were not equal with men at this time. They were so far from being equal that they could not even vote until 1918, and then only if they were aged thirty or more. Yet they were equal in this regard: they could be hanged.

At the very end of 1922 – a time when the question of female execution was dominant in the news, and becoming almost dangerously emotive – a document was drawn up by a senior Home Office civil servant, Sir Ernley Blackwell, and sent to Sir John Anderson. Its intention, as usual with this issue, was to codify and calm. It listed the women who had been convicted of murder in England and Wales since 1890, excluding infanticide (the specific crime of a woman killing her baby within a year of birth had recently ceased to be a capital offence: there was a dim understanding of the wretchedness that might lie behind it). Twenty-three names were typed on the document, together with a brief description of what they had done, and whether or not they had been executed for it.

Nine of the women had been hanged. Six of these had murdered other people's children, a seventh was a sadistic mother. Condemnation was therefore an easy business. Of the remaining two, Mary Ann Ansell had poisoned her mentally incapacitated sister for £11 in life insurance – unarguably cruel again – while Emily Swann was executed, alongside her lover in another double hanging, for the murder of her husband.

Therefore fourteen women were 'respited', as the legal term had it. One was deemed insane and another, aged seventy-two, had dementia. Two were reprieved on grounds of drunkenness. Mercy was recommended and given to one who cut the throat of her husband's lover; this was a crime of passion, which implied lack of premeditation. The same reasoning was applied to two women who knifed their common-law husbands. And two child-killers were reprieved, thanks to a twist of circumstance that surely struck even the sober men of law: they were pregnant.

So might a kind of logic be discerned? The authorities executed women who had become 'unwomanly'; who had behaved in a manner

so unnatural that it rendered them equal indeed with men, and obliterated any special privilege of gender. Throughout this thirty-two-year
period a total of 457 men were hanged in England and Wales (plus
sixteen in Scotland), which shows the rarity of the female murderer,
and the straightforward shock value accruing to crimes that subverted
the feminine ideal. With Mary Ann Ansell the home secretary actually
spelled this out, saying that the law must take its course because 'sex
alone should make no difference in such a case'.

Nevertheless there were inconsistencies. Two servants who suffo-
cated an old woman in the course of a robbery were reprieved in 1902.
As for Fanny Gilligan, another woman who murdered her lover – was
it passion or premeditation that caused her to coat the man in paraffin
and set him alight? Yet she received the benefit of legal doubt. The home
secretary respited her in 1911, 'with particular regard to her sex'. Perhaps
this was to do with the god-awful hopelessness of some of these women,
the low class of life that they inhabited; as with those who murdered
when drunk, reprieve became a function of patronage (foolish creatures,
they know no better). If, however, the woman was thought to have displayed agency, rather than passivity, it usually went badly for her.

Given this, however: was it an easy thing to judge? Particularly in
the cases of dual enterprise, in which women were accused alongside a
man and the challenge was how to apportion blame. To take a familiar example: who is more culpable, Macbeth or his wife? Are they
in fact equally guilty, under what would become the legal doctrine
of Common Purpose? Possibly, but here is a slightly different question: what would a court have decided, had it tried them both for the
murder of Duncan? The evidence of joint action was slim. A verdict
would almost certainly have come down to demeanour – what the
courtroom made of them – whether Lady Macbeth looked more like
her husband's dominatrix or his victim. In the real world of 1910, Ethel
le Neve was acquitted of being an accessory to the murder of Cora
Crippen, although she had fled the country along with Cora's husband
and worn the dead woman's jewels. Dr Crippen took all the blame,
and it may be rightly so, but Le Neve's appearance – pale, doe-eyed, as

if in need of smelling salts – would have assuredly helped her evade a charge of full conspiracy.

In two other cases of dual enterprise – in 1900 and 1918 – the woman was regarded as the more guilty party. One was hanged, the other saved only by pregnancy. Significantly these were child-murders. Otherwise it was all rather wayward, but then the law is never quite as consistent as it likes to claim; and what truly goes on between two people, high on amorousness and excitation, is well-nigh impossible to know. In 1903 Emily Swann was tried for murder after her lover, John Gallagher, killed her husband with a poker. Swann was considered equally guilty. She had been present at the murder and was said to have shouted encouragement. As the judge put it: 'one does not commit murder only with one's hands. If one person instigates another to commit murder, and that other person does it, the instigator is also guilty of murder.'

This was the law. 'It was,' wrote Sir Ernley Blackwell, 'laid down by Serjeant Foster in his "Crown Cases" as long ago as 1776.' Yet Mary Stone – also convicted in 1903 – was respited after the murder of her lover's wife. There was deemed to be doubt as to her share in the crime, but the same could have been said of Swann. What may have counted most strongly against Emily Swann was her age: she was some twelve years older than Gallagher, and therefore assumed to be the domi-nant partner. Conversely – and contentiously – in September 1922 the young Elsie Yeldham had lured an ex-boyfriend to a remote place in Epping Forest, where her husband-to-be killed and robbed him. This sounded very much like malice aforethought; but, as Blackwell commented, 'the judge thought the woman acted under influence of the man'. This could only have been an opinion, as the trial was a shambles. Mrs Yeldham's reprieve was not quite the Scottish verdict of 'not proven'; she had, after all, been convicted. It was more like 'not quite proven enough for the state to hang you for it'.

This, at any rate, was the best guess of Mrs Yeldham's judge, Mr Justice Shearman. The home secretary, Edward Shortt, a lawyer himself and a man of some compassion, concurred with the legal opinion. 'On this and in view of her sex, it was decided to commute.'

★

It was the state that hanged the criminal, that smooth bureaucratic entity with its painstaking observances, its measuring tape wielded against the rope. The job of the state was to preserve the moral workings of society, and this meant judicial hanging.

The trouble was that it was not the state, in the end, that did the deed. Dry and calm as the workings of the execution were supposed to be, there was nonetheless the physicality of it… One person had to take hold of another, handle them, march them, look them in the eye. These were the moments when the grip of the law became slippery and parlous. The coroner would ask at the inquest if the sentence of death had been properly carried out: 'Was there any hitch at all?' The answer would come: 'None of any kind. Death was instantaneous and there was no delay in carrying out the execution.' The grip was resumed, all was well again. And yet. There was still the implicit sense of what lay within those words. And when the executed person was a woman, soft of voice and body, the giver of life and the fireside consoler of men – men who now had to steady her, urge her to her feet, feel her resistance, feel the flesh of her arm still warm and working, touch her in a way that would then have implied erotic intent…

The law knew, perfectly well, that there was no problem about any of this. By stripping the convicted woman of her forename and title she was rendered almost sexless. She was her crime, and the hangman understood as much. Henry Pierrepoint wrote comfortably of Walters and Sach that they were 'baby farmers of the worst kind and they were both repulsive in type. One was two pounds less than the other and there was a difference of two inches in the drop which we allowed. One (Sachs) had a long thin neck and the other (Walters) a short neck, points which I was bound to observe in the arrangement of the rope.' So, a job well done.

The document sent to Sir John Anderson in 1922 was intended, although it did not say so, to justify the execution of women, to bolster official courage. That is probably why the list began in

1890 rather than the more obvious 1900: the total was thus almost doubled, from five women to nine. The comments – 'Gilligan might have been exed & very nearly was!' – were also designed to show the essential firmness of the law. At the same time the number of reprieves was increasing steadily. The final phase of the death penalty can be said to fall between the last public execution in 1868 and the last executions of all: in 1955 for a woman and in 1964 for men. During that period the reprieve rate for women rose from roughly 25 per cent to 90 per cent, about twice that of men. Until the Homicide Act of 1957 narrowed the definition of what constituted a capital crime, every person convicted of murder had to be given a death sentence, even though reasons not to carry these out – such as diminished responsibility – were becoming more common. In early twentieth-century crime fiction the implication is that almost any killer will be hanged – therein lies much of the moral force of Golden Age detective novels – but in truth this was not the case, especially with regard to women. In late 1922, when the Home Office list was being typed up, two prisoners were under sentence of death at the jail – one of whom, Daisy Wright, had thrown her daughter off Tower Bridge – but at that point no woman had been executed for more than fifteen years. Indeed it looked quite likely that Rhoda Willis, condemned for baby farming in 1907, would become the last to be hanged.

Without admitting as much, the authorities had allowed loopholes to replace nooses. They feared 'sentimental' public reaction – there had even been a petition to save Willis – and then there was this other aspect, the illogical sense that it was somehow worse to hang a woman than a man.

Because it *was* illogical, and because it did implicitly dictate policy, at the same time it had to be explicitly fought. Therefore accompanying the typed list of twenty-three names, the executed and the respited, was a long memorandum. It argued that the second woman under sentence of death at Holloway should be hanged.

The only possible argument that could be urged for the reprieve of this woman may be summed up in the expression 'We don't hang women nowadays'. This is an entirely fallacious idea which is due to the fact that for fifteen years there has only been one case in which the execution of a woman was or could have been seriously considered. That was the case of Fanny Gilligan...

As regards the execution of women generally, the trend of recent legislation has been all in favour of equality between the sexes... On general and constitutional grounds I doubt myself whether it is open to the home secretary to advise the King to respite the capital sentence in the case of a woman merely on the ground of her sex. In this case it would be absolutely impossible, to my mind, to give any other grounds.

If the capital sentence in the case of women is to be abolished, this must be by legislation and not by the exercise of the Prerogative of mercy.

★

As much emotion as possible had been sucked from the death penalty. As much dignity as the system deemed appropriate was accorded to the prisoner. In turn it was hoped that the prisoner would behave with dignity: that the most difficult process of all would pass off without undue distress to those concerned. Everything was supposed to be upright and steely and signed off with a handshake.

Albert Pierrepoint, who executed more than 400 people, believed that a woman was as capable of that forbearance as a man. The only person whom he described kicking up rough was a German spy, who fought like a bear with those who sought to put him to death. 'It was unfortunate. He was not an Englishman.' By contrast Pierrepoint recalled 'young lads and girls, working men, grandmothers. I have been amazed to see the courage with which they take that walk into the unknown.'

In fact at least one other man behaved inappropriately at the last: Patrick Mahon, hanged in 1924, tried to jump off the trapdoor before it opened. Nevertheless, if what we are told is true, a surprising number of the condemned did conduct themselves with ramrod restraint at the end. Pride, straightforward will, disdain for the only-obeying-orders performances of those around them, may have got them through. Or they may have felt that there was no point in giving way. Easier for them if they held on. Easier for everybody. Indeed there is a sense, in reports of these stiff, stalwart, spirit-swallowing endings, of the condemned prisoner behaving well out of a kind of terrible courtesy. It is an echo of the aristocratic pardon given to the axeman, and it is consoling, even to us, who no longer have to bear the collective guilt of a death penalty enacted in our name. Easier, even for us, to read of Ruth Ellis – the last woman to be hanged – smiling at Pierrepoint on the gallows.

'You might make it a double, old boy,' is said to have been the last request of Neville Heath, a sex-murderer who nonetheless knew how to behave. This was the gallant way, the gentlemanly way, which incidentally might also be assumed by women. Emily Swann relied on brandy to pull herself together before she joined her lover on the drop at Armley jail. 'Good morning, John,' she said, civilly, as she approached him. 'Good morning, love,' was the reply.

Eleven months earlier, at the double hanging at Holloway, Annie Walters is reported to have spoken with a similar bravura: 'Goodbye Sach,' she called, as one waving a friend on to an omnibus. Walters, a woman in her fifties, left her life stoically. Or so we are told; at any rate her behaviour was contrasted with that of the other prisoner, some twenty years her junior, who was not brave. She may have intended to be, but Amelia Sach was unable to control her emotions. The reality of death hit her differently from Walters: it hit her completely.

And why the hell should I make it easy for them, Sach may have thought; although more likely she thought nothing at all, she simply felt. Which meant inhabiting a state of mind so impossible that the only way out was oblivion. The end too terrible to assimilate was, at least, the end to the suffering that it bred.

By 9.01am, or so the innocent living would have been told, it was all over. Skip-hop-skip, went Edith Graydon on her way to school.

★

Sixty-eight years later, after Holloway was rebuilt and its graves disinterred for reburial, she would share a burial plot with Annie Walters and Amelia Sach. At the bottom of the typed Home Office list of names, hers was added in public school script: the tenth woman to be executed since 1890. In adulthood she thought often about destiny, and not always with optimism. Nevertheless the nature of her own hovered in a sphere beyond her imagining.

She had lived in a state of conflict about how far she could create her own future. This is true of many people, but it was peculiarly marked in her. She did it in the most banal of ways, scattering shillings on bets ('even in horse racing the fates are against me') and, at the start of 1922, musing 'What will the New Year give', as if the year were an impersonal force (like the law). She did that thing known as tempting fate, as for instance when she pranced about in widows' mourning hats at her place of work – a milliners' warehouse – where nobody else 'had the pluck… they all say it is unlucky – so because of it being unlucky to them I thought it might be lucky to me and tried them all on. I think they all think terrible things are going to happen to me now… I wonder who will be right, they or I?'

Sometimes she sensed that 'they' *would* be right, that fate was indeed against her. 'That hand of fate is always held up at me blocking out the future,' she wrote in a letter of May 1922. A week or so later, she quoted a sentence from the Koran that she had found in a novel: '"The fate of every man have we bound about his neck."' This struck her, forcefully, and she asked her correspondent if he believed it to be true. 'I darent think…' she wrote, as if in trepidation, like a child half-relishing a distant lurid thrill.

As it happened the quotation *was* true: literally true. She, of course, had not thought of it in that way. She had been merely playing with the idea. Seven months later, seven yards from the apparatus that was her fate, she would write another letter in which she recalled the phrase that she had encountered from a place of safety: 'Somewhere I read "The fate of every man hath he bound about his neck", and this, I suppose, I must accept as mine.' Like the Hamlet of Act V, she had become, perforce, submissive to destiny. Her words on the page were slow and heavy: 'what is to be will be'.

She had time, then, for thinking. She may have remembered her restless fear that fate might hedge her in, that she could be stopped at any turn by predestination – in her case, by the twin forces of class and gender. Yet it is never quite that simple, as she may also have recognized. There was the more shadowy fate spinning blindly in the dark, the one that lay within her nature. The concept of a 'nature' is as fraught as that of destiny. Again there is the question of how far it can be overridden: whether or not it is immutable. All one can say is that outward circumstances were not the whole story here. Because of how she was – and because she had the genetic blessings of a bright brain and a powerful allure, surely not given to her for nothing? – she had sought to direct their traffic.

She was one of those people who seek to make their own destiny. This is rarer than one might think. Passivity is more common – that hopeless smiling shrug of 'what can you do?' – and especially for a woman born into the lower-middle class. Acceptance, called contentment, would have been expected of her. It was the attitude of her mother and her aunts, lively women but born into a world of fewer opportunities, and without her vital inner sense that the world might just be theirs to conquer. She knew the dangers of striking out, but she didn't really heed them. She ploughed on through her world of hope. She considered the power of fate – the fact that it might overwhelm her, a working London girl as she was, circumscribed by train carriages and the marriage tie – but at the same time she did something that thumbed a nose to it.

She wrote her story. This was the defining act of her life. She wrote it in thousands of words' worth of correspondence. Almost all of this was sent to her lover Frederick Bywaters, who spent most of the sixteen months of their affair away from her, on the ships where he worked as a clerk or steward. These were remarkable love letters, of the most intense and beautiful and individual kind. On the face of it, the affair itself was her autonomous act, and her intention in writing was simply to bring Bywaters close, to 'talk' to him. But romantic love is always a solipsistic business: that is its paradox. With Edith – whose emotions flowered in periods of separation – the letters were *for* Bywaters and *about* something more. Her talking, as she put it, was a conduit for self-expression, in which she discovered and uncovered herself with moment-by-moment candour, and created an alternative life more real than reality. The words of her letters are what remain of her, and in them she still seems breathtakingly alive. They were – are – the evidence of her desire for self-determination. Later they became evidence, pure and simple. 'They played a great part in hanging her,' wrote the detective who charged her with murder.

To make a life in one's head is regarded, by those who do not do it, as somehow inferior to dealing with life as it is. It is seen as the act of a fantasist, somebody who dreams their life away and fails to live it.

The irony, then, is that these letters – with their loose, sensual, imaginative conjuring of alternative lives – should have been taken so literally: to the point where they became the most stern and unyielding reality. But to her they always *were* real, in the way that a book was real. 'We live and die in the books we read...' To her a life inside the head was not inferior; she knew that to dream as she did is a creative act. The problem comes with the need for expression, the desire to offer one's dreams to another person, because one is almost bound to be misinterpreted. For the reader has autonomy also.

Yet what truly signified, rather than the letters themselves, was the nature that wanted – needed – to write them. She assumed that they would be destroyed, after all – the idea that their contents would be read almost a century later would have confounded her. It would also surely have pleased her, that finality had not been final; nevertheless the letters were not written for posterity. They were the waste product, as well as the life's work, of a nature too big for its circumstances ('mine is a real live cage...'). In a world that began small for her and, after an illusory expansion, grew much smaller, this nature is what hanged her.

She wrote out of frustration, and sometimes palpable despair, but still, she wrote. She did so because she had a fierce driving sense of what could and should be hers: the things beyond her grasp that nonetheless winked at her, so close and so elusive, like the lights on Piccadilly Circus, the last thing she saw before she descended into the underground on the night of 3 October 1922 and never emerged again. She wrote letters, but really she was seeking to write her story: to catch hold of it, seize it by the shoulders and control its course. 'In your mind make your own end,' she wrote to Bywaters, of a novel whose conclusion seemed to him unsatisfying. 'Its lovely to do that...'

She also wrote that 'the endings are not the story'. Which is sometimes true. Her own end, indeed, was so apparently remote from what had gone before that in fiction it would seem scarcely credible. At the same time the connection was there. It was precisely because she tried to control her own story that its final chapter was snatched from her, along with every last vestige of autonomy. She had tried to grasp the numinous, as artists and lovers do. Doing so took her to the finite, to an ending place as graceless as an abattoir.

★

She had made a grave mistake, believing that she had more power and freedom than she actually had. This is true of many women – indeed it is still true today, however much we might wish otherwise – and it begins to explain why Edith Graydon, later Thompson, became a kind of Everywoman figure: not just in her own era of the 1920s, but ever since, whenever her story is told.

She was so ordinary and so extraordinary. Her fate was so predictable and so random. She got under people's skins, as some women can do, with their flagrant, poignant admixture of display and mystery. Everybody had an opinion about her – everybody she knew and encountered; everybody who read about her – nobody was indifferent to her.

She was hanged for murder, but she was the kind of woman that other people want to kill.

THE TRIAL

WITHIN THE CENTRAL CRIMINAL COURT,
OLD BAILEY, LONDON,
WEDNESDAY, 6TH DECEMBER, 1922.

Judge---

MR. JUSTICE SHEARMAN.

Counsel for the Crown---

THE SOLICITOR GENERAL.

MR. TRAVERS HUMPHREYS.

MR. ROLAND OLIVER.

(Instructed by the Director of Public Prosecutions.)

Counsel for the Prisoner Frederick Bywaters---

MR. CECIL WHITELEY, K.C.

MR. HUNTLY JENKINS.

MR. MYLES ELLIOTT.

(Instructed by Mr. Barrington Matthews.)

Counsel for the Prisoner Edith Thompson---

SIR HENRY CURTIS-BENNETT, K.C.

MR. WALTER FRAMPTON.

MR. IVOR SNELL.

(Instructed by Mr F. A. S. Stern.)

[*Copy Indictment No.* **1**]

THE KING

AGAINST

FREDERICK EDW^D FRANCIS BYWATERS
AND
EDITH JESSIE THOMPSON.

CENTRAL CRIMINAL COURT

Presentment of the Grand Jury.

**F. E. F. BYWATERS and E. J. THOMPSON are charged
with the following offence:--**

STATEMENT OF OFFENCE
MURDER

Particulars of Offence.

F.E.F. BYWATERS and E.J. THOMPSON on the 4th day of October, 1922, in the County of Essex, and within the jurisdiction of the Central Criminal Court murdered Percy Thompson.

[*Copy Indictment No.* **2**]

THE KING

AGAINST

FREDERICK EDW^D FRANCIS BYWATERS
AND
EDITH JESSIE THOMPSON.

CENTRAL CRIMINAL COURT

Presentment of the Grand Jury.

**F.E.F. BYWATERS and E.J. THOMPSON are charged
with the following offences:--**

FIRST COUNT:
STATEMENT OF OFFENCE.

**Conspiracy to Murder contrary to sec. 4 of the Offences
against the Person Act, 1861.**

Particulars of Offence.

F.E.F. BYWATERS and E.J. THOMPSON on the 20th day of August, 1921, and on divers days between that date and the 2nd day of October, 1922, in the County of Essex, and within the jurisdiction of the Central Criminal Court, conspired together to murder Percy Thompson.

SECOND COUNT:
STATEMENT OF OFFENCE.

Soliciting to Murder contrary to sec.4 of the Offences against the Person Act, 1861.

Particulars of Offence.

E. J. THOMPSON on the 19th day of February, 1922, and on divers days between that day and the 1st day of October, 1922, in the County of Essex, and within the jurisdiction of the Central Criminal Court, did solicit and endeavour to persuade and did propose to F.E.F. Bywaters to murder Percy Thompson.

THIRD COUNT:
STATEMENT OF OFFENCE.

Inciting to commit a misdemeanour.

Particulars of Offence.

E. J. THOMPSON on the 10th day of February, 1922, and on divers days between that day and the 1st day of October, 1922, in the County of Essex, and within the jurisdiction of the Central Criminal Court, did unlawfully solicit and incite F. E. F. Bywaters unlawfully to conspire with her, the said E. J. Thompson, to murder Percy Thompson.

FOURTH COUNT:
STATEMENT OF OFFENCE.

Administering poison with intent to murder contrary to sec. 11 of the Offences against the Person Act, 1861.

Particulars of Offence.

E.J. THOMPSON on the 26th day of March, 1922, in the County of Essex, and within the jurisdiction of the Central Criminal Court, did administer to and cause to be taken by Percy Thompson certain poison or other destructive thing unknown with intent to murder the said Percy Thompson.

FIFTH COUNT:
STATEMENT OF OFFENCE.

Administering a destructive thing with intent to murder contrary to sec. 11 of the Offences against the Person Act, 1861.

Particulars of Offence.

E.J. THOMPSON on the 24th day of April, 1922, in the County of Essex, and within the jurisdiction of the Central Criminal Court, did administer to and cause to be taken by Percy Thompson a certain destructive thing, namely, broken glass, with intent to murder the said Percy Thompson.

EDITH

'Poirot asked:

"*What* do you see so plainly? The witnesses?
The counsel? The judge? The accused standing
in the dock?"

'Fogg said quietly:

"That's the reason, of course! You've put your
finger on it. I shall always see *her*…"'

From *Five Little Pigs* by Agatha Christie

I

'To the Puritan, all things are impure.'

From *Etruscan Places* by D. H. Lawrence

S
O THERE WERE five official counts against Edith Thompson, of murder, conspiracy and attempted murder, but in fact there were two others not named on the charge sheet. She had been conducting an adulterous affair with a man eight years her junior. And she had celebrated that affair in letters that were perceived to redefine the concept of shamelessness.

Thus, exposed as she was by the trial, she became the ordinary and extraordinary Everywoman, the London girl who walked the streets like the rest of us but who embodied these giant and eternal sins: the interesting ones, the stuff of the Old Testament and the shilling-shocker. In an age before images on a screen she was a figure to compel a nation. Most murderesses were seen as merely the flotsam and jetsam of life. But this one, with her grace and decadence: she had it all. She was a woman tied to the railway line in one of those early silent films, with the added bonus that she deserved to be there and the train might really run her over. Placed behind the dock she was as mesmerizing as any heroine ever created, an Emma Bovary or a Messalina according to taste, and she aroused in her audience every emotion that femaleness can. Her unravelling drama could be read in the newspapers – pages and pages of it – or, if one were especially lucky, watched at the Old Bailey. There was a black market in tickets for the trial; members of the London unemployed would spend the night in the queue and sell their seat for £5 to what were then called 'society women'. 'It was the atmosphere of a first night,' was the recollection of the writer Beverley Nichols, who attended as a young journalist on the *Sunday Dispatch*.

The evidence against Edith as presented at the trial was weak, and indeed has subsequently been questioned or even ridiculed. But when it came to the other accusations – counts six and seven – she was guilty beyond question, as it then seemed beyond redemption, and according to her counsel Sir Henry Curtis-Bennett she was 'hanged for adultery'. Prejudice directed the trial, as it all too often does, making a mockery of the law's worship of its own impartiality. Prejudice suffused the soul of the judge, the jury, the public gallery and indeed the air in that lecture room of a court, whose atmosphere – like any proudly antiseptic environment – succumbs so easily to the viral.

'May I humbly beseech Your Majesty as last resort to exercise your Royal prerogative of mercy towards my daughter Mrs Thompson now under sentence of death I am broken hearted at the terrible injustice of her sentence caused entirely by prejudice.' So wrote Edith's mother, in a telegram to King George V at Sandringham – and a replica sent to his wife Queen Mary – two days before the execution. Her analysis was pretty much correct, but the most terrible thing about prejudice is that there is so little to be done about it. It can be argued against – legislated against – but it cannot be stopped, and the devil of it lies in its shape-shifting quality. Even those people who believe themselves to be devoid of it are likely to hold other prejudices, which appear not to be so, because they are socially acceptable within their own time. Race and gender prejudice are recognized and guarded against; they happen, quite possibly as much as they ever did, but they are deemed to be wrong. What about the other prejudices, however, the ones supported by moral sanctimony? What about the mood that gripped the nation when any ageing comedian, any jaunty television personality of the 1970s, was liable to be swept away by the hurricane that was the Yewtree inquiry, in which the presumption of innocence became a mere irritating *bagatelle* getting in the way of all the righteous outrage? That was what Edith was up against: that strength of desire for condemnation, for scapegoats for some perceived societal affliction, for the processes of logic to be bypassed.

Prejudice does not go away, it shape-shifts. If – let's say – a Lord Lucan were brought to trial today then prejudice against the posh bastard would be frankly overwhelming. Indeed one can feel, just writing the words, the hypothetical prejudice rising: the newspaper columns that permit catharsis while engendering the need for more of the same; the social media ravenous for its victims' vital organs; the self-importance in the tone of the official commentators and the sneer in the voice of the right-on – all of them feeding the same belief, irrational but oh-so mysteriously satisfying, that there are certain people who deserve what they get, who need to be made an example of, who may or may not be guilty but fuck it, what the hell, who cares, let's hang them for what they are – what they represent – what they would have done given half a chance, you bet your life... When Edith Thompson stood behind the dock in December 1922, a milk-white fawn watching the approach of the hunt, that same dirty tide washed over her, again and again, in repeated unstoppable waves.

★

Letter to *The Daily Telegraph,* published June 1951:

> On the direction of the judge about 120 typed foolscap sheets of the whole of Mrs Thompson's correspondence were handed to the jury to be studied by them, and it was my duty to read them to the members of the jury, which included two women. 'Nauseous' is hardly strong enough to describe their contents...
>
> The jury performed a painful duty, but Mrs Thompson's letters were her own condemnation.
>
> ONE OF THE JURY, London EC1.

Daily Express pamphlet on the Thompson-Bywaters trial, published December 1922:

Even the case-hardened lawyers wore an air of contemptuous disgust as they toiled through the sewers of sensation. Their very wigs looked cynically derisive as they took the wash of the unspeakable.

Let us be realists, not romantics, as we hold our nose, for all this ordure is the product of the dregs and scum of romance in putrescence. The death of Percy Thompson is not the worst thing in this apocalypse. His bloodstained corpse is not the supreme horror. No! It is the festering soul, the mind diseased, the hard heart, and the wanton surrender to the baser and more brutish senses. It is the degradation of love into a vile caricature of its own image. It is the stricken misery of an old father and two old mothers gazing at the moral ruin of their offspring. And behind it all is the vision of national decay, for there can be no hope for a race that loses its ancient bearings in a sea of sensual anarchy.

But our prejudices today are different, and how therefore do we understand that a love affair, and love letters that were passionate but in no way pornographic, could have caused such a monumental reactive surge that this juryman still remembered it – felt it indeed – nearly thirty years on? Why, in that convergence of man-made law and natural law, which from time to time demands a sacrifice to cleanse the public soul, was she the person thrown to the hounds?

It was all of a piece with that imponderable – the role of women – which in the early twentieth century was in a state of revolution that caught Edith Thompson in its wayward spin.

★

When she took her husband till death did them part, making the vow in the little red brick St Barnabas church on the edge of east London – an unlikely place, it now seems, in which to ignite such a conflagration – there would have been no thought but that the marriage was for life. Divorce was so rare as to be statistically almost non-existent. In a population of some forty million, there were about 800 divorces a year. They were extremely hard to obtain, and on the whole people preferred it that way: marriage was sacred, even to the irreligious. It was the status quo, it was social cement. Grounds were so limited that in 1922 a Mrs Norman Rutherford was denied a divorce from a husband who had been sent to Broadmoor. Then there was money: still a major factor today in the procedure, but in the early twentieth century most people were unable to afford the procedure itself. It might cost as much as £50, more if contested. And what happened afterwards, when what God had put together had been ripped asunder? Financial uncertainty, a limbo status, social stigma. Divorce was almost all about adultery; the notion of incompatibility would have been met with incredulity; and marriage to a person who had been named as one's co-adulterer was perceived as near-fatally damaging to the reputation. Again in 1922, the scientist J. B. S. Haldane was sacked from his post at Cambridge University after he divorced and remarried. He was the 'guilty' party but, even to the partner without fault, divorce carried a shame that can barely now be understood, and could only be shaken off by those of the right disposition or class.

'The one thing they shrank from,' wrote Sir Ernley Blackwell, at the very end of 1922, in the long internal Home Office memorandum about the convicted murderers Edith Thompson and Frederick Bywaters, 'was a scandal or overt elopement which might affect their material positions.'

On the whole, divorce was a rich person's game, and separation was for the extremes of rich and poor. Similarly, affairs were conducted most freely by those who did not worry about other people's opinions: the upper and lower classes. Women like the sexually bohemian Lady Dorothy Cavendish (wife of future Prime Minister Harold Macmillan) or the serial cohabitants of the *demi-monde* – they kept their beds casually open, and shame did not touch them; nor of course did it touch their men. But for people like Edith and Percy Thompson the marriage tie was as close as bindweed, adultery was a fumbling, unacknowledged secret, and divorce was a cataclysm whose fallout was almost comparable with that of murder. That is why women like Adelaide Bartlett in 1885 and Florence Maybrick in 1889, men like Dr Crippen in 1910 and Herbert Armstrong in 1921, poisoned their spouses rather than trying to divorce them.

'I'd love to be able to say "I'm going to see my lover tonight."' So wrote Edith to Bywaters, a day before her husband's murder.

> If I did he would prevent me – there would be scenes and he would come to 168 [her place of work at 168 Aldersgate Street] and interfere and I couldn't bear that – I could be beaten all over at home and still be defiant – but at 168 it's different. It's my living – you wouldn't let me live on him would you and I shouldn't want to – darlint its funds that are our stumbling block – until we have those we can do nothing.

Nevertheless divorce was in the air, which was why people were so worried about it. The law, which had stood since 1857, was beginning to be liberalized. An important change came in 1923, when Edith was recently dead; it would have made little or no difference to her particular case, but it did make wives equal with their husbands before the law. Before 1923 a woman had had to prove a secondary grievance on top of adultery – incest, desertion, other such trifles – while a man could obtain a divorce on the grounds of adultery alone. Now, after the passage of the Matrimonial Causes Act, anonymous girls could be hired to spend a night with a man, traditionally in Brighton, so that a divorce could be obtained without naming the real cause of it: Agatha Christie's first husband gave her a divorce in this way, as he did not want his girlfriend to be named in the petition, but it was Agatha herself who felt the shame and failure of it, and never again took communion in church. The equality principle of the new law had been urged by early feminists, and it was quite widely opposed. 'Is there any man in this House,' asked an MP, 'who is the father of a son and a daughter, who would regard the sin of adultery on the part of his son as being as severe as the sin of adultery on the part of his daughter?'

He was shouted down, but a lot of people – women included – would have agreed with him. The sole female MP, Nancy Astor, didn't want to back the bill but felt that she should.

So divorce became less rare, and after 1923 more wives became petitioners, although the number remained very low: fewer than 3,000 a year. The subject was debated more freely, but alongside that went an intensified resistance to the whole idea. As is the way when almost any change is proposed, this resistance was unduly stubborn, and had the air of being emotive rather than reasoned.

★

Edith was born upon a brink, when change seemed almost like a natural law: it was the end of the Victorian era, the end of a century, the beginning of new freedoms, not all of which were illusory. The foundations had been laid, however, in the age of corsets and ankle-flashing. When Edith's mother, Ethel, was born in 1872, a wife did not really exist in law – her identity was fully absorbed into that of her husband, who owned both her body and her property – yet by 1897 a legal commentator was able to write: 'Woman was born in chains and, behold, now on every side she is free. The Victorian epoch may claim with justice the gratitude of enfranchised womanhood; a gratitude, moreover, that will at least be leavened by a lively sense of favours to come.'

Which was true, up to a point. But there is an implied passivity in that word 'gratitude', singularly inappropriate to the agency-seeking suffragists – who emerged in the same year as this proclamation – and still more so to the more hardline suffragettes, whose campaigning began in 1903. These women showed contempt for the chains that society had placed on them. Society threw all that it had back at them, again deploying the principle that they had rendered themselves sexless, and could thus be banged up in Holloway and fed with tubes through their noses. Nevertheless in 1918 they achieved near-equality, representation for women aged thirty or more, which meant an electorate that was 40 per cent female; Edith never exercised this right to vote, as she died at the age of twenty-nine, but she would of course have expected to do so, to have had her say in the push-pull between Stanley Baldwin and Ramsay MacDonald that continued throughout the 1920s (and which of them would have got her support? Hard to say: she had aspirations toward a higher class and loyalty to her own). As a follower of racing, a regular gambler, she would have had her fancy for the 1913 Derby, in which Emily Davison took a death plunge beneath the king's horse; she may also have seen the Pathé newsreel footage; she would have felt the force of the suffragette's physical courage – a quality she herself lacked – and of all that blind impersonal passion.

The vote, for which Davison died, was the surest, purest sign that women were acquiring autonomy. The term 'feminism' had first been used in the 1890s. Later it would be espoused by Edith's near contemporaries: Rebecca West, a year older, one of the many who would offer her opinion on Edith Thompson, and Vera Brittain, born four days later on 29 December 1893 (Edith cited her birthdate of Christmas Day as another signifier of bad luck). Brittain was a feminist who understood the ambiguities of femaleness, better perhaps than did the idealists who preceded her. She was a wife, she took pride in her extremely attractive appearance, and she worked: she regarded all these things as compatible in the life of a woman. So too did Edith, who had the same gifts, denied full expression by the dead hand of class.

Still: the life that she could grasp was immeasurably different from that of her mother. Ethel Liles – the daughter of a police constable – was born into half a terraced house in Hackney with neither electricity nor bathroom; into a world in which women wore corsets and few cosmetics (perhaps a touch of *papier poudré*); in which they used menstrual 'rags' and did their washing in the scullery 'copper' (a metal container for heating water, with a handle to turn and achieve arduous washing-machine-type motion); in which they fought an ongoing war with dirt and damp; in which they were tyrannized by fires, making them, stoking them, containing the constant chaos of ash and smuts and smoke; in which they gave birth at home in terror of puerperal fever, paying a midwife or doctor in a one-off sum or instalments; in which they waited, fatalistically, to lose their teeth and their looks and to die at sixty with luck. Those would have been Ethel's expectations. Her family was respectable and solvent – by the 1880s they had moved north to Hornsey, to a bigger house with single occupancy – but it was a fact that, for women without servants, the means simply did not exist to make life easy. Of necessity they were domestic creatures. Aged eighteen Ethel worked as a dressmaker; but jobs were for unmarried girls or widows. Wives did not work outside the home. It was almost axiomatic.

Yet Ethel saw, and to some extent benefited from, changes that she could not have imagined, and that her daughter accepted without thought as a fine new normality. For a start: clothes. As a very young woman Edith still wore the wretched corset – a 'health' corset as it had become, which is to say it did not strangle the vital organs – and blouses with necks full of bones sticking into the flesh of the jaw; she wore skirts almost to the grimy London streets, sometimes streaming with material, sometimes clinging tight as if quite literally to hold back, like a pair of ankle-cuffs, the female progress. But even before the war all this was becoming otiose, and by 1919 the idea of clothes as alluring swaddling was dead and gone. Skirts hovered between calf and ankle (Edith once cut out a newspaper article headed 'Battle of Calves and Ankles', and sent it to her lover Bywaters), dresses became lighter, hats shrank, hair was shorn; the whaleboned odalisque was toppled by the tube-shaped flapper, alarmingly active, lean as a stalk with her drooping tulip head. The transition to this silhouette was still happening while Edith lived – her post-war photographs show her in soft, rather Bloomsbury dresses, boat-necked and loose-skirted, airy and simple and acutely feminine (or perhaps that was just her) – but the real shift had been made: woman began the century in corsets and, behold, now on every side she was free. Floating along without her cuffs. Playing tennis like Suzanne Lenglen. Vamping and aping the lithe satiny goddesses of the silent screen, although some feminists were not so keen on this kind of thing. Equality was not, they considered, about behaving like men while flaunting whatever made one different from them. Why the 'boring obsession with sex', wrote Winifred Holtby. The liberation of the 1920s, wrote Sylvia Pankhurst, was too much about 'absurdities of dress which betoken the slave woman's sex appeal rather than the free woman's intelligent companionship'.

Such words were a sign that the role of women was, indeed, becoming imponderable. Not just for society, for men, but for women themselves, who had begun to doubt and suspect each other, not so much personally as politically (although, as the flagrantly non-ideological Nancy Mitford understood, the personal and the political are rarely to be separated). The debate was on. It is still happening. And in these early schisms, a central question was implicitly asked: what is a woman supposed *to do with* her femaleness? Enjoy it? Use it? Ignore it? Make a weapon of it? Accept the limitations that it imposes? Relax into them? Rage against them? Seek to undermine them? Seek to override them? Do all of these in turn, dancing forwards and back as one negotiates the game of gender... That was how Edith played it, moving deftly between roles in a way that women still do, however much we might say otherwise. It served her well, and it served her ill; which again is familiar to us. We would not expect such calamitous consequences, but then nor did she.

The small freedoms, though... They amounted to something that *looked*, at least, like a brave new world. Women like Edith smoked, they took their meals in Lyons' Corner Houses, they took aspirin rather than suffer a headache or period pain, they lived in houses with electricity and running water, they shopped at the Co-operative stores rather than traipsing from butcher to grocer to baker, they wore lipstick and block mascara, they shaved their underarms and later their legs, they used Hartmann's Hygienic Towelettes for Ladies or Southall's sanitary towels, 'indispensable to Ladies travelling'. For without these products – basic to the point of outright banality, but miracles nonetheless – how was any sort of freedom possible? Women knew themselves, felt themselves to be at the mercy of their bodies. Their procreative destiny was a gift but it was also the most terrible nuisance. Did biology have to run everything, all the time? Only when power over *that* had been achieved could they seize the reins of their lives. Only birth control, in fact, could truly change the game; as it did, or began to do, in the early twentieth century.

Ethel Liles was one of nine children. Edith was the eldest of six, but by the time her generation reached maturity, the average number of children would be two or three. Having been incompetently practised for centuries, birth control had become widely used. It was also feared, as against nature and society: the 'Malthusian uterus' was condemned by the church and by doctors. Gynaecologists warned that contraception was harmful. Those who advised on the subject were liable to be prosecuted. Nevertheless in 1921 Marie Stopes opened her first clinic, for married women only, in London's Holloway. (Edith almost certainly never attended this clinic, although she knew the area well; in fact she died just a couple of miles from where she was born.) Stopes offered measures more reliable than *coitus interruptus* or *reservatus*: her own brand of diaphragm, soluble quinine pessaries and sponges soaked in olive oil. It was primitive stuff, of course – as were the douches and condoms that were also thrown into the mix – and the levels of ignorance were still blistering. There was no concept of the safe time of the month. Information, such as it was, came from other women, as a kind of whispered female folklore; unless one was a woman like Edith, private, non-gossipy, mysteriously innocent, who wrote to Bywaters in February 1922: 'I've never had experience in such matters and I never discuss them with members of my own sex as so many girls do therefore I suppose I'm rather ignorant on such subjects...'

Unwanted pregnancies happened all the time. Naturally. Then women were back in the dark ages, brought up hard against the separate will of their antique destiny. They swallowed quinine, raspberry leaf, purgatives and gin; they bought medicines such as 'Madame Drunette's Lunar Pills', advertised openly but in a coded manner as – for instance – 'menstrual regulatives'; they threw themselves down the stairs or tried to dilate their cervix with candles; they galloped wildly on a horse, if they had one; they boiled and steamed themselves in the bath, if they had one; and, if necessary, they took the tremulous road to the abortionist, whose primary trade was often that of midwife. One estimate, admittedly not much more than guesswork, suggested that 100,000 women tried to procure or induce an abortion in the years before the First World War. These things had been going on since Hippocrates advised pregnant prostitutes to jump up and down with their legs tucked under until they miscarried. Abortion was then a fact of life, because it was not thought that a foetus itself *had* life. In the nineteenth century, by which time medical understanding had advanced, abortion was made illegal – it was briefly a capital offence – and the Offences against the Person Act of 1861, under which Edith was tried, specifically prohibited the procuring of drugs or implements to that end. The law and religion united in condemnation of a crime that did not merely end a putative life, but did so in order to gratify the whim of the woman whose duty was to nurture that life. The daughters of Mary did not abort; to do so was an aberration, an offence against the person and against God. Only in secret, in the dark corners of sculleries and bathrooms and rooms off alleyways, did women pray for the loosening of pain and blood that would set them free once more.

★

Some of these conceptions were within marriage, but not all. It wasn't just Edith Thompson. Women had extramarital sex; they just didn't talk about their affairs in the way that they would today. They also had premarital sex. One estimate suggested that almost 40 per cent of women did so in the decade between 1915 and 1925. This figure is naturally impossible to verify, but the point is clear: sex outside marriage was far more common than society cared to acknowledge (in part thanks to Stopes). In 1920, a seventeen-year-old typist named Irene Munro took a solitary holiday in Eastbourne, clearly with the intention of attracting male companionship, and was brutally murdered on a stretch of shingle by two young men when the fun got out of hand. Four years later, in a house overlooking the same Eastbourne beach, a thirty-nine-year-old secretary named Emily Kaye was killed and dismembered by

Patrick Mahon, the married man by whom she had fallen pregnant. Women took lovers. Not just the Lady Dorothy Cavendishes and the Edwina Mountbattens (whose butler asked her 'but what shall I do with the other gentleman,' when a third lover turned up while she was entertaining one in her bedroom and keeping another at bay in the drawing-room). Not just the Fanny Gilligans and the Mary Stones who dodged the hangman's noose. Not just a serial mistress like the writer Jean Rhys, a near-contemporary of Edith Thompson, whose escape to Paris after the war saved her – temporarily at least – from a life that she called 'useless and boring', and could have done the same thing for Edith. 'If she had been a Frenchwoman,' an observer at her trial wrote (inspired by her image to floridity), 'she would have been long ago taken out of her humble working life and been at once the slave and the ruler of some connoisseur in extravagant caprice.'*

No: affairs were conducted by ordinary women, what the world would call decent women, teenage typists and middle-aged secretaries: women who went on buses and carried shopping baskets and sought something in their lives to make them just a bit more fun, or simply bearable. Some of them even sought other women. In 1921 there was an attempt to legislate against lesbianism, although it was blocked in the Lords in case it gave people ideas.

As with divorce, the sense of all this was in the air, and what had brought it out was the war.

In the aftermath, when people were rather wondering what the last four years had all been for, a kind of moral chaos was deemed to rule in Britain. It is very familiar, this panic that seizes society after seismic events: the sense that things are on a brink and the desperate desire for them to return to normal. To be as they were before the world went mad. To expunge those elements that collude with an unstable future rather than a reassuring past. As today, so it was in 1919. Authority was questioned. The monarchy was advised that it must justify its

---

* Filson Young, in *The Trial of Frederick Bywaters and Edith Thompson* (William Hodge & Co. 1923).

existence to a less deferential country. Strikes, including by the miners and the police, led to a genuine fear that the all-too-recent events in Russia were influencing workers. Illegitimate 'war babies' were fat little exhibits in the case proving social decadence. Modernism was sending the arts into places where no nice person should go. There was a rather queasy boom followed by a long, heavy, hopeless slump. Moral certainties, at such a time, became accordingly hallowed. And central to these was the role of women. When society is in an almighty panic, what better to soothe it than the image of a virtuous female presence, steadfast and smiling, at the heart of the home?

Yet the war had done the *really* destabilizing thing of allowing women out of their cages. Ordinary women again – bright smart vital girls, some of whom had anticipated nothing more from life than a housemaid's uniform and the courtship (please God) of a handsome footman: because of the need for labour, sexless labour, in munitions or on trams, they had been pushed out of the home and into the world; and it had left them, after the war, with this extraordinary idea that they might escape literal servitude, find work that offered a relative freedom. Vera Brittain called work the twentieth century's 'great gift to women'. It could not have happened without Southalls and Stopes, but what also made it possible was war.

Then, in 1919 – the year that the Sex Disqualification (Removal) Act allowed women to hold any civil or judicial office – more than three-quarters of a million female workers lost their jobs, because it was considered unpatriotic not to hand them over to the returning men. There was a logic to that, what with post-war unemployment and men being the designated breadwinners. Nevertheless women had begun to see work in a different way. Some pretended to be single, because the convention was to sack them as soon as they got married. Some turned down jobs in service, although they were obliged to back down when their benefits (paid at a lower level than to men) were withdrawn. It was other jobs that they wanted, however. Not necessarily careers, as such; that shift had not quite happened; but the possibility that it might had begun to seem possible.

The backlash was powerful and concerted and – yet again – not entirely unfamiliar. Women had been let loose during the war: fair enough. They had been given the vote: also fair (or so one was obliged to say; although the means, the suffragette antics, only *barely* justified the end). They could become magistrates, jurors, even solicitors if they really wanted. Nevertheless the war was over, and it was time to ruffle the hair of any incipient Boadicea and gently push her back towards the altar. Newspapers presented female emancipation as a threat to a social order that had already been sufficiently destabilized, thank you very much, by the Kaiser. Being a wife, proclaimed *My Weekly* – one of the lifestyle magazines that were starting to proliferate – was the 'best job of all', while a female writer lamented the shorter hair and skirts, the shunning of household occupations: 'Many of our young women have become desexed and masculinized.'

There was a problem, however, with this urge to marry everybody off. The carnage of the Western Front had left Britain with 1.9 million more women than men: 'Our Surplus Girls', as the *Daily Mail* described them. It was suggested, as a solution, that these girls should propose to soldiers – presumably the poor incapacitated rejects – which carried an odd echo of wartime behaviour, when of their own free will girls would write love letters to soldiers whom they didn't even know, and amuse themselves no end with those whom they did. Oh yes, the war had let something loose all right... Even the newly founded Women's Institute was viewed with wariness, as a possible hotbed of subversion. Lord Reith's BBC banned all references to birth control as well as to atheism (a censor sat in the studio with a finger hovering over the cut-off button). The newspapers kept in libraries pasted over the horse racing cards and results (it was illegal to gamble off-course, and would have been yet another mark against Edith that she had regular bets, placed for her by the driver at her business premises). 'Ain't We Got Fun' was the title of a popular song, quoted by Edith in a letter to Bywaters; and the general opinion was that the fun needed to stop, here and now.

It was familiar stuff, all this semi-hysteria, this equation of female freedom with immorality, of immorality with lawlessness, but it had consequences.

> …This perplexing creature had a long suffering husband and a cosy home. There was no apparent reason why she might not also have had a happy husband and a happy home… it was not a case of Romeo and Juliet or a Paolo and Francesca… it was the case of a mature wife who was weary of her husband and who ached with romantic longing for release from her duty and her obligation…
>
> Her illicit passion devoured her… There is no evidence of the restraining influence of religion or honour or morality. These things were not there. They may have been there at one time, but they do not come into this wretched story.
>
> What is still more disquieting is the utter absence of them in the whole environment. Everybody in this milieu seems to be morally helpless. There is no stern voice, no warning entreaty, no austere censure, no rebuke, no reproof. Where were all the old anchors and moorings in this grimy surge of moral anarchy? It is a glimpse of a modern London without a conscience or an ideal. This is our life and this is how it is lived.

So wrote the editor of the *Sunday Express* in December 1922, in his pamphlet – price 2d – about the trial of Edith Thompson and Frederick Bywaters.

★

A couple of years later the game was up, in some small but essential way. A veritable mass of young women were enjoying what older feminists would doubtless have called flapper freedoms: watching Clara Bow in cinemas, mimicking her outlandish *chutzpah* as she batted her eyelashes without fear at any man in sight, shortening their skirts until their silken knees were out and proud, taking jobs as typists and waitresses, taking their vote for granted, powdering their noses with compacts embossed with pictures of Rudolph Valentino, listening to jazz, imagining a *lèse-majesté* dance with the Prince of Wales (who would himself come up hard against the stigma of divorce). *They*, those girls born when the age of Victoria was truly over, were the ones who slipped the leash. Of course they were less free than they believed themselves to be. Of course the newspapers sighed and agitated for them to be brought into line. But the moral panic, however thunderous, was not quite as absolutely real as it had been in the five or so years after the end of war, when Edith had made her strike for freedom. 'She was a very capable woman,' her employer, Herbert Carlton, would tell the Old Bailey. Oh yes: capable of anything.

As with the politicized intelligentsia who were her contemporaries, she had refused to accept a role chosen by society. She certainly didn't think that being a wife was 'the best job of all'. She wrote to Bywaters that she didn't 'believe in' housework, describing it as 'drudgery'; which it was, even for a woman who could afford to send clothes to a laundry. She had, she wrote, spent the weekend 'amusing herself making jam – chutney & mincemeat with the apples from the garden'. But she wasn't really amused, she was simply filling the time in an unhappy home, and 'it doesnt even help to stifle thoughts now'. In the very same paragraph she wrote that she was waiting, thank God, for the arrival of a maid. It was a request to which her husband had finally agreed, which would have established Edith for good and all as one who had risen to a higher class. The maid arrived at Paddington, to take up her new job, on the day after Percy's murder.

That same year, 1922, the first issue of *Good Housekeeping* had informed its readers that 'we are on the threshold of a great feminine awakening. Apathy and levity are alike giving place to a wholesome and intelligent interest in the affairs of life, and above all the home.' This was a clever compromise, suggesting that a woman lured by the feminist creed might find fulfilment in the role of domestic goddess. Which indeed she might. Nothing wrong with that at all: as long as it was the woman's choice, and it wasn't Edith's.

Like Vera Brittain, her near-twin, she wanted to work as well as be married; and she did not want the jobs that would have once been her fate, dressmaking or taking in laundry or other such female stuff. She wanted to be out in the world. She started at the age of fifteen, working in Southwark as what the 1911 census described as a 'Clerk, folding box manufacturers, cardboards'. She learned bookkeeping, and aged about eighteen she was given a job at Carlton & Prior, wholesale milliner, in Aldersgate Street near the Barbican. She became a buyer, worked with skill and success. She bustled to and fro on the train to Fenchurch Street, back and forth every day, one of the noble commuters of London, going to her place of business even when the sun beckoned her to a delirious leisure or the snow fell in vicious clumps, even when her body let her down – when the agonies of her menstrual cycle caused her to swell and faint – or her mind yearned to wander in the dreamscapes of her own conjuring... Always, throughout almost exactly one half of her life, she worked. She showed up, five and a half days a week. If she didn't, if the monthly corkscrew probed too deep for endurance, it was noteworthy. 'On Saturday I was so ill. I had to stop away – its not very often I give in so much as stopping away from business but on Saturday I really had to...' She earned a good wage of £6 a week, plus bonuses. She played her part upon the commercial stage of the City of London. She would have called it a job, but today it would probably be called a career, for it carried prospects and it defined, completely, one part of her complex soul.

Approximately a third of women worked in the early 1920s, but for married women the figure was about one in ten. So Edith was unusual. Still more so because her salary was slightly larger than that of her husband. They were a modern couple in that sense, joint owners of a house, joint contributors to its running; and she with her precious peck of independence. Her job at Carlton & Prior was effectively sexless – the only 'female' thing about it was that the business dealt in millinery – and to have held it down, with nothing to help her but native wits, no higher education or contacts along the way, was an achievement by anybody's standards: man or woman. She was somebody who could claim sisterhood with the feminists, although she would not have seen it that way; and nor, apparently, did Rebecca West, who at the end of 1922 commented that she 'was, poor child, a shocking little piece of rubbish, and her mental furniture was meagre… I am not asking for sympathy for Edith Thompson. She is a poor, flimsy, silly, mischievous little thing.'

Oh, the evil of class! Like West, who had a long affair with H. G. Wells, Edith was a working woman with a lover. But still there was this judgement. Her opportunities were manifold – they made her life overwhelmingly different from that of her mother and aunts, who admired her as a glorious flower of new womanhood – but the difference was still not enough. She left school aged fifteen and went immediately out to work; no Somerville or Girton for her.

She was a lover of books, music, theatre – she performed Shakespeare with an amateur dramatic society, she read Dickens in her death cell – and perhaps culture meant more to her than it did to the highly educated, because she became so absolutely lost in it. It helped her to live, which is surely the point? ('arent books a consolation and a solace', she wrote). She compared them with life, rather than with other books. 'She would read a book and imagine herself the character in the book,' as Bywaters said at the trial, which was surely true, but did not go deep enough: she had a writer's imagination, which sees real life merely as an option among others.

But her taste was not shaped by the rarefied intellects of the ladies' colleges. She responded with sentimental ease to a popular lyric – 'One Little Hour' was her song, *their* song – and she quoted it as if it were 'Un Bel Dì'. 'One golden hour! For that eternal pain!' She could lose herself in a show, a performance. Not with the same intensity as she did in books, but when – for instance – she heard a song with the title 'Feather Your Nest', she wrote to Bywaters: 'I wished we could just you and I – but we will yes, somehow we must.' It was the same childlike intensity, a sort of magnetic literalness, which led her to write – as one offering up an *aperçu* – a sentence of this kind: 'two heads are better than one is such a true saying.'

She assembled pieces from the newspapers, some of which would feature as evidence at her trial. 'You heard them read, gentlemen; they are scraps from newspapers,' Justice Shearman would later say, querying the headlines as one echoing a voice from another planet: 'Battle of *what*?' 'Battle of Calves and Ankles, my lord.' This particular article was not cited as evidence; nor was 'Do Men like Red Haired Women?', nor 'An Ideal Love Letter', nor 'Women who Always Act', nor 'Masterful Men', nor 'The Best Wines that I have drunk'. But these headlines were read, nonetheless, from the little scraps cut out painstakingly for Bywaters – a childlike act, again, and moreover pathetically private – not intended for judgement.

She went to the West End theatres, and on the night of her husband's murder attended a Ben Travers farce at the Criterion. She went regularly to variety shows at the Holborn Empire, the Ilford Hippodrome, the East Ham Palace; she was out for pleasure, although she was not uncritical. She told Bywaters about a joke made during a 'pierrot entertainment' at the Hippodrome: 'A man on the stage said this last night "Marriage is the inclination of a crazy man to board a lazy woman, for the rest of his natural life". Rather cutting I think, but there it came from a man.' Again there was this intense engagement with what she saw and read, even when the material was too insubstantial (flimsy) to merit it. She sent novels to Bywaters then 'discussed' them in subsequent letters, ostensibly with him but at least as much with herself.

> About "The Slave". I didn't know what to make of that girl – yes
> I think she is possible – perhaps and apart from being happy with
> her body – he was quite happy seeing her with those jewels. They
> were 2 similar natures – what pleased him – pleased her – not
> English at all, either of them… she had never lived and she didn't
> live did she? not in the world as we know living… I don't know if
> you will understand this, it seems a bit of a rigmarole even to me.

So much perception – ! albeit scattily expressed; and not without relevance to her own life. But was *The Slave* worth it? The book was by Robert Hichens, whose works she referenced frequently. He was an elegant stylist by today's standards, admired incidentally by the schoolgirl Jean Rhys; he was also something of a sensationalist, and certainly far too successful to be acceptable to the literati. 'No one can write a best seller by taking thought,' as Rebecca West once put it, thus explaining in part her attitude towards Edith's mental furniture.

West called herself an 'old-fashioned feminist' (that slightly joyless thing). She wanted the novelist Elinor Glyn to be banned from libraries. Glyn, whose books fairly heaved with sex, was reviled by the post-war puritans as a quasi-pornographer, but she was also despised by a woman like West – who would doubtless have called herself a free thinker, and went in for 'free love' with the married H. G. Wells – because she demeaned sex, in the worst possible way: by making it the stuff of bad literature.

Edith was a far better writer than Elinor Glyn, or could have been. 'The letters of Mrs Thompson were, in passages, remarkably well written,' the *Daily Chronicle* commented, 'and indicated a curious degree of sensibility in one who at the same time was plotting to commit a singularly cruel murder.' Her mind was sincere, one might even say Lawrentian, in her reaching towards sex as something that should carry no shame (an attitude that helped push him out of the country and her on to the gallows). In carrying on an affair with Bywaters she too was practising free love. But she did so instinctively, rather than on modernist principle, and it is more than likely that Rebecca West objected to Edith in the same way as she did to Glyn. How could such a woman, with her belief in the potency of cheap music and her absorption in romantic fiction, presume to understand love and desire? As a 'shocking piece of rubbish' she failed to understand that these sacred things were about the free woman's intelligent companionship – indeed the way in which *she* wrote about them showed that ideal up as something of a mirage, and acknowledged instead a dangerous truth, that relations between men and women are not, in fact, susceptible to the principle of equality.

You know best about that darlint, and I am going to leave everything to you – only I would like to help you, can't I…

I'm wanting that man to lean on now darlint, and I shall lean hard
– so be prepared…

Yes, you are a bully – but sometimes – only sometimes I like it. I
like being told to do this by you…

Whats more now I'm the bully aren't I? but its only fun darlint –
laugh.

That word, 'darlint'. It was a contraction of 'darlingest' – the darlingest
boy – and it came so often in the letters as to constitute the punctua-
tion that was otherwise an irrelevance (there were assuredly those who
thought that Edith simply didn't know *how* to punctuate. In fact she
only rarely committed actual errors in grammar or spelling).* And
darlint was objected to: not specifically by West, although her feelings
may be inferred, but by F. Tennyson Jesse, the woman who wrote *A
Pin to See the Peepshow* (1934), a supremely sympathetic novel based
upon the Thompson-Bywaters case. So if Tennyson Jesse, who was in
Edith's corner, could write a letter to *The Daily Telegraph* some thirty
years after the event, admitting – in almost jocular fashion – that her
nerves had been frayed by all those 'darlints', and implying that they
were the product of a slightly inferior sensibility – how then might a
sterner commentator have reacted?

Yet Edith was a natural born writer. The sensuous stream of consciousness of her correspondence was the instinctive, unschooled kin
of *Ulysses*, published in Paris in 1922. As Frederick Bywaters astutely

---

* I have reproduced all Edith's idiosyncrasies, as to regularize her style would
be to harm it. The only one that needs explanation is her occasional habit
of leaving a space between sentences rather than use a full stop; Frederick
Bywaters did the same thing.

put it: 'when writing letters to me she did not study sentences &
phrases before transferring them to paper, but, as different thoughts,
no matter what, momentarily flashed through her mind, so they were
committed to paper.' He was compelled by her letters, as many people
have been since. Yet Edith, who wrote to be read by Bywaters alone,
and wrote in the main for herself, had no thought of being judged on
this correspondence of hers. She made no claims for it. She would have
agreed that it was shapeless and formless, and that she lacked the dis-
tanced awareness required for a 'proper' writer. Nevertheless she had
a gift. Her ability to express herself *even as* she thought was innate,
something preordained. Some of the cadences that she conjured in a
moment, as it were without awareness, with the mysterious breath of
creativity, have passed into a kind of immortality:

> Darlint, I've surrendered to him unconditionally now – do you
> understand me?

> We ourselves die & live in the books we read while we are reading
> them…

> I just tried to make you live in my life…

> He has the right by law to all that you have the right to by nature
> and love…

> Darlint – do something tomorrow night will you? something to
> make you forget…

The subject matter condemned her, of course, but there was more
than moral outrage in Rebecca West's words: there was snobbery, and
a kind of wishing of Edith away; a feeling expressed by many people.
Quite simply, she did not fit. Still, today, women are supposed to fit,
although the spaces designated for them are more diverse and forgiving in shape. But a woman who did not fit into the England of the early

1920s? Well. Best that she did not transgress, draw attention to herself, make herself vulnerable: or else. 'Even those who objected in principle to her execution can hardly regret her absence from this sphere,' was the last sentence of a book review, published in 1923, of the edition of the *Notable British Trials* series featuring the case.

Edith's prison visitor, Margery Fry – sister of the Bloomsbury Group's Roger, and later the Principal of Somerville – was a truly good person, one of the great and good as we now would say. She was, as she wrote at the time, '*terribly* exercised about the Thompson case'. Yet there was no meeting place between the two women, as they sat together in the condemned cell at Holloway. How strange and appalling those hours must have been, in the yellow-grey glare of the perpetual light. The attempts at conversation, the clean, clipped Roedean accent ('are they giving you all that you need?') and the soft London voice full of self-improvement ('oh yes, they let me have cigarettes'), the fierce brow-knitting concern on the one side and the blankness on the other. Later, in the 1950s, Margery Fry described how she had tried to feel her way towards Edith's 'flimsy personality': that word again. Fry was not cold, as Rebecca West was, but she was equally judgemental. She was a woman whose life was spent in public service – with the Howard League for Penal Reform; at Oxford – but she was a product of her class and of the English education system, and for all her goodness she dealt in abstractions. Her mind was crystalline, impersonally forgiving, unable to bend and crack into that understanding which comes with a consoling Guinness in a shabby saloon, or a popular song that swoons and envelops, or a Cup-winning goal. Epistolary love affairs belonged in the pages of Laclos, not in the fervid scribblings of a bob-headed little bookkeeper. Fry was perplexed, baffled, frustrated by the woman whom she wished to offer her compassion, who seemed to her as banal and unreachable as a dusty mannequin behind a shop window.

To these Frys and Wests, with their cool and ordered views on life, their inner resources fortified by *Middlemarch* and Mozart, Edith was a thing of straw, self-absorbed but without the power of self-analysis. Unlike another contemporary, Dorothy L. Sayers (who also transgressed sexually, and had the illegitimate son to prove it) she had no reverence for scholarship and none for God. These things were not in her sphere. She revered life: what it was, and what she dreamed it to be. The only thing that limited her dreams, her means of expression, was class. Within those circumscribed barriers she ran astonishingly free. So it was a question, with her, of whether one saw the externals – the transgressions, the follies, the clichés – or the complex impulses beneath them. This became the question that would decide whether she lived or died.

★

Edith was not pitiable, which Fry probably wanted her to be. She was not really what anybody wanted her to be; she could not be categorized. Unlike those poor wretches who had been spared the gallows because they were full of gin, or empty of morals, Edith could not be excused for knowing no better. Nor could she be in receipt of *de haut en bas* patronage. Indeed her social position was designed to irritate the intelligentsia rather as the self-made Thatcherites would do some sixty years later. She belonged, in fact, to what was effectively a new class: working-cum-lower-middle, but defined as never before by its aspirations. She was a beneficiary of the shift within Britain from tenant to property owner. Even more than the middle classes it was Edith's class, the New Aspirants – the clerks and milliners whose worlds had been shaken up by war and who no longer fancied the old order – who seized the opportunity to buy their own home and signify respectability, achievement, with a see-your-face-in-the-Brasso-shine front-door knocker.

Edith wanted to move upwards, in the real world, as well as out towards Shangri-la. She was a skilled climber. With her mimetic intelligence she noted the way that people outside her *milieu* behaved, and did the same herself. As the trial observer put it, 'she had the secret of looking like a hundred different women according to the nature of her environment.' She was like a girl today who studies the red carpet at the Oscars and within days has a replica dress from Asos; she was one of those gleaming

London magpies with a survivor's facility for picking up what was what, who was who and where it was at; and from the know-your-place streets of suburban London she travelled a long way – as far as her class roots would allow her to go – down the perilous path to success.

Admirable, then. Yet there is a suspicion in this country of what can, in the wrong mood, be defined as 'uppishness'. Edith was one of the self-reliant, the go-getters, in a society that has a weakness for victims, dependants, people who don't get above themselves, or fancy themselves. In 1922, when the longing to return to some sort of pre-war *status quo*, in which women stirred a pot on the stove and everybody knew their place, such feelings were high. Edith was not born in chains, but she *had* been born in a tiny terraced house on the Islington–Hackney border, and now here she was, flitting between her £250 double-fronted villa and her £6 plus bonuses City job, parading herself at Lyons' Corner Houses and West End hotel bars, attending Henley Regatta at a lunch party hosted by Stanley Baldwin, no better than she should be and in fact a damn sight worse... She was, as they say, having it all. The job, the home, the lifestyle, the husband and the toyboy – two men, at a time when 1.9 million surplus girls didn't even have one! Having it all has the capacity to enrage today. A hundred years ago it touched a big old nerve, the nation's sciatic nerve.

'It makes one feel that we are going rotten at the bottom as well as at the top, and that the paganizing process of moral decadence has gone further and deeper than we had suspected,' wrote the editor of the *Sunday Express* in his pamphlet. Edith, he informed readers who wanted to hear exactly this, 'stood forth as the creature and creation of a hectic and hysterical age.'

But there was something else. Margery Fry described Edith as ordinary, while Rebecca West dismissed her as such. That this was not quite the case is suggested by a kind of bewilderment and vehemence in their verdicts.

She was ordinary, and she was also extraordinary. She was Everywoman. She negotiated the game of being female, at a time when the rules of the game were changing and complicating; when the role of women was being re-defined in many new ways, then redefined what it had always been. But she was Everywoman in some other, more nebulous sense, which again served her well and ill: mainly ill.

All women are female impersonators to some degree, said the US feminist Susan Brownmiller – a brilliant remark, but not true of Edith. Femininity is a choice, a construct, it is now said – also untrue for her. Femaleness rippled through her genes, her flesh, her nature. She was lush with it, yielding with it. And her letters, which were her, stream with this quality. It was instinct in her. Indeed it is not something that can be faked, although many women are able to assume it. It is there in everything she writes: every word has a sensory weight, and so powerful is this still, almost a hundred years after she died, that reading her scattered thoughts – flashing as Bywaters said through her mind – one can actually *feel her feelings*. Her emotions, her sensations; which anyway with her were co-mingled. One feels the rhythms of her menstrual cycle – when she was heavy with it, light with it; when it made her fat, faint, agonized, heady with relief – she seems always to have been aware of it working within her body, its potential to betray – and even when she writes 'I got your complaint badly… all my teeth ache and my head and neck,' she somehow implies the proximity that transmitted this cold, or whatever it was, from Bywaters' body to her own. Even the weather becomes eroticized (which is something more than merely erotic): 'today is cold and dull and I feel cold too – not in the flesh – in the body inside I mean…'

Because Edith's femaleness took itself seriously, by extension it took maleness seriously also. Bywaters would have liked that, almost more than anything. He was eight years her junior – the difference signified in many ways, but in this particular regard it made him her slave: no girl of his own age would have treated him with this absolute absorption, which still throbs today with its slow sensual pulse.

Ive made a bruise on each side of my left wrist, with my right thumb and finger, but it doesnt do any good, it doesnt feel like you...

I am just dried up wanting to see you and feel you holding me...

I do so want you to talk to me today, I keep on looking at you to make you talk, but no words & not even thoughts will come...

Its such a starving sort of feeling darlint – just living on a picture...

I will do as you say about when I want you, I'll even bruise myself, as you used and then take myself to Court for cruelty to myself, eh darlint?

After tonight I am going to die   not really...

There was nothing overt about her. She was not deliberately soulful. Her seriousness was nothing to do with being humourless, it went far deeper than that. She was great fun, in fact. 'Darlint, your own pal is getting quite a sport,' she wrote, after a day of races and cricket on a work excursion to Eastcote, northwest of London, the last Saturday of June 1922. She ran and played so hard that her muscles became sore ('this time last year you were able to rub me & gradually take that stiffness away do you remember?'). Two days earlier she had attended a garden party in Wanstead, closer to home. 'They had swings & roundabouts & Flip Flaps cocoa nut shies Aunt Sallies – Hoopla & all that sort of things I went in for them all & on them & shocked a lot of people I think. I didn't care tho'...' On the way home one of her male companions suddenly said that he fancied 'some fried Fish and potatoes – I'd got rather a posh frock on – wht georgette & tied with rows & rows of jade ribbon velvet & my white fur & a large wht hat, but all that didnt deter me from going into a fried fish shop in Snaresbrook & buying the fish & chips.' What a picture she creates – ! all that life, that irruption of dressed-to-the-nines vibrancy into the little shop hazy with heat, the other customers with their oily mouths falling open with disdain or nudge-wink amusement or lust.

Yet she was not obviously sexy-looking. She was tall and very slim – the prison record, taken when she entered Holloway after the trial, gives her height as 5 feet 7¼ and her weight as 118 pounds – although this was after a week of probably no food to speak of. In her letters, in her days of freedom, she gives a tender, intimate sense of a perpetual swelling and subsiding: with the time of the month, with her appetites – she ate a pound of marrons glacés given to her by an admirer ('I really did enjoy them'), French almonds from another man, Turkish Delight from Bywaters ('its all gone now & I'm sorry I was so greedy') – and with her emotional state, which she believed could affect her physically: 'darlint do you put on flesh when your heart is aching, I suppose you must if I am fatter because my heart aches such a lot.' She was well-dressed, naturally elegant, and a lover of fashion – in tune with the times that she thought she inhabited rather well – which is not always something that pleases men. Yet her clothes give the impression of voluptuous caress: a brown musquash collar wrapped high around her throat, as if to protect its vulnerability; a black velour hat brim dropping gently over her eyes; an ostrich feather following the long curve of her cheekbone. Her face was protean, different in almost every photograph (she hated being snapped; had some photos taken for Bywaters but 'although you say you like them darlint I dont really – especially that one I look so fat in. Tear it up please...'). In one picture she is laughing at a family party with her husband's arm thrown around her shoulder, a girl like any other. In the picture on this book's cover, seated between husband and lover, she is a girl to catch at a man's heart.

'She had beauty, you know?' So the writer Beverley Nichols recalled on the radio, with a catch of wonderment in his voice.* He was speaking fifty years after the event, with no diminishment of memory. 'One of the most beautiful things about her was her neck. And that was not a very happy thought to have, when you knew the outcome... I

---

* The radio programme in which Beverley Nichols featured, along with other interviewees including Edith's sister Avis, is mentioned *passim*. It was entitled *Hanged for Adultery?* and broadcast on BBC Radio 4 on 21 July 1973.

wish I could think of somebody she reminded me of. I think, rather, a Rossetti drawing. And at the same time I think she had a slight resemblance to Diana Cooper... A beautiful woman. With a sort of innate quality of aristocracy.' And then: according to one of the detectives who would later charge her with murder, resolutely indifferent to her spell, 'she was not a woman a man would turn round and look at a second time.' Which may have been true. But it was not the point.

She had this quality, almost invisible to the casual eye, palpating through her words and her presence. A femaleness that was innate, an allure that could not be anatomized as item: dark reddish hair; item: well-shaped brows; item: unusually long eyelashes; item: pale skin. Perhaps more than anything, this quality formed her destiny. It was beyond her control, although she allowed it to direct her course. Any woman would, whatever Rebecca West might say. Her boss Mr Carlton was susceptible to it. It would have helped her to get the job, when she walked smartly into his office and he recognized her for what she was: a good business head, a good worker and something else altogether, something to enliven the nine to five with its everyday mystery. One of her husband's friends, an insurance broker named Sidney Birnage – he saw it, took her to lunch then turned up at her office a couple of hours later, asking to take her to tea. A man called Mr Derry, whom she knew from a local pub – he saw it too. He tried his luck when he met her by chance one day in Southampton Row. 'He wanted me very much to have lunch with him there, and I only got out of doing so by saying I had mine. However I consented to go into the buffet with him and had a Guinness with a port in it, and two ports afterwards... You're not cross are you darlint?' It was part of the push-pull of a love affair that she would test Bywaters in this way – he did the same to her – but Edith could not resist male admiration, it was not in her to do so. She exerted her femininity with the unconscious luxuriant ease of a cat flexing its claws. She loved that responsive male glance, that quickening, just as she loved the sight of St Paul's on her way to work: it was a sharp sunlit moment picked out of the grey.

And as with her letters, this quality of hers was open to interpretation. It depended on the man who encountered it. Herbert Carlton was a worldly sort, who carried on dalliances of his own, and he could appreciate Edith as he would a glass of good brandy. He had enough male confidence to enjoy her. His son, who spoke about Edith to the radio fifty years after the trial, took a narrower view. 'I think she rather liked the men, and I'm sure the men liked her.' The tone, the laugh, pinched at the memory as at a quick taste of snuff. Another voice on the radio was more explicit still, spelling out what others left to be inferred. This man had encountered Edith only briefly but remembered her well: 'A *very* attractive woman. In fact I thought at the time – we had an expression for that type of attraction in those days – I wouldn't mention it here...' And then there was the young homosexual Beverley Nichols, who saw in her the yearning black narcissus head of a Jane Morris, the thoroughbred refinement of his friend Lady Diana Cooper, whose fine-boned white face had been called the most beautiful in London. Nichols liked and appreciated women, as in his quite different way did Herbert Carlton. But liking so rarely goes with lust, lust is so much more common than liking, and thwarted lust is so very, very dangerous.

'Darlint I know you called me "fast",' she wrote to Bywaters. As with many men, he was capable of seeking to criticize what he himself found attractive. At the same time he knew the truth, that she had no interest in actual advances except his own. She had plenty of opportunities if it was sex that she craved – as many people believed was the case. In fact the London equivalent of the *cinq à sept* would have been an affront to Edith's nature (and her class, which was precisely the one that took fright at such things). She wrote that 'a good woman who had a husband or a lover who really loved her & whom she really loved – would never sin with another man – because she felt that other man wanted her.' Even with Bywaters – whom she did adore physically – she found it hard to abandon herself, to lose her self-awareness. What signified for her was in the mind, the imagination. She took love deadly seriously. That was part of her attraction, even to the men who saw her as easy pickings.

'I think you misunderstand me when you think I thought you were cross with me for going out No, darlint, I didnt think you were cross for that, but cross because something happened or might have happened to me, that would happen to any girl who took the risks I take sometimes...' She knew her own *faiblesse*, although she didn't *really* think that she was at any risk. She was a canny, clued-up London girl. She referred to being taken for a meal by 'the usual type of man, that expects some return for a lunch,' and whom she had no difficulty whatever in choking off.

Nevertheless it was not quite so simple. There was something more on offer with Edith than straightforward 'return' for a veal cutlet at Frascati's. She could play that particular game on autopilot, but so could lots of girls, and sex appeal alone would not have generated quite so much calamitous energy in her life. Nor would it have caused the reaction that it did in a man like Nichols, who held her wavering aquatint image in his mind's eye for half a century.

It was the unknown man she encountered in the foyer of the Waldorf Hotel, the one who asked her 'Good afternoon, are you Romance?', who came closest to putting his finger on it. He was searching for the respondent to a lonely hearts advert, but his question had an unconscious resonance. Edith's allure *was* romantic. Far rarer than being merely erotic, and potentially far more destabilizing. It was there in the sweep and cling of her clothes, in her disturbingly changeable face, and in her rapt dedication to her role as lover. In other circumstances – not this country with its giggling pornographic puritanism, not the uneasy fearful post-war years, not the tight respectable laburnum-lined suburban streets, certainly not all three of these lumped together – it might have constituted her great gift. It should have been a power, not a weakness. It got under the skin of men; not least the ones who decided to resist it, who fairly hated her for it, like His Honour Mr Justice Shearman, and the jury whom he led with such relentless witchfinder zeal.

('We are inclined to think,' wrote the *Daily Chronicle*, whose even-handedness carried an undertow of dry cynicism about the whole business, 'that only a British jury would have had the strength of mind to find both Mrs Thompson and Bywaters guilty of murder. The verdict shows how little the jury was influenced by the unwhole-some glamour which Mrs Thompson's very remarkable love-letters had thrown over the case, that the average English jury-man, unlike the Frenchman, is quite unwilling to condone crime because it sprang out of an overmastering passion of love or lust, and, in a word, that the sternest moralist need not wring his hands over the immense popular interest which this case has aroused. The faults of a British jury are rather excess of convention and lack of subtlety.')

And it got under the skin of women, of whom there were two on the jury, besides all the others (which meant almost every woman in the country) who were fascinated by the case. Too many of them saw nothing pitiable about Edith, however much she became somebody to be pitied. They couldn't help it – as with the male reaction, it was as animal as the raising of a dog's hackles – Edith was one of those whom other women instinctively mistrust. Too much romantic allure. Too much like the girl who would captivate one's husband in some myste-rious way that could not be countered, it could only be shut out. Who *was* this Thérèse Raquin who caught the 8.34 to Fenchurch Street? That fluid yearning femaleness didn't go with being a capable business person, it didn't go with being lower-middle-class, it didn't go with having only-just-above-average looks: it didn't go with anything much, to be frank. It was a rogue factor, putting Edith Thompson impossibly outside the sisterhood.

She had a couple of good female friends, and a sister who proved exceptionally loyal when most needed. Before that, however, the sister had played a more ambivalent role; while a woman betrayed Edith to the police, apparently out of simple malice. In her letters Edith displayed staunch solidarity with her own sex – 'I usually stand up for them *against* you' – and from the way in which she described her future betrayer, a fellow working girl, she had no sense whatever of the threat that might lurk in that quarter. But then she had no reason to fear, at that time, the emotions that she aroused simply by existing.

A woman like Margery Fry, wise yet unworldly, would probably not have resented this quality in Edith, which anyway by the time that they met had been dimmed and drugged out of her along with everything else. Fry was stunned by her ordinariness. But that in itself implies a recognition that in some scarcely definable way she was *not* ordinary, else why be stunned? As for Rebecca West, who was not without allure herself – although it surely did not have that same blind and fatal aspect – who knows what dark blend of spite and snobbery compelled her to make that terrible judgement upon another woman, again a fellow worker, but one who could not be stamped with the mark of female approval?

And then, like Lady Macbeth, Edith had no children.

So all in all, when she was charged with murder, conspiracy and attempted murder – when, worse yet, she was found to have conducted an adulterous affair with a man eight years her junior – worse still, to have celebrated this affair in letters that redefined the concept of shamelessness: all in all, she never stood a chance.

II

'...when you are young you think of marriage
as a train you simply *have* to catch...'

Elizabeth Bowen to her friend Molly Keane

EVEN TODAY, A childless woman is a slightly marginalized figure. The very word 'mother' carries its soft and overwhelming emotional heft (not a woman but 'a mother' was attacked, the newspapers will tell us; 'as a mother myself I felt for her,' an interviewee will say). It drags its religious undertow and casts its serene Raphaelite blush upon all mothers, any mother, except the one who harms her child and is defined as an aberration. But the childless woman, the Ruth with her briefcase and her alarming separate identity, is also against nature. She stands aside while society coos and melts at her fellow female, the one whose stomach is swollen with her true destiny. She is questioned and may be judged by both men and women. In a dock she would still, today, stand apart and undefended, suspected just a little from the start. Imagine, therefore, 1922. The childless woman is herself alone (and why does she want to be, what is she up to?), ungraced by that sacred mother word: sexless, except that Edith Thompson was not sexless.

She grew up in a close family, in a household full of younger children, but she did not create such a thing herself. The 1911 census describes them thus:

Edith Jessie 17 Clerk, folding box manufacturers, cardboards
   b. Stoke Newington

Avis Ethel 15 Waitress, dining rooms, light refreshments
    b. Stoke Newington
Newenham* Eustace 12 b. West Ham
William George 10 b. West Ham
Harold Albert 8 b. West Ham

What stories lie within the lists of officialdom. Here is another one:

Graydon Edith J to **Thompson Percy**, West Ham Essex, first
    quarter 1916.

And, because of that marriage, two more:

Deaths registered in October, November and December, 1922:
Thompson Percy, 32, Ilford Essex

Deaths registered in January, February and March, 1923:
Thompson Edith J, 29, Islington

She was born at a terraced house, 97 Norfolk Road, London N1, also in
Islington. One of her aunts, after whom she was named, assisted at her
birth; it was to Edith Walkinshaw that the niece wrote from Holloway
jail – 'Dear Auntie' – saying that she finally understood the truth of
the phrase: ' "The fate of every man hath he bound about his neck"…
I'm glad I've talked to you for a little while.' Norfolk Road itself no
longer exists, although the area at the top of Islington's Essex Road,
just before the right turn leading to Hackney, is relatively unchanged,
one of those rare places – like a breathing space in the city – that
has eluded the reach of the corporate hand. The old, real London is
discernible – the stalwart brick and fatalistic fighter's spirit – and the
ordinariness is a proud thing. This is where Edith spent her first five

---

* The unusual name was held by several of his Irish forebears.

years, emerging on to Essex Road and feeling the tough little rush of life that blows through every main street in London. She was baptized at St John's church in Hackney's Mare Street. Then, in 1898, the Graydon family moved east to what was then the suburb of Manor Park, at the very extreme edge of London.

Today, Islington to Newham would be a financial step down. Then it was improvement. Like everybody in this story the Graydons wanted to move up, but not in the New Aspirant way of their daughter. That came later, after the 1919 Housing Act that helped the shift from tenant to owner, and facilitated social mobility for people like Edith: those whom the *Daily Express* pamphlet called 'the humdrum clerks and humdrum milliners whose life is lived on a few pounds a week,' the ones who were getting above themselves. The Graydons were not like that. They still had deference in their souls, but they also had the self-respect that sits with respectfulness. They wanted to move from working class to lower-middle – a vital difference – and they achieved it through property ownership. Even before the war, overcrowding in London had meant that the outskirts were being colonized. The Edwardian years were the age of the garden city, with its seemly image of tended greenery and air fit for children to breathe. The development of Manor Park was a less exalted precursor of the same ideal. It was a miniature new town, an affordable offer of a 'better life': that familiar human desire, so necessary, so admirable, and sometimes so full of hidden hubris ('we're going to start a new fresh clean life together soon darlint, arent we tell me we are...'). South of the main Romford Road, with its shops and its public library, the streets were given names to inspire and uplift – Byron Avenue, Ruskin Avenue, Wordsworth Avenue – and a school was opened in 1901. Edith attended it between 1903 and 1909. Like St Barnabas church on Browning Road, where she went to Sunday school and later was married, it was a mere few steps from her home at 231 Shakespeare Crescent.

This was an imitation *en petit* of the great creamy crescents of affluent west London, a shallow curve of red brick houses tight-packed as a row of encyclopaedias. Like its neighbours, the Graydons' house had disproportionately large front windows – identical on ground and upper floor – a thin back garden, three tiny bedrooms, an indoor bathroom but no electricity or fridge. Today the area has changed because of the ethnicity of the residents. In the little wild garden outside St Barnabas church – which stands adjacent, as it were without reverence, to a terrace of houses – women in burkas sit taking the air beside their pushchairs. But the look of the place has not really changed. Above all it is ordinary. One imagines the girl emerging from that neat narrow façade every day – hop-skipping to school, walking smartly to the end of the road to catch the tube at East Ham, smiling polite good mornings to the neighbours – and the imagination falters, at the thought that the girl from these streets would create a story to shake and compel the nation.

But she had, said the writer Beverley Nichols, 'anything but a lower-middle class mind, and she had not a lower-middle class appearance.' He said this without snobbery – in fact he claimed social kin with her – although his own rise out of his background was more successfully achieved. And she, despite her yearning for more, that nameless *more* in her life, always craved the sanctuary of '231', as she called it. As only one's family home can be, it was home.

Almost every Friday night she went to Shakespeare Crescent for dinner, usually accompanied by her husband, and in the refuge of the parlour the breach between the Thompsons became easier and more distant, as these things do in the presence of a kindly older generation. What her parents, William and Ethel, thought about it all is hard to fathom. Not until the cataclysm that fell upon their lives do they step – Ethel in particular – step into a fierce light. Before that the impression is of decency, good nature and perhaps insufficient alertness to what was going on with their sparkling star of a daughter; there is the faintest sense that they were out of their depth with her. Exactly how much they suspected about her relationship with Frederick Bywaters – whom they had known since his boyhood – is unknowable. Although they were clearly aware that *something* was going on, they would have believed (hoped?) that whatever it was would come to nothing.

Fifty years on Beverley Nichols recalled the figure of William Graydon. 'He was quite a little man. I met him on the night she was arrested, and he was standing in this dreary little house, in a dreary little room, under a bright gas lamp, and he was on the verge of tears. And he said to me something which was so simple and yet so revealing. He said: "To think that this should happen to people like us." '

Ethel, born in 1872, was five years younger than her husband. Within the strata of class she was slightly his superior – the police constable father, Alfred Liles – and from early childhood she was a north Londoner. Her family mostly stayed in that area – Tottenham, Stamford Hill – although one sister married in West Ham and was later registered as living, without her husband, with a 'stepson' born some thirteen years before the marriage. It is hard to know, in an age when secrets were kept so well, but this may suggest an illegitimate Liles in the cupboard. Ethel, who valued respectability, instinctively shielded herself from any hinted similar lapse in her daughter's morals. She was one of those women whom *My Weekly* would have approved as doing the best job of all, although there is no sense whatever that she thought Edith should do the same. She was conventional, but she was also easy-going. She saw her daughter's free spirit, and she probably felt that in the end Edith would revert to type.

After the trial she became a different kind of mother, burning with the fires of a figure from Greek tragedy, confined within a world where the outlets were not curses and calls to vengeful gods but letters, written with shaking cramped fingers, to authorities as unmoveable as a row of antique statuary. She fought as hard as she could for Edith's life, as did her daughter Avis and the sisters to whom she was closest, Edith and Lily. On the night of the murder Lily and her husband, John Laxton, had accompanied the Thompsons to the Criterion Theatre. Three months later Lily wrote a letter to the government, imperfectly spelled but so perfectly sensible that the only response could be to dismiss it: 'Gentlemen, my real plea is on behalf of the parents... These things or crimes are only committed in a moment of passion & not premeditated. The punishment of years of confinement is bourne by the offenders, but the punishment of hanging, is bourne by the parents & relations.'

There is, in Edith's letters to Bywaters, a constant subliminal sense of closeness to her parents, although they are rarely more than shadowy figures. Ethel featured directly only once, in a letter from March 1922, in which Edith – as was her occasional urge – dramatized an incident and brought it to quick, vivid life. It began when her mother offered her a cigarette; '& I said, "Where did you get these they look posh". *She* "Never mind I had them given me".'

In fact the cigarettes had been a present from Bywaters, and apparently contained opium (which was then used quite happily to soothe babies). The letter continued:

> *Dad* He's sailed now, went out today. By the way "Have you had
>   a row with him?"
> _ *Me* Have I no, the last time we met we were pals (this is right
>   isnt it darlint).
> *Dad* Has Percy had a row with him then.
> *Me* Yes – he did.
> *Dad* & is it over yet. I thought it was when Percy came back to
>   say good bye just before Xmas.
> *Me* No, its not over & not likely to be – but still I'm sorry I
>   didn't see Freddy. I should like to have done very much.
> *Dad* Yes, I sure you would & I'm sure he would like to see you.
> *Mother* What do you think of the fags?
> *Me* Not much they are scented & I dont care for such posh ones.

> Mother was quite indignant with me darlint & said "If they'd been given to you you'd like them," so I said "Would I" & smiled Darlingest boy, you know why I smiled.

> *He* [Percy] came in then & mother offered him one – he looked
>   & said "Amive" Oh they're doped cigarettes…

What to make of this? The clues are thin, but they imply a kind of weak probing anxiety by the Graydons as to the state of play between Bywaters and the Thompsons.

However – and this is the heart of the matter; of the *entire* matter – the scene as described by Edith raises another question, which is how much of it was actually true.

Back to William Graydon. He was born in 1867 to Irish parents – not unexpected, that dash of the romantic Celt in Edith's blood – and had some of the Irish lack of embarrassment about being oneself: . he took the occasional gig as a Master of Ceremonies at the Savoy Hotel. He was also, as the phrase had it, good on his feet. He taught ballroom dancing, as sometimes did Edith and, later, her younger sister Avis. They did this for a Mr Warren, who ran an academy in East Ham with his two sons. Mr Warren was a loyal friend, and he adored the Graydons. Later he would be unable to restrain himself from writing two anonymous letters – on his own headed paper – to the brother of Percy Thompson, Richard, who had given a series of vengeful interviews to *Lloyd's Sunday News* characterizing Edith as not merely a murderess, but a woman of almost fathomless depravity, a gambler and a spendthrift, even an amateur prostitute. When Richard Thompson took the letters to the police, asking for protection against the threats that they contained, Warren admitted immediately having written them. 'He explained,' ran an in-house memo from Scotland Yard, 'that he was an old friend of the Graydon family and was very much annoyed to read the letters [sic] written by Mr Thompson... making attacks upon the character of the woman who had been executed, and he wrote the letters to Mr Thompson thinking to induce him to make a public apology and retract the statements.' Richard Thompson did nothing of the kind, although he did drop the complaint against Mr Warren.

William Graydon, who was raised in two rooms in Clerkenwell and started work as an office boy at thirteen, was a dance teacher on the side only; his real job was as a clerk with the Imperial Tobacco Company. When his three sons came back from the war unhurt – the two youngest were in the merchant navy, the oldest had been at the front – he surely believed that he had dodged the worst that life could throw at him.

His answers at the Old Bailey, where he appeared during the case for the prosecution, give a sense of a man holding himself together. He was dignified and courteous (somewhat more so than the judge, who later in the trial asked vaguely: 'Who is William Graydon?' 'The father, my lord,' replied Edith's counsel). The most important part of his evidence concerned a couple of paragraphs in one of his daughter's letters, a correspondence of which of course he had been unaware, and was obliged to hear read out before the giggling and half-crazed public gallery. The passage related to an episode, described by Edith to Bywaters, in which her husband had visited Shakespeare Crescent alone and complained about her.

> I rang Avis yesterday and she said he came down there in a rage and told Dad everything – about all the rows we have had over you… Dad said it was a disgraceful thing that you should come between husband and wife and I ought to be ashamed. Darlint I told you this is how they would look at it – they dont understand and they never will any of them.
>
> Dad was going to talk to me Avis said – but I went down and nothing whatever was said by any of them. I told Avis I shd tell them off if they said anything to me I didn't go whining to my people when he did things I didnt approve of, and I didn't expect him to – but however nothing was said at all. Dad said to them "What a scandal if it should get in the papers" so evidently *he* suggested drastic measures to them [meaning, Percy suggested such measures to Edith's parents and sister].

Having read this out to the court, Edith's counsel Sir Henry Curtis-Bennett said:

'Now Mr Graydon, is there any truth in those two paragraphs?'

'None whatever.'

At which point the judge, who in his footling yet lethal way intervened regularly to occlude any point made by the defence, put in: 'It
is not what this lady had said; it is what she said the witness had said
to her.'

'I am taking it by steps at present, my lord,' said Curtis-Bennett,
no doubt with a prayer for patience, before returning to his witness.
'If anybody reported that – I will put it in *that* way – it would be quite
untrue, would it not?'

'Quite so.'

'Pure imagination by somebody – I will not use the word pure –
imagination by somebody?'

'Exactly.'

In other words, Edith had invented an entire episode in which Percy
told her parents that she was seeing Bywaters in secret, her father
reacted with extreme anger and then never mentioned any of it again.
If William Graydon's denial in court was true, it was one of the most
significant answers given at the trial, implying that not everything
his daughter had written should be taken literally. Accordingly it was
completely overlooked.

It is possible, of course, that *Avis* invented the episode – as hinted
at by the judge – but that is another story, for a little later, and anyway
highly improbable. In court Avis took the same line as her father.
Asked if she had ever related this incident to Edith, she replied: 'It is
pure imagination on my sister's part.'

And there is another, pretty much provable instance of Edith's fantastical imagination; apparently insignificant, easily missed, buried in
a letter that was anyway not put in evidence. It lay within her description of the garden party in June 1922, the one that ended with her
entrée into a fried fish shop dressed in white georgette tied with jade
ribbon. The picture is superb, a creation of the most absolute vitality. It
is as convincing as a passage in a novel, and because some parts of the
story are impossible to disbelieve – as when Edith evokes the embarrassing smell of the fish on the bus ride home – the reader is compelled
into believing that it was *all* true.

Earlier in the letter, however, Edith had told Bywaters about how she made a trip 'up West to buy a frock for the outing'. She often described her clothes for him, asking him whether or not he fancied the sound of them ('Ive also had a new navy costume made. I dont think you will like it because its a long coat – but I bought a cream gabardine skirt (not serge) to please you darling so I thought I could please myself this time. Am I right?'). On this occasion she bought a pale mauve voile, which she wore to the works picnic at Eastcote two days after the garden party. The mauve dress, she wrote, was 'from the shop [where] I saw the White & jade frock I told you about & I asked them if they had still got it – they had & showed it to me – it was lovely & so was the price – 12 guineas – so it had to stay in the shop.'

It was Edith's habit, when writing to Bywaters, to carry on with the same letter over a period of days. She would lay it down, pick it up again, until the accumulated entries might total two or three thousand words. So it is *possible* that – having decided she could not afford the dress, which (according to her) cost more than two weeks' wages – she nevertheless returned to buy it. But the way in which the letter is written makes this unlikely: she describes the dress so exactly, as it was in the shop, and just a few hundred words later describes it equally exactly, as it was on her own body – no mention of having returned to buy it, oh I couldn't resist darlint and so on – and this was a woman who offered up to Bywaters every last detail of her life. It is as though, having evoked the white georgette in all its tantalizing beauty, she could not resist plucking it from its West End display and clothing herself in it. So clearly did she see the picture that she made (accessories and all) that she conveyed the image to Bywaters – precisely, splendidly, with her swift swooping gift – and made it more real than reality.

Try explaining that to the Old Bailey.

*

What is truth, said jesting Pilate… a question never more aptly put than in regard to Edith Thompson's letters, although one that is rarely at the heart of legal trials. Most of *her* judges never even bothered to ask it, let alone try to answer it. Their job was to take her literally. Her father and sister told them not to, and instead to ask what is truth. The only one who took notice of this was her own counsel, although even he may not have entirely believed in the premise of his client's mendacity. He certainly did a pretty terrible job defending her.

But it is easy to say, in a vague kind of way, that Edith's letters are a mixture of different realities. Far harder is to decipher these. When she wrote such-and-such a thing, was it literal truth, part-truth, invention, wish fulfilment – ? How to know? Did she herself always know? All one can do, with these thousands of words of hers, is look for external corroboration – of which there is very little – or use one's instinct, as to whether a phrase or sentence carries the flavour of actuality. Sometimes, as with the fried fish and white dress episode, truth was the river from which the tributary of imagination flowed. Probably.

*

To Avis Graydon, the letters *in toto* were a phantasmagoria, created by somebody who did not merely conjure alternative lives, but who was an alternative Edith. In her way, Avis took the letters literally, and was one of the millions who condemned them. Fifty years after the event she said:

'I just couldn't believe that my sister... could have lent her name to anything like this. I – *disbelieved* her writing the letters.'

But she did write them, said Avis's interviewer.

'Yeah!' Her voice, even in her late seventies, was vigorous old London, strong black tea with a spoonful of the ladylike. Edith's accent must have been the same, but softened and shaped by her wider social sphere. 'It was her writing! I saw them. That was the only thing that convinced me. Because I said – she never wrote those letters. I *said* so.'

Even the strongest emotions are filtered through who we are, and Avis's agony about the revelation of the letters was poured into the taut mould of her respectability. 'I couldn't lift my head up. I couldn't believe it. It knocked me back to such an extent.' That was the reaction of her class, sad and humbled and ashamed, hopelessly in thrall to the opinions of the other people whom one cannot escape. It permeated everything, every encounter that she had in the neat little streets that encompassed her world. A good morning from the greengrocer standing outside his shop, from the postman with his mailbag – it would never again be just a pleasant greeting – it would hold that flash of prurient excitation, the sudden realization that this quiet young woman – such a lady, you'd never think it! – was the sister of the one who wrote the sexy letters. Later, of course, she would become the sister of the one who swung, who copped it; but that greater cataclysm would not eclipse the mortification of the other.

Manor Park stood at the polar opposite to the world of publish and be damned. When Edith's letters were quoted with such delectation, in the press and at the Old Bailey, the situation was very similar to the 'criminal conversation' actions of the eighteenth and nineteenth centuries. In these proceedings, a party was sued for adultery – usually as a precursor to a divorce, which then had to be granted by Parliament – and evidence of their misconduct was given in a public court. Servants, reporting their observations of a couple lounging on a silken sofa with their clothes in disarray, would testify that this 'manifested unequivocally the guilty intercourse which had just passed between them.' Such details, which could be enormously salacious and were about anything but 'conversation', were reported and read with the same avidity that would later be given to the Thompson-Bywaters trial. They were the soap operas of their age. They must have caused agonies of suffering to the sensitive, while others no doubt pranced in the spotlight of their sexual success. But the damage to their reputations was not fatal. However deep the shame, the stain of it would not spread throughout every inch of their lives; they would not have to creep and sidle around it every day. They could shrug it off, ride it out, or if necessary go to a villa in Italy. They were upper class, their carriages kept them aloft from the streets, and the knowing, winking glance of the tradesman need never meet their eye.

Conversely Edith, had she been acquitted at the Old Bailey, would have had no life at all. Not that such a knowledge would have consoled her: like almost anybody who expresses a wish to die from unhappiness ('we'll leave this world that we love so much…') when the time came she would have taken being alive on any terms whatever. Nevertheless, the class to which she belonged would have destroyed her. And it was class, that prison, which forced her to spend the brief span of her adulthood with Percy Thompson. She married him on 15 January 1916, in the one truly stupid act of her life. Other things that she did, which might be called foolish, were driven by emotion. But she entered into that marriage in cold blood, it was contrary to her nature and she should have known better. Had she followed her instincts – something that she was otherwise rather good at – she would not have tied herself to this man; and three people who met ghastly deaths might have lived to see men walk on the moon.

Class decreed it. It would have been inconceivable that she might look beyond the 'boy next door', which Percy was. He lived in nearby Clements Road with his widowed mother, younger brother, two sisters and a brother-in-law, a family as ordinary as the Graydons although somewhat less likeable: tight-lipped rather than smiling. Percy was the best of them. He met Edith in around 1910, probably because they both used East Ham underground station every morning on their way to the City. So by the time of the wedding they had been 'walking out' for six years or so and, well, there it was, Edith had to marry somebody and he was the nearest to hand. The casualness is at such odds with the near-irreversibility. The might-as-well marriage still goes on today, not infrequently among people who have been together for six years or so, but never with the sense that the experiment could not, if necessary, be mercifully cancelled. Yet there it is: it happened.

At twenty-two, Edith was by no means on the shelf. Nevertheless marriage had become an expected next step. That was true for girls of any background; they all wanted a husband, or at any rate felt that they ought to want one. The irony is that Edith might well have had *more* freedom – belonging to the class that she did, midway through the destabilizing war – had she dared at that point to choose it. She was not marrying for any material reason. She felt no pressing desire to get away from the family home, where anyway she would live with her husband until they found a place of their own. She was not acquiring a financial supporter, nor did she need one, as she had a good job that she did not intend to give up. She was not moving up, or on, or changing anything much, except the fact that she would be sharing a bedroom with Percy rather than Avis. She knew that there was a world beyond Manor Park; she saw the top-hatted City men every day, looking down at her from their public school Olympus, occasionally with a sharp glare of appreciation. So she could have waited, if she had only shown the autonomous impulse that would later reveal itself. Instead she drifted up the aisle in her embossed white dress as if tugged by a force stronger than she knew how to resist. It was only after her marriage that she displayed the desire for self-determination, by which time it was fundamentally too late.

'Were you happy with him after you fell in love with Bywaters?' she was asked at the Old Bailey in December 1922.

She answered: 'I never was happy with him.'

But youth is all too often a time of blindness, in which a sort of bright hailstorm flies around one's life – only when it settles do things become clear, and this can take years. When Edith met Percy, in that haze of youth which makes everything scintillate with promise, he was a boy of twenty or so, exactly the same height as she (5 foot 7¼), not bad-looking, and his sheer masculinity would have been enough to light a flame. He wasn't much of a dancer – unlike her – but he could sing, and he enjoyed amateur theatricals with Edith. Like her, he was out to better himself. He had done so already. The Thompsons lived near the Graydons but they had climbed harder to get to Manor Park: Edith's childhood was cosseted compared with Percy's. His mother Margaret, born in Sunderland in 1854, had moved to east London with her merchant seaman husband and was widowed in her forties. The family of four children were left with nothing, just a derisory pension. At the start of the century they were living in Charles Street, close to the docks. It was real poverty, grimy and candlelit and pest-infested, and the way in which the Thompson children pulled themselves out of it was very impressive. The youngest son, Richard, became an accountant. One sister married a jeweller, the other a son of a church minister. And the child who had shown the way was Percy, who left school aged thirteen, in 1903, and found a job with a shipping company in the City – the sort of work that he would do all his life. The money that this brought in made all the difference in the world to his mother, who like most poor women was old at fifty, but nevertheless outlived her son.

So Percy was not a 'catch', but Edith in all her complexity may have liked the idea that *she* was the more desirable party in the marriage. Some people do. It is a comfortable idea, although it does not always work out so straightforwardly. She had a husband whom she could (as she thought) manage, who was dependable and dutiful. The value placed upon such qualities was strong. It still is, in many quarters, but then, again, it was more important because the decision was for life. The last thing a wife wanted was a man who was going to misbehave. Edith had already asked Percy to promise that he would never drink too much. In some part of herself she was a woman like her mother and aunts, full of London street sense, and she knew what no-nonsense demands to make. She knew about the aunt who had ended up living with a mysterious 'stepson' and no husband. And she was, apparently, reconciled to the sort of steady man that most of her female relations had married: Ada with her railway clerk George, living in Tottenham; Lily with her furniture store manager John, in Stamford Hill; Edith with her stock keeper William, also in the furnishing trade, in Highbury; and her mother. All these women slid uncomplaining into their destiny and stuck it out until the end: happily or unhappily, nobody would ever know, nothing would ever be heard of dissatisfaction except a whisper over the teacups or a glass of Bass, a guarded spurt of confidence in a sister or a friend, a brief receipt of sympathy and then – finish. Back to get the old man's tea. The only one among them who didn't marry was Avis. 'How could I?' It was the voice of respectability again, in all its small and terrible tragedy. 'Would you

like to have to tell a man – that your sister – had been in trouble with
the police, to the extent that she had been? I couldn't bring myself to
tell a man. It's too great a thing to tell him.'

And then Avis had also been attracted to Frederick Bywaters:
indeed it is possible that he exerted the same power over her as he did
over her sister.

Bywaters was thirteen years old, newly out to work, kicking restless heels at his home around the corner from St Barnabas church on
the dull January Sunday of Edith's wedding. He must have heard the
bells. He may even have seen the bride and bridesmaid, the two girls
whose lives he would later wreck, in the open car that took them from
Shakespeare Crescent to the corner of Browning Road – a journey that
can only have lasted a couple of minutes, but that lent a short spurt
of pomp to a workaday occasion. A wartime wedding, of course. It
was only because Edith was in the trade, in the know, that she wore
such rich white finery, such a splendid white picture hat shaped with
plumes. What did she look like in the tumbril that took her to Percy,
with her pure pre-Raphaelite jawline lifted to the grey skies? As out of
place as a Derby winner in a suburban back garden? Perhaps. Probably.
The guests walked to the ceremony, then ambled off to the pub or back
to Shakespeare Crescent. The party included family – Avis with her
plainer, humbler version of her sister's looks, the handsome maternal
aunts with their spry and cheerful husbands, the charmless brother-in-
law Richard with his undertaker's aspect – and the boss, Mr Carlton,
the man with whom she probably should have had her extramarital
affair. He would have looked after her, and no association with him
would ever have led to the gallows. Cynical? Yes, but a healthy dose of
realism would have been far more use to Edith in the management of
her explosive erotic force than the romanticism that surged through
her veins and flew up in the face of Bywaters.

There is nothing to suggest that she felt even a shadow of this passion
for Percy Thompson. Why *him* – ? however much one may rational-
ize it, the question remains unanswered – as with so many marriages,
which to an outsider are frank mysteries. Why him, why her, why did

these two separate beings think, with such childish credulous folly, that they would be happier together than apart?

But the wedding, despite the inauspicious setting, was probably a jolly affair; they usually are; it is when they are over that the trouble starts. When the married couple went to bed in their hotel in Westcliff-on-Sea, they probably congratulated each other on an occasion that had 'gone off all right'. Then there was the wedding night. It is quite likely – statistically speaking – that Edith and Percy had already slept together, although obviously that cannot be known for certain; either way this, too, was probably an ordinary occasion. The fact that Edith would later loathe and dread her husband's advances does not mean that she always did so: '…he puts his arm round me & oh its horrid. I suppose I'm silly to take any notice, I never used to – before I knew you – I just used to accept the inevitable.' This was written five years after the wedding. At the time, when she only knew Percy's touch, she probably didn't mind it at all. Nevertheless: what Bywaters let loose in her could not have been so extreme, had it not been so unlike anything she had ever felt before.

'He asked me why I wasnt happy now' – she wrote in November 1921 – 'what caused the unhappiness and I said I didnt feel unhappy – just indifferent, and he said I used to feel happy once. Well I suppose I did, I suppose even I would have called it happiness, because I was content to let things just jog along, and not think, but that was before I knew what real happiness could be like…'

Whatever the honeymoon was, happy or content or indifferent, above all else it was short. The Thompson marriage was about to be broken up before it had even begun. The culprit, at this early stage, was the war. When Edith took the decision – if one can call it that – to accept Percy's proposal on Christmas Day 1915, she knew that conscription was inevitable. The Compulsory Service Bill was introduced just a couple of weeks later. So even if she had been growing a little bored with Percy – if the hailstorm of youth had begun to settle upon him, revealing his stolid silhouette and basic unsuitability – now a whole new whirl of excitation had arrived to obscure any calm view of the future. An engagement lasting just three weeks? Yes, because of the war. A marriage, to the only man she had ever 'courted'? Yes, because of the war. The relentless daily destruction of scores of young men had given an air of unnatural eligibility to any that remained, even those who, like Percy (according to his army enlistment papers) had the physical trait of 'acne on back'. Well, such was life. The Edith who dreamed of a man to unleash her soul was dormant still. And she most certainly did not want the war to deprive her of a husband: to become one of those women who, after 1918, would say that whoever she had been *meant* to marry had died at the front. One of the *Daily Mail*'s 1.9 million surplus girls? That was not for her. Becoming a war widow was something else, it was sad but not shameful. And when she agreed to marry Percy, instant widowhood was a real possibility. That is not to say that she wanted him to be killed, of course she didn't; although had he caught a bullet it might have been a more merciful end than the one he eventually did suffer, to say nothing of the one that consequently befell his wife.

But Percy swerved that particular fate. Even by the end of 1915 he had been moving close to 'white feather' territory, as one of the 650,000 men who had so far resisted the call to arms. Very sensibly, one might now say; yet the image of the gallant clear-eyed soldier was so powerful, and the lists of the fallen so long, that even the strongest sense of self-preservation was liable to succumb beneath the weight of public opinion. Whether Edith was also applying pressure is unknown. In any event, by the time of her marriage she knew that Percy's enlistment papers were being processed, that he was doing his bit at last: he had signalled his virtue by volunteering for the London Scottish regiment. Conscription had been heading to meet him anyway, but he could at least spend his wedding day in the anticipatory guise of one of our 'brave boys'. He may, however, have already been planning his escape route.

Seven years later, his wife would be waiting to discover if the system that had condemned her to death might allow her to live. Percy Thompson, who was himself – after a fashion – condemned in early

1916, also sought to evade his sentence. Unlike her, he was successful. After six months he was discharged from the army and, as war raged on the Somme, he resumed his aborted honeymoon.

He got out on health grounds, which were a matter of dispute. He himself claimed to have a bad heart; claimed also that Edith made it worse with her antics. She thought him a hypochondriac, staging relapses after what he called 'unpleasantness', and she said as much in her letters to Bywaters. 'On Thursday – he was on the ottoman at the foot of the bed and said he was dying and wanted to – he had another heart attack – thro me. Darlint I had to laugh at this because I *knew* it couldn't be a heart attack.' So she wrote in June 1922.

Yet it is possible that he did believe himself to be an invalid of sorts. 'He had always, as long as I had known him, complained of his heart,' William Graydon told the coroner's court in October 1922, explaining that his son-in-law had been rejected by the army 'as medically unfit with heart affection'. Thomas Booth, who ran the company for which Percy worked as a shipping clerk, spoke similarly in his police statement: 'When he returned to the firm after leaving the Army he led me to believe that his heart was not strong enough for active service. I formed the opinion this was the cause of his discharge.' Meanwhile Fanny Lester, one of the sitting tenants at the house bought by the Thompsons in 1920, told the police: 'Occasionally he had heart attacks, or I should say what I was told were heart attacks.' That sounds sceptical – Mrs Lester herself would probably have called them 'funny turns'; they were certainly not heart attacks in the accepted modern sense. In fact both Edith and Percy were prone to fainting. With her, the cause was probably her excruciating periods. As for him: his brother, Richard Thompson, told the police that 'his heart had been affected since his birth,' and this would appear to be a fact, coming as it did from within the family. Mr Justice Shearman also referred to Percy's 'weak heart' as if it were a proven condition. But it was *not* proven, as the judge would have known from the post-mortem report of the Honorary Pathologist to the Home Office, Bernard Spilsbury.

'I found,' wrote Spilsbury, 'slight fatty degeneration of the heart muscle, liver and kidney... The fatty disease of the heart muscle, liver and kidney may have resulted from disease, but no disease was found in the body which would account for these changes.'

The phrasing is careful (and will later be re-examined). Nevertheless it does not suggest a heart affected for some thirty years. The heart was not perfect, it was slightly enlarged, but the word 'weak' was frankly emotive. Nor was any specific issue discovered during Percy's time with the 14th Battalion of the London Scottish. Indeed he passed the medical when he first arrived at his regiment's camp in Richmond Park. Yet he was hospitalized quite soon afterwards, with what was suspected to be cardiac trouble: the best guess of the medical officers, in an age when diagnosis was vague, and what was then known as a 'dicky' heart might be soothed with opium or stimulated with strychnine.

The story went like this. Although just twenty-five at the time of his enlistment, Percy was not a healthy specimen. He was a sedentary smoker and his early years, spent in dank sordid lodgings just a few steps from the Thames, may well have generated physical weaknesses that his adult lifestyle did nothing to improve. In any event, by increasing his cigarette intake to around fifty a day, he managed to bring on breathing problems during army training. He started a game of spoof with his doctors, which ended in the decision that he was too ill to serve his country.

It was a wheeze, in both senses of the word; and if he was trying it on then who can blame him? If he dodged the fate that had been chosen by the authorities for know-your-place Private Thompson – was this not, in its more underhand way, the same bid for autonomy that Edith later attempted? Percy refused to face a preordained obliteration. Well: good for him.

Except, of course, that other young men had to fight in his place, and by 1916 they were assuredly just as reluctant as he. And the story goes on. Instead of keeping his mouth shut after his discharge, Percy is said to have revelled in boasting about it. Back at Shakespeare Crescent, where he lived with Edith until the spring of 1917, he came to near-blows with a friend of William Graydon – that same Mr Warren who would later defend Edith with his valiant anonymous protests, whose two sons had fought at Gallipoli, and who found Percy's triumphant crowing to be in extremely poor taste. Mr Graydon himself, whose oldest son Newenham fought in France, can hardly have thought differently. As for Edith – what embarrassment and shame did she feel about this new husband of hers, celebrating his freedom over yet another fag in her parents' parlour, her slightly portly clerk in a world of khaki?

★

If the story is true. Who is to say, when everybody is dead, and when those who spoke during their lifetime had an agenda, as surely as the defence and prosecution did at the Old Bailey?

There is probably truth in it, however. It may have become exaggerated in the telling, but to invent a story completely is difficult; especially for people like the Graydon family, from whom it must have originated. It is in character with much of what one reads about Percy Thompson (as opposed to the dim saintly figure portrayed at the trial). And it is important, because so little is known about the man as he was before the summer of 1921, when Edith began her love affair with Frederick Bywaters. Percy, too, is defined by that relationship. Almost every reference to him falls within its sixteen-month span. He comes across as an unattractive man, to which one might say that he had cause at that time to behave badly; to which one might then say that Edith had cause to stray, given the shabby little story of the call-up evasion, and what that implied about her husband's nature. 'He said we were cunning, the pair of us,' she wrote in November 1921. The same could have been said of Percy.

Nevertheless it is awful, really, how hard it is to feel compassion for a murder victim. 'Think of the man who was killed,' urged Frederick Wensley, the detective who headed the Thompson-Bywaters case; he wrote this in his memoirs because he was all too aware that sympathy had strayed so far to the executed wife ('a good deal of false sentiment was invoked'). However dreadful what happened to Percy Thompson, it was not a death laced with the choking taste of foreknowledge.

But, as a commentator astutely put it: 'Husbands are seldom news'. In a story of this kind – the old, old story of the love triangle – the unwanted husband is usually cast in the worst role of the drama. He is the cuckold, the *commedia dell'arte* buffoon, the sitcom suburbanite in buttoned-to-the-neck pyjamas, the obstinate fall guy outwitted by the nimble lovers, the metaphorical eunuch. The subtext is: bad luck, loser, you should have been able to keep hold of your woman. If Percy had been different, Edith would not have looked elsewhere. That is why the court, the police, the authorities sought to write a different story altogether, because they recognized the uncomfortable truth within that subtext. They may even have recognized themselves. Mr Justice Shearman, for example, had rather a lot in common with the Percy of Edith's letters: the smallness, the obstinacy, the querulousness, the misogynist's rage that flared beneath his references to women as 'the fair sex'.

Again, with these letters, there is the issue of how far and in what sense Edith was telling the truth. That central mystery is never more impenetrable than when she wrote about her husband. For sure, a major event – the one in which he was said to have turned up at her parents' house and railed against her – was dismissed out of hand at the trial by both her father and sister. Almost certainly *they* told the truth. But the implications of this were ignored, and accordingly other incidents featuring Percy were accepted as plain fact. The court was swayed by the cumulative nature of what Edith wrote about him, as much as by the substance. And it had a point, but perhaps not a legal one. All that is for later. For now, and for the question of what Percy Thompson was actually like – the man, not the murder victim – there is again an accumulation of evidence. As this is not a question of law, merely of judgement, it is reasonable to trust it. Not entirely, because Edith was not an objective witness, and nor were her family. But there

is something about the *way* in which Edith describes Percy, something
flowing steadily within the stream of her consciousness – the echoing
of her husband's vocabulary, the catching of his moods, the repeated
'*he… he…*' – which one instinctively recognizes as real, feeling as it
were how she felt, as she heaved the weight of him – metaphorical,
literal – off her chest.

Darlint, I've been beastly ill again this week… I caught it from
him, I asked him when he had his if he would sleep in the little
room and he said "No, you never catch my colds, I always catch
yours" so we remained as we were and I caught it badly.

Do you remember the pin incident [when Bywaters fetched a pin
for her sewing] and the subsequent remark from him "You like to
have someone always tacked on to you to run your little errands
and obey all your little requests"…

…I was told I was impudent & all sorts of things bad & that I
must have a very good tutor – that is quite a favourite phrase and
is often used… Anyway he sulked for 2 days…

…he told me he was going to break me in somehow – I have
always had too much of my own way and he was a model husband… He also told me he was going to be master and I was to
be his mistress and not half a dozen mens (his words).

…he came in looking, well you know how with that injured air of
mystery on his face attempted to kiss me and then moved away
with the expression "Phew – drink".

…Mr Dunsford [a buyer] offered to take me up in the Car and let
me stand on the roof of it to see the Prince [of Wales, proceeding
through London after a trip abroad]… He did make a fuss – said
he objected & a lot more nonsense & asked how I was going to

get on to the roof – I darent tell him Mr Dunsford was going to hoist me up – he would have been "terribly shocked".

…he gets jealous & sulks if I speak to any man now.

This last was confirmed by Avis, speaking fifty years later. 'I've never known a person so jealous, for no reason whatever. Now you might meet her, and shake hands with her, and hold her hand for just a second longer than he'd think you should – He'd go up and say, that's *my* wife! What I call – *inanely* jealous. For no reason whatever.'

To which one might say – hang on there Avis, the man did have reason – which again raises the conundrum: Percy was as he was, but to what extent did Edith make him still more that way? The remarks that he made, the rather old-womanish snideness and the attempts at patriarchal dominance, they were after all provoked by the knowledge that he was losing her to another man. He had good qualities. He had had enough about him to want Edith in the first place. He was a devoted son, going out to work at thirteen to save his mother from destitution. There was nothing lazy or feckless about him; in his way he was upwardly mobile, an achiever like almost everybody in this story. 'He was a most conscientious worker of a very quiet and reserved disposition,' his employer Thomas Booth told the police. Faint praise, perhaps, but still. Then there was this, from William Graydon, in a statement made after identifying Percy's body at the mortuary: 'He was a cheerful, happy and pleasant disposition and as far as I know had no objectionable habits.' It was hardly the time to be criticizing him, nor did Mr Graydon want to give the impression that Edith had had problems at home. Possibly he did think that Percy was a reasonable husband, as husbands went. A slight oddity, however, is that in mid-1922 Mr Graydon took to staying overnight at the Thompson house, which perplexed Edith somewhat. 'It's becoming a regular thing now – I wonder why?' There is absolutely no suggestion that he did this to get away from his own marriage; he may, however, have been keeping an eye on his daughter's.

Marriage! What an undeservedly good press it still gets, so wildly at odds with its capacity to cause misery and destruction. Two people who might otherwise be kindly and contented can become truly monstrous, simply because of their conjunction; proximity alone can stir up the dregs of their natures. Yet with a different wife, Percy could have been a nicer man than his single self. All he wanted, really, was a space in which to let his ordinariness blossom. He had thought that he wanted Edith, who was not ordinary at all, and it could be said (certainly would have been in 1922) that he had gone a long way to accommodating her in what was then a highly unusual marriage. There is no evidence that he tried to stop her working, felt emasculated by her salary or nagged her to have a baby. That may well have been because he didn't fancy the idea of an income sliced neatly in half. Nevertheless he would have been viewed – with some justification – as an extremely liberal husband.

In late 1921 Edith wrote to Bywaters, telling him that her employer, Carlton & Prior, now required her to work half-days on Saturdays: 'He's grumbling fearfully about it – "No home comfort whatever you'll have to stop at home", no other man's wife wants to gad the town every day" They all find enough interest in their home".' That sounds rather more unreconstructed. But the word 'gad' – which presumably Percy did use – implies that he was less worried about Edith going to her job, and more about what she might get up to after she had finished it. In the year before his death he became increasingly suspicious (never an appealing trait). In February 1922 he checked with Herbert Carlton's partner, Ellen Prior, as to what time his wife finished work during the week: 'Miss Prior told him we had not worked after 5 since last year and he mentioned this to me – as much as to say "How do you account for saying you worked late some weeks ago"...'. Of course she had been using work as an excuse for meeting Bywaters. So again, Percy's desire to control his wife could be seen as proceeding from a wholly legitimate cause, and his normal behaviour as quite remarkably tolerant. He was with her at the works party and the garden party that ended in the fried fish shop; on both these occasions she behaved with an extreme exuberance that might well have riled some husbands today, and indeed, on the way home from Eastcote: 'he started to make a fuss – says I take too much notice of Dunsford & he does of me & created quite a scene. I am really sick of this sort of thing – he gets jealous & sulks if I speak to any man now.' The letter in which this was written did not appear in evidence at the trial. Had it done so, however, the court would to a man – and to most women – have sympathized with Percy.

The image presented in court was, implicitly, of forbearance in the face of persistent outrage. As the *Daily Express* pamphlet put it, Edith 'had a long suffering husband and a cosy home. There was no apparent reason why she might not also have had a happy husband and a happy home.' Percy stood for marriage, and all that marriage stood for in that time of flux and fear. He was honour and rectitude. What sort of a man he had been was utterly irrelevant: he was the husband, the upright pillar that the act of adultery snatched away from an entire society.

Perhaps, in the end, it comes down to whether or not a person is truly suited to the married state, which in those days was not really a question for consideration. Percy undoubtedly was. Edith was not, although she thought that she was, and indeed that she had to be: everybody got married. Today, when relationships are malleable entities, a woman like Edith would be able to move from man to man, serially serious about them all in turn – believing herself in love, finding out that love is part-illusion, deciding whether or not the illusion contains enough reality to be sustained – and no great harm would be done. But in a society where marriage is imbued with a power that almost everybody is obliged to accept – even those who know in their hearts that it is a false god: what terrible harm can ensue.

★

And one can feel pity for Percy, although it does not necessarily flow easily. Not just because he died young, but because he was simply unable to cope with marriage to Edith. He was not the first man to want an unusual woman then want her to change, because she was just too difficult. He tried everything to stop her slipping through his hands, and seems to have believed that he could do so: if Edith was telling the truth, Percy 'seemed astounded' when she told him that she didn't love him. He then asked her if they might start again, 'start fresh' – the thing that she wanted to do with Bywaters – 'so that when another year has passed meaning the year that ends on January 15/1922, we shall be just as happy and contented as we were on that day 7 years ago. These are his words I am quoting...' It was not Percy's fault that effort in a relationship is the thing most precisely designed to kill it.

'He said he began to think that both of us would be happier if we had a baby, I said "No, a thousand times No" & he began to question me, and talk to me & plead with me, oh darlint, its all so hard to bear, come home to me – come home quickly & help me...'

This was written in December 1921, when Edith was pregnant by Frederick Bywaters. Again, the letter was not put in evidence at the trial, but it is more damaging than many that were, because it makes Percy's suffering real.

Yet at the same time, if Avis Graydon is to be believed, the desperate frustration caued to him by his bright, blithe, sexy, elusive wife had turned him into what would, today, be called an abusive husband. 'He wants me to forgive and forget anything he has said or done in the past...' wrote Edith, which implies that even Percy recognized that there were things to be forgiven.

Avis saw quite a lot of her brother-in-law, both at Shakespeare Crescent and at the Thompsons' home. There is no indication that their relationship was fractious (although both Percy and Edith could be snippy about each other's family; not unusual within a marriage). After his death, however, she let her views be known. She was not impartial; how could she be? Nevertheless this, from a letter sent after the trial to the Prime Minister, Andrew Bonar Law, is convincing. 'It is untrue,' she wrote, 'that my sister was happy until Bywaters came into her life.'

She was rebutting the portrayal of the marriage as given in court, as some sort of template that would satisfy any normal, decent woman.

'Mrs Lester [the sitting tenant] can prove, & also others with whom she [Edith] lived before, that she was unhappy; only her great respect & love for her parents prevented her bringing her troubles home.'

In her stilted way, so poignantly unlike the loose unfurling ribbons of Edith's sentences, Avis continued: 'I should like to say, that Percy Thompson being of a peculiar character had no friends of his own, & naturally very soon disagreed with my sister's friends.

'The man is dead, but why should he die blameless...'

It was a good question, steamrollered beneath the symbolic weight given to Percy as the emblem of wronged virtue. The Home Office notes made upon Avis's letter showed exactly what authority felt about any attempt to undermine this victim status: 'PT is described as a popular young man without an enemy in the world.' In fact nobody gave the impression that Percy was popular, or indeed that he was peculiar. His character simply didn't arise as a factor in the investigation. Avis's contention, that he fell out with Edith's friends, may be true although nobody else made such a claim. The Thompsons socialized in the usual way – they dined for instance with the Birnages – Percy was surely aware that Sidney Birnage had his eye on Edith, but he was a useful man to know, a social superior with a generous nature, and nothing was ever said. On another occasion, however, the Thompsons were invited to spend a day with friends of the Graydons; Percy accepted and then 'a few days later said "he wasn't going" – he wouldn't have me making arrangements to go anywhere without first consulting him, and obtaining his consent.' This does indeed sound peculiar to an outsider. It is typical of the power struggles that go on within happier marriages than Edith's; although Percy may have had another reason for changing his mind.

For, in her written plea to Bonar Law, Avis suggested that Edith was not the only one enjoying an extramarital dalliance. 'His case was just the same as my sister's which you can see by the letters, not produced.' This referred – far too obliquely, but that was Avis – to a mysterious girl with whom Percy worked at his firm in Eastcheap. In a letter from August 1922, Edith wrote:

...he sulked for 2 days and on the Sat. Avis came down and during the course of conversation she said to him, "My friend Bessie Hughes saw you in Lyons [Corner House] in Bishopsgate the other Friday evening." *He* "Oh did she, its quite possible." *Avis* Yes & you were with a short fat girl in a brown costume with a white stripe (This is Miss Tucknott). *He* Oh yes, I took her in to have something to eat as it was late after working at the office & it was my last night in town for a fortnight. I told him afterwards that I was not the only one who was deceitful, but he wont have it...

On other occasions Percy returned home inexplicably late; as, for example, on the day when he suddenly refused to go out for the day with Edith. This is not to say that he was conducting an actual affair. That is highly unlikely, not least on logistical grounds. The girl sent a wreath to his funeral, but that did not make her his lover. But what a shame for all concerned that he didn't take up with the stout little Agnes Tucknott, ten years his junior and doubtless grateful for his manly attentions! Class, again, and the stubbornness that was both his strength and his folly, would never have permitted such a step off the road.

This flirtation of Percy's was mentioned, rather obscurely, at the Old Bailey during Frederick Bywaters' evidence. 'Mrs Thompson related to me he [Percy] had taken a lady out to tea, and I made the remark "All people's tastes are alike".' However, as this was said in the middle of immensely damaging cross-examination, it would have been hardly noticed. Even if it had been, the assumption would have been that Percy had every right to do such a thing in the circumstances.

Fifty years on, talking about the case in 1973, Avis went much further in her accusations. 'I never had much time for him,' she said robustly. 'He was a drinker for one thing.' So much for Percy's promise to Edith not to drink excessively, and William Graydon's statement that he had no objectionable habits. 'He was a violent tempered man,' said Avis. 'If my father had the least inkling that this was going on, he'd have gone and taken her away and he would have applied to somebody, to see that he didn't molest her!' This sits strangely with Mr Graydon's frequent presence at the Thompsons' house; although it is possible that he *did* have an inkling about his son-in-law's behaviour and was keeping a watch in order to keep Percy in check. Edith would not have said anything to him, but she may not have needed to. It was a theme of Avis's, however, this lamentation of her sister's folly in confiding to nobody except Bywaters. She expressed it, clumsily, in the letter to Bonar Law: 'no doubt after Bywaters seeing her unhappiness, she turned to him for sympathy. Her great mistake being – afraid to confide in her family who loved her above everything.'

As for Percy's heavy drinking: nobody except Avis mentioned this. There was the evidence of the post-mortem, what Spilsbury called 'the fatty disease of the heart muscle, liver and kidney', which may have been exacerbated by alcohol. But most damning of all were Avis's reiterated references to Percy's temper. 'Very violent. I put that down to the drink! If the police had've known that, that would have been something – for her. But oh no, they didn't want to find out anything *for...*'

At the Old Bailey, Bywaters had mentioned that Edith feared 'being knocked about when she was asking for a separation or divorce.' The remark was not examined. Nor was a further statement, that Bywaters had 'extracted a promise from him [Percy] that he would not knock her about any more and that he would not beat her.' Then there was this, from Edith's last extant letter to her lover: 'I could be beaten all over at home and still be defiant...' – explicit enough, one might think, but again completely overlooked. Another letter, not used in evidence, referred to the infamous 'Russell case' of 1922, in which a wife accused of adultery made a counter-accusation that her husband had subjected her to what she described as 'Hunnish' sexual practices: 'I have found it very interesting & a portion of the evidence on enclosed slip struck me as being very similar to evidence I could give – does it you?'

But the strongest support of Avis's allegation came during an account, at the trial, of a cataclysmic marital row on 1 August 1921. Bywaters testified that 'Mr Thompson threw his wife across the morning room, and on her passage across the room she overturned a chair.' Edith herself said that Percy 'struck me several times, and eventually threw me across the room.'

Her counsel made absolutely nothing of what today would have been prime evidence, a means both to mitigate the charges and to shift the balance of sympathy. There might not have been much point, however, back in 1922. A Home Office memorandum written after the event referred to this row, and did so in terms that suggested it was Edith's own fault. It had arisen because Bywaters was in the house, and Percy was justifiably suspicious. The unstated implication was that Percy's violence was also justified, indeed not even worthy of comment.

The story of this row – and indeed of other arguments – was corroborated by the sitting tenant, at the marital home, Fanny Lester, who told the Old Bailey: 'I would not say that Mr and Mrs Thompson were on very good terms at any time.' On 2 August 1921 she saw Edith's arm, which had been bruised when she was thrown across the room. It was, said Mrs Lester, 'black from the shoulder to the elbow.'

Edith had shown her the arm, presumably in order to get a bit of sympathy from somebody without worrying her parents. Nevertheless she minimized the incident. She was not the type to complain, except in a brief and shrugging way; she knew that she could expect little pity. There was no such concept then as 'domestic violence', no notion that a husband should not demand sex from his wife when he chose. It was only as recently as 1895 – within Edith's own short lifetime – that wives had been fully protected in law against physical assault, which of course continued to happen. And anyway the class rigidity in Edith would have kept her mouth shut. She was from precisely the wrong background to make a fuss, steeped as she was in a blend of working-class stoicism and lower-middle-class respectability. Even as her more refined self shrank from her husband, the tougher part of her would have accepted his behaviour as par for the course, a wife's lot; especially a wayward wife such as she was. Given that there is no evidence of how Percy treated her before the liaison with Bywaters, she may well have felt that she did, indeed, deserve some of what she got.

So Percy's character would not have presented itself as a means to escape. Legally it was little help to her, and morally she was not affronted by it. She understood her husband, however much she sometimes could not bear the sight of him. To characterize the story as a straightforward diagram, a triangle in which Percy was the corner that had to be rubbed out, is to underestimate its complexity. The game of push-pull played by Edith and Bywaters was also there within the Thompsons' marriage, which many onlookers described as happy. 'I believe he thinks Im quite jealous,' she wrote, about her husband's Lyons' Corner House rendezvous with Miss Tucknott, and indeed her reaction was not quite indifferent. 'She would do peculiar things,' said John Carlton, the son of her boss. 'Like when she was sent out [on an errand]. She would send herself a telegram back, saying something like "I'll meet you tonight darling, such and such a time". Send it to the office. And leave it in a pocket for her husband to see. To cause a little bit of jealousy.'

'Why didn't they go away together and let him live?' It was the question asked by the editor of the *Sunday Express*, in his pamphlet about the Thompson-Bywaters trial. It was not that simple.

III

'What you get married for if you
don't want children?'

From *The Waste Land* by T. S. Eliot

BEFORE ALL THAT came the ordinary years, which later seemed to Edith like a mere existence: 'I was content to let things just jog along, and not think.' Later still, when there was nothing much to do but think, she may have wished that she had never tried to grasp something beyond that daily routine of streets, work, streets, home. Or perhaps not. Frederick Bywaters killed her, but without him there would have been nothing extraordinary; there was life, but no aliveness. So she may have thought.

After Percy's discharge from the army in July 1916, the Thompsons lived at 231 Shakespeare Crescent. This was common practice for young couples – Percy's family home had accommodated a brother-in-law – but it was an odd way of starting one's marriage, and there was scant space in that house. Avis, who had previously shared with her sister, could use her brothers' room while they were away; otherwise she would have camped in her parents' bedroom or slept downstairs. As usual she had a raw deal. Percy was family now, and therefore to be welcomed, but his dodging of service must have caused tension. Also he seems to have been rather boring about his health, surely in part to justify the decision of the army medical officers. He paid frequent visits to Dr Preston Wallis, the Graydon family's doctor, whose surgery was at the end of Shakespeare Crescent, and who was at that time living out a story that might – with less luck – have ended similarly to Edith's.

Certainly it could have created a comparable scandal had the full beam of prurience been turned upon it. Probably Dr Wallis was protected by his professional status: that respectful little community would have turned a willingly blind eye to the fact that he was involved in a love affair with his nurse, Ada Bolding, who lived with him at the surgery while her curate husband studied at Oxford. In 1921, the Reverend Bolding was offered a position at Lingfield in Surrey. Dr Wallis moved in with the couple, at around the same time as Frederick Bywaters moved in with the Thompsons. Bywaters lasted just a couple of months as the lodger, Wallis a little longer. At the start of 1922 Bolding was found dead, full of hyoscine, the drug used by Dr Crippen to kill his wife.

A cutting from the *Daily Sketch*, dated 9 February, later became Exhibit 15a in the Thompson-Bywaters trial. It read:

Curate's Household of Three

Mystery of his Death still unsolved.

Wife and Doctor

Woman asked to leave the Court during man's evidence.

Death from hyoscine poisoning, but how it was administered there is not sufficient evidence to show.

This was the verdict last night at an inquest at Lingfield after remarkable evidence and searching cross-examinations...

'What about Dr Wallis's case,' Edith wrote to Bywaters a month later; 'you said it was interesting but you didn't discuss it with me.'

Despite the open verdict, the general belief was that Bolding had discovered the affair and committed suicide. Both Dr Wallis and Mrs Bolding were cleared of suspicion of murder. Unlike Percy Thompson, the Reverend Bolding presented an ambiguous corpse to those required to make judgement upon it. Nevertheless it could have turned out very differently for the lovers.

But back in 1916 Dr Wallis was living in sin, the Reverend Bolding in ignorance, and the Thompson marriage was in a state of health not unlike Percy's: could be better, could be worse. Wallis suggested sea air as a tonic. He may have recognized that Percy was unduly fearful of living beneath the Zeppelins that hovered over Manor Park – his hands were said to shake when he played cards – and needed an acceptable excuse to escape them. So in the spring of 1917 the Thompsons moved into lodgings at Westcliff-on-Sea, in Essex, where Herbert Carlton lived with his family. The three of them travelled into the City together. If Carlton was eyeing Edith over his copy of *The Times* every morning, Percy would have had the sense to take no notice. He was the man in possession, and there was no reason to believe that this would ever change.

Thus the Thompsons saw out the war. Percy's life was as untouched by it as it was possible to be, although save resigning his job there was nothing he could do to dodge the bombardment of the City of London. Edith had her brother Newenham at the front, and as much as anything she would have been affected by her parents' worry. She visited Shakespeare Crescent every Friday, as she would do all her life, and when Newenham returned in 1918 she was there with Percy for the party, ecstatic despite rationing. Soon afterwards she was on the streets as the bells pealed for victory, part of the London crowd that danced and shrieked and became oddly aggressive in the celebration of peace. She was an intuitive girl, alert as an animal to atmosphere; she would have felt the tilt of turbulence in the country, seen what was in the eyes of the demobbed soldiers, heard the prayers for the scarcely fathomable numbers of beautiful dead boys, whose likeness she would soon encounter in the form of Frederick Bywaters. She would have sensed the push for change – that nebulous thing, which never quite brings what is expected of it – and the desperate cling to certainty. The nation voted in Lloyd George and prepared to grapple with aftermath. Edith, whose life had been so unchanged by war as it was happening, would be vastly affected now that it was over. Favourably so, as it seemed. She would become one of the lucky ones, climbing from the wreckage with all her men alive and well, clutching her future like a shiny new sovereign, a member of the New Aspirant class that could never have emerged so suddenly without all that destruction and upheaval. It was entirely unforeseeable that she, too, would later become a casualty – it might even be said one of the war's last casualties: felled by the collective public mood as it swung, with hefty solemnity, towards a prelapsarian morality.

★

Before that, however, there was Ilford.

'Ilford, albeit of mushroom growth, has a pretty conceit of itself,' said the *Evening News* in 1907. 'Its street vistas are beautifully monotonous; every front garden is a replica of its neighbour; while the names of the thoroughfares have a poetry and distinction that will be found hard to beat elsewhere.' It was quite true that Ilford – just across the border from east London – was a dream of homogeneity, long straight streets crossed by other long straight streets, the grid system of Haussmann's Paris replicated in a couple of miles of Essex. It was also true that these villa-lined streets had names of aristocratic seemliness: Belgrave Road, Seymour Gardens, Stanhope Gardens, De Vere Gardens, Mayfair Avenue. They would form the landscape, pleasing and spacious and poster-bright, traversed by Edith almost every day for three years.

What had been a village was developed alongside a branch of the Great Eastern Railway known as the 'Fairlop loop', which opened in 1903 and was intended to encourage these new Essex settlements (Chigwell was another). Ilford was, therefore, one of several Edwardian suburbs. Yet somehow it became *definitively* suburban: a place where people mowed their lawns every Sunday, raised children and geraniums, kept cats that perched sleekly on garden walls, played bowls on the green in Valentine's Park and died without fuss in their beds. It is impossible to overstate the importance of this *milieu* in pushing the Thompson-Bywaters case to prominence. 'The Ilford Murder' was what the case was called, always and only, as if nobody could quite believe that such a thing had happened in such a place. 'Ilford Murder Mystery': so the story began in *The Times*, on 5 October 1922. Then, as the days ticked on: 'Ilford Murder Charge'; 'Ilford Crime'; 'Ilford Inquest'; 'Ilford Exhumation'; 'Ilford Murder Trial'; 'Ilford Verdict'; 'Ilford Executions Today'.

'Thanks to your Courage, Statesmanship & sense of duty you deserve well of the Commonwealth for having hanged the Ilford Scoundrels,' was a letter sent to the home secretary in January 1923. 'Allow me to congratulate you on the wisdom & courage which have led you to confirm the death sentence on the 2 Ilford murderers' – that was another, written by the foreign secretary Lord Curzon, who had incidentally conducted a long love affair with the married 'pornographer' Elinor Glyn. Of course people knew the names of Edith Thompson and Frederick Bywaters, but 'Ilford' was the key word, a kind of synecdoche: it represented not just a suburb but all suburbs, and all that suburbs stood for, which had been undermined and ripped apart by the behaviour of the 'Suburban Messalina' and her young boyfriend. Had these events taken place in the East End, or the West End, or indeed pretty much anywhere other than a place like Ilford, the shock would have been less extreme, and accordingly less damaging.

What the equivalent would be today, it is hard to say, because the passion for shiny door knockers and everything nice has somewhat lessened (or perhaps respectability simply takes other forms). Running a brothel in Kew might fit the case. A gangland shoot-out in Lyme Regis. Meanwhile Ilford itself is so different now – its population mainly Muslim and its high street dominated by a generic shopping centre – that the symbolic weight that it carried in 1922 can scarcely be comprehended. Since 1965 it has been officially Greater London, incorporated into that untidy overhang, that chaotic spread contained by the M25. The North Circular Road slithers through it like a fat grey snake: it is all about cars and buses and getting to somewhere else. What remains of the past is the town hall, at which the inquest on Percy Thompson was held, a building of proud municipal bombast with its domed roof and doors inset with stained glass. And a certain atmosphere remains, if one imagines just a little. Unchanged is the shape of the residential streets that Edith walked every day, from her home to the train station and back again: the long Belgrave Road, intersected at intervals as regular as a pulse by streets that are wide, flat, becalmed, oddly lifeless, more like an open-air stage set than a human environment. Some of what she saw can still be seen through her eyes; for instance the view ahead of her when she stepped from Ilford station on the night of her husband's murder, the darkness stretching out and away, quite remarkably far for this small square of suburbia, leading as to some undisclosed infinity.

★

Ilford was another world from Manor Park, although it was physically close. Little Ilford Lane led south from Romford Road to the church where Edith married Percy; the walk from 231 Shakespeare Crescent, made by Frederick Bywaters on the night of Percy's death, took about half an hour. A plan shown to the trial jury contained this information:

'From 231, Shakespeare Crescent to scene of crime 2 miles 370 yards (approx.)

Time taken to walk same 31 mins. 28 secs.'

The Thompsons first moved to Ilford in September 1919. It is unclear why they didn't simply rent a place of their own; perhaps it still seemed normal to them to live 'with family'. They spent ten months as paying guests with Percy's sister, Lily, her husband Kenneth Chambers and their son Graham, who lived at Mansfield Road just a few minutes' walk from the station. As might have been predicted, this arrangement did not end well.

Chambers, whose father was a church minister in Stepney, and who himself worked for a bank in Highgate, gives the impression of being a mild and civilized man. Avis liked him, and there is nothing to suggest that Edith felt differently. She had known him since before her marriage, as his father ran the amateur dramatics society to which she and Percy had belonged; so too had Lily, whom Edith did not like. She did not get along with Percy's family. They were uptight, which always had a bad effect on her: for example in July 1922 she went on holiday with her husband and sister to Bournemouth, and found it so appallingly stuffy that she persuaded Avis to climb a tree with her in front of a row of boarding houses, whose inhabitants were suitably stunned. Her parents would not have approved of tree climbing – attention-seeking – but they were good sports, they knew how to throw a party, they had a piano in the parlour around which people would have a sing-song ('It's a Long Way to Tipperary', 'If You were the Only Girl in the World', Irish ballads) and a bit of a laugh. They were both respectable and fun, in a peculiarly old London way. When Ethel Graydon was given cigarettes full of opium by Frederick Bywaters, who presumably wrote to Edith to ask if her mother had minded, she replied that 'Mother wasnt cross a bit... in fact she laughed it off as a huge joke and said I had three yesterday and they didnt hurt me.' But the Thompsons had yanked themselves up from the docks and they were not going to put a foot wrong. Richard – Percy's accountant brother who also lived in Ilford, at 49 Seymour Gardens – was intensely prissy, one of those men who found Edith's mere existence something of an affront and who later played the leading role in her downfall. In June 1922 she spent an evening at his house: 'I went to 49 last night and sat and listened to ailments for about 2 hours – its awfully exhilarating especially when you feel blue.' This was some sort of grisly family party – Richard and his wife, possibly his older sister Margaret – anyway there were enough Thompsons present to put Edith on the defensive. At one point Percy asked why his nephew Graham did not come to visit him; 'and I said "Why do you ask for him to come round when you know he's not allowed to."

'This led to words of course and I was told that neither his mother [Lily] nor his Father [Kenneth] would tell him not to speak to me – my retort was that I knew his Father would not but It would take more than any of them to convince me his mother would not, and I wish to God I didnt have to go there – I feel really bad tempered when I come away.'

So: Edith and Lily did not get along. Nothing very surprising about that; women rarely took to Edith, and she herself did not care for competition. Lily had been the star of the amateur dramatics society, she had married well (better than Edith in truth) and her position as landlady may have made her cool and superior. The inference, therefore, is that it was tensions between the sisters-in-law that brought the stay at Mansfield Road to an abrupt end. A further nonsense – of the kind to make one wish all family ties sunk in the deepest ocean – arose when Edith and Percy discussed employing a maid in late 1921, and Edith suggested a girl called Ethel Vernon who had previously worked for the Chamberses. No, said Percy, it could not be Ethel 'because my people wont like it'. Possibly Edith *had* been out for trouble. There were other maids besides Ethel Vernon. Nevertheless Edith continued to press for her, and the girl arrived to take up her job almost a year later, when Percy was on a mortuary slab and Edith immured within Ilford police station.

According to Avis Graydon, however, the real falling-out with the Chamberses was not between Edith and Lily. The problem, in fact, was Percy: 'he was so bad-tempered and he got on so badly with his family,' as Avis put it. Support for this version of events came from Mrs Lester, the Thompsons' sitting tenant, who claimed that they had left in a hurry 'owing to a quarrel they had one night in the bedroom, when Thompson was knocking his wife about and his brother-in-law told them to go.'

This does not accord with what Kenneth Chambers told the police, but then he was a discreet man. He gave no reason as to why the Thompsons left his home, although he did say: 'Neither I nor my wife have been to see them at their address since they left here, and they have not visited us here' – in other words, there had been no real contact between the couples for more than two years, despite the fact that they lived less than a mile from each other. Chambers went on to say that 'Mr Thompson was a very reserved man and he never discussed his domestic affairs. As far as I could see, they were a very happy and affectionate couple.' Which he may, or may not, have believed.

Avis's claim, that Percy got on badly with his family, is not generally borne out. It was possibly true of Lily, but most definitely not of Richard, who told the police: 'I frequently lunched with my brother in the City.' For the best of reasons, Avis was not an entirely reliable witness. Nor did Mrs Lester care for Percy. According to Edith's letters her husband tried repeatedly to evict his sitting tenants, and in September 1922 (by which time Mrs Lester's husband had died) matters came to a crisis: 'she is not attempting to get out and its nearly 2½ years now – so *he* told her if she wasnt out by *Dec* (she promised to get out for certain by this September) he would take the matter to Court.' However this grudge extended to Edith also: 'she's horrid to me – of course she cant do anything to irritate him, as he hardly comes into contact with her – but I do – & she's so nasty.' Which implies a certain grim impartiality from Mrs Lester. She was capable of disliking everybody, but in the end she disliked Percy more than Edith. And she was in a position to observe a great deal, when the Thompsons moved into 41 Kensington Gardens in June 1920.

★

Three years later, in September 1923, when the couple were both dead and Mrs Lester gone at last, a sale of the Thompsons' possessions was conducted at the house. The local auctioneer was a Mr Bailey. One of his assistants later recalled the occasion, to which so many people turned up that they spilled out into the garden and on to the pavement.

> They were going mad. I remember Mr Bailey was elated by the fantastic prices he was getting – for the most odd items that were being auctioned – like garden forks and flower pots and old beds. Particularly the bed that was thought to have been theirs... The privet hedge was left bare, because the people who attended wanted to say they had something from the house.

The house was ordinary: of course. Built at the very start of the Edwardian era, it was a textbook suburban villa with its four large windows (not quite symmetrical; bay windows on the right side of the house only), its neat front lawn behind a low wall and gate, its large back garden full of pear and apple trees. It presented a façade, self-respecting and respectable, but also replete with upward mobility. It still does. Today the front garden has been paved over to make parking spaces, the windows have been replaced and the frontage painted, but the aspect of the house is the same. Amid properties that have peeled and rotted around their Sky dishes, it is a single-occupancy bandbox. It is the kind of house that makes murder more interesting: the kind at which the imagination fairly goggles, as it conjures the police walking leaden-footed through the dark towards the front porch, congregating behind the gently swollen bay window, emerging again with the woman staggering in their charge.

As a sign of achievement, a starter home, for a childless couple aged thirty and twenty-six, it was hugely impressive. At that age the Graydons had been about to buy their house in Manor Park but '41', as Edith called it, was a different proposition altogether. The doll's-size rooms at Shakespeare Crescent could have fitted like bits of fiddly jigsaw into the airy spaces of the marital bedroom and drawing-room. And this house in Ilford cost £250: less than Edith's annual wage. It would have been more expensive without the nuisance of the sitting tenants – Mr and Mrs Lester plus their daughter Norah, who paid a risible thirty shillings a month plus half the rates – but they were given six months' notice; there was no sense at this time of what tremendous sticking power Mrs Lester would show.

'I have resided at the above address since 1st January 1919,' she later told the police. 'I then occupied the whole house with my husband (since dead) and my daughter Norah, now age 31. The house, which is double fronted, consists of eight rooms, including the scullery.' She continued, for all the world as if she were the one in possession: 'I arranged at the time of purchase to allow Mr and Mrs Thompson to occupy three rooms, viz:- the front drawing room on the right of the house, the back morning room on the left of the house and the front bed-room, over their drawing room, together with the use of scullery and bath-room.' In fact the bathroom had to be shared, although Edith would use it as a private place in which to write her letters. 'As Mr Thompson kept pressing me to move out, I gave up to them the back bed-room, over their morning-room. This they said was for a maid.' In fact it would be used by Avis Graydon, William Graydon and, for a brief span, Frederick Bywaters. It was in this room, ceded by Mrs Lester, that Edith and Bywaters began their love affair.

Edith paid half the price of the house. She could have bought it on her own, but that would have been inconceivable. Anyway legally it belonged to Percy. His name was on the deeds. This was one of the downsides of being a woman in 1920; it allowed Richard Thompson to suggest that Edith had not merely wanted rid of her husband, she had wanted his 'estate'. But as long as she kept her sense of realism – did not expect too much – it was an unprecedentedly good time to be an ordinary girl seeking to get on in the world. The very word 'ordinary' was being redefined. It had begun to imply agency rather than passivity. The Housing Act of 1919 had led to a building boom; homes were affordable, and the shift within Britain from renting to owning was becoming powerfully entrenched. Or rather, the *desire* to make that shift. Then, not everybody could do it; now, hardly anybody can do it. That a home so close to London might be bought, outright, is an idea straight from fairyland. Nevertheless the New Aspirant urges of Edith Thompson are entirely recognizable. There is something of her in every young woman gazing into the window of an estate agent, working for a down payment, yearning for the sound of the key – one's own key – opening the way to that precious proud possession.

Yes, she was only half-owner of half the house. The proximity of the tenants – in the kitchen, where Mrs Lester helped Edith in an attempt to make herself indispensable; in the corridors; in the bedroom and morning-room that lay adjacent to her own – was a clamp on freedom, although again she could never have dreamed that this would last throughout her entire tenure. And her pride in the house is still palpable in the list of contents sold by Mr Bailey. She bought many of these with her own money – notably a mahogany bedroom suite plus washstand, made intricately and to last, as furniture was in those days; except for the mirror on the dressing-table. This broke not long after the incident, in May 1922, in which Edith paraded in mourning hats in front of the girls at Carlton & Prior. 'Talk about bad luck – Mother came over to hang some clean curtains for me and in moving the dressing table – the cheval glass come off the pivot and smashed the glass into a thousand pieces – This is supposed to mean bad luck for 7 years – I am wondering if its for us (you and I) or her. What do you think about it?' Edith was fascinated by luck, that flashy cousin of fate. She tempted it constantly with her bets on the Guineas, the Derby, the City & Suburban – all the major races that then were at the forefront of the national consciousness, including the puritan tendency – 'really I have no luck' was the constant refrain, when yet another horse failed to play its part in her vision of the future. She backed the winner of the Oaks in June 1922, and the bookmaker was never seen again. Like all good gamblers she accepted the reversal; it added to her belief that luck was against her, but she could not resist trying to change it. Her brother-in-law was right to call her a profligate in this regard, when he gave his interviews to *Lloyd's Sunday News* in January 1923: a typical bet of ten shillings each way was one-sixth of her weekly salary, far more than most hard-working people (especially women) would put on a horse. Of course Richard Thompson meant to imply that she was scattering Percy's money around in this way. The point was that she had her own money, which to a certain type of man – not entirely extinct – was the real insult. Edith's contemporary, Agatha Christie, also enjoyed the money that she earned; but before that, as a very young woman, she had been told by her grandmother always to keep a stash of five-pound notes somewhere secret, away from her husband. Without that, independence was illusory.

'He had plenty of the most necessary thing money' – so wrote Edith to Bywaters, a throwaway comment on a character in a novel. She did not have enough for true autonomy, as she was only too aware. But she had the joy of hard-earned disposable cash with which to gamble on making more, regularly visit theatres and cinemas, buy presents for her family, dress herself and her home. It was surely Edith's decorative instinct, the one that gave her a flair for clothes, which imbued her half-house with a taste both luxurious and refined. She imprinted the rooms with her extraordinariness. Like a rich woman, she had a ten-piece *service de toilette* in her bedroom, and a cabinet filled with Limoges in the drawing-room. She had another mahogany suite in the drawing-room, expensive-sounding again with its 'silk upholstery'. She graced this solidity with the fashionable: black cushions of both velvet and satin, ebony elephants, Japanese prints. Again something of her can be glimpsed today in magazine lifestyle features – the female professional in her contemporary surroundings, at one with her times and herself – or in the self-reverence of the internet. Except that she was not quite such a woman. Is anybody, even today, when image is all? Lifestyle can only deliver so much. In the end it is not the same as a life. In the end one has to find a way of occupying the space of one's existence, even if that space is a beautiful arrangement of carefully chosen accoutrements. In the end life is difficult, for those who are not naturally contented. It seems something of a cliché, perhaps, this discontentment; but a cliché is nothing of the kind to the person who inhabits it.

For Edith, pride in her achieved surroundings was not enough. She did not call the Ilford house 'home': that was only and always 231 Shakespeare Crescent. 'I am getting ready to go,' she wrote in November 1921, before leaving work on Saturday lunchtime, 'no not home, but to 41 to get dinner ready, first and then do shopping and clean the bedroom and dust the other room and do God knows how many more jobs, but I suppose they will all help to pass the time away.' This was not always how she felt about the place, but too often it was. The morning-room where she ate her meals, with its French windows leading out to the garden and its 'glasshouse': it was like something from a photo shoot, the long slatted blinds, the tiger stripes of light and shadow upon the table at which she would entertain, the lovely lady of the lovely house. As a girl beneath the gas light she would have dreamed of such a configurative perfection. It would have seemed the very ideal of achievement, a setting for a life that had become just as it should be; and here it was; yet it left her restless as never before, because this was the endgame, and yet life went on.

★

She was too big for her world, but some of it she enjoyed. The routine was hard, as it is for most people, but she had plenty of stamina and vitality. Every morning she passed through the front gate, walked for twelve minutes or so to Ilford station, perhaps ticking off the street signs as she neared her destination – Endsleigh, De Vere, Courtland, Mayfair, names that would become part of the evidence at the Old Bailey – carrying an umbrella or parasol, shaded in a hat, tip-tapping in her barred shoes that could cut a chilblain 'right in half' (later she bought laced shoes for walking: 'no don't make a face darlint, they are rather nice ones'). She took the train to Fenchurch Street, emerged with the City workers at the exit leading to the underground at Tower Hill, then four stops round the Circle Line to what was then called Aldersgate Station – now Barbican – situated beside her place of work. It was a far longer journey than the old one from East Ham, but that was the suburbs for you. At her lunch hour she moved among the workers down Cheapside and Poultry, streets bracketed by the stern masculine glory of St Paul's and the Bank of England, then perhaps on to the corner of Lombard Street and King William Street, past the Hawksmoor church... 'And each man fixed his eyes upon his feet/ Flowed up the hill and down King William Street/ To where Saint Mary Woolnoth kept the hours...' *The Waste Land* appeared in 1922; it is doubtful that Edith knew much about it, although it is in part a comment upon the sensibility that was attributed to her, the modish morality as thin and cheap as rayon: 'at my back I hear/ The sound of horns and motors, which shall bring/ Sweeney to Mrs Porter in the spring.' T. S. Eliot was another who felt compelled to have his say about her. His letter to the *Daily Mail* was published the day before her execution: 'On the Ilford murder your attitude has been in striking contrast with the flaccid sentimentality of other papers I have seen, which have been so impudent as to affirm that they represented the great majority of the English people...' How she offended these intellectuals, with her aspirations and her emotions!

She offended plenty of people, and long before she became public property; that is the lot of the audacious and attractive woman, to enrage as well as please. Many of the staff at Carlton & Prior disliked her. She was not one of the girls, part of the workroom gang on the two upstairs floors. She was management, the only member of staff to have her own office, and doubtless it was suggested that she was favoured (or worse) by the boss ('the only person in this world that is nice to me is Mr Carlton'). Miss Prior, the junior partner, who had one good hand and one made of wood, would only have liked Edith in so far as she was a reliable and efficient worker. She wasn't pretty in that schoolgirl-crush-worthy way that other women admire; one can almost imagine the sibilant whispers of 'well *I* don't think she's good-looking,' designed to console for the fact that men so clearly did think it. She was said – more whispering – to show off her mass of dark hair, bobbed to reveal her lovely neck in the spring of 1922: 'Mr Carlton likes my hair cut – he noticed it, and told me so immediately he saw me, I told you nobody but Lily did didnt I...'

Lily Vellender, a good-hearted Jewish girl a couple of years Edith's junior, was also on the managerial staff at Carlton & Prior. She was one of the few women to be a true friend to Edith (outside her family there were only two such: Lily and a childhood friend called Bessie Akam). The Thompsons mixed socially with Lily and her husband Norman, who lived in Islington; there is no actual evidence for Avis Graydon's assertion that Percy 'disagreed' with Edith's friends which does not mean it was completely untrue. Later Lily would become party to knowledge that she surely did not want, that Edith was involved with Frederick Bywaters. There is a suggestion that she tried to dissuade her friend from the affair, issuing an indirect and – as it turned out

– acutely ironic warning against Percy's capacity for violence. 'Lily had a dream the other day that the Birnages came to 168 [her place of work] to warn me that he was going to murder me – as he had found out that I had been away from home for a night with a fair man': so Edith wrote in April 1922.

But Lily gave nothing away to the police and the Old Bailey. She was loyal. Her evidence was solely concerned with sightings of Bywaters; including on Monday 25 September, eight days before the murder of Percy Thompson, when she saw him standing outside Carlton & Prior.

'He was alone,' she stated to the police. 'Prisoner Thompson said to me, "Fred is outside, would you like to have a cup of coffee with him." I went and joined him… Mrs Thompson remained at the business but later came over with her hat and coat on and I left leaving them there.

'I next saw Bywaters the following Friday before the murder, about 4.50pm in Fullers [a tea room opposite]. I went into Fullers alone and I left him there. When I returned Mrs Thompson was dressed ready to leave, and I saw her go in the direction of Fullers…'

Another girl at Carlton & Prior, Rose Jacobs, was also brought casually into the secret. 'Rosie', as Edith called her, was a young milliners' assistant, who later testified that on Friday 29 September Edith had written a note in her presence, telling Bywaters to come and meet her at 5pm. 'She gave it to me unsealed and said "Will you take this note over to Fullers, Mr Bywaters will be sitting just inside the door?" I went to Fullers and handed the note to Bywaters.' This happened at about 4.30pm. The note, which was wrongly dated the 30th, read: 'Come in for me in ½ an hour.' It was not necessary to send such a note, as within twenty minutes Edith would be asking Lily – as above – to hold the fort at Fullers once again. There is a kind of whirling excitation about Edith's desire to write to Bywaters (as if she didn't do that enough), to involve the girl, almost to want to impress the girl, to dance with danger. And it *was* danger; as the rest of Rose's evidence would make clear.

Rose assuredly resented the glamorous Mrs Thompson and the young man who sat obedient as a spaniel in Fullers, stirring his coffee with his eyes on the door. It was a kind of jealousy, and that emotion makes almost any other possible. Why, Rose would have thought, should Edith have this Bywaters boy at her beck and call? She knew that Edith had a perfectly good husband; she had seen him at the works outing at Eastcote, where his wife behaved in a way quite inappropriate to a woman of nearly thirty: leaping through the races, acting as MC for a cricket match. 'I... made a megaphone of my hands & just yelled – nothing else – Mr Carlton said all that shouting was worth 2 long drinks afterwards so I had 2 double Brandies & Sodas with him.' Mr Carlton again... He was so obviously up for dalliance, but Edith had the gift of keeping men at bay while giving them the come-on (another reason for women to dislike her). 'On Saturday Mr Carlton took me home by road,' she wrote in May. 'It wasnt his car but a friend of his. A real posh car youd have liked it. Im afraid if Miss Prior knew she might want to give me the sack. However I shant tell her and Im sure he won't...'

Later, when this letter was Exhibit 51 in the Thompson-Bywaters trial, the judge pulled his trick of reading out some of Edith's words in order to make them sound as ridiculous as possible. 'A real posh car,' he quoted. Then added: 'Whatever that might be.'

Unlike Mr Carlton, who also had an inkling about Bywaters and kept his counsel, Mr Justice Shearman was petty. He belonged to the class of man who could not deal with Edith, or could only deal with her by in some way destroying what she represented. Oddly enough, Carlton's son John was also such a man. He saw through Edith, as he thought, but he did not *see* her. 'She was a very clever woman. Lived in a little bit of a world of her own... Peculiar woman.' He perceived a threat in her – which was correct, although not the whole story – and Richard Thompson took a similar blinkered view. In his first statement to the police he described her as 'a highly strung girl. I mean that she has burst out laughing for little cause and has got hysterical at times.' This was before any charge was made against her. Later he became more venomous. One might say he had cause, but his allegations were nonetheless characteristic: among more serious claims he suggested that his sister-in-law had undressed in full view of her neighbours. As with the accusation of gambling, there may have been a factual basis to this. Apparently some of the men in Kensington Gardens did like to glimpse Edith's soft silhouette through the venetian blinds. Richard Thompson might well have done the same thing, hating himself all the while, although not as much as he hated Edith. She was a woman who revelled in her physicality – sometimes felt it to be cramped and thwarted – teach me to swim, teach me to play tennis, she would write to Bywaters, and the sense is of a bursting need to free her body, to let it loose as she had once done on the dancefloor (but Percy, of course, could not dance). At the same time there was something more powerful: the need for an audience. As when she climbed the tree in Bournemouth, she wanted to kick up her hooves; and to be seen doing it. To be watched as she took off her clothes – admired yet untouched – yes, she would probably have liked that. It was the counterpoint to her writing, where the audience was intended to be Bywaters alone, or indeed her own self.

She was restless, even at the theatres where she herself was part of the audience, where she watched the plays of the moment such as Michael Morton's *Woman to Woman* at the Globe ('Darlint it was a lovely play'), or the film *The Glorious Adventure* screened at the Royal Opera House, starring the Lady Diana Cooper whom she was thought to resemble, or the entertainments at the Ilford Hippodrome and East Ham Palace. But she liked playing her part in the life of the capital, being the savvy young woman about town. She knew her way around commercial buying – could hold her own with what Mr Carlton described as the 'large number of travellers coming to our premises' – and her business acumen did not fight against her romanticism, it sat mysteriously alongside it. She knew the shortest distance from Fenchurch Street to Tower Hill, her way around a Lyons' Corner House menu, the right place to have a meal, the bar of the Regent Palace and the tea dancing arena of the Waldorf. She would never dare to stay at these hotels, however. She was not a class rebel – not rebellious enough, in fact – her marriage, her refusal to upset her parents by talking to them: she pulled back from what she also craved. Despite her yearnings, her actual horizons were always restricted. Although there was nothing to distinguish her from any richer, higher-born girl when she stepped smartly into those West End foyers, in her heart she felt different, and she was never truly to transcend the limitations of class.

But Ilford was aspirational, and she liked it for that. A part of her variegated soul enjoyed the order and the decorum. She mingled happily with the *bourgeoisie* whom she also sought to *épate*. She liked watching the tennis players, white shapes moving between the sun and broad shadows of Valentine's Park. She liked dining with Sidney Birnage and his wife, who also lived in Ilford and whom the Thompsons had met while staying with Kenneth Chambers. 'On Saturday we went to the dinner party at the Birnages,' she wrote in April 1922 – 'it was a very posh affair for a private house – full course dinner and she cooked everything herself – I think she is awfully clever.' Another part of Edith admired this creative domesticity. She was intrigued by the feel of other lives; she coveted them, thinking to wear them as she might a beautiful dress; but she would have struggled to fit into that of Mrs Birnage. 'On Sunday I cooked a chicken my very first attempt at poultry,' she wrote in May. This was after six years of marriage. She had been proud of her jam and chutney-making – she was good at most things that she attempted – but also deeply bored. Or perhaps the problem was simply the person who ate these offerings? 'I thought about you the whole time and wished I had cooked it for you.'

A conventional thing to say. But then Edith, the Everywoman, *was* conventional, as well as iconoclastic. She was typical and she was nothing of the kind. Some commentators at the trial compared her with Emma Bovary: 'Madame Bovary in a bunshop!' was the phrase used by the *Daily Express*, illogical in its implication that a canonical literary figure was tainted by the association. After all, Emma Bovary herself was ordinary. And she and Edith were indeed near-identically trapped, in a class fatally lower than the one to which they were suited.

It might also be said that both women died because of their inability to separate illusion from reality (not uncommon, but rarely taken to such extremes). Then there was the symbolic weight that they both carried, their profound and unconscious quality of femaleness. Nevertheless the Madame Bovary comparison is not quite right. Edith was more average, possibly therefore more complex. She was a worker; she had an immense capacity for everyday pleasure; she liked a glass of wine and a chat about the Derby form with the Mr Derrys and Mr Dunsfords; she was paradoxically rooted in what she sought to escape; and she would never, ever, have got into the kind of debt to which suicide was the only solution. 'Money was never made to stop with me,' she wrote, after a couple of losing bets, yet she denied herself the white and jade georgette dress. She bought a fur coat for £27, using all her £13 of savings and repaying the rest at £1 a week, but a good coat was an investment. In the winter of 1921 she wrote: 'I don't think Ill be able to buy that watch for you by Xmas, darlint, Id like to ever so much, but as things are, Im afraid I cant afford to...' She did buy the watch, but only when she was able to do so. Not even love was worth financial hardship; which was part of her problem.

Moreover: unlike Emma Bovary, she had no child. She lived – perversely as it then appeared – with a husband, and three people to whom she was entirely unconnected. Without her salary, 41 Kensington Gardens would not have been affordable. Still, the choice of the empty family house, rather than the smaller home with its warm family chaos, was unusual. It would be so today, in fact, although the contemporary woman does not pay such a high price for her choices. It was this childlessness of Edith's that signified to the world her troubling urge for autonomy; until, that is, the world was able to read her letters. And the 'world' – that anomalous mass of post-war opinion – would have offered a straightforward remedy for her restlessness. Children.

Instead of which, she was obsessed with herself rather than her family; in that respect she did resemble Emma Bovary, for whom even motherhood brought no fulfilment. They were both women who longed for more, demanded more (silly women, it would have been said; might still be said), and because of this discontentment they were led – as it seemed inevitably – to commit adultery. The *Daily Mirror* said as much in an editorial of 12 December 1922, the day after the conviction for Percy Thompson's murder: 'There are thousands of fiction-fed women who believe that, by some mysterious decree, there is "a right of nature and love" which is supreme over the "right by law". They are the Madame Bovarys of real life who regard it as impossible to love the men they have chosen to marry.'

So was that it? Was Edith actually something rather simple: a woman who liked almost everything about her life, except the inescapable husband? Was it because of Percy Thompson that 41 Kensington Gardens was not the electric-lit nirvana that it ought to have been, that she was in fact in the house very little, that she spent her hours of leisure pretty much anywhere as long as she was not with him, *à deux*?

She herself seems to have thought as much. As she admitted to the Old Bailey, she had 'taken an aversion' to him. The irruption of Frederick Bywaters into her life created overwhelming problems. Nonetheless she believed it to be the solution to the intricacy of her nature.

Such is the sweet lunacy of love.

*

Bywaters was born on 27 June 1902. Like all the main players in this story, he grew up in Manor Park and he had aspirations. The Kensington Avenue School attended by both him and Edith was a good establishment; *pace* T. S. Eliot and Rebecca West, it instilled some of the fundaments of learning into its most famous pupils. Edith and Bywaters were not scholarly, but they had their own minds, and they expressed themselves with a directness and sincerity superior to that of many more highly educated people.

'Now sir' – wrote Bywaters to the home secretary, at the start of 1923 – 'if I had, for one moment, thought or imagined, that there was anything contained in Mrs Thompson's letters to me, that could at any time, harm her, would I not have destroyed them? I was astounded when I heard the sinister translation the prosecution had put to certain phrases, which were written quite innocently.'

Very few of Bywaters' letters to Edith survive. She destroyed them; as he should have done. 'You don't know what sort of letters he was writing to me,' she flashed at her mother from her cell at Holloway, when Ethel Graydon's sense of shame momentarily broke through the enormity of her distress, and she asked how Edith could possibly have written those things. Indeed the question of what Bywaters wrote to Edith is one of the great imponderables in this story. Up to a point it can be inferred from her replies, but her voice was the only one that could actually be heard, and this had its effect.

From 1901 the Bywaters family lived very near the Graydons, at 72 Rectory Road. According to a boyhood friend of Bywaters called Pat Dixon, this was 'considered part of the elite district', and Kensington Avenue School was 'considered a little bit of the elite'. This meant stand-offs between the more upmarket boys, who wore caps, and those who attended Essex Road School nearby, who did not. Dixon, speaking on the radio some sixty years after the event, recalled a fight on the corner of Browning Road between an Essex Road boy named Lawt and the thirteen-year-old Freddy Bywaters: 'Bywaters gave him a really good licking.' He was much smaller than Lawt – his eventual height was just 5 feet 6½, although he muscled up to nearly eleven stone – but 'evidently he knew how to handle himself. He'd had instruction, I should think.' And was he, asked Dixon's interviewer, an aggressive boy? 'No no no. He was always very well-dressed, because the family as we knew them were quite a respectable family.' This apparent *non sequitur* had its logic in the world of Manor Park boys. If one was well-dressed and respectable, one was not aggressive. In the larger world, of course, the logic did not follow. Dixon also said, with a kind of gracious male admiration: 'He was always a very very handsome young boy.' As with Edith, these looks were in some degree his destiny.

The person who had given Bywaters his instruction in boxing was presumably his father, also called Frederick. He was born in 1878, the son of a coachman, and like most of the men in this story he went out to work at thirteen. He became a ship's clerk, so was frequently abroad. He is a somewhat shadowy figure. When his son was awaiting trial at Brixton jail, a report was made by the Senior Medical Officer that began: 'I am informed by the mother of the accused that his father was at one period of his life intemperate, and attempted suicide when in drink: that the father had relations who were eccentric from drink...' The respectability discerned by Pat Dixon was therefore relative, rather than absolute; it was not that of the Graydons.

Meanwhile Bywaters' mother, Lilian Simmons, was a woman of substance. She may not have been as pleasant as her acquaintance Ethel Graydon, but she was far worldlier. From the first she was alert to the threat in her son's association with an older married woman ('is she your Mother any judge of whether "I'm no good",' wrote Edith in April 1922). Her father had been a warehouseman in Bethnal Green; but this family too was trying to climb. Somewhere along the line it acquired a double-barrelled name, Hall-Simmons, and one of Lilian's brothers eventually ran his own catering business, having been a manager at a hotel in Aldersgate Street, very close to Carlton & Prior. Lilian could have surely done the same thing, had everything been different.

She was born in 1874, which may have given Freddy the idea that an older woman was a desirable norm. Given what her son looked like, her mysterious husband may also have been very attractive; and he was physically brave, another quality possessed by Freddy Bywaters. He served from the early days of the First World War in the Royal Field Artillery, fought at the Somme and in Palestine. Although he was invalided out with lungs ruined by gas (not smoking), he returned to the war. He died of a pulmonary haemorrhage in a convalescent hospital in March 1919. From that point Lilian's life became parlous in the extreme. As Percy Thompson's mother Margaret had learned some twenty years earlier, the safety net for widows was as insubstantial as a spider's web. Freddy, almost seventeen, had been working for more than three years by this time; his sisters Lilian and Florence, aged eighteen and fifteen, were able to take on dressmaking and cleaning jobs; but the youngest, Frank, was not yet seven. So Lilian sold the house in Manor Park, where she had lived in relative ease, and made what would still be a huge move within the tight postal districts of London. She went southeast, to the very cheap area of Upper Norwood, and bought a tiny property at 11 Westow Street. There she set up what she called a costumier business. It was impressive: she had a lot about her. It must also have been nightmarish. When the greater disaster came she blamed the war, in part, for having laid her son so open and vulnerable, with no father as a guide, and a mother whose driving need was to make a living.

'Had my poor boy a father to advise him,' she wrote to King George V at the end of 1922, 'this terrible thing would never have happened, but my husband made the supreme sacrifice in the great war, leaving me with a family of four young children to support. I have done my best for them and brought them up respectably.

> Freddy, my eldest boy, went out into the world at the age of 13½ yrs. When only 15, he joined the merchant Service (he was not old enough for the Army), and stayed in the P&O co. until Sept 23rd of this year, his character all the time being excellent.
>
> He has always been the best of sons to me and I am proud of him, but like many other boys of his age fell under the spell of a woman many years older than himself, who has brought all this terrible suffering on him.
>
> Your Majesty, I implore you to spare his young life. I have given my husband for God's sake leave me my boy...

She included documents to verify her husband's war record. The Home Office, to whom these were forwarded by Buckingham Palace, made this comment upon the letter: 'Her husband's death in service is not sufficient grounds on wh. to respite her son for such a cold blooded and deliberate murder.'

★

As outlined briefly by his mother to his king, Freddy Bywaters had gone to work in a shipping office at the age of thirteen and a half, around the time that Edith married Percy. The firm was in Leadenhall Street close to the Fenchurch Street station that he too would have used.

At that point the age difference between Thompson and Bywaters was a chasm, which five and a half years later it was a near-sickening thrill to leap.

Edith had known Freddy Bywaters since about 1915, when she was twenty-one and he thirteen. She would certainly have seen him before that time, a high-cheekboned little nuisance kicking a ball around the streets of Manor Park: her nemesis. This familiarity makes the passion of their congress all the more astounding. It is unusual to fall in love with a friend of one's little brothers. Freddy was the same age as Harold Graydon, although it was Bill – a couple of years his senior – to whom he was closest, and would later see occasionally on overseas voyages. 'I knew the Graydon boys,' said Lilian Bywaters in her police statement, 'through them calling at my house to go to school with my boy Fred.'

All three of these young men entered the merchant navy during the First World War. Freddy, fired up rather than unnerved by his father's example, had tried to join the convoys in 1917 but was prevented by his mother, who refused to give her consent. Then, as she said: 'When he was fifteen years old he went to sea.' He did so without telling her. After a very brief period in an office at Royal Albert Docks, in February 1918 he was off. He signed a statement to the effect that he understood the implications of sailing in wartime, and left for India on a P&O troop carrier, the SS *Nellors*, on which he was described as 'a general servant and writer'. He stayed with P&O for the next four years and seven months, the rest of his working life.

Whatever had driven his father to plunge into the turbulence of oceans and the carnage of war, it was in Freddy Bywaters also. He was a wanderer, a rover. He had Edith's restlessness, filtered through the masculine, and he gave into it completely, allowing it to take him to India, Sri Lanka, Australia, France, Aden, Egypt. That he should have begun to do this aged fifteen now seems highly remarkable; that he should have covered so much of the world in five years – have lived a full man's life by the age of twenty – is barely conceivable; but a century ago it was not so unusual. He was a little like the pub waiter hero of Patrick Hamilton's *Twenty Thousand Streets Under the Sky*, a handsome young man made for higher things, whose story ends on a breathless urge to escape the circumscribing destiny of class: 'The sea! The sea! What of the sea! The solution – salvation!' Bywaters had that yearning for unreachable horizons, and the desire for betterment, although in practical terms his ambition was small: his last promotion, which he was never to take up, was to linen storekeeper. But the person he seems most to have resembled was the absent father. Probably Lilian Bywaters was right to stress the significance of this bereavement. It was hardly unique after the war, nor did Frederick senior sound the steadiest of role models. Nevertheless he might have done what Lilian could not, talk straight to his son.

With the typical male desire for the women in his life to get along and give him a quiet time, Freddy had tried to bring Lilian and Edith together through their jobs. Edith seems to have been eager enough; Lilian not.

'My son Fred told me she was in the millinery line,' she said to the police, 'and suggested I should do some business with her. I ordered a hat which she sent on from her place at Aldersgate Street... the hat did not suit me and I wrote her to this effect. She then suggested I should meet her and we met by appointment at the Strand Palace Hotel. This was some time last year about the Autumn, but I cannot remember quite when.' What a ghastly occasion that must have been, the tight, polite conversation between mother and lover – who in a basic female sense understood each other very well – in the Art Deco foyer. 'I have seen her since on several occasions but have merely said Good morning or words to that effect.'

It was around that time, in the autumn of 1921, that the mother and son had a conversation in which he said how unhappy Edith was with her husband: 'he asked me,' she told the trial, 'if I could tell him how she could get a separation from her husband.' Her reply was cautious and intelligent. 'I said that there was no law to compel her to live with a man if she was unhappy with him.' Lilian saw what Freddy did not, that it was not merely a question of unhappiness, that for Edith to leave Percy required a courage – a *desire* – that she did not quite possess. Drowning as he was in the dark honey of Edith's allure, Freddy was wholly uninterested in any of this. But his mother saw the complexities, and she also saw danger.

In March 1922, at the end of one of Freddy's shore leaves, she made her most serious attempt to dissuade him from seeing Edith. There was a tremendous row, whose effects lasted six months. Immediately afterwards, Freddy had made his allegiances clear by writing this letter, which he also forwarded to Edith ('When & if you write to your Mother I want a copy of the letter please, yes I do...'):

Dear Mother,

I am writing to you though at the cost of my dignity, to remind you of the foul, unjust and spiteful allegations you made against one, whom you do not know.

You have a passing acquaintance and I suppose you conjure anything from that, anything that your mind may suggest; and without thought or reason but with unmitigated disdain, you slander.

I ask you, I tell you, and warn you, not to interfere in any manner or form, with me or my private affairs.

You do not seem to realize that I am now of an age when I live my own life – not a life to be mapped out and planned by you, though if it were, I know it would be done with the best of good intents.

Mum, do please try and realize I am not Frankie.

If you do want to answer Mum, please think about what you say or do.

Your ever affectionate son, FEF, Frederick Edward Francis.

Lilian did not reply directly, but her reaction is given in a letter from Florence Bywaters, then eighteen and living at Westow Street:

> Mum has been very ill for about three weeks Doctor coming every day... Just one thing I want to tell you Mick [the family called him by this name]. The night before you left well of course I couldn't help hearing it said. But leaving out what you said to Mum even but I happened to hear a little remark which I think concerned me. It was this "My sister! They only want me for what they get out of me." Well you know best yourself whether this is true or not. But all I can say is that if it were true I have been very patient in waiting for what I get from you...
>
> Mum wants me to tell you she had your letter but it came at rather a bad time she being that day at her very worst... she was suffering from a nervous breakdown together with blood-poisoning.

This last sentence is almost funny – why not chuck in diphtheria for good measure? – but what lay behind it was not funny at all. This attachment was rupturing the Bywaters family: 'you know I always felt responsible for the break,' wrote Edith in September 1922. When the worst did indeed happen, Lilian's anguish – that she had not managed to prevent it – must have been intensified almost beyond endurance. But the obstinate loyalty of a man to his lover can override all other considerations, especially when that lover writes so tenderly and sadly: 'I have returned copy – thank you darlint. The part that hurt most was "that woman".' If Freddy had felt any doubts, when his mother launched her lacerating verdict, Edith could dispel them in a moment with her soft erotic force. Lilian and Florence were the voices of good sense (Florence's ripostes were sharp indeed) who cut the nineteen-year-old boy down to size; Edith built him back up again. Small wonder he preferred her.

'Of course darlint I love all you've said about me, about giving up what people cherish most for me... I feel proud when I read it that you say it about me – proud that I have someone that thinks so much of me – its so nice darlint...'

But she was deeply bothered by Lilian. Perhaps she feared the mother's influence. Perhaps, she recognized that the mother had a point; *she* knew that the relationship between her and Freddy was a thing of beauty, but she also knew that nobody else on earth would see it that way, and that in some terrible future that truth might have to be confronted. The two women would see each other from time to time in the City, where Lilian did her own buying, and the necessary courtesies became progressively more strained. In May 1922 Edith wrote to ask Freddy how he would like her to behave, if she were to meet his mother in the street.

> When I asked you that question darlint I had already seen your Mother – but I really wanted to know what you would like me to have done.
>
> As it was – I hardly knew what to do – I couldnt pass her unrecognized without being absolutely rude so I just said "Let me smell, how are you?" and passed on, I didn't stop to shake hands. She had a large bunch of red roses in her arms...

Two months later Edith claimed that Lilian had cut her dead. It may not have been true; may have been an attempt to glue Freddy to her side in the battle. But the sudden dispersal of her ladylike loftiness – the retreat to the feisty little girl from the streets of Manor Park – feels wholly believable:

'...as she came up I just smiled, bowed, said "How do you do" – she just took no notice whatever and walked on. I can't explain how I felt – I think I wanted to hit her more than anything...'

Such were the passions raised by Freddy Bywaters, and such the conviction in his mother that he should have no dealings with Edith Thompson.

Lilian was right, more right than she could have known, but she handled it badly. Giving advice is one of the hardest things to do

because nobody wants to take it, unless it accords with their own inclination. Possibly, just possibly, Frederick senior could have made his
son think rather than feel. He would not have displayed the jealousy
that Lilian could not quite hide; man to man he might have admitted
to an admiring envy, that's quite a woman you've got there and so on;
nevertheless he could have given the whole business a kind of context.
He could have reminded Freddy that the world was full of girls, and
that even the best of them is – astonishing though this may seem
– replaceable. He might also have told him, in his own way, that unat-
tainability can make the most ordinary person seem extraordinary.
And that love, which is part-illusion, is not worth losing something
real over, such as one's life.

The irony, however, is that the father who might have tamed the
situation was also the person who had given Freddy Bywaters his wildness. For instance it was not quite true to say – as his mother did – that
his behaviour was always deemed to be excellent (although Pentonville
jail would mark his conduct at the highest level).

Lilian gave evidence to that effect, in relation to his time at
Kensington Avenue School. There Freddy had indeed been a good
pupil, the odd fight notwithstanding. Her son's counsel Cecil Whiteley
KC asked:

'When he was at school did he get a good character from the school?
'A splendid character; every report was marked Excellent.'
'Was the report as to his character always Excellent?'
'Yes, I believe always, as far as I remember.'
'We have got them here, if necessary.'

It was not much, a few school reports in mitigation of a murder
charge; but in fact Whiteley was convinced of his client's fundamen-
tal decency. When he requested a meeting at the Home Office on 23
December 1922, offering new evidence in relation to Bywaters' conviction, the notes on the internal file contained the sentence: 'Mr Whiteley
also said Bywaters is a good chap & that his father was killed in the
war.' His solicitor, Mr Barrington Matthews, thought similarly. Also
on 23 December, he wrote to the Home Office presenting a petition

for a reprieve, saying: 'I only desire, on behalf of my client Bywaters, to state that until he was brought into the unfortunate contact with Mrs Thompson he was a boy who had never given his mother a moment's anxiety, and bore the very highest possible character.

'Unfortunately his father was killed in the war and he has therefore been at a very impressionable age entirely without a father's guidance and care...'

The Home Office memo on the letter read simply: 'There is nothing new here.'

Again the death of Bywaters' father had been cited as a factor, but the real blame – in the opinion of Barrington Matthews, as with all his client's many supporters – lay with Edith Thompson.

Further evidence as to his good character, this time during his period of employment, was given at the Old Bailey. Exhibit 46 was a formal record from the SS *Orvieto*, on which Bywaters worked between February and June 1921; and the SS *Morea*, the passenger liner that employed him on four voyages as a writer, baggage steward and laundry steward, starting in September 1921. On six occasions he received a 'VG' – very good – for both conduct and ability.

What was not mentioned at the trial – not that it would have made much difference – was the sizeable blot upon all this well-scrubbed perfection. In a police statement, a man named Arthur Newbury, chief clerk in the P&O Pursers' Department, confirmed that at the start of 1921 Bywaters had been suspended. He had jumped ship: left the SS *Malwa* while it was docked in the Thames at Tilbury.

It was a serious offence. The reason for it happening is unknown. The obvious guess is that it was something to do with Edith, although their relationship is 'officially' deemed to have begun in June 1921. She did send a telegram to the *Malwa* on 22 September 1920 – 'Chief away today cannot come' – the chief presumably being Herbert Carlton – which may have referred to a romantic assignation. And in April 1921 Edith was signing a telegram 'PEIDI', the pet name given to her by Freddy. So they were engaged upon some sort of flirtation by that time; but that is a very different thing from a full-blown affair, and from the peripheral evidence of the letters it is as certain as can be that the relationship proper began in June. Why, anyway, should he have jumped ship on her account? What would it have facilitated? He could hardly have disappeared with her to the Brighton Metropole.

The more likely explanation, therefore, is that Freddy Bywaters jumped ship because he fancied doing so, because a rush of blood to the head drove him to act in a way that might have ruined his life, had P&O not seen fit to forgive his youthful idiocy. As it happened it was none other than Percy Thompson who intervened on his behalf, asking the son of his sitting tenant – another P&O employee – to find Freddy a berth on the *Orvieto*. For this, Freddy rewarded Percy poorly. Like his lover, he was a complicated person. Decency was rightly attributed to him; and to those who regarded him as Edith Thompson's plaything, which was the vast majority of people in late 1922, it was the whole story. In truth it was nothing of the kind.

IV

'What really torments civilized people is that they are full of feelings they know nothing about; they can't realize them, they can't fulfil them, they can't *live* them. And so they are tortured. It is like having energy you can't use – it destroys you.'

From 'The State of Funk', essay by D. H. Lawrence

T HE PICTURE THAT these two, Thompson and Bywaters, presented in the dock of the Old Bailey could scarcely have been better designed to arouse emotion in the onlooker. The mere sight of them lit a touchpaper within the collective soul of the nation. They seemed to melt and tremble with sex. They sat apart but the knowledge of their relationship, which had become as public as Hyde Park, made this separation seem more erotic than if they had been jammed up against each other.

Beverley Nichols, who had reacted so sensitively to the sight of Edith, was almost as compelled by Bywaters. 'The principal effect Bywaters gave was of a sort of smouldering masculinity. He was obviously a very virile, and I should think an extremely passionate man, who might have that effect on a great many women.'

In fact Frederick Bywaters alone was a figure who fascinated. Like Edith, he belonged to the class of 'humdrum clerks and humdrum milliners' – as the *Daily Express* defined the *milieu* of the case – although his position was considerably less elevated than hers. As a ship's writer and steward he earned between from £5 7s 6d and £13 15s per month, according to the position. At the time of his arrest, when the *Morea* was docked at Tilbury and his contract for the voyage was terminated, he was employed on the ship as a 'daily servant'. He lived in a part of London that was then not even dignified with the description of 'suburb'.

Yet he had, like his lover, a quality of the extraordinary. He was marked out, and as such Edith found him out. When he became a public figure – as a killer, because he never denied that he had killed Percy Thompson – he was nevertheless found desirable, poetic, poignant, honourable; and troubling, not because of his crime but because of his beautiful masculinity. He had an air of carnal experience, doubtless acquired in overseas brothels, but with Edith he took sex seriously, regarding it as something important and intrinsic. To be so physically at ease with oneself was rare in this country. To be so confident, full stop, was rarer still for a boy who belonged to what had always been the deferential classes. 'You understand this letter as entreating you still to be her lover?' was an intervention made by Mr Justice Shearman at the trial. 'No, it was not entreating; it was stating facts; that was all.' Bywaters was twenty years old, but he was not confounded by the judge, nor by any of the questions put during a prolonged cross-examination, which he knew perfectly well were systematically fashioning a noose. He never broke down or lost his head. He held on to his sense of self. 'Do you seriously suggest that, Bywaters?' 'I do.'

Like Edith Thompson, he aroused not just emotions but conflicting emotions. Like her he divided opinion, although mainly within his own sex. The judge felt a pinched and needling urge to disempower him, to nullify his swagger. Detective Inspector Wensley, who headed the investigation into Percy Thompson's murder, disliked him outright; and squared up to him, as the boy Lawt had done on the corner of Browning Road. In his memoirs Wensley described meeting Bywaters for the first time at Ilford police station.

His attitude, as he greeted us, was full of self-assurance, and there was a kind of studied arrogance in his tone. 'What do you want with me?' he demanded sharply. In his ordinary life I should imagine him to have been rather a conceited and dictatorial young man, and I cannot say that the defiant air with which he confronted me impressed me very much in his favour. I was a man old enough to be his father, a chief of police seeking for information about a cowardly murder, and no ordinary person would have resented my inquiries.

Wensley's book was dedicated to the two sons whom he had lost in the war. Again, the times were playing their part in this case. The very fact of Bywaters' aliveness – his likeness to so many of the dead with his clear eyes, his strong brushed-back hair, his musculature, his over-powering youth – and then the decadent use to which he had put that precious physicality: to some, this was an affront in itself.

Yet other men, such as Bywaters' solicitor and counsel, found him almost irresistible. They knew that he had gone wrong, but believed that wrongdoing was not truly in his nature. They responded to his looks and manner with benevolence, almost admiration, as to a sporting hero on a cigarette card; or a son. 'I liked the boy,' said the Governor of Pentonville, who spent time with him on the night before his execution. So compelled by Bywaters was Mr Eliot Howard, Chief Magistrate at the Police Court in Stratford – where the case was heard before committal to the Old Bailey – that he wrote to the home secretary a couple of days after the trial verdict.

Although there is no doubt of Bywaters' guilt, I desire to make an earnest appeal for Mercy on the following grounds.

As a youth of 19, of previous excellent character, he was exposed for many months to the malign influence of a clever and unscrupulous woman 8 years older... An impressionable youth of that age would need to be of unusual strength of character to resist such solicitations.

This was in remarkable contrast to DI Wensley. But Howard's attitude was the more prevalent; and still more so among female observers.

Overwhelmingly they took Bywaters' side. For, as with so many calamitous relationships, it was all about sides: whose was the greater fault, who deserved the more sympathy. The women saw the handsome doomed boy, and frankly there was no contest. Not one female voice spoke up for Edith. Even if they pitied her, they did so in an abstract way, shaking their heads sorrowfully while holding what she represented distastefully between two fingers. They certainly did not empathize with her, at least not publicly. She was too threatening; even, in the spotlight of the dock, too obscurely enviable. 'Thank you for defending the honour of my sex,' a woman wrote from Belgravia to the home secretary, applauding his decision not to reprieve Edith Thompson.

'I do not think,' wrote the civil servant Sir Ernley Blackwell, 'we have a single application from any one of the women's societies in favour of the reprieve of Mrs Thompson, and I believe that so far as those women societies are concerned any differentiation between these prisoners, purely on the ground of sex, or the respite of both prisoners on the ground that one of them is a woman and therefore if she is not executed the other ought not to be, would be bitterly resented.' Ah yes: equality cut both ways, as these women were obliged to accept.

And that, in essence, was the issue. Both Thompson and Bywaters had been convicted of a capital charge, and the death sentence was therefore mandatory. Increasingly it was not carried out, but reprieves were problematical in cases of joint enterprise; as the Home Office list of executions had made clear. Blame had to be attributed within the guilty partnership. This was extremely difficult, and rarely had much to do with actual evidence. After the Thompson-Bywaters trial, much of the loudest handwringing was about the vexed issue of hanging a woman. But then – said the commentators sadly – given that young Bywaters had to hang, how was it fair that she should not? This was the outward mood. Yet the secret, excited mood of the country held the reverse view: it wanted to hang Edith, and this meant that it also had to hang Bywaters.

A huge petition was got up for his reprieve by the *Daily Sketch*. It was submitted to the Home Office, and an internal memo noted that it had been signed 'by some 900,000 persons'. Nevertheless it was dismissed as a semi-stunt: 'it is said to have been signed sometimes over and over again by the same persons, and in many cases (I am told in about half) the signatures are those of children.' In fact a long queue of signatories had formed immediately at the newspaper's office. 'Bywaters must not be hanged,' was a headline on 15 December 1922, together with a long article 'written' by his mother. Even if the number of names was exaggerated, it was absurd of the Home Office to deny that the *Daily Sketch* had touched a nerve. Meanwhile the *Evening Standard* wrote on 12 December, the day after the verdicts:

> It is unpleasant to hang a woman – at least, that is the general feeling among males; what women themselves think is quite another matter – and petitions for the reprieve of Edith Thompson might possibly not be extensively signed by members of her own sex. But if the woman were to be reprieved, would it be just to hang the man, who, much younger than herself, and possibly of weaker character than herself, undoubtedly, in the view of many, acted under her influence?

The *Daily News*, which admitted to a degree of doubt about Edith's conviction, nonetheless wrote: 'Morally, no one can have any illusions with regard to Mrs Thompson; morally, the figure of her lover appears quite engaging in contrast.'

This made no sense at all, strictly speaking. Both had engaged upon an adulterous affair and both, according to the verdicts, had committed murder. To be precise, Bywaters had physically killed and Thompson had incited him to do so: that was the gist of it. There was, of course, the fact that he was seven and a half years her junior. Even now this would be a noteworthy factor, lending a thick layer of luscious prurience to the scrutiny – as if this pair weren't already sexy enough, what with their looks and their letters, why, the woman was a cougar on the prowl…! Oh yes, one can imagine the commentary today, the suburban Messalina who was also a suburban Marschallin; and so on.

And no question, sympathy would still be with Bywaters among the majority of the population. No doubt about that whatsoever.

Almost a century ago, however, the notion of a woman of twenty-eight with a boy of twenty was not merely titillating; it was so outlandish that Edith could only be rationalized as a sorceress, a praying mantis. The murder simply *had* to be her doing, because that was the dynamic of the relationship. As the *Daily News* put it: 'If the verdict were to be on moral blood-guiltiness, there is perhaps a case for placing at her door, and not at her dupe's at all, the fate of her unfortunate husband.'

And then, as if in confirmation, Frederick Bywaters' own words were offered up as Exhibit 30 at the Old Bailey: 'Peidi you are my magnet – I cannot resist darlint – you draw me to you now and always... Darlint Peidi Mia Idol mine...'

Yet the sight of the couple in the dock, the trembling woman and the self-possessed man, did not quite fit the image. Many relationships are power struggles. It is rare to find an equal partnership, and they are not necessarily as idyllic as they sound, although Edith, with her sweet reiterated cooing of the word 'pal' – the best pal a girl ever had, from your pal Peidi, the palship of two halves – made a good fist of portraying this affair as some sort of Platonic ideal, which was about the last thing it was. In fact it was a near-definitive power struggle. This was partly because both parties were so intense in their feelings, partly because they saw so little of each other; but also because the woman was so much older. When the traditionally dominant male is in that particular submissive position, the balance of the relationship almost inevitably shifts. On the one hand the woman is in charge, she knows how to play the game, she has the craft and the control; she can play at mystery and femaleness in a way that a contemporary would not accept, having seen it all before; she is taken majestically seriously. On the other hand she has intimations of mortality: the awareness of loosening and softening flesh, the fear that his hand will encounter something it rejects, the sense that at any time, out of the corner of his young man's eye, he may catch sight of something taut and casual and *equal...* One of Edith's letters confronts this, in that acute and sensory way that makes the reader feel it with her:

> My veriest own lover I always think about the "difference" when I'm with you and when I'm away sometimes when I'm happy for a little while I forget – but I always remember very soon – perhaps some little thing that you might say or do when we're together reminds me. Sometimes I think and think until my brain goes round and round "Shall I always be able to keep you". 8 years is such a long time – it's not now – it's later – when I'm "Joan" and you're not grown old enough to be "Darby"...
>
> Don't ever take your love away from me darlint – I never want to lose it and live.

This was one letter, written in July 1922, but the fear implicit within it spread further, and her defensive question – 'I hadn't mentioned the subject any more had I?' – suggests that she did indeed mention it when they were together, when she could not avoid the sense that her own beauty was shaded by his animal glow. It may not have been true, and she did not feel it all the time, but the vulnerability was there. Then *she* was the supplicant. The older woman was not wielding power, she was admitting to the fact that she might lose it.

At the Old Bailey, Bywaters was asked what he thought that Edith had meant by the July letter, and he answered bluntly: 'Her age and mine. She was eight years older than me, and she felt it.' That cannot have been an easy thing for her to hear, even in circumstances that should have rendered it an irrelevance. And those in court should have heard it properly too, the young man's cool unthinking cruelty and what it meant within that relationship.

Sometimes, as it wound its complex course, she had actually seemed to be the younger one, or rather the more dependent. It was a game, but there was also something real going on. 'I'm not bullying I'm deciding for you Chère,' he would say; and she found it both thrilling and consoling. Among Edith's many contradictions was the fact that she was a stoic, seasoned adult who retained direct access to her child's self; and she expressed this not to her parents but to a boy barely out of his teens, with whom the reversion to helplessness was both eroticized and genuine. 'Why and how was I a "little girl" – darlint I always feel that I want you to take care of me, to be nice to me, to fuss hold me always in your arms, tight, ever so tight...' Lovers do make themselves childlike to each other. Nevertheless there is something truly and touchingly unsophisticated about Edith, that murderous temptress, when she wrote: 'Lunch time I went to Queen Vic. St. to get some "Toblerone" to send...'

Sending chocolate to one's boy overseas – that is also, of course, the action of a mother. Edith wrote indulgently of how she liked to ruffle Bywaters' hair, and of 'how much I wanted to be with you, so that I could love you that "Mothering feeling" came over me.' But it would be wrong to think that she diverted a maternal impulse towards him. Contrary to received opinion, childless women do not invariably seek an alternative outlet, whether it be a toyboy or a toy dog. Edith did occasionally muse on the subject of babies, but only as a possible means to keep her lover by her side. She was not the motherly type, she was far too fascinated by herself. In a subsequent letter she wrote that she had sent one bar of Toblerone and kept another, so perhaps they could eat it together, bite into it at the same time, while thinking of each other. Was that maternal? Not so much. Yes, she believed that she could control and school her younger lover, but many women feel this way about their men. At the same time they usually know, deep down, that the belief is delusional.

Filson Young, who edited 'The Trial of Frederick Bywaters and Edith Thompson' for the *Notable British Trials* series, wrote this in his introduction:

> A great deal of play was made about their respective ages, and it was suggested that she was an experienced woman corrupting a young lad. That is not the way I see it... In some ways he was the older of the two, as he was certainly the more masterful. He was an almost excessively virile, animal type.

The words of Beverley Nichols, stripped of their romantic yearning. And DI Wensley, who was crude but shrewd, wrote something similar: '[Bywaters] cannot be set down as an unsophisticated youth, for he was experienced much beyond his age, and of strong and dominating character.' Wensley acknowledged the woman's influence, as she could hardly be let off the hook by the detective who had brought her to justice. Yet at the same time he equivocated, subtly but significantly: '*Whichever of them first thought of murder* [my italics] there is no question that she had such power over him that he was prepared to do her bidding.'

Within the push-pull of passion, dominance and supplication shift like the shadows on shot silk. Who is to say, for instance, where the true seat of power lies in a passage such as this:

> Yes, we are both going to fight until we win – darlint, fight hard, in real earnest – you are going to help me first and then I am going to help you and when you have done your share and I have done mine we shall have given to each other what we both "desire most in the world" ourselves, isn't this right, but darlint don't fail in your share of the bargain, because I am helpless without your help – you understand.

Or this:

> Darlint this is the one instance in which I cannot stand alone I cannot help myself (at first) – the one instance when I want a man to lean on and that one man is and can only – always – be you.

Those who saw the couple on trial were similarly conflicted, mesmerized by the nature of the invisible connection between these two alarmingly attractive people, whose outer facings hinted at their unruly emotional capacity. The woman, slightly worn with her parched face; had she really lured that unabashed young man beside her to his fate? To those who studied the story, it seemed so. Her age, her letters, her shamelessness in writing the letters, her age... And yet, to look at them, one would not be sure. Which of them had led the other – was it really possible to say? Of course it was not.

But the decision was made to blame the woman, because although she may have been the supplant she must have been the dominatrix. In the three months between the murder and the executions there was almost no deviation from that line. Almost everybody accepted it, even those who saw the threat in Bywaters – a puritanical older man like Shearman, a man inured to charming villains like Wensley. Almost everybody saw him as his lover's victim. Unlike her, he was not a victim of prejudice. There was not the same desire to destroy him. He had to be destroyed, but there was not the *desire* to do it. The qualities that in her were so hectic and intolerable were, in him, acceptable. Simple as that.

★

And what would have happened to the extraordinariness of Edith Thompson, if Frederick Bywaters had not re-entered her life in 1920? She flowered after that point, so it is possible that without a stimulus she would have reverted to type, 'settled', and become completely the ordinary person who was also in her. More likely she was looking for a stimulus, and alighted upon him for that purpose. Love is circumstantial, not absolute.

In fact the true outlet of their love affair was her writing; the act in which she uncovered and discovered herself, and developed alternative lives more real than reality. But that would never have happened had she not sought to 'talk' to Bywaters. Without him, or somebody like him, she would probably never have written anything, never attempted to grasp the numinous, as lovers and creatives do. And she would probably have lived to her late sixties, like her mother who died in 1938, or her mid-seventies, like her father who died in 1941. She would have aged, the thing that she feared (Everywoman again), although without a younger lover it would have mattered less. An unrecorded

and unremarked life, therefore, with Percy Thompson and perhaps
in the end a baby to push in its pram through Valentine's Park, or on
longer walks up to Wanstead Park, by the City of London graveyard
in which she would have been quietly buried alongside her husband.
Anonymity, or notoriety, were the only alternatives for a woman born
into Edith's world. How different it would be today for a girl of her
kind, a good-looking New Aspirant with a gift for self-expression! She
would still trouble people, because she still would not 'fit', but outside
the prison of class – perhaps outside her own conflicted country – the
damage would be survivable.

And class, once more, played its part in her choice of lover (for it was
a choice; there were other candidates). She never in her life met a man
who could respond to what Beverley Nichols called her 'innate quality
of aristocracy'. This was not a snobbish remark, it was about something
in Edith that sought an outlet, and believed itself to have found one
in Freddy Bywaters: another boy next door. It just so happened that,
having been around the world, he returned to Manor Park at the start
of 1920 with an air of expansive newness, a metaphorical smell of the
salty exotic. He also returned as an unusually handsome young man,
with that blend of the vulnerable and the hard-edged that is peculiarly desirable. Nevertheless she could have aimed a lot higher. It was
strange that she should succumb in the end to a teenager with a streak
of aggression and a salary about a quarter of her own (he was generous with it, buying her presents and lunches, but basically he had no
money). She was a woman of refinement, despite the hoydenish behaviour that she sometimes could not resist. Bywaters had a brain, he had
manners, he could express himself; nevertheless he was a very rough
diamond when compared with the Mr Carltons and Mr Birnages. He
belonged to the open air and seas. On 14 October 1922, possessions
found in his quarters on the *Morea* were opened at Limehouse Police
Station, as reported in a statement by Detective Inspector Francis Hall:

'I opened them by means of keys found on prisoner Bywaters when
he was searched... The trunk and brown paper parcel contained
Clothing. In the ditty box I found 5 bundles of letters, some of which

contained newspaper cuttings; an automatic pistol; 25 rounds of ammunition...'

'I was,' Bywaters wrote to the home secretary at the start of 1923, 'in the habit of carrying either a knife or a revolver.'

Beneath his aspect of a chiselled young princeling, an amateur cricketing hero, a Rupert Brooke of the oceans, there lay something coarse and unlovely, something of the thug. In an earlier age he might have been a highwayman, adored by the girls as he stood firmly on the gallows. Edith was such a girl, although at the same time she tried to elevate him. She wrote a long letter in April 1922, in the course of which she referred to a remark he had passed on, made by the ship's barber and presumably somewhat ribald. 'I suppose in a way the barber was right darlint – he does know you better than I do – that part of you that lives on ships but I know you – the inside part that nobody else sees or knows and I dont want them to yet awhile at any rate.' The bit of rough was also capable of the most pure and ardent emotion; which again was highly attractive.

Although Edith would later torment herself over the age difference, at the start it would have been exhilarating to command the interest of this boy. There is no idiotic thrill quite like the knowledge that one is fancied by somebody fanciable; it is like a perpetual first sip of champagne, and covers the world in the bubbling, popping mist of the freshly poured glass. This was the glancing male gaze that she knew so well, but made deeper, fleshier, by reciprocity.

So his youth made him physically desirable – made her feel physically desirable – but perhaps the real point about Bywaters' age was this. He freed Edith to be herself, which included the assumption of roles. Through him she could feel what she longed to feel. In that sense he *was* her plaything, because he let loose yearnings that were in the end solipsistic, that existed most powerfully when she sat alone in the bathroom at 41 Kensington Gardens, writing writing writing herself into a different world.

And outside the window, putting a hand to his lower back as he stood up with his spade, was her husband. Of course Freddy Bywaters could not have been more unlike Percy Thompson. The contrast was such as to make Percy seem worse than he was, a pompous cliché of an English husband. 'He is a clean-looking fellow,' was reportedly his judgement upon Bywaters, after an evening at Shakespeare Crescent in around May 1920. It was the first time that the Thompsons had seen Freddy in a couple of years: the first time, effectively, that they had met him as an adult. Percy liked Freddy; Freddy liked Percy: the murderer and his victim enjoyed a glass of Bass together in the company of the woman who would destroy them both, who both destroyed her, whose feelings at this early stage are unknowable.

★

Her sister's feelings are clearer. In January 1920 Freddy Bywaters had called at the Graydons' house to look up his old friend Bill. The last time Avis Graydon met him, she had barely remarked him. Now she did. At least six months before he engaged the attention of the glamorous Mrs Thompson, he had commanded the tentative affections of the waitress Avis.

She too was considerably older than he – almost seven years – but nobody within the family seems to have taken any notice (so many of the men of her own age were dead, after all). Freddy was undoubtedly very mature. A boy of seventeen and a half who had travelled round the world was, in fact, a man. His horizons were literally broad. He was already experienced, and became much more so. In Marseilles and Port Said he disported himself in the bordellos alongside his fellow crew members. In Australia he took up with a girl whose letters Edith demanded to see; somewhat immature behaviour, but she apparently could not help herself. 'Darlint, Australia frightens me.'

It is possible, even likely, that Freddy Bywaters was keen on this girl, although his willingness to hand over her letters implies that they were hardly the same kind as Edith's own. 'I'm beginning to think I'm rather silly to have asked you for them because you do love me – I know that – Do you think I am silly?' No doubt he liked the Australian girl when he saw her, but Edith could stay in his mind when he was away from her: that was a woman's gift, not a girl's. And both she and Freddy found pleasure in tormenting each other, and being tormented, with reminders of how alluring they each were to the opposite sex. Her letters were punctuated with pinprick references to the man who took her to Frascati's, or the man who took her to the Holborn Restaurant, or the 'Waldorf man'. Freddy did the same thing. According to Proust there is no love without jealousy. They both liked to drip fuel on to that particular flame: a dangerous game. Lovers are compelled to check that jealousy is all present and correct. What they forget is that it then has its own ideas on how to behave, it is a third party that must be managed and kept away from the strong liquor, but how easily this is forgotten, in the sharp nervous joy of seeing its arrival on the scene!

'I felt quite jealous that she should remember you all this time,' Edith wrote, of a nameless Ilford woman who had asked after 'that nice curly headed boy'. The woman herself was not exactly threatening, but her fond remembrance underscored the way in which every female – or so it seemed – fell a little bit in love with Freddy Bywaters. Edith claimed not to be jealous of the Australian girl, but that was only after Freddy had shown her the letters, and anyway the reassured feeling did not last. She was astoundingly open about it. Playing it cool was not in her repertoire. With her other male admirers she was elusive and enigmatic and they chased her all the more for it. With Freddy she laid herself bare; because of the strength of her feelings, but also because she was essentially unattainable, and therefore to remove herself further was to risk alienation. There was a magnificence, even a pride, about her sumptuous abasement, which must have aroused corresponding sensations in her lover.

In her near-infinite complexity Edith was both splendid and small. When she wrote about the Australian girl she made of her petty panic something perceptive, even prescient, despite the disorderly idiom.

Darlint, I did have a doubt about Australia – doesnt doubt show great love sometimes? I think it does, its that sort of doubt I had

– perhaps "doubt" is the wrong word – its fear more – fear of losing you – a woman is different [from] a man – a man says "I want
it – I'll take it" – a woman wants to say that – but an inborn feeling of modesty is it? makes her withhold her action perhaps
you'll not understand this. Men are carried away on the moment
by lots of different actions, love, hate, passion, & they always
stand by what they have done…

Then she could write this, about a local girl named Molly who had
previously gone out with Freddy.

What is she doing to herself? She looked awful – her face and lips
are rouged terribly and thick black lines pencilled under her eyes
– and her face is fearfully thin fallen in under the cheek bones.
Perhaps its working in the West end. She certainly looks years
older than her years and I shouldn't say she was pretty now – Oh
darlint I do think it is a shame don't you?

The cattiness was dumbfounding. In an obscure sense it was
designed to flatter Freddy, making him feel that Edith – the sophisticate – cared about him so much that she was reduced to attacking
a little girl he had once smooched with in a cinema. More directly,
she was irritated by Molly because in some ways they were uncomfortably similar. The girl was literally on her turf, had seen her
walking around with Freddy, sat giggling behind her at the Ilford
Hippodrome – 'is she affected in her conversation? She was very
much on Saturday and I wondered if it was put on for special benefit.'
This was the ordinary Edith in full flow. Within her streamed
something entirely unremarkable, the sort of woman who noticed
people whispering together and worried about it: for instance she
reported seeing Molly and her admirer Mr Derry at Ilford station
one morning – 'I bowed – said good morning to him as I passed and
have since been wondering if they have told each other what they
know about me.

'Never mind, a little more bad feeling cant hurt – there is so much of it to contend with…'

Here, in less lethal form, was the judgement of the Old Bailey and the British public. Edith was the kind of woman that other people disliked, talked about, wanted to put down. At this point she rather revelled in it. It proved that she was different, even when she was behaving just like everybody else; and particularly with regard to her sister Avis. Sometimes, in her letters, she described Avis in terms not wholly unlike those that she used for Molly.

> Avis came to tea Sat. as I've already told you & went again at 7.30 to keep an appointment she said.
>
> In the afternoon we went shopping together & she spoke about you a lot. She seemed to be quite friendly with you.
>
> She mentioned she saw you on the station every morning & what a lot it must cost you for fares & it would be cheaper she thought if you lived in East Ham & then they would be able to see a lot more of you.
>
> Also you had on a diamond ring & seemed to have plenty of money altho "I know writers dont make more than £5 per trip she said" she also told me you asked after Peggy & that she told you all about it & that she went round & had a drink with you she didn't see why she shouldn't as you could be pals (her interpretation) if nothing else.
>
> She said lots of small things connected with you – which aren't important & I didn't remember.

This outbreak of mentionitis from Avis, conveyed by Edith at her nastiest and funniest, took place in early April 1922, when Freddy had just sailed after a two-week shore leave. So much of this time had been spent with Edith that she knew herself to be the woman in possession, and therefore could condescend massively to the babbling Avis. At the same time she was slightly put out. Nobody likes to hear that their darlingest boy has had a drink with their sister, especially a drink that they knew nothing about at the time. But then Avis, who knew far more than she was telling, was being catty also. The handsome Mr Bywaters had, in fact, managed to create all manner of upheaval within the lives of these sisters.

'One night I dreamed that you had married Avis – because she found out how much was between us (you and I) & threatened to tell everybody unless you married her...'

That was written in August 1922. A couple of months earlier, William Graydon had sent a letter to the *Morea* in Australia, asking Freddy to meet up with his son Harold – then working in a café in Melbourne – and pass on a bag:

> I'll leave it to you to make the best arrangement you can, and I've no doubt you will. Well now what of the voyage so far, are you comfortable and a full ship, and does there seem a prospect of making say half a fortune this trip. I hope you will be successful and do yourself a real bit of good this trip as it is a long one, and that next time we meet you will be able to report progress.

Not to overstate the case, but there is the merest hint of the prospective father-in-law in Mr Graydon's tone. He knew Freddy Bywaters, and he seems to have been fond of him. Also – he may have thought – if he married Avis then he would stop whatever he was doing with Edith.

At the age of twenty-four, Avis was looking more and more like a 'surplus girl'. The dynamic irruption of Frederick Bywaters into the gas-lit parlour at 231 Shakespeare Crescent must have been the answer to a prayer – a far simpler solution to *her* problems than he would later be for Edith's – until Edith halted the progress of this alternative story. Having done so, her attitude to Avis became complex. There was guilt (not too much of that), resentment of said guilt, wariness, a particularly unjust envy, a desire to patronize; and then the unstoppable female arrogance that comes with knowing that one is the more desirable woman.

'Avis has just been round here [Carlton & Prior],' she wrote in July, '& I was in the office having a brandy & soda with Mr Carlton; he asked her to have one too – I think she feels very flattered am I horrid I really believe I am – tell me – but everything in this world seems so topsy turvy – Id give anything to be her – free I mean & I think shed change places with me this minute if we could...'

As for Avis's attitude to Edith at this time: one can only guess.

Later, when her sister sat beneath the perpetual light of the condemned cell, she shoved to one side whatever had gone before and become a support as absolute as her mother and aunts. After Edith's execution, an event which effectively ended Avis's own life, she was silent for some fifty years. Then she gave a couple of interviews, in which she was vehement in her sister's defence: Edith was innocent of murder, and indeed of many of the other sins of which she was convicted.

Avis could not deny the adulterous affair, but she was so contemptuous of Percy Thompson as implicitly to justify it. And that was generous in the extreme; because Edith's behaviour – or perhaps it was simply Edith, who provoked so much, as it were without volition – had ensured that Avis would die alone, in August 1977, in a house just north of Valentine's Park. There had been no escape from the little world at the eastern edge of London, just as there had been none for her sister.

Her closeness to the dead Edith was intense. 'Sometimes I think I'll go to that door, and she'll be coming in,' she said in 1973. Indeed the two girls had always been close, born just twenty-one months apart and similar in appearance; although the impression is that Edith was always the princess, the star turn, while Avis took the role of handmaiden. Edith looked like a woman who knew how to be beautiful, whereas Avis was unselfconscious, not blessed or cursed with the power to spark fires. There was a companionable ease between the girls, who shared a bed when Avis stayed at Edith's marital home. Yet this powerful bond could pull tight with tension; especially where Freddy Bywaters was concerned.

In May 1920 he moved into 231 Shakespeare Crescent as a paying guest. His ship – the SS *Plassy*, with which he had visited China and Japan – was in dock at Tilbury. He was required to work on it every day, and travelling from Upper Norwood was a logistical nightmare. From Manor Park, the journey could hardly be easier.

'After he moved here he found it rather a long way to come home from Tilbury and he arranged to stop at Mrs Graydon's,' his mother told the police on the day of his arrest. 'He would then come home for the weekends… so far as I remember he stayed with the Graydons after coming back from about three trips. He was very reserved and very rarely mentioned anything about the Graydon family.'

It was this custom of Freddy's, to stay in Manor Park on his shore leaves, which led Avis to suggest (as per the letter of April 1922) that he should move back to the area – preferably to the Graydon house. In fact he never again lived at Shakespeare Crescent, although on his two subsequent visits home he spent plenty of time there. In every way it was easier than being with his mother; it was a house visited by Edith; and it was inhabited by Avis. By September 1922 – his last leave – he may well have been wishing that he had chosen her for his correspondent, instead of her fascinating sister, whose personality seemed to have no solution, no resting point, no end. On the night of Percy Thompson's murder he asked Avis to go out with him on the following evening. He was arrested at the Graydon house, where he had turned up to keep the date. He was complicated indeed; although – as will later be suggested – there may have been another reason for this strange, sudden invitation.

But before that, in the fractious little idyll that was the summer of 1920, the cross-stitch of deceit was first sketched in chalk upon the fabric of their lives. Little is known of actual events; only that in the eight weeks before Frederick Bywaters sailed to India in July, both Avis Graydon and Edith Thompson had started to take an interest in the lodger, and he in them. Avis liked Freddy and perhaps began to dream of marriage. Freddy liked Avis and possibly thought the same thing, but in a much vaguer way. Edith liked Freddy and by September 1920 was sending him a telegram ('Chief away today cannot come') cancelling an invitation of some kind, probably lunch. Freddy liked Edith and was intrigued by the richness of her response to his gaze. Percy liked Freddy, doubtless saw him as a means whereby poor old Avis might be lifted from the shelf, and was ignorant as to the rest – which was, indeed, almost nothing at this point.

It was not good, needless to say, that Edith was prepared to flirt in her usual way with the man whom her sister sought to attract. But that was Edith: which is why so many people, including Lilian Bywaters, thought of her as a bad lot (although Lilian's cynicism was in part because she knew of what she spoke. On the evening of her son's arrest she was at a pub in Hammersmith – which today sounds so innocuous, but was unusual then for a woman, and especially one without a husband; a widowed Ethel Graydon would never have done it).

The defence, that there was no real intent in Edith's flirtatiousness, collapses with regard to Freddy Bywaters. He made the play for her, but even he would not have dared to do so without the near-certainty of success.

She did, as she believed, fall in love with him. Not at first sight – that was attraction – but thereafter. The circumstances were right. The stars were aligned. Despite the fullness of her life – Ilford to Fenchurch Street to Aldersgate Street to West End to Manor Park to Hippodrome to hairdresser to dress shop to restaurant to cinema to dance and so to bed – she had reached the point where full and fulfilled had become two different things, and the sense of vacancy was yearning to be shored up by a suitable candidate. That did not mean that she was unable to resist Bywaters. Of course she could have done. Love is not an act of God (although it is an act of faith). But she may have thought, if she thought at all, why should I?

'Whatever name is given to it,' said her counsel Sir Henry Curtis-Bennett, in his closing speech for her defence, 'it was certainly a great love that existed between these two people.'

By the spring of 1921 Freddy was calling for her at Carlton & Prior, as Edith's boss would testify to the police. Stating that he had noticed the young man outside the premises a few days before the murder, Mr

Carlton continued: 'I have seen Bywaters once before, about eighteen months ago, when Mrs Thompson mentioned to me that she had a friend who had called to see her. He came into the shop on this occasion but left soon after I came into the shop.'

By the high point of summer, it had become clear to all concerned that Frederick Bywaters' interest lay not in Avis Graydon, but in the more glittering and elusive prize of Edith Thompson.

★

The catalyst was that most innocent-sounding of things, a week's holiday on the Isle of Wight for the two 'couples': Edith and Percy, Avis and Freddy. Whether Edith engineered this arrangement is impossible to know. She may have wanted Freddy there for added interest, somebody at whom to bat her silky lashes; she may have encouraged her husband to extend the invitation. Or Percy may have had the idea himself, when Freddy returned from Australia at the start of June 1921. If so, if Percy thought to please Avis and/or gain himself a convivial drinking companion, then he rushed his own fate upon himself in a way that is almost tragic.

Eleven months later, when Edith was facing the truly deadly prospect of a Bournemouth boarding house with Percy, Avis, no drinks licence and no Freddy, she wrote:

> when I try & contrast my feelings of going away this year to those of going away last year – I really wonder if Im living in the same world – I suppose I am – but its not the same world to me darlint – that world last year didnt contain a pal – just one only, to whom I need not wear a mask – but this year does... I wonder if there ever will be a time when I shall appear as I really am – only you see me as I really am...

The poignant eternal cry of the lover; which as she embarked upon her holiday on 11 June was about to be heard.

That Saturday, the party travelled down from Victoria station and met the Vellenders, Lily and Norman, at lodgings in Shanklin named Osborne House. A gang of pleasant young Londoners, enjoying their nice little yearly break. Innocent indeed. Yet would the shift from flirtation to affair – the decisive move of white knight to black queen – ever have been made had this holiday not been taken?

The island was not 'abroad' – it was not Paris, where morals might be expected to run free – yet with its cliffs and slopes, its skies lifting lightly with their peerless promise, it held enough sense of pagan liberation to make it possible. Edith, drifting along the seafront in her airy dresses, protecting her face but letting the back of her neck recklessly burn, had time and space to accept anything that might be offered.

'It's Friday now, darlint,' she wrote on 16 June 1922. 'I am wondering if you remember what your answer was to me in reply to my "What's the matter" tonight of last year.' She meant the Friday night of 17 June 1921, the last night of the holiday, when she and Freddy had somehow managed to lose the rest of the company; perhaps on the pier, perhaps while smoking together on the Esplanade outside the theatre, perhaps speaking quietly into the soft sea air on the verandah of the boarding house.

'I remember quite well – "You know what's the matter, I love you".'

And yes, that was hard to resist from the beautiful young Bywaters, who at last treated Edith in the way she most wanted: as somebody special. Not just a sexy girl who might be up for a bit of fun; but extraordinary. What Sir Henry Curtis-Bennett, in his address to the jury, called 'one of the most extraordinary personalities that you or I have ever met'. Sitting in a boarding house on the Isle of Wight.

Almost certainly it was the furthest that she ever travelled (the story that she went to Paris as a buyer before the war is hard to credit; it would have been a vast responsibility for an inexperienced nineteen-year-old). Here, again, was the limit of her horizons. The pretty island, on which she was literally and metaphorically cut adrift, lay thereafter within her imagination as a calm and futureless paradise: 'you remember the Shanklin times, when neither of us had any cares, or worries, personal ones I mean, altho' we hadn't learned to know ourselves or each other...'

What chance did Percy have – or Avis? Physical destiny cast those two ruthlessly aside and brought the yearning profiles of Freddy and Edith together for a first kiss – the chasm sweetly leapt – in the sharp shadows of the cliffs. It had been prefigured, quite clearly, in a photograph taken during the journey, between train connections, on the beach at Southsea. Percy reclined beside Edith on a bed of pebbles, their shoulders not quite touching. He grinned unselfconsciously into the camera, pipe clenched between his teeth. His wife, looking into the distance beyond the lens, as it seemed into another world, had one hip raised in its soft summer dress. Upon it she cradled quite openly the head of Freddy Bywaters, who lay on his side like a young animal with his eyes half-closed. The photograph, with its great erotic charge still pulsing through the dead *chiaroscuro*, sets out all that would happen on this holiday. Yet even then it could have been avoided; the story of Thompson and Bywaters was still theirs to will and control; which most unfortunately they did.

For Avis, realization may have begun even as she was taking the photograph, although she would have convinced herself otherwise. She knew for sure when the Thompsons went back to London after a week and Freddy, with whom she had expected to stay on, said that he too was leaving. She remained alone in the boarding house, grappling with the knowledge that the plans in her head had borne no relation whatever to his; and with the suspicion that her sister was the cause of it. When she returned, Freddy met her at Victoria and told her that he wanted to be friends, or some other such evasion. Yet she did not quite give up on him. Whether she would have done so, had it been any other girl who had come between them, is impossible to say; but she could not quite accept that particular situation.

Percy, meanwhile, had seen nothing. He had not yet looked through the lens. If reports of the holiday are true, he had spent some of it getting drunk, behaving like a certain type of Briton off the leash; and on the way back to London, on Saturday 18 June, he transmuted into a cuckold out of Restoration comedy. Yes, he said, it was a damn fine idea to let the spare bedroom at 41 Kensington Gardens to his clean-looking young friend Freddy Bywaters. Let's do it!

Nine days later, Edith and Freddy became lovers.

★

Later they would deny this to the Old Bailey. 'Was it on the holiday which you spent with her and her husband at Shanklin when you first fell in love with her?' was the question put to Bywaters by the Solicitor General, Sir Thomas Inskip, for the prosecution, to which the answer was 'No'. The solicitor general then asked:

'When do you say you first felt or declared your affection for her?'

'I first told her just before I went away in September 1921. That was after I left her husband's home.'

Reading Edith's letter – Exhibit 25 – in which she recalled the evening when he confessed that he was in love with her, the solicitor general said:

'Was this a true or an untrue statement, that a year ago, in June 1921, you and she had declared your love for each other?'

'That is not right.'

The solicitor general had one last go, quoting from another of Edith's letters written in August – 'Does that satisfy you that your evidence is wrong as to the date you told her you loved her?'

'No.'

Like much of Bywaters' evidence, it was catastrophic: sometimes he had the air of a man insisting that the world was flat. His own counsel, Cecil Whiteley, had allowed him to obfuscate. 'I think her husband knew we were meeting... I was fond of her. I had never mentioned it to her, though,' was his description of the relationship during the summer of 1921. But the epistolary proof said otherwise. How could Bywaters – and more to the point, Whiteley – have thought that the lie would not be exposed? This was not an instance in which a witness could say – as William and Avis Graydon would later do – that Edith had invented an episode. She could hardly have related an imaginary declaration of love to the person whom she claimed had made it. Anyway there was more: for instance Exhibit 23, in which Edith wrote of how she hated the idea of the Bournemouth holiday. 'I'll always be thinking of Shanklin and then of our tumble down nook' (this was a recurring phrase, no doubt much tutted over by Rebecca West and T. S. Eliot, taken from a popular song: 'you remember that wonderful holiday we were going to have in 22, and that little flat in Chelsea that you were coming home to every time and that "Tumble down nook" you were going to buy for me, one day.' Domesticity with Freddy presented itself to Edith as a kind of heaven, but that was because it was unattainable, unreal).

Then there was Exhibit 63, written in August 1922: 'Fourteen whole months have gone by now, darlint, it's so terribly long. Neither you nor I thought we should have to wait all that long time.'

The solicitor general read this to Edith, who also upheld the lie as to when the relationship had begun. 'Does that not satisfy you,' he asked, 'that you and Bywaters declared love to each other in June, 1921?'

'Not at all.'

It was absurd, but it was also deeply damaging. The line of questioning came in the middle of cross-examination, and the demonstrable deception spread to infect answers both before and after.

It was done, one can only think, to avoid the impression that they had been cavorting and misbehaving under what was technically Percy's roof. Hence Bywaters' specific reference to when he first declared his affections: 'That was after I left her husband's home.' The issue for the defence, as so often in this trial, was to judge what impression any admission by these two would make upon the jury. 'Thank God, this is not a court of morals,' Sir Henry Curtis-Bennett said in his closing speech, but of course that is exactly what it was; which is why it was in the balance, as to whether it looked worse for Thompson and Bywaters to be exposed as liars or as the sort of people who conducted an adulterous affair in the murder victim's house. There would be another such decision taken within the evidence; more damaging still. Today the defence as conducted looks frankly pitiful, but in 1922 its room for manoeuvre was frighteningly limited.

Other letters, not given in evidence, written a year later in a mood of languorous remembrance, tell something of how Edith and Freddy glided through the second half of June and July, newly wrapped in the golden cloth of their mutual adoration, which was to be wrenched violently aside at the start of August.

'Today is Friday darlint,' she wrote on 23 June 1922, 'by the *day* not the date the day you took me to lunch at the Holborn – first time when I let you see and told you some things that no one else knew.' This was the Holborn Restaurant, an establishment of glorious gilt and Edwardian proportions: an aspirants' rendezvous. There, five days after the return from the Isle of Wight, Edith flowered tremulously beneath Freddy's ardent gaze and spoke – not without a degree of pleasure, at this early stage – about her marriage. What did she say, one wonders. That Percy drank? That Percy's touch made her shudder? She would not have lied. Despite everything she never badmouthed her husband in the letters, as some women might have done, but the impression that she gave was somehow worse: of a stubbornly immovable object, blocking out the light in her life. Whatever she said at the Holborn, Freddy can hardly have been surprised – he obviously knew that she was not happy with her husband – but he would have been flattered by her confidence and she by his attentiveness. At the table, the small space between them would have quivered with the desire to be closed.

Nine months later she wrote, in a coda: 'Since finishing my letter to you I have a confession to make.

'Today I've been into the Holborn Restaurant – no don't be cross darlint, not to lunch –'

So Freddy was capable of jealousy, and she took a certain delight in provoking it. It was part of the power struggle within the relationship, but it was also Edith's nature. It was like the telegrams that she sent to herself and left for her husband to see; although at the same time it was nothing like, because between her and Freddy the emotions ran naturally high, and his surging youth pushed them to run still higher.

★

Freddy had returned to England on 4 June 1921. A bare two weeks later he had declared love to a remarkable woman, found it to some degree reciprocated, and been invited to live at her house as a paying guest. It is unsurprising that he quelled his usual desire to sail abroad. Instead he paid a token visit to his mother – at which he failed to inform her of his changed address – then settled into his new circumstances: accommodation for just £5 a month in a house twice the size of any he had previously known, an easy journey back and forth to Tilbury, the lush, magical lady of the house... 'As I said last night,' she wrote in September 1922, 'with you darlint there can never be any pride to stand in the way – it melts in the flame of a great love – I finished with pride Oh a long time ago – do you remember? when I had to come to you in your little room – after washing up.' Those last three words are the essence of Edith. She would not have thought of them as bathos, they were simply what had happened and therefore they were said; her imagination danced alongside her honesty, as in her willingness here to admit that she had advanced the love affair. On 27 June, Freddy's nineteenth birthday, she made the final move towards their first sexual encounter. It is possible that he was not quite bold enough to take that last step, that she had to play the Duchess of Malfi's part and reassure him of her willingness, her daring. Perhaps they had reached a kind of *impasse*, which had to be either accepted or broken through.

At the trial Bywaters gave an account of the day, surely true in part.

On 27th June, 1921, Mrs Thompson told me she was unhappy, and I said, 'Let me be a pal to you, let me help you if I can.'... Mrs Thompson and I had been having an argument, and she suddenly burst into tears, and I advised her to wait, not to give up hope, and not commit suicide.

References to suicide, and to a suicide pact – a vow that the lovers would kill themselves after a certain time if nothing had 'changed' – recurred within Edith's letters. 'I suggested it as a way of calming her,' Bywaters told the court, 'but I never intended to carry it out.' No more did Edith. Whenever she mentioned the pact in her evidence, it gave an uneasy impression of melodramatic insincerity. As for the 'argument' to which Bywaters referred, this was surely about whether they should give up on the not-quite-affair; Edith brought the argument to an end by beginning the affair. In one of his rare surviving letters, written during his last shore leave ('yesterday or tomorrow' referred to meetings between the couple) Freddy recalled 27 June 1921 in lovers' language:

> Darlint Peidi Mia – I do remember you coming to me in the little room and I think I understand what it cost you – a lot more darlint than It could ever now. When I think about that I think how nearly we came to be parted for ever, – if you had not forfeited your pride darlint I dont think there would ever have been yesterday or tomorrow.

The date became hugely significant to Edith. It was Freddy's birthday, and for her too the start of a new year, even a new life. She marked the 27th of each month in her letters, for instance in August 1922: 'Darlingest boy, to-day is the 27th and it's on a Sunday, so I am writing this in the bathroom, I always like to send you greetings on the day...' (when this letter was read out at the Old Bailey, and Bywaters confirmed that it was an 'anniversary' greeting, Mr Justice Shearman expostulated: 'But this is August.')

However June was *the* birthday, as she wrote in a short letter headed that date in 1922:

'The birthday of the Palship of 2 halves.

'This is the real birthday darlint just the same as I always wish I wish today & hope everything will not always be in vain.'

More prosaically, the reason that the affair began at this time is that the Lesters, the three sitting tenants, were away on holiday. Edith too must have taken a day off, or more likely half-day. Then, according to Herbert Carlton's police statement, she was 'away' from the evening of Friday 1 to Monday 11 July. She took two weeks' holiday in 1922, so here was her second week in 1921. 'I had no idea where she had been,' said Mr Carlton. She had been in London, mostly, and in bed with Freddy Bywaters: this was their honeymoon, in which the illusion that the light-filled Ilford house belonged to them could be sustained, at least until Percy's key was heard in the door. Edith seems to have found Freddy a delightful domestic creature as well as a lover. He was, she wrote a few months later, 'a man to lean on… such things as wiping up, getting pins for me etc, all counted, darlint.' In the early days of love a man holding a dishcloth *is* an object of desire; although the implication is that Percy never did any such thing, and that Edith was genuinely entranced.

But when the Lesters returned – probably around the 11th – the opportunities to have sex would have been hard to find. This, of course, was part of the headiness of the whole business: the dodging and darting and significant looks across the breakfast table. Mr Lester was an invalid, and his daughter scarcely features in this story (so who knows what she saw or thought), but his wife was a great one for appearing where she was least expected. Nevertheless she seems to have been unaware of anything going on between Edith and the lodger. Her impression was that Freddy was a friend of both Thompsons – as he was, at first.

'About the latter end of March, 1921,' she told the police,

I remember the time as my son Frank William was home from sea, Bywaters who I know more by the name of Freddie [this was how the name was spelt in the police documentation] came to the house one evening. Mr Thompson introduced him to my son and asked him if he could give Bywaters a berth on board one of the Orient Steam Ships.

This is a little confused, as Freddy had actually set sail on the *Orvieto* at the end of February. Nevertheless Mrs Lester's story can scarcely have been invented – although she may have exaggerated her son's importance – and the friendship shown by Percy helps to explain why she accepted Freddy's presence at the house.

'My son told him before leaving to call the following morning at the Orient Office at Tilbury, where he (Bywaters) was given a position on board the same ship (I forget the name of it) as my son was on, as baggage steward.'

Mrs Lester's statement gradually made its way to June 1921, and the Isle of Wight holiday.

Mr and Mrs Thompson were only away a week, when they returned Bywaters was with them. All then were very friendly. Mrs Thompson told me that her husband had invited Bywaters to stay with them... sleeping in the back bedroom I gave up to them for the maid. He stayed for about six or seven weeks.

During the time he was here she left home for business at 8.15am. Her husband left home about 9. Bywaters never accompanied either of them... He generally left the house about midday, but very often came home with Mrs Thompson about 6.00pm. Mr Thompson came home soon afterwards. They all seemed happy together till about the last week.

On 31 July 1922 Edith wrote: 'This day last year [a Sunday] I was at Kew with my pal'. The day after that – after the sun-steeped, sultry, steamy wanderings among the orchids – the storm broke.

It was 1 August, Bank Holiday Monday. Lunch was over, and Percy, Edith and Freddy were in the back garden in Ilford. Edith, seated demure as a medieval princess on her wicker chair, was sewing and found that she needed a pin. Freddy, the courtly lover in flannel trousers, offered to go into the house and get it for her. Such is the complexity of human nature that out of such incidents, which cannot be dignified with the word 'trivial', a conflagration can ensue: something in the manner of Edith's demand and Freddy's hop-to-it response collected together the disparate threads in Percy's consciousness and told him some, at least, of what was going on.

The storm began to rumble.

'I could hear Mr and Mrs Thompson quarrelling,' said Mrs Lester to the police. 'Bywaters was present, but I could not hear what was said or what the quarrelling was about.' Then she and her family went out for a few hours; possibly, on her part, reluctantly.

This incident of the pin, which was of course about a great deal more than that, provoked Percy to say to Edith: 'You like to have someone always tacked on to you to run your little errands and obey all your little requests.' Graceless words, but what a fool the man must have felt. Freddy – ! who had been as he thought his friend, whom he had invited to the Isle of Wight, for whom he had exerted himself with Mrs Lester's son, who was Avis's beau… Avis was due to come to tea that afternoon, but she did not turn up. She too probably felt a fool. The raging argument between the Thompsons had dropped by teatime, or rather had been suspended, as these things usually are; according to Edith's evidence at the Old Bailey, it was Avis's failure to arrive that started it up again.

'I wanted to wait for her, but my husband objected, and said a lot of things to me about my family that I resented.' Few people will stand to hear their relations criticized – doing it oneself is different – and anyway Edith was hugely protective of the Graydons. With regard to Avis she would also have been feeling very guilty. What Percy said can only be guessed at – they brought you up badly, they had it easy compared with my mother – but two things are certain: that they were not his real target, and that Edith retaliated in kind.

Then the row seems to have moved into that stage where control is lost. The knowledge that the Lesters were not there to hear was liberating. What was said is again unknowable, but Percy surely accused Edith of inappropriate behaviour with Freddy – her sister's young man, the sister that she was supposedly so fond of – and in turn she probably said that she was so unhappy in her marriage – his brutishness, his lack of understanding – that she turned to Freddy for sympathy. As the cause of the argument retreated prudently outside, so the Thompsons screamed at each other in the morning-room, where the French windows opened on to the garden; according to her statement Edith was then hit several times, and according to corroborated evidence she was thrown across the room, overturning a chair with the force, knocking her arm against the table on which the meals were served – on which the tea things stood ready for Avis – and bruising it from shoulder to elbow. Freddy heard the bang and ran back into the house. Edith ran upstairs. The two men squared up to each other.

Freddy's reaction to Percy's behaviour, as described in his first police statement, was characteristic. 'I thought it a very unmanly thing to do and I interfered.' It was a similar remark to the one that he made in a subsequent statement, in regard to the second and fatal showdown. 'The reason I fought with Thompson was because he never acted like a man to his wife. He always seemed several degrees lower than a snake. I loved her and couldn't go on seeing her leading that life.'

On this occasion it is unlikely that any blows were struck; it was Edith to whom Percy had been the aggressor. But he was not at all cowed by this younger and fitter man. He had feared the western front, but he did not fear his future killer. He demanded that Freddy leave the house. Freddy immediately walked out without any of his possessions.

'We were all out on the Bank Holiday Monday till about 7pm,' Mrs Lester told the police. 'Bywaters was out when we returned, Mrs Thompson left the house shortly after... followed soon after by Mr Thompson who appeared in a temper. All three returned together about 11 or 11.30 and retired to bed.'

What happened in the early part of the evening is a mystery. Edith may have spent some time alone with Freddy, whose young man's rage was intense. Percy had become his opponent, and an unworthy one. Edith herself was almost a cipher: simply the woman whose honour he was impersonally defending. She may have calmed him down. She must have done, because at some point in the evening they were joined by Percy, and for the first time the issue of separation, or divorce, was openly raised. It had been mentioned before between the Thompsons, according to Edith 'very often', although that is unlikely to have been true; but now it was about more than unhappiness or incompatibility. A new factor had created a different equation. The threesome probably spent the later hours in a pub – where else? – and there is downright oddity in the image of them discussing the end of the marriage in congenial surroundings, like a debating society, amid the Bank Holiday crowd, while the two men took turns to get in their round at the bar. As Freddy told the Old Bailey: 'Mr Thompson said to his wife, "We will come to an agreement and have a separation," and she said, "Yes, I should like that…"' Rather like a medical operation, an immense row can leave people cleansed, light of head and heart, even cheerful. It is a deceptive mood; not one that lasts.

It was the aftermath of cataclysm: the first, prefiguring struggle, in which the three protagonists were left bruised, fundamentally changed, but alive.

'I think you said,' Freddy was asked by his counsel, 'that you and Mr and Mrs Thompson discussed a separation?'

'They discussed it; I listened.'

But the idea that the events of 1 August would lead to a formal ending of the Thompson marriage was inconceivable in that world, at that time. A different kind of ending, however, had become a distant possibility.

V

'It's them pills I took, to bring it off, she said.'

From *The Waste Land* by T. S. Eliot

O N FRIDAY 5 August 1921, Frederick Bywaters left 41 Kensington
Gardens for good. Exhibit 49 in the trial, the earliest-dated of the
letters to be put in as evidence, was written to him six days later.
For the next fourteen months the love affair between Thompson
and Bywaters was conducted mostly by correspondence. The actual
number of letters between these two is unknown. Twenty-seven of hers
and three of his became exhibits, along with a number of telegrams and
cuttings. Twenty-nine others written by Edith – plus two postcards
and a couple of telegrams – survive, but were not submitted as evidence. The length of the letters varied hugely: some were two or three
thousand words, one or two were just a sentence. They were written on
different types of paper ('I cant help this paper being another colour –
its the only pad the stationer had in stock'), in fountain pen ('this is a
vile nib'), in a surprisingly neat, legible, almost schoolgirl hand, sloping
to the right in the usual way, with slightly florid 's's and 'f's.

Of Bywaters' letters much can be inferred; not least that Edith was
right to snap with defensive pride at her mother: 'You don't know what
sort of letters he was writing to me.' This, for instance, was written after
a physical (not fully sexual) encounter, and every sentence is like a ripple
of half-sated frustration.

Darling Peidi Mia... darlint I was afraid – I thought you were
going to refuse to kiss me – darlint little girl – I love you so much
and the only way I can control myself is by not seeing you and I'm

not going to do that... darlint when you suggested the occupied carriage, I didn't want to go in it – did you think that perhaps I did – so that there would have been no opportunity for me, to break the conditions that I had stipulated – darlint I felt quite confident that I would be able to keep my feelings down – I was wrong Peidi. I was reckoning on will power over ordinary forces – but I was fighting what? not ordinary forces – nothing was fighting the whole of me   Peidi you are my magnet...

He had taken on Edith's tone and idiom although one is aware, by contrast, of her guiding intelligence; as it were, her writerliness. A second letter, written a few days later and this time after sex the previous day, is calmer but still propelled by the aftershocks of passion, the words trying to handle a near-ungovernable excess of feeling, as only a very young man would need to do:

Peidi Darlint,
    Sunday evening. Everybody is out and now I can talk to you. I wonder what you are doing now my own little girl... Peidi Mia I love you more and more every day – it grows darlint and will keep on growing. Darlint in the park – our Park on Saturday, you were my "little devil" – I was happy then Peidi – were you? I wasn't thinking of other things – only you darlint – you – was my entire world – I love you so much my Peidi – I mustnt ever think of losing you, darlint if I was a poet I could write volumes – but I not...
    My darlint little girl I love you more than I will ever be able to show you   Darlint you are the centre – the world goes on round you, but you ever remain my world...

Could she not tell that she was playing with fire? This, of course, is the question, what effect the letters written by the one had upon the other.
    But what an affront, really, to have exposed these words to the frigid interior of the Old Bailey, and the ravenous consumers of the Thompson-Bywaters soap opera. The letters were evidence in a murder

trial (although Sir Henry Curtis-Bennett fought for them not to be). Percy Thompson was dead. Yet it seems such an insult, all the same, that they had to be read out in their agonizing entirety by the various counsels, whose cultured accents intoned them with a dogged display of non-embarrassment; that they were tutted over by a titillated and determinedly scandalized jury; that they were pass-the-parcelled around the court in a way that caused the judge to fuss and fret... 'I really think the best way, Sir Henry, is to provide, of course, a volume. We do not want this strewn with odd letters.' Shearman became obsessed with the letters, not what was in them but how many copies were to be taken, how the jurors were to read them: 'The important thing is that they should have them to study before the case is finished. I do not want to do anything in a hurry, and without full consideration.' Meanwhile Thompson and Bywaters sat in the dock, listening to this embodiment of the law, this pedantic old man, fiddling interminably with the pages on to which they had written their souls.

The letters were evidence. Yet what tantalized was the way in which they held their sense of privacy, close as the scent of a violet pressed within a book. They were aware of nothing except themselves. Therein lay their innocence, even when their subject matter was anything but. Frederick Bywaters was by his own admission a killer; and yet to read the words that he wrote in his tiny bedroom in Upper Norwood, beneath the grubby glow of the gas, while his body was still softened by the imprint of his lover's... it is hard not to feel the shift, between the intimacy of his intention and its monstrous exposure to the light.

As for Edith: it is possible that the greatest suffering of all was caused by the reading aloud of her letters.

Why he did not destroy them, as she had asked, is one of the bigger mysteries in this story. Bywaters wrote to the home secretary that he would have done so: 'if I had, for one moment, thought or imagined, that there was anything contained in Mrs Thompson's letters to me, that could at any time, harm her...' Nevertheless the fact that Edith was disposing of *his* letters surely suggested that he should do the same – except that he had no wife to nose around and find them;

he must have felt safe, but still it is odd. Were the letters so precious to him that he wanted to preserve them? Did he envisage a time in which they might be of use? Blackmail is perhaps too strong a word, but they would certainly have constituted a hold over Edith. It depends on one's view of his character. He had a sense of honour, but he could also be dishonourable.

She, who told the court that she always got rid of her letters, whoever the correspondent, was caught with the two cited above by mischance: they had been received very recently. The third quoted at the trial was a sort of blind. Dated 1 December 1921, it read:

> Dear Edie,
>   Do you remember last Xmas you wrote to me wishing me all the best ... I want to wish you all that you can wish yourself   I know all those wishes of yours will run into a deuce of a lot of money Such things as fur coats, cars and champagne, will be very prominent on the list – anyhow, good health and I hope you get it... I shall be about 2 days this side of Suez. Never mind I will have a drink with you...

This teasing tone was probably typical of the social animal Freddy, the good chap who like so many of his time aped something of the public school lingo, who wore a manly façade that Edith told him she had penetrated to get to the 'real' him. There was not a darlint or Peidi Mia in sight. It was cleverly done and deliberately kept, as she later wrote: 'the only one I have is the "Dear Edie" one written to 41 [Kensington Gardens], which I am going to keep. It may be useful, who knows?'

Asked at the trial what she meant by that, Edith replied that she wanted to show the letter to 'my people', meaning the Graydons. It would certainly have been 'useful' to show it to Avis, and still more so for Percy to have seen it.

The rest of Freddy Bywaters' letters were disposed of, probably burned in the grate in Edith's office at Carlton & Prior. It was possible to do what is so difficult with today's communications, get rid of them as if they had never existed. It could so easily have been that nobody, except the lovers themselves, ever knew a single word of what they had written to each other. The terrible thing is that one is glad that Edith's letters were *not* destroyed, even though they destroyed her; that is a great paradox within this case, that she achieved immortality through the thousands of words that helped to end her life.

The letters defined the love affair, so much so that Edith would write to Freddy even when he was actually in England: when she had either just seen him, or would soon do so. It wasn't that he was more real to her on the page, but she could express herself more as she wished to do when not confronted with his reality. Without a doubt, she felt barely controllable excitement at the thought of his physical presence. Yet this very young and in some ways very ordinary man could not possibly fulfil the intricacies of desire that she wove through her writing: that was not quite the point of him.

Her feelings for the real Freddy were real. She *felt* them. But what, exactly, was she feeling? Something that she herself had created. That is always true of love – it has to be: when a person becomes magical to another, that transfiguration is in the eye of the beholder. The beloved is not simply his or herself, they are what the person in love with them wants – needs – them to be. But when Edith Thompson fell in love with Frederick Bywaters she was in a state of receptivity so heightened, so complex, that there was scarcely a man on earth who could have *really* engaged with it. He came closest to what she craved, and so she allowed sexual attraction to become love, as people do, except that in this case love evolved through the letters, which were not the same as Bywaters himself.

All love is illusory, really – the feelings within one's heart are not of the same order as a heart attack – it is something that lovers nurture until it takes on solidity. So it is a question of degree, of how far illusion and solipsism have overtaken reality. A thin coat of Vaseline upon the lens is one thing, a whole jar is another; yet the mysterious thing is that illusory feelings can be just as strong as any others. By the time

Edith had gone through fourteen months of attenuated separations, snatched reunions and writing alternative realities into life, she had bound her destiny so tightly with that of a nice-looking hot-blooded ship's clerk-cum-steward that she was no longer capable of seeing the truth: that she did not want him quite as much as she thought she did. She wanted what he represented to her, which was not quite definable. If this whole story had been about Thompson's love for Bywaters then she would have run away with him. Simple as that. If those fourteen months had been spent living together in a cramped furnished flat, rather than a plush palpating dreamscape in which the space between them became more erotic than congress could possibly be, and non-fulfilment acquired its own addictiveness, then Thompson would have had what she never had: a chance to get over her passion for Bywaters. As it was: she did not.

Love is circumstantial. Romeo and Juliet's emotions are pushed into overdrive by the pressure of prohibition. The First World War had only recently conjured love from the fear that people would never see each other again. For Thompson and Bywaters, after 5 August 1921, the circumstance was straightforward difficulty; the world around them wielded its secateurs, chopping off every outlet and possibility, and the plant of love grew stronger. They saw each other so seldom that they had to write instead, although for Edith that too became problematic. Whereas today her phone would be flashing continually with messages from her darlingest boy, then she had to find a way to receive communications that were easier to obliterate but harder to explain away. They were sent to Carlton & Prior, of course, and her shrewd, worldly boss had a pretty fair idea of what was going on. In April 1922 Edith described how he had

> said to me at 11.30 today – "I have news from your brother for you" – I wasn't thinking of the mail being in and said "How have you got news?" and he just gave me your envelope. I thought the remark rather strange and can't quite make out if he really thought it was from my brother – or was being sarcastic.

Edith's brother Bill was in the merchant navy, but Herbert Carlton had seen Freddy at the premises a year earlier, and he would have sussed the situation with his practised eye; not that he would have interfered. He knew the ways of the world, and of a woman like Edith. Miss Prior, whom Edith described staring at the seal of one of Freddy's letters 'all the time she was bringing it down the stairs', may have also had her suspicions, but she said nothing. As long as the capable Mrs Thompson did her work, the rest was nobody else's business.

Circumventing Percy, however, was not so easy. In June 1922 Edith wrote:

> We're both liars he says and you are making me worse and he's going to put a stop to all or any correspondence coming for me at 168 [Aldersgate Street]. He said "Its useless for you to deny he writes to you – because I know he does" – hence my wire to you regarding G.P.O.

This referred to a telegram of the previous week: 'Send everything Fisher care GPO call Monday.'

It was not the first time that Percy had threatened to intercept Edith's mail. 'Im afraid he'll ring up and ask them to stop anything that comes for me so I must get Jim on my side.' Jim – James Yuill – was the firm's driver, who put on Edith's bets and distributed the post; he would have been easily handled. Nevertheless Percy could have been a danger to her at work. In February 1922 he questioned Miss Prior as to what time they shut up shop – catching his wife out in a lie – and in March he started taking the same train into Fenchurch Street. She could not be sure, in fact, of what he might do. He was in the sort of mood to employ a private detective, although the idea (and the expense) might have frightened him.

So in June 1922 Edith, doubtless vastly enjoying herself, invented an *alter ego*, a Miss P. Fisher, who received correspondence at the General Post Office near Aldersgate Street. In typical fashion – quite remarkable, how inconsequent this capable businesswoman could be! – she

was amazed when the GPO refused to hand out mail to somebody who
merely claimed to be Miss Fisher.

> I never have a thought about having those letters sent to GPO   I
> called there on Monday [12th] and was told that unless I could
> prove I was Miss P Fisher I couldnt have them.
> I thought, this is a devil of a mess and wondered what to do.
> Eventually I decided to have some cards printed (this cost me
> 6/6) dont laugh darlint, and I also got Rosie to address an enve-
> lope to me at 168 in the name of Fisher...

Rose Jacobs, that obliging young Judas, later told the police all about it.
'Some time in June,' ran her statement,

> Mrs Thompson and I were in the basement. She said "Would
> you mind writing a letter for me and address it to Miss Fisher
> c/o Carlton and Prior." I wrote at her dictation – "Dear Miss
> Fisher, I beg to call your attention to our next Committee
> Meeting which will be held on Friday (and a date I can't remem-
> ber) and your presence will be required. Yours truly, R. James."
> Mrs Thompson sealed it in an envelope and kept it. I've no idea
> what the letter meant...

'Darlint,' Edith continued to her lover, 'I think it would be best to
address all letters there until I tell you otherwise, dont you?' In fact
this particular charade did not last very long; Freddy began writing
to Carlton & Prior again. As James Yuill told the police: 'About once a
week – on the average – either a registered, or ordinary letter arrived
for Mrs Thompson, which I always put into her desk. They generally
have foreign post marks. I do not know the contents.' Jim was not the
type to speculate on another person's affairs. He probably suspected
a boyfriend, but to the police he said staunchly: 'I have known Mrs
Thompson since she has been with the firm. I also knew her husband.
He has called at the shop for her, and I have also seen him at the

annual outing of the firm. They always appeared very affectionate, and I thought them a very happy couple.'

★

So from August 1921 until October 1922 the love affair that ended three lives was conducted, in the main, by letter; it is almost shocking how seldom the couple actually met throughout this period. Bywaters' leaves were as follows: 5 August to 9 September 1921; 29 October to 11 November; 6 January to 20 January 1922; 16 March to 31 March; 25 May to 9 June; 23 September to 3 October. That is to say, fourteen and a half weeks out of just over sixty. The couple saw each other on several of these days (it is impossible to know how many) but by no means all. So they were separated throughout more than three-quarters of this period, in which 'love' pushed events to their murderous climax. Furthermore, after Bywaters left Kensington Gardens, they would have found it very difficult indeed to have sex. Nobody knows where they went – Wanstead Park? The basement at Carlton & Prior? – but wherever it was, it would have been a place in which discovery was always a possibility, and where *coitus interruptus* or a kind of advanced *frottage* was more likely than intercourse. It is probable, indeed, that after August 1921 the notorious Thompson and Bywaters – the lovers whose names represented the godlessness of adultery, who had threatened the sacred institution of marriage – had full sex with each other perhaps three or four times.

The longest period that they had together was the three months between Freddy Bywaters' arrival in England on 4 June 1921, and his departure with the *Morea* on 9 September. Even then they were chasing opportunities. There was the Isle of Wight holiday, between 11 and 18 June – during which they were not alone, but also not suspected except by Avis – followed by Freddy's arrival at 41 Kensington Gardens on 20 June, and the beginning of the sexual affair on 27 June. There was the honeymoon week of 3 to 10 July, which was interrupted only by the necessity of spending evenings in the company of Percy Thompson. The return of the Lesters, and Edith's return to work, meant that the

three weeks leading up to 1 August were more circumscribed. But it
is unsurprising that Edith should have looked back to the summer of
1921 – the fervid blue heat of its skies, the sun falling like gold upon
the suburban plains – and recreated its lush, fertile memories, living
them again through the corresponding days of 1922: 'Darlint this
month and next are full of remembrances – arnt they?' she wrote in
June. The shock of separation in August was sharp; it was an ending,
as she may have intimated; and shock is never quite assimilated. She
had not expected to lose Freddy in that way. She yearned thereafter for
the corporeal presence that had been stolen from her so suddenly. The
subsequent meetings were simply too brief and unsatisfying to make
up for that loss, the wrenching apart of the palship of two halves.

> Darlint you say you realize what it was for me after Aug. 5th I am
> glad you do, in a measure, it was & still is too awful, I darent think
> too much I should always be weeping & that wouldn't do, would
> it? because you told me to dance only sometimes to dance is
> much harder than to act & think.

Mrs Lester, who in matters of this kind was a reliable witness – her
towering inquisitiveness having made her so – described to the police
what had happened in the aftermath of the August Bank Holiday.

> Mrs Thompson took her husband's breakfast to his bedroom. This
> caused me to ask Mrs Thompson if her husband was not well. She
> replied, 'He is all right, but will not have his meals in the same
> room as Freddie.' Bywaters had his breakfast in the morning room
> with Mrs Thompson. After they had left for business, Bywaters
> packed his attaché case came down stairs and said, 'Goodbye Mrs
> Lester I am leaving.' I said, 'Oh, have you got a ship.' He said, 'No'.

Having described how Edith showed her blackened arm 'when she
came home from business,' Mrs Lester continued: 'She gave me to
understand that they had words over Bywaters, that Mr Thompson

had pushed her across the room and that Bywaters had interfered. The following week... they appeared cool to one another, and had very little conversation. After this they appeared to be on more friendly terms.'

In a letter dated 4 August 1922 Edith wrote to Freddy – 'the bestest pal a girl ever had' – with again that masochistic inhabitation of the previous year: 'I wonder if you remember what today *by the day* is, I keep on thinking about it & of you & wondering if youre thinking as well about leaving me all by myself at 41 for good.' Freddy left the Ilford house on Friday 5th, although Mrs Lester's account wrongly suggests the 2nd; yet that is the more logical date, as how on earth did Freddy stay at 41 Kensington Gardens for three more days after that row? By keeping out of Percy's way, clearly. With her willingness to confront bathos Edith wrote of their parting, 'when Morris Avenue corner became one of the treasured spots in our memory...' This road is in Manor Park – by the church in which Edith was married – which suggests that Freddy may then have visited the Graydon house, probably the place at which he was most relaxed.

> Last Tuesday was the memorable 1st [August] such a lot seems to have happened in that little time – & yet such a little – everything that we wanted to happen hasnt & everything that we didnt want to happen has
>
> However perhaps this coming year will bring us the happiness we both desire more than anything in this world – & if it doesnt? we'll leave this world that we love so much – cling to so desperately.

She was referring to the suicide pact that she and Freddy had vowed to fulfil after a certain, shifting span of time. Her prophecy was accurate, although not in the way that she had meant; and she had not in fact meant it.

After 5 August, despite the sudden change in circumstances, the couple still managed to meet regularly. 'Come and see me Monday lunch time, please darlint   He suspects,' was the single-line letter posted to Norwood on the morning of Saturday 20th. Percy had rid the house of the wretched lodger but was very much on his mettle. Edith had returned home late the previous day, after a tryst with Bywaters in the darkening early evening of the City streets. 'I usually saw him on Fridays,' she told the Old Bailey.

Then – after that short note, and another line sent in August – there are no letters at all until a prolonged outpouring of some 2,600 words in November 1921 (undated, but the mention of a racing bet enabled the police to establish when it was sent; they ponderously took a statement from the relevant horse's trainer in Newmarket, although a check with the newspapers would have given them exactly the same information). Yet Freddy was away between 9 September and 29 October, and he told the Old Bailey that he and Edith wrote to each other during those seven weeks. It was just before he left, he said untruthfully, that he fell in love with her.

So a cache of Edith's letters was lost; probably literally. It could happen easily enough, although there is another possibility. Freddy may have disposed of them as instructed, as she did with his. This is mere speculation, of course. He kept the two little notes sent in August, although these were of scant importance. But if he *did* deliberately get rid of the September and October letters, what changed him thereafter, and led him to preserve what he had formerly destroyed? Was it in any way connected with a visit to 41 Kensington Gardens on 5 November, the last time that he went to the house, and – aside from a gathering at the Graydons a couple of days later – the last meeting between him and Percy until they became murderer and victim?

After the evening of 1 August, and the strange pub seminar at which the Thompsons discussed ending their marriage in Freddy's presence, the subject of separation was held in a kind of limbo. As there are no letters from the months of September and October, it is impossible to know if it was raised again between Edith and Percy. It was raised between Edith and Freddy, however, when he returned to England. As he told the Old Bailey:

When I came back in October Mrs Thompson and I spoke about the desirability of her getting a separation from her husband. I said to her, 'Can you not come to any amicable understanding or agreement with your husband to get a separation,' and she replied, 'I keep on asking, but it seems no good at all'...

Then it was raised between Freddy and Percy.

I went to Kensington Gardens on a Saturday afternoon [5 November] and made a request to him that he should have a separation. I had taken Mrs Thompson out previously; apparently he had been waiting at the station for her and he had seen the two of us together. He made a statement to Mrs Thompson, 'He is not a man or else he would ask my permission to take you out,' and she repeated that statement to me the following day. In consequence of that I went and saw Mr Thompson, and as he had said that I had run away from him, I told him that I did not see him at the station. Mrs Thompson was present part of the time.

This is Bywaters' account only. Yet its absurdity – Percy's spying on Edith at Ilford station; his accusation that Freddy was not a 'man', no doubt in return for Freddy having said something similar back in August – has an air of antler-clashing reality.

After this opening skirmish the two men sat together in the house and engaged in their free and frank discussion. It was almost as though they were uneasy enemy allies, the husband and the lover.

I said, 'Why do you not come to an amicable agreement; either have a separation or you can get a divorce,' and he hummed and hawed about it. He was undecided and said, 'Yes – No – I don't see it concerns you.' I said, 'You are making Edie's life a hell. You know she is not happy with you.' He replied, 'Well, I have got her and I will keep her.' Eventually I extracted a promise from him that he would not knock her about any more and that he would not beat her, but I could get no understanding with regard to a separation or divorce.

'He came to the house,' said Mrs Lester to the police, 'and saw Mr and Mrs Thompson. Mrs Thompson told me that her husband and Freddie "had made it up". I opened the door to him, and have not seen him since. He only stayed about two hours. More or less since, Mr and Mrs Thompson have been short tempered with one another.'

So there the situation remained. Effectively it did not move from that point for the next eleven months. But did something about that conversation with Percy lead Freddy Bywaters to keep hold of Edith's letters, in case they might be useful in the future? They were evidence of adultery; they were also evidence of Percy's inadequacies. They portrayed him as a poor thing. He was a blusterer, a threatener. Freddy despised him, and in some obscure way may have thought that the letters were a hold over him, as much as over Edith. It is a far-fetched idea – quite likely there is no significance at all in the fact that he kept Edith's letters from November 1921 – but the motives behind Freddy Bywaters' more extreme behaviour *are* obscure.

In her evidence, Edith stated that after the meeting between Percy and Freddy she asked for a separation or divorce. This was probably true; although there is no knowing how, or how often, she made the request. 'I asked him to give me my freedom, and I even went so far as to tell him I would give him the information to get it.'

'You had told your husband that you had been unfaithful to him, or would be unfaithful to him, and given him grounds for divorce?'

'I did.'

She was the adulterous party, so it was necessary for her husband to divorce her. If he refused to do that, she was stuck, unless she simply left him; which would have cost her everything.

Of course it is blindingly obvious, now, that the best thing that Percy Thompson could have done was to have called his wife's bluff: said to her all right Edie, off you go, here's your separation or divorce, we'll sell the house, it's too big for us anyway, I'll be free to see Miss Tucknott whenever I want and you can carry on all over town with young Bywaters. Suits me fine. Bye! How, then, would Edith have reacted? How long would the affair with Freddy have lasted? How would they have dealt with the social stigma, the sorrowing eyes of their families and the cold shoulders of their class, the financial constraints, the realities of a 'tumble down nook' which took pennies for the meter? Why didn't you run off with her, asked an old lag who slept in a ward with Freddy at Brixton jail. 'He said, well, his mother wouldn't have approved.' Sometimes Edith wrote of her willingness to go abroad, and Freddy told the Old Bailey that she had asked him to look for situations in his various destinations: Bombay, Marseilles and Australia were all suggested. Her brother Harold had worked in Australia, and Mr Graydon had a sister there, so it was not infeasible. 'I don't want to stop in a hat shop always – if things are different,' she wrote. In fact Mr Carlton would probably have kept her on, and overridden any objections from the junior Miss Prior. A friend, one of Edith's admirers, had asked her if she knew anybody to take his flat in Bayswater, three rooms at 35 shillings a week: 'Darlint it is just the thing we wanted. I do wish I had been able to take it.' She could have done, in fact; there was nothing *really* to stop her. But if she stayed in London, what would Freddy have done? Would he have looked quite so desirable with his dishcloth when wielding it was a case of necessity? Would he have wanted to wield it? 'I'd like to see you at the top – feel that I'd helped you there' – what did she mean by that, if anything? Why did she spend her entire savings – £13 – on a fur coat when they could have paid for seven weeks' rent in Bayswater? These were the questions that danced around the lovers and that they never quite confronted. What would have happened, had they suddenly been forced to do so?

But Percy did not call Edith's bluff. It was not his nature, just as it was not hers to be a wife. He cannot possibly have been happy himself. The situation was untenable, so too his frustration with it, and despite his unattractive character he was deserving of pity; he had known that his marriage was not a success, but the betrayal was still a cruel one. Apart from anything else he had been made to look so silly. Unmanly. And Freddy Bywaters, cool as a cucumber, hard as nails, a cad but a somehow impressive one, refused to admit to any shame over that; while Edith contrived at deception in that soft, yielding, wicked way of hers, which still aroused his desire. Like his wife, he was obsessed with what he saw as a halcyon past: 'He wants me to forgive and forget... He wants me to try as well and so that when another year has passed meaning the year that ends on January 15/1922, we shall be just as happy and contented as we were on that day 7 years ago.' She had married him, after all. Why had she done that, a girl like Edith Graydon, if she had not loved him once?

It was a good question, but it was very difficult to answer, and anyway it had become irrelevant. If only Percy had not believed in marriage as an entity, as signifying more than the two people who were in it! It was normal that he should do so; society did the same thing. But if only he had let his anger guide him, drive him off to freedom! For he was trapped just like Edith. What on earth did he think that the rest of his life would be with her? He should have washed his hands of it all. He would have saved everybody's lives – it was within his gift to do that – but his defining characteristic was obstinacy, and he refused to be the one who gave way. He preferred the pointless patriarchal stance that he had taken up, the observation point at Ilford station, the questioning of Miss Prior and later of Avis, the sulkiness in company, the self-righteous flirtation with the fat little office girl, the attempts to control a wife who slithered through his hands like her silken camisoles, the grim-jawed knowledge that if he was miserable then at least she was too. In a way he was probably enjoying it. Many marriages are a fight, and his had become a peculiarly engrossing one, with an opponent whom he both lusted after and loathed. And of course he had right on his side. Nobody would have expected him to behave any differently. He could have killed her, and an Old Bailey jury would probably have recommended mercy. Did he ever want to do that, or did he always exercise a degree of restraint when he hit out at his wife?

'I've run away and left you.' So Freddy Bywaters wrote to Edith after sailing for Bombay (as it was then called) on 11 November 1921. It implies guilt, a wrench between the necessity of departure and the urge to stay; also, just possibly, a barely acknowledged relief.

Whatever it was, Edith was having none of it. In the long, long love letter written a week later – the first, aside from the two August notes, that Freddy preserved – she quoted the remark back at him, then wrote:

'Darlint I don't like you to say and think those hard things about your-self… Truly darlint, I dont, I know whatever you say – that its Fate – its no more your fault than it is mine that things are still as they are…'

This letter, compiled over several days – partly, as she told him, in a lunch hour – was so typical of many that followed that some passages are reproduced, as a means to convey the way in which Edith talked, as she put it, to her lover: the touchingly childlike seriousness, as when she wrote the words 'Pour Vous' on the envelope; the sensuous stream of consciousness, through which she expressed herself even as she was thinking; the gift of immediacy, with which she found the spark of life in a moment or an incident; the suddenness of her leaps from one thing to another, as if her mind – set free from the commonsensical demands of her job – could flit and settle, flit and settle, tapping its wings with the delicate ferocity of a butterfly. She recalled a meeting with Freddy – perhaps in the alley, now called Bartholomew Place, that ran alongside Carlton & Prior, which itself is now the site of a carpark – when she was alone with him for the first time after more than seven weeks.

> Darlint you say do I remember? that Monday Oct 31 I'll never never forget it, I felt – oh I don't know how, just that I didnt really know what I was doing, it seemed so grand to see you again, so grand to just feel you hold my shoulders, while you kissed me, so grand to hear you say just 3 ordinary commonplace words "How are you" Yes I did feel happy then…

Earlier in the letter she had referred to the suicide pact, which neither had any intention of carrying out but which it consoled her to think of:

> All I could think of last night was that compact we made. Shall we have to carry it thro'? dont let us darlint. Id like to live and be happy – not for a little while, but for all the while you still love me. Death seemed horrible last night – when you think about it darlint, it does seem a horrible thing to die, when you have never been happy really happy for one little minute.

I'll be awfully miserable tonight darlint, I know you will be too, because you've only been gone one week out of 8 and even after 7 more have gone – I cant look forward can you? Will you ever be able to teach me to swim and play tennis and everything else we thought of, on the sands in Cornwall?...

Last night I booked seats for the Hippodrome – the show was good...

Continuing the next day, a Saturday, now a work half-day ('He's grumbling fearfully about it'), she began with a reference to Freddy's photograph, which she kept in her desk.

'When I looked at you to say "good morning" an irresistible feeling overcame me, to put my fingers thro your hair and I couldnt. I love doing that darlint, it feels so lovely – you don't mind do you? most men dont like it, in fact they hate it, usually, but I know youre different from most men...' She was unable, even then, to resist that little provocation – who were all these other men whose hair she ruffled? – and was at it again as she slid into a different tone, the yeah-but-no-but idiom of the suburban girl:

Avis said at the class [dancing] Mel mentioned he had seen me "with a friend of yours" he said to Avis, but when Avis was telling me she said "I asked him who it was and he wouldn't tell me" She didnt actually ask me to tell her, so of course I didnt mention you, but she knows I am sure.

On the Friday you left [November 11], Mel rang me twice and both times I was out, he hasnt rung again...

'Mel', who recurs in the letters and always with the same troublemaking note in his voice, stood somewhere near the bottom of her hierarchy of admirers – and knew it, there was a thwarted quality to his teasing – but nonetheless Edith did not really discourage him; that, too, was something that she could never quite bear to do. It was interesting, however, the general awareness of her friendship with Freddy. She seems to have worried very little about hiding it; almost in fact to have flaunted it, despite her careful destruction of the letters. Soon Mel would accuse Edith of seeing more of Avis's 'fiancé' than Avis did herself. Freddy was not engaged to Avis, nothing of the kind. Mel was the kind of man who said that kind of thing. Nevertheless in that small world – where the Graydons were known and the Bywaterses remembered – the incipient attachment of Avis to Freddy had been noticed. No doubt there had been a certain amount of oh, poor old Avis, she's got someone at last – bit on the young side but he knows his way about – and so on. And then something else had been noticed: the movement of Freddy's gaze towards the girl-made-good Edith. Oh yes, definitely something in the wind there... well, who can blame him, she's got the come-hither in her eye... Percy would have known all this, and minded it considerably, although it is somehow doubtful that the Mels and Mollys would ever have dared to say anything to him. Avis, however, was a sitting target. She helped her father at the dancing school in east London, where Edith occasionally still put in a sweeping, stellar appearance, and if a man like Mel decided to say his piece to Avis as they waltzed around the room there was nothing to be done about it. She too was unhappy, and for her there was no way out: the Isle of Wight had been a week in solitary rather than a libera-tion. Yet Edith, who envied her sister's freedom to marry Freddy, even though Freddy did not want to marry Avis – although who knew what the pressure of class might achieve, in the end? – was unable to resist one more low thing: the occasional jab at a sister whom she adored.

How ordinary it all was, though! How in the name of God could this little love drama, with its chorus of east London spies and gossips, its words scribbled lightly on to pages, have ended in murder and a double hanging?

In her letter of November 1921 Edith wrote, as it were *en passant*:

'Yesterday I met a woman who had lost 3 husbands in eleven years and not thro the war, 2 were drowned and one committed suicide and some people I know cant lose one.'

Then she wrote:

'Bess and Reg are coming to dinner Sunday...'

But it had been said: it had begun.

★

It was surely not the first time that Edith and Freddy had mused upon how much better life would be if Percy did not exist. Not if he were dead, exactly. The reference above is casually indirect: 'some people I know cant lose one...'

It is the sort of thing that might be said by a wife to her lover, or indeed by almost anybody in a certain mood. To suggest that it implies any serious intent would be almost insane. What complicated matters, however, is that in the same letter, which eventually became Exhibit 62 at the trial, Edith had gone on to write this:

'Thank you for giving me something at some future date, when both you and I are ready.'

The sentence was separated from the one about losing her husband by more than two thousand words. In between was a characteristic variety of other thoughts, to which Edith drifted and hopped as the urge took her.

He asked me why I wasnt happy now – what caused the unhappiness and I said I didnt feel unhappy – just indifferent, and he said I used to feel happy once. Well, I suppose I did, I suppose even I would have called it happiness, because I was content to let things jog along, and not think, but that was before I knew what real happiness could be like, before I loved you darlint. Of course I did not tell him that...

I am glad you liked "Maria" I thought it was lovely... Perhaps you do know how she felt darlint, I'm not sure, you know a man never feels like a woman about anything...

...I know nothing ever comes right in this world, not right as we want it to be... Perhaps I ought not to write at all when I feel like this.

I'm sorry you asked me about a photograph, really sorry, because I never make a good one, darlint...

...Avis just phoned and asked me to go and see Grandma [Deborah Liles, who was close to death and living in Stamford Hill with her daughter Lily]... I suppose I shall have to go – altho I dont like it much, I'd far rather remember her as I saw her in the Summer.

Why dont you want your mother to ring me darlint?

Yes, I think I do feel a bit no not cross – but what shall I call it – disappointed about the lady and the mail bag. For a start I dont like the expression about the coffee and milk coming from you to me – from you to anyone else – perhaps yes and after all is she any worse for being a native?... I thought you were beginning to think just a little more of us than you used.

Immediately after this admonition to Freddy – revealing in its way of her superior mind – for his dismissive description of a girl, probably a North African encountered during a stop-off in Marseilles, came those words:

'Thank you for giving me something...'

The 'something' was, almost certainly, a drug: a substance or herb, no doubt picked up on his travels from one who knew about such things, something that had abortifacient properties.

Here, then, was the second choice that had to be made by the defence. In the interests of appearances it had permitted Freddy and Edith to lie about when they began their love affair, a risk that didn't really pay off. But the second choice was even more outrageously invidious; and it was this. Was it better for Edith to have received a drug from Bywaters in order to bring about a miscarriage, or to administer it to her husband for the purpose of poisoning: in order to 'lose' him?

★

For all the frankness of Edith's letters, many of the passages were obscure. This might have helped her defence, although in fact it did not. Once the decision was taken that she must not be known to have self-aborted, that particular obfuscation made everything that she said seem like evasion. But in the moral climate of 1922, which had already made her the very emblem of decadence, admitting openly to what thousands of women did in secret was simply not possible. Hypocrisies of this kind do not go away, they merely metamorphose; or perhaps not, in this case. Even today a defendant who testified that she had had an abortion would be judged for it, not by everybody but by some. There would be some, still, who would think that she had valued her freedom, her work, herself to the point of unnaturalness.

Edith had fallen pregnant during Freddy's two-week leave in late October–early November 1921. By her own account they had sex on 3 November. Where they went is unknown, as is why they did not use precautions. Freddy was experienced, he knew all about condoms and withdrawal – life on the ships would have given him this basic know-how – and Edith's childlessness, after almost six years of marriage, suggests that she must have used contraception quite regularly, probably a diaphragm. But it would seem that, after the first long separation of their love affair, the sheer thrill of being together again got the better of them. Perhaps, in some subliminal way, Edith sought to intensify the risk and hand a hostage to fortune. Certainly she was aware from the first that conception was a possibility. She fainted at work on 7 November, which she may have seen as a sign of very early pregnancy. Of course she could not know yet for sure, which is why she thanked Freddy for giving her something 'at some future date'. Nevertheless her ignorance and inconsequence are startling. She was a sophisticate, and she knew almost nothing.

'I'm glad you told me you wouldn't worry about me darlint, Yes of course I will tell you everything, when the time comes, but you wont worry about it, will you darlint, because I dont and wont.' Presumably this referred to the miscarriage that would happen – as it were of its own accord – at some point in the future. A kind of modesty seems to have prevented her from spelling this out, even to the man who had caused the situation in the first place; what is also quite bizarre is how sure she was that the miscarriage *would* happen. Had she done it before? Perhaps, although her tone does not suggest that either.

'…its still the same & I've not done anything yet,' she wrote in a letter dated 6 December, not put in as evidence. 'I don't think I shall until next month, unless you tell me otherwise…'

More incredible inconsequence. The situation had been confirmed – a missed period does not definitely mean pregnancy, but she would have thought that it did – yet she was preparing to wait, to carry on as normal. It was almost as if she was subconsciously nurturing the month-old speck inside her, having guarded her body so strenuously against Percy; who ironically, now that she was carrying another man's baby, was pleading for a new start in their marriage. He was in part genuine and humble – 'he asked me why I wasnt happy now' – although this did not last. He was also impelled by a desire to sleep with Edith again. They had never stopped completely, but of late sex had been very infrequent. When the mood of conciliation wore off, Percy's insistence upon what he called his 'rights' would become the chief battle within their warring marriage.

Edith, who put up with things that very few wives today would accept – certainly not wives with independent means – found this a kind of torment: an outrage. In May 1922 she replied to a question from Freddy about a book they had both been reading (*The Shulamite* by Alice and Claude Askew). 'You asked me if Deborah described her feelings rightly when she was talking about Kullett making love to her.' He had surely been thinking about Percy Thompson.

'Darlingest boy, I don't think all the feelings can be put on paper because there are no words to describe them. The feeling is one of repugnance, loathing not only of the person but of yourself.'

That was how she reacted to her husband's touch, which previously she had tolerated and which now – like the acne-covered back compared with Freddy's smooth young skin; the short-cropped bristly

head compared with Freddy's thick waves of fairish hair – no, really, it
was not a fair fight – seemed to her scarcely bearable, a kind of prosti-
tution. 'All that lying and scheming and subterfuge to obtain one little
hour in each day – when by right of nature and our love we should be
together for all the 24 in every day.' For this, the judges and jurors in
the Old Bailey were unable to forgive her: she had found them out, all
those unromantic men with their pipes and slippers and predictability.
What if their wives felt similarly about them?

In June Edith described a ludicrous and rather ghastly episode:

> I said I was going to sleep in the little room – we had a scuffle – he
> succeeded in getting into the little room and on to the bed – so I
> went into the bathroom and stopped there for ½ an hour – he
> went downstairs then and I went into the little room quickly –
> locked the door and stopped there all night.

Oh, these marriages, and the madness of believing that there was
virtue in keeping them intact! She would, she said, have made a dash
for the spare bedroom every night:

> but even a little thing like that Fate was against us – because Dad
> was over on Sat. and asked me if he could stay the night – sug-
> gested he should sleep with *him* in the big bed – but Dad would
> not hear of it – so sooner than make another fuss – I gave in.

Back in November 1921, when Percy was trying his luck less aggres-
sively, Edith's reaction was not merely nervous – 'he said I was fearfully
strung up' – but illogical: 'I resisted, because I didnt want him to touch
me for a month from Nov 3rd do you understand me darlint?' If this
meant anything, it was that she did not want Percy to be able to claim
paternity of a baby that she intended to get rid of. As if in recognition
of the absurdity, she wrote in her very next letter: 'I gave way this week
(to him I mean), it's the first time since you have been gone. Why do
I tell you this? I dont really know myself, I didnt when you were away

before, but it seems different this time, then I was looking forward –
but now well I can only go from day to day and week to week until Jan
7th...' This was the day of Freddy Bywaters' return to England. The
letter – undated, written in early December – continued:

> We had – was it a row – anyway a very heated argument again last
> night (Sunday). It started through the usual source, I resisted –
> and he wanted to know why since you went in August I was
> different – "had I transferred my affections from him to you"
> Darlint it's a great temptation to say "Yes" but I did not...
>
> You know darlint I am beginning to think I have gone wrong
> in the way I manage this affair. I think perhaps it would have
> been better had I acquiesced in everything he said and did or
> wanted to do. At least it would have disarmed any suspicion he
> might have and that would have been better if we have to use
> drastic measures darlint – understand? Anyway so much for him.

It was a passage of this kind that allowed the police and the prosecution to portray Edith as definitively duplicitous, seducing even as she
sought to destroy. It was true, in a way.

In a letter dated 3 January 1922 she went further still.

> Darlint, I've surrendered to him unconditionally now – do you
> understand me? I think it is the best way to disarm any suspicion,
> in fact he has several times asked me if I am happy now and I've
> said "Yes quite" but you know that's not the truth, dont you

What Freddy Bywaters thought, in fact, can only be guessed. He was
not jealous of Percy as a man – how could he be? – but these details,
these descriptions, which presumably were true and certainly read as if
true – did *those* make him jealous? She knew what she was writing, but
she did not know what he was reading. She was like any other writer,
believing herself to be in control of her words and in fact nothing of
the kind, not once they were received by another person.

She was pregnant still when Freddy saw her, for the first time in more than eight weeks, on Monday 9 January, the day – *to the day*, as her phrase had it – on which they would both die the following year. And she was still pregnant when he sailed again, on the 20th, when they both had 354 days of life remaining. During that leave she had, Freddy told the Old Bailey, 'complained of being ill treated; she said "Things are just the same; they get no better." She said that the chances of getting a separation were very small, that Thompson would never agree to it.' She may also have discussed the fairly important business of the baby growing inside her, but he could not allude to that.

The day after his departure on the *Morea*, Edith miscarried. In a letter not used in evidence she described what had happened on Friday 21 January:

> About 10.30 or 11 a.m. I felt awfully ill – I had terrible pains come all over me – the sort of pains that I usually have – but have not had just lately – do you understand.
>
> These continued for about an hour & I stuck it somehow – feeling very sorry for myself – until about 12 o'c I went off then into a faint. They managed to get me to with brandy – then I went off again, & again, making 3 times in all. Everybody here [Carlton & Prior] was fearfully frightened & eventually went for the doctor...

Edith was then driven home by James Yuill.

> Darlint, I was lying flat on the floor inside, with the water bottle.
>
> When I got home I went straight to bed & about 7 something awful happened, darlint I don't know for certain what it was, but I can guess, can you, write & tell me.
>
> On Saturday, I felt a bit better, but not much. I didn't know what to do or take to get better & I looked awful. In the evening I dressed & went out & really enjoyed myself... It was a very cosmopolitan crowd darlint & I wish I had been with you there...

The fact that Edith should have pulled herself together and gone to an evening at the Holborn Empire (sending Freddy a programme of the show) almost defies belief. Freddy said as much. But what choice did she have? This was the reality of her double life: she had to have the guts to cope with it. Nobody knew about it, and nobody was going to sympathize. A doctor coming to work was one thing – it had happened when she fainted in November, when the bill of 10/6 had appalled her – but the prospect of somebody coming to the house, seeing the grotesque effusions of blood and knowing exactly what they meant, was entirely terrifying. She was used to pain – her symptoms suggest that she suffered from endometriosis, which can lead to fainting, and at its worst is very much like the wrenching sickness of an early miscarriage – and she was used to dealing with it, she was tough in some ways. Once the extremity of pain was done, a sensation of wrung-out relief would have made her able to lipstick over the cracks. On 15 February she wrote:

> …I suppose I'm rather ignorant on such subjects but I'll tell you everything about it when I can look at you & you mustnt be cross with me darlint about getting up. I can say I did know it was dangerous or whether I didn't I just didn't think about it at all, I fought and fought with myself to make myself keep up & I think I succeeded, darlint. Put yourself in my place darlint & see how you would feel if you thought by stopping in bed and not making an effort a doctor would have been called in would have said well what have you & I think he would someone else not you would have taken the blame & the pride for the thing they did not do.
>
> I imagine how I would feel about it, I'm afraid darlint I would not have been able to keep silent…

This last was for Freddy's benefit: she defended herself against his accusation that 'it was ridiculous for you to get up' by claiming that she could not bear Percy to think that the baby had been *his*. She was appealing to her lover's masculine pride, which was clever. Of course the truth was that she did not want Percy to think she had miscarried at all. At that point he did not suspect an actual affair with Freddy – at least, he may have suspected it, but he did not really believe his suspicions – but a doctor consoling him about his lost baby would surely have given him ideas. So Edith made light of her suffering, she cleaned up the bloody bathroom, she crossed her fingers that Mrs Lester would keep her nose out and her mouth shut, and she took the familiar journey: walk down Belgrave Road, train to Liverpool Street, tube to Holborn, every step and jolt a little knife-rip of the stomach.

But the real question about this episode is how Edith, who had danced her way blithely through a family Christmas – also her twenty-eighth birthday – and through her lover's shore leave in January ('Yes, darlint, it was real lovely on Thursday'), had managed to bring her pregnancy to its convenient end. In the letters that survive she did not explain. She would not have explained anyway. Possibly, given that she did not understand the body with which she was so deeply in tune, she *could* not have explained. It is odd that the miscarriage happened the very day after Freddy's departure; one would suspect a visit to an abortionist, except that this hardly squares with the words 'real lovely' to describe their last evening together. More likely Freddy brought her another supply of an abortifacient, no doubt recommended by a fellow sailor who had had a girl in trouble. Something, after all, did the trick.

In a letter from the previous month, Exhibit 27 at the trial, she had written:

'I had the wrong Porridge today, but I dont suppose it will matter, I dont seem to care much either way. You'll probably say I'm careless and I admit I am, but I don't care – do you?'

When this passage was read at the Old Bailey, the decision not to acknowledge Edith's desire to self-abort proved immediately problematical.

VI

'...hot blood begets hot thoughts, and hot thoughts beget hot deeds, and hot deeds is love.'

'Is this the generation of love? hot blood, hot thoughts, and hot deeds?'

From Shakespeare's *Troilus and Cressida*

THE QUESTION OF what was meant by the 'wrong porridge' was raised on the first day of the trial of Thompson and Bywaters, 6 December 1922, in the opening speech for the prosecution. The Solicitor General, Sir Thomas Inskip, quoted the relevant paragraph from Edith's letter then said to the jury:

The unexpectedness of the passage, the inappropriateness of the passage as it stands, is startling. It will be for you to say whether the line of thought that was in Mrs Thompson's mind was that the existence of her husband was a bar to the happiness she thought she could attain.

When her own counsel, Walter Frampton, quoted the passage at Edith and asked to what it referred, she replied: 'I really cannot explain.'

The damage was instant and very deep. Frampton attempted to mitigate it with further questions, which did not improve matters particularly.

'The suggestion here is that you had from time to time put things into your husband's porridge, glass for instance?'

'I had not done so.'

'Can you give us any explanation of what you had in your mind when you said you had the wrong porridge?'

'Except we [she and Bywaters] had suggested or talked about that sort of thing and I had previously said, "Oh yes, I will give him something one of these days".'

At this point Mr Justice Shearman intervened, for once with good cause. 'Do you mean', he asked Edith, 'that you had talked about poison?' She replied: 'I did not mean anything in particular.' To Frampton she said: 'We had talked about making my husband ill,' and he resumed:

'How had you come to talk about making your husband ill?'

'We were discussing my unhappiness.'

'Did that include your husband's treatment of you?'

'Yes.'

'Now you say you probably said that you would give him something?'

'I did.'

'Did you ever give him anything?'

'Nothing whatever.'

But one can see, reading this exchange, why Sir Henry Curtis-Bennett had done everything in his power to try to stop Edith Thompson from testifying in her own defence.

★

There is no way of knowing the truth about the 'wrong porridge'. But the point is that Edith could have explained it away, if she could have admitted to the attempts at self-abortion. She could have explained a great deal away – not quite everything – by saying that she was trying to end a pregnancy, or possibly to avoid one. Instead she had to answer as above.

Whether she did, in fact, put an abortifacient in the porridge then give it to Percy by mistake is open to question. For a start, the defence

proved that Mrs Lester made the porridge at 41 Kensington Gardens.
'I never knew Mrs Thompson make it,' she said. She had been specifically recalled in order to emphasize that point. Before her husband
died in May 1922, she made breakfast for him 'and Mr Thompson used
to have a plate of porridge out of it. One time he took a fancy to porridge and I said to Mrs Thompson, "don't you trouble to make it; I will
make enough for the two" and I made it with Mr Lester's.'

She added: 'Sometimes Mrs Thompson would have it as well as Mr
Thompson.' The defence was showing that Edith had scant opportunity to poison a substance under Mrs Lester's charge; a point that
was naturally ignored, but that also makes it less likely that Edith
should have dosed the porridge, and furthermore managed to mix up
the bowls. It is not impossible. Putting a drug into the stuff was just
feasible. Putting glass into it, as the prosecution would allege, was out
of the question; which the defence, in its tip-toeing and nervous way,
made clear; but nothing like clear enough.

Most likely of all, one would say, the entire episode had been
invented by Edith. This was the contention of Curtis-Bennett. Yet it
does not quite account for her answers, in which she seems both to
deny and not deny that something had happened. She had not tried to
poison her husband's porridge, but she could not explain what she *had*
done. Which brings one back to the attempts to miscarry: the thing
that must not be told.

The fact is, however, that this paragraph about the porridge was the
first of many of its kind in Edith's letters, not all of which could have
related to the need to terminate a pregnancy. Even after the miscarriage in January – soon after it – the letters were full of such references,
punctuating the text like a litany, breaking through with the gentle
insistence of waves. 'Darlint – You must do something this time – I'm
not really impatient – but opportunities come and go by – they have
to – because I'm helpless and I think and think and think – perhaps
– it will never come again.' Even if the miscarriage could have been
admitted to in court, that would not have been the end of the matter;
the lie about it was the first twist of the rope that made all the others

feel inevitable, but in that courtroom they probably *were* inevitable. If there could have been openness about that one event – if the letter detailing the miscarriage had been put in evidence, instead of being anxiously pushed to one side by Curtis-Bennett – then a kind of maturity and understanding might have permeated the whole business. But that was precisely what was never going to happen.

All the complexity of Edith Thompson was poured into those letters, and over the course of eleven months – between November 1921 and October 1922 – the pattern that she wove of facts, fantasy and falsehoods still defies disentanglement. Nobody knows what she meant by much of what she wrote. Her gift – a writer's gift – for creating alternative scenarios means that the letters float forever in a beautiful occlusion, striped occasionally with clarity. Their mystery, as well as their loveliness, is enduring. Certainly there was no elucidation at the Old Bailey. 'What is your meaning here?' the solicitor general asked their creator, quoting yet another sentence, but the context of the trial was too far removed from the one in which the letters had been written; no real answer could be given within that limited sphere.

She tried to obfuscate, but her questioners too were fundamentally in the dark. They worked backwards from the fact that a murder had been committed, which was only right, but their line of travel did not lead to enlightenment: it swerved and circumvented and lurched about as if in a London fog. In the case of the defence, its desperate manoeuvres were intended to dodge the multiplicity of incriminating remarks that Edith had made – to find explanations, to assemble little theories, to nudge her by any means possible on to a grass verge of safety – whereas the prosecution did the opposite, doggedly picking up every scattered phrase and sentence, gathering them together until they accumulated into a sign marked Guilty.

None of it had much to do with truth, but then what is truth? A man had died, justice was required. The letters, which formed almost the entirety of the evidence against Edith Thompson, made something else as well: a narrative that could be followed, as long as one knew what to look for: a countdown to murder.

★

'Darlingest boy, its Wednesday now,' wrote Edith on 25 January 1922, 'the last for posting to Marseilles.

'I'll be thinking & thinking, wishing such a lot of things tomorrow – late – when I shall know you have arrived. You will help me darlint you won't fail me this time.'

She was feeling 'bucked' as she put it; recalling Freddy's last leave, in which they had spent Saturday the 14th playing with snowballs in the slushy grey streets, having drinks in a 'low common place' in the City and buying sweets – 'I know you called me "fast" & the man in the confectioners thought I was terrible spending all your money & darlint I will be terrible, when you have a lot of money for me to spend.' How innocent she sounded, like a grown-up child; as she did a couple of days later, when she sent one of her 'birthday' greetings on the 27th.

This letter was not put in evidence. It referred to Percy only once, directly, mentioning that they had gone out to the Birnages a few streets away – 'for a hand of cards. They were very nice, but the strain of keeping out family matters (owing to the rift with Lily) was rather trying.' That was her ordinary life with her husband, the tamely enjoyable evenings with other couples, the silly niggling friction with in-laws: the façade, as one might say, although it was a little more than that. It *was* a life, this chain of events that she took part in with Percy. It was not leading anywhere or up to anything, but was simply the circular round of marriage; this chain never broke, it was still in place on the night of the murder, which happened after just such another outing to the theatre, where the Thompsons were described – as they always were by those who saw them – as a happy couple, a normal couple.

Yet a couple of weeks later there was this, in a letter sent to Aden dated 10 February: evidence again.

...we had words – in bed – Oh you know darlint – over that same old subject and he said – it was all through you I'd altered.

I told him if he ever again blamed you to me for any difference
there might be in me, I'd leave the house that minute and this is
not an idle threat.

She may not have actually said this. The noble stance was not quite
Edith; although what followed must be true, in some measure at least.

About 2am. he woke me up and asked for water as he felt ill
   I got it for him and asked him what the matter was and this
is what he told me – whether its the truth I dont know or whether
he did it to frighten me, anyway it didnt   He said – someone he
knows in town… had given him a prescription for a draught for
insomnia and he'd had it made up and taken it and it made him
ill. He certainly looked ill and his eyes were glassy. I've hunted for
the said prescription everywhere and cant find it and asked him
what he had done with it and he said the chemist kept it
   I told Avis about the incident only I told her as if it frightened
and worried me as I thought perhaps it might be useful at some
future time that I had told somebody
   What do you think, darlint   His sister Maggie came in last
night and *he told her*, so now there are two witnesses, altho' I wish
he hadn't told her – but left me to do it
   It would be so easy darlint – if I had things – I do hope I shall
   How about cigarettes?
   Have enclosed cuttings of Dr Wallis's case   It might prove
interesting darlint, I want to have you only I love you so much try
and help me
   PEIDI

Dr Wallis was the man whose lover's husband was found poisoned;
the coincidence of somebody, whom Edith knew quite well, becoming
involved in a situation so like her own was inevitably exciting to her.
As for Percy: she did not show an excess of sympathy for her husband,
but then why would she? She thought him a hypochondriac, and the

post-mortem on his body (fatty deposits aside) confirmed her opinion. She probably also thought that he *was* trying to frighten her. He had an array of tricks, poor man, designed to get her attention if nothing else. The reference to Avis, however… Mr Justice Shearman read it out in his summing-up on Monday 11 December, thus:

'"I told Avis about the incident only I told her" (look at these words) – "as if it frightened and worried me" – not that it had frightened her, but she pretended it to convey that, and you will have to consider in a good many of these things whether she was genuine or acting.'

Along with the *Daily Sketch* about Dr Wallis, Edith had sent a couple of other newspaper cuttings; for instance an extract from the *Sunday Pictorial* headlined 'Poison Chocolates for University Chief'. In a case straight out of early Golden Age detective fiction – not Edith's style, she preferred romance – the vice-chancellor of Oxford University was sent chocolates 'filled with ground glass and what is believed to be an insidious form of Indian poison'.

The judge cited the headline from this cutting, then said, in his scrupulous little way: 'I only allude to it because somebody else alluded to it.' The 'somebody else' was the prosecution: far fewer allusions were made to any point raised by the defence.

In fact, as Detective Sergeant John Hancock told the Old Bailey, there were 'some fifty enclosures' sent by Edith, 'referring to a variety of subjects. Of these cuttings about ten referred to cases which were more or less in the public eye at the time.' So the extracts relating to 'The Poisoned Curate' and 'Poisoned Chocolates', to 'Drugs for Brother in Hospital' and 'Girl's Drug Injection', were outnumbered around four to one by those such as 'Battle of Calves and Ankles', 'The Wedding Season' and 'Do Women Fail as Friends'; these latter cuttings, the lifestyle or women's page extracts, what the judge referred to as 'scraps', were listed by DS Hancock but not put in as evidence: only the scraps about poison made it that far.

Similarly excluded was a letter of 15 February, from which can be inferred Freddy's reaction to the miscarriage: 'Please dont worry, darlint I'm alright really now – only a bit shaky – & I dont like the way you say "It was ridiculous for you to get up" etc because I'm not going to let you bully me so please take note monsieur & dont transgress again.' This was a love letter, pretty much pure and simple: 'oh, I understand darlint the one pal you've got understands everything'. She didn't, of course. She knew less than she realized about her darlingest boy; but at this stage, when winter was soon to give way to spring and Freddy was halfway through his tour, she was buoyant *malgré tout*; her longing had a sensuous quality, there was as yet no aridity in it. 'There's nothing but ordinary every day things to tell you darlint oh except one thing just that I love you so much but you know that...'

A week later, in a letter dated 22 February, she wrote that she was ill again: 'only with a cold tho... I caught it from him.' Oh, him –! the inevitable and immutable *him*, who refused to sleep in the spare bedroom because that meant giving way, and thus gave her his cold. Then – because his moods were so variable, and because he did care for the wife whom he also sort of hated – 'you mustn't laugh I was given my breakfast in bed'. And then, another mood: he cornered Miss Prior at Edith's place of business and asked what time they finished work each day.

During this visit Percy had seen a little bronze monkey that Edith kept on her desk, a gift from Freddy. Now in full-blown officious mood, he asked for Freddy's address – wrote it in his 'note book' like a policeman – 'he also said "Have you anything whatever belonging to him – anything mind you" (I knew he meant our monkey).' Naturally Edith denied this:

it wasn't a lie was it, because the monkey belongs to us doesn't it and not to you or to me, and if it was a lie I dont care, I'd tell heaps and heaps and heaps to help you even tho I know you don't like them...

Darlint, do you think I like telling them, do you think I don't hate it, darlint I do hate this life I lead...

Darlingest boy, the thing I am going to do for both of us will it ever – at all, make any difference between us, darlint, do you understand what I mean   Will you ever think any the less of me

– not now, I know darlint – but later on – perhaps some years hence – do you think you will feel any different – because of this thing that I shall do...

Im not hesitating darlint – through fear of any consequences of the action, dont think that but I'd sooner go on in the old way for years and years and years and retain your love and respect.

Evidence again.

Sorry that Ive got to remain inactive for more than another whole month, and I had thought by that time I should be seeing you for just as long and every time you wanted me   However, for that glorious state of existence I suppose we must wait for another three or four months Darlint, I am glad you succeeded   Oh so glad I cant explain, when your note came I didn't know how to work at all – all I kept thinking of was of your success – and my ultimate success I hope.

I suppose it isnt possible for you to send it to me – not at all possible, I do so chafe at wasting time darlint...

Obviously, this time, Edith was not pregnant.

Therefore this letter was not easily susceptible to explanation.

'The meaning of that is for you to judge,' said Mr Justice Shearman to the jury; 'you will fully understand it is not for me to tell you what the letters mean; you are the judges of that, not I; there is no law about it whatever.' A remarkable statement, the last one. What on earth did it mean? What were they all doing there, analysing these barely comprehensible letters, if there was no law to guide them? There was, however, legal opinion – or at any rate opinion from a legal brain. The judge had plenty of it, as for instance in reference to Edith's line about 'the thing I am going to do for both of us'. He told the jury: 'It is said that the meaning of that is, "If I poison him is it going to make any difference to you afterwards"; that is what is suggested is the plain meaning of the words.'

There was no plain meaning to the words whatsoever: the judge had interpreted them, that was all. But in the absence of plain meaning, and in that courtroom, he had been pretty much bound to do so.

On 6 March, a letter not put in at the trial referred again to the miscarriage. 'I suppose I have been ill probably more so than I thought but I wouldnt give way because I wanted to keep that illness all to ourselves thinking that helped to keep me up.' She alluded to her periods, which had started again on 26 February: 'I did feel really ill darlint, I think it was worse than before what happened... I didnt stop away from 168 [work] because I thought of your letters and I knew they would forward them to 41 [home] if I was not there so I managed to get in every morning & went early...' It can't have been easy, making that journey to Aldersgate Street – not long, but complicated and gruelling, like most commutes – making herself attractive as both she and the world demanded of her, pushing her body, depleted and anaemic as it now was, through the cold (1922 was a cold year – snow in April), smiling on and dancing through. Somebody to talk to would have made it better. As much as anything, that was what Freddy Bywaters was all about, yet it was because of him that she could not talk to anybody else – particularly her sister. And was she, really, talking to Freddy Bywaters? Yes and no. She was expressing herself, through writing; his response was important to her but it was not the whole of the matter; she had no idea, much of the time, what his response could possibly be. What she wanted was a response identical to her own. But Freddy was an interpreter, like the judge.

And what he also read was that her life went on: she went to a show at the Palace Theatre, to a dance with friends at Shoreditch Town Hall ('he came too'), to Percy's office to help with his accounts, to other friends in Tulse Hill with the Graydons for a hand of whist. All this normality and competence and a certain amount of fun – 'I enjoyed it dancing with Reg and Mr. Philpot' – and at the same time, all this other: 'darlint longing much more for you to be here to see you, for you to hold me so tight I cant breathe.'

It was not long until another leave. 'Oh darlint, even the looking forward hurts,' she wrote on 14 March – 'does it you? every time I think of *Friday* and onwards my inside keeps turning over and over – all my nerves seems like wires continually quivering.' By this time the *Morea* was at Plymouth, the man was imminent: no feeling quite like that one. Edith told her husband that she had written to Freddy, asking him not to try to see her during this leave. A lie, naturally. On Friday 17 March the lovers met for the first time, then intermittently over the next fortnight. There is the faintest sense that this leave was disappointing to Edith – how could it not be, when the Freddy of her imaginings was now a creation some seven months old, and had acquired such substance? She had forgotten, for instance, that he had a life beyond her control. Again she asked to see the letters sent by the 'Australian girl': 'I did not look at them – except at a small slip of paper...' This unknown girl on the other side of the world became a pawn in their game, a means to keep their desire for each other topped up to the brim. Freddy wielded the weapon, Edith reacted; Freddy laid down his arms, Edith relaxed; and for a moment equilibrium was achieved.

'I do like to hear you reassure me,' she wrote at the end of March, while he was actually in England. 'I like you to write it – so that I can see it in black and white... its just a vain feeling I have to hear you say things to me – nice things – '

She had read his letter – the one that reassured her – at quarter to six that morning. She had slept on it unopened. Edith, Percy and Freddy's words, all in the same bed.

Then the leave suddenly bloomed, on the very last night – Thursday 30 March – and in a letter dated 1 April Edith wrote as if in raging disbelief, that what had suddenly become magical again had been snatched away from her. As ever there was no attempt to hide what she felt, to play it cool. She was above that.

'I was fighting all night long to keep your thoughts with me darlint I felt all the time you were not with me – didnt want to be... I cried and cried and cried, until I eventually went to sleep, but I had heard the clock strike five before I did so...'

Percy was beside her throughout this sleepless night of longing for Freddy. It is hard not to think that he was aware of Edith's restless, voluptuous misery, and it was directly afterwards that Lily Vellender, her friend at work, told her of a dream in which Percy wanted to murder her: 'as he had found out that I had been away from home for a night with a fair man (her expression).' As Lily must have suspected, this was what had happened – very nearly – on the last night of Freddy's leave. Nearly but not quite. Something had held Edith back – the proscriptions of her class, the fear of entering reality – and had held Freddy back also; it was almost as though he too had become addicted to frustration. But the hours of passionate unsated congress were still heaving through her body as she wrote:

> About that Thursday – had there been anywhere to stop in Ilford – I should have said, "Take me there, *I won't* go home", and you would have said, "Yes I will" but darlint before we had arrived at the Hotel, I should have thought about things and so would you and I can hear you say just when we reach the door "Peidi, you're going home" pour moi   just this once darlint and I should have gone.
>
> Darlint you're not and never will be satisfied with half and I don't ever want to give half – all of every ounce of me that lives to you…
>
> Darlingest boy you said to me "Say no Peidi, say No" on Thursday didn't you – but *at that very moment* you didn't wish me to say "No" did you? You felt you wanted all me in exchange for all you. I knew this – felt this – and wouldn't say "No" for that very reason.
>
> Half an hour afterwards or perhaps even ten minutes afterwards you'd really have wanted me to say "No" but not at that especiall moment.
>
> Darlint I feel that I never want to withhold anything from you   if you really want it and one of these days youre going to teach me to give all and everything quite voluntarily arent you? Please darlint.

What erotic power this woman had – ! and how fearsomely strong this lack of fulfilment made it. Freddy could never get enough of Edith because, quite simply, he never got enough of her. It was all very well to cavort in seaport brothels with prostitutes who knew every trick in the book, to have sex like a heedless pagan; but with Edith, whose sensual gift gleamed like jet from beneath veils of inexperience, innocence, conventionality, residual shame – who had to be uncovered, trapped, instructed in how to enjoy her gift to the full, and who could so seldom be any of those things... At times the sheer difficulty of the whole affair made Freddy Bywaters want to chuck it, but more often the desire to win this particular game was uppermost. He was full of self-love, taut with masculinity, and everything that he felt was charged to the height. Whereas Edith's emotions were modulated, his were not. He was sharp and keen as a weapon. She seems never to have feared her ability to handle him, and in a way his youth made him malleable, but at the same time it was a little like owning a pet wolf. Thrilling, of course.

And then there was the other man: *him.* He too was dangerous in his heavier, more ponderous, bear-like way.

'He knows or guesses something,' she wrote, in a letter not used in evidence dated 4 April,

how much or how little I cant find out. When I got home & went upstairs I found him not there.

As I was getting into bed a car drew up outside & he came in looking, well you know how with that injured air of mystery on his face attempted to kiss me and then moved away with the expression "Phew – drink". He had been to a Theatre – he had a programme – what I imagine is – waited for me on the 11.30 found I wasn't on it & caught the next – of course was surprised to find me home. If he has any sense he could easily put 2 and 2 together. Your last night last time & your last night this time – I went to a theatre on both occasions.

By which she meant that she had pretended to go to the theatre on 30 March, and had in fact spent the evening with Freddy Bywaters. Which Percy knew only too well. He *had* put two and two together.

He also made a good guess at where his wife had gone that Thursday night; having pretended to be at the theatre with her school friend Bessie Akam, whose husband was away, she most likely spent part of the evening with Freddy at Bessie's house. Whether or not Bessie was there too, whether or not their sexual fumblings took place there or outdoors, another person was in on their secret. Bessie could be trusted – she was a friend to Edith up to the end – but still the network of deception was growing, as it always does.

I said "A remark you passed at tea time about Bess what do you mean by it I want to know." *He* "You want to know do you – well you shant you can just imagine how much I know & how much I dont & I hope you'll feel uncomfortable about it"

I'm afraid I let go then & said several things in haste perhaps it would have been better had I held my tongue & finished up with "Go to Hell" – you can only keep good tempered when you – getting what you want a case of sugar for the bird & he sings. I was told I was the vilest tempered girl living & "you used not to be, but you're under a very good tutor"...

'Oh,' she wrote of her husband, 'it's a rotten spirit.'

This was the first weekend in April: 'how I got through Sunday I dont know living with banging doors & sour silent faces will turn me grey.' A couple of days earlier Freddy had returned to Norwood before sailing, and had his almighty row with his mother. The people around the pair were becoming obstacles at every turn. Mr Graydon was asking tentatively if Freddy had fallen out with Percy, Avis was prodding crudely, hinting that Freddy saw other women ('he was always knocking about with some girl or other before he knew me, and now he doesn't see me and he probably does the same'), Mrs Bywaters was telling Freddy to cut 'that woman' out of his life, Percy was using all his limited resources to make Edith a facsimile, at least, of a proper wife. But opposition is a friend to love, just as prohibition is a friend to passion. The idea that people can be persuaded out of an attachment is simply absurd. The only thing that really works is allowing it to run its course. And in this case, where constant separation meant that the affair never became everyday, its spark might drop to a smoulder but it would not go out; because dreams of what their lives could be, which Edith Thompson experienced so intensely, and communicated with such intensity to Frederick Bywaters, would always re-ignite it.

And Edith, that virtuoso of the imagination, had many tunes to play on this particular theme.

'Don't keep this piece,' she wrote, in her letter of 1 April.

'About the Marconigram, do you mean one saying Yes or No, because I shant send it darlint I'm not going to try any more until you come back.

'I made up my mind about this last Thursday.'

Then she described a visit to Percy's mother in Manor Park: 'he puts great stress,' she wrote,

> on the fact of the tea tasting bitter "as if something had been put in it" he says. Now I think whatever else I try it in again will still taste bitter he will recognize it and be more suspicious still and if the quantity is still not successful it will injure any chance I have of trying when you come home
>
> Do you understand?

There followed a passage in reply to Freddy's last letter, in which he mentioned a man called Dan:

> Darlint, don't trust him. I don't mean don't *tell* him anything because I know you never would. What I mean is don't let him be suspicious of you regarding that – because if we were successful in the action – darlint circumstances may afterwards make us want many friends or helpers and we must have no enemies – or even people that know a little too much. Remember the saying, "A little knowledge is a dangerous thing".

What this referred to is unclear.

> I wish we had not got electric light. It would be easy.
>   I'm going to try the glass again occasionally when it is safe I've
> got an electric light globe this time.

In the closing speech for the prosecution, the solicitor general stated: 'I am bound to say to you that this letter of 1st April is one that deals entirely with this idea now occupying so much of her attention, that her husband must be got rid of. The passage is full of crime.'

During questioning about the letter, Exhibit 17, Freddy Bywaters testified to the Old Bailey that he had given quinine to Edith during his leave in March 1922. 'It was in the form of 5 gram tabloids, white.' It is possible that 'Dan' was involved in obtaining this quinine; if of course the statement was true. Asked why he had given the drug to Edith, he replied that she had talked frequently of wanting to commit suicide and had badgered him for some means. He chose quinine because, with that particular substance, 'I knew she could not hurt herself.'

It has been suggested that this quinine was really wanted as an abortifacient – which is scarcely possible, given that Edith had only recently miscarried – or possibly as a contraceptive; also unlikely, given Freddy's nervousness about having full sex ('say no, Peidi') during that March leave. In fact there was another explanation for the 'quinine', offered by Freddy a couple of weeks before his death.

During his cross-examination by the solicitor general, he was asked about Edith's reference to the tea tasting bitter. 'What did you understand by the passage?'

'That she had taken quinine and it had tasted bitter.'

The solicitor general, exaggeratedly patient, read the sentence again and said as to a recalcitrant child: 'To whom did it taste bitter?'

'Mrs Thompson.'

'Do you suggest that, Bywaters?'

'I do.'

Walter Frampton, asking Edith about the incident, asked simply:

'Was there ever any time when your husband complained to his mother about the tea tasting bitter?'

'Not to my knowledge.'

'Was this an imaginary incident then that you were recording?'

'Yes.'

★

On 5 April Edith replied to a letter received on Saturday 1st, her half-day at work, which must have been written just before Freddy sailed:

> I was prepared to wait till next Monday to hear from my own man, but at 12.15 just as I was going to leave your letter came. It bucked me up such a lot I thought to myself well it will help me to get thro the 'inevitable weekend' & it did help me darlint…
>
> Darlint that ache which you and I share & you speak about – not a sharp stabbing pain that lets you know it is there & then gone – but just a numb feeling a feeling of inactivity like a blind that is never more than half raised just enough to torment you with the sight of a tiny bit of light & sunshine.

Freddy had described the row with his mother and sister, and asked if it worried Edith, which it did: 'after all darlint – but for me it never would have happened I'm always the cause of pain to you & perhaps to myself as well but always to you ever since you knew me you've never really been happy & perhaps had you known me less you might have been.'

She was surely hoping for a denial when she wrote this, and she probably got one. Nevertheless it was true, and they probably both knew it.

> I'd like you to tell me darlint just how you feel when you move out of dock – what are your thoughts when you begin to move

when you must realise that you're not on England... You told me you were sailing about 2 & about that time I began thinking how you were feeling if you were hopeful and not too downhearted & I thought about everything connected with the last fortnight, some things I was sorry about & some things pleased. How did you feel?

It was a pity that this letter was not part of the evidence. There was no 'crime' in it. It was devoid of crime. Instead there was Browning – 'What poet was it who wrote "Oh to be in England now Spring is here" I wish he were alive and feeling as miserable as I' – the snow was falling as she wrote, 'thick lumps'. There was talk of leaving the country: 'you know I could do practically anything to earn just enough to keep myself for a little while.' There were books, *The Shulamite* and *The Woman Deborah* – 'I await your remarks' – there was Turkish Delight, 'much better than the last lot', there was a woman who came into Carlton & Prior who told Edith that she hadn't aged in five years, 'but I'm sure by the way she said it, she doesn't think it.' It was an ordinary letter, or as ordinary as Edith could be. So too was the one dated 12 April, written at speed before the firm closed for the Easter break. 'We're fearfully busy here – I was here till 7 the last 2 nights & still we have such a lot to do before the holidays.' It was a love letter; nothing more.

But what was read at the Old Bailey was this, from the 24th:

'I used the "light bulb" three times but the third time – he found a piece – so I've given up – until you come home.'

The solicitor general, cross-examining Freddy Bywaters, asked:

'What did you understand by that passage?'

He answered: 'She had been lying to me again.'

'She had been what?'

'Lying to me, lying.'

'What did you understand the lie was?'

'It was melodrama on her part, trying to persuade me that she had taken broken glass.'

Again, therefore, Freddy was insisting upon Edith's declared desire to kill herself, as an explanation for her words. Again, as one restraining his formidable incredulity, the solicitor general read out the sentence about the light bulb, then said:

'You understand she meant her husband had detected her in an attempt to commit suicide?'

He was unfazed, prepared to push his own lack of logic to a logical end.

'Yes.'

'"So I have given up till you come home." Do you suggest that she was going to wait for your arrival home in order that you might co-operate with her in committing suicide?'

'I might give her something more, more quinine.'

'That would be a strange idea to you, Bywaters, if that is right?'

'Yes; I do not know her idea.'

And that, at least, was the truth, unlike everything else that he had said.

★

The Easter holiday was not as bad as Edith had been fearing, or pretending to fear; mainly because of the presence of her parents, with whom she always felt safe, and Avis, whose enduring interest in Freddy both irritated her and piqued her vanity. She related the events in the letter of 24 April: tea dancing at the Waldorf on Thursday the 13th, then clothes shopping with Avis; spring cleaning on Good Friday followed by a concert at the East Ham Palace, Mr Graydon's treat; Edith's repayment on Saturday at the Ilford Hippodrome, where the ghost of Freddy hovered like Banquo. His ex-girlfriend Molly sat behind her and a music hall song entitled 'He makes me all fussed up' put him into her mind – was it part of his repertoire? 'Of course Avis remarked about you and the song...' Avis, poor handmaiden Avis, stayed in Ilford for the rest of Easter – sleeping with Edith in the marital bed, where Percy brought them both a cup of tea...

Also, this happened.

> Bye the way – what is "Aromatic Tincture of Opium" – Avis drew my attention to a bottle sealed in the medicine chest in your room [that is to say, the spare bedroom].
>
> I took possession of it and when he missed it and asked me for it – I refused to give it him – he refuses to tell me where he got it and for what reason he wants it – so I shall keep it till I hear from you.

The incident, which took place on Easter Monday, was described more fully by Avis at the Old Bailey. Percy had hit his finger with a hammer when the two of them were out in the garden, knocking apart the case of the grand piano; he asked his sister-in-law to go upstairs and find a bottle of what he called 'New Skin'. That was when she saw the opium, about half a pint of it. She went down to tell Edith, advised her sister to 'nip up and get it', and on returning the New Skin found that the opium had been removed by Edith from the chest. It was standing on the sideboard in the drawing-room. Avis told the court:

'I said, "I will do away with this, so there can be no more trouble", and I took the bottle and went to the scullery and poured the contents of the bottle down the sink. I then put the bottle in the fire in the morning room.'

Opium was taken for heart problems, which Percy believed himself to suffer from, and it may be that this bottle of medicine was what had caused the episode in February, when he woke his wife complaining of illness. If Avis did indeed pour the stuff away, perhaps she had thought to avoid a repeat of this event (which Edith had told her about). Perhaps she believed that opium was in part responsible for Percy's erratic behaviour towards her sister. She knew that something was wrong in the marriage – why, for instance, was *she* helping the man to smash up a piano case, while Edith sat indoors by the fire? – and her opinion of Percy was not high; at the same time she knew that something was going on between her sister and Freddy Bywaters, that Percy had cause to sulk or be angry; that the situation was, in fact, extremely loaded. To imagine that she feared the presence of opium in the house, that either of the Thompsons might use it against the other, sounds absurd. Yet the newspapers were full of tales of domestic poisonings – the solicitor Herbert Armstrong had just gone on trial for dosing his wife with arsenic – and of deaths from drug use, as Edith's collection of cuttings went to show. In some vague, unacknowledged way, Avis may have felt that it was simply *better* to get rid of the opium. Her instincts were right, although – as so often with these things – she would not really have believed them to be.

Incidentally if Avis's evidence was true, that she poured the opium away, then Edith's claim – that she 'took possession of it' – was a lie, a piece of fantasy. Written for Freddy.

In her letter of 1 May, Edith described being ill yet again. It was as though the miscarriage, and the absence of recovery time, had removed her resilience. This time she had a sore throat and 'I've got practically no voice at all – just a little very high up, squeak.'

Then she wrote: 'About those fainting fits darlint, I don't really know what to say to you.' This was her menstrual cycle once again, obstinately refusing to give her peace.

> I'm beginning to think it's the same as before – they always happen 1st thing in the morning – when I'm getting up and I wasn't as ill as I should have been last time [her period in April], altho' I was a little – but not as usual.
>
> What shall I do about it darlint, if it is the same this month – please write and tell me I want to do just what you would like.
>
> I still have the herbs.

These, of course, were the remainder of whatever Edith had used to induce a miscarriage (not quinine, therefore). The trial was not told this, although it was almost impossible not to infer it. But if Edith really believed that she had fallen pregnant again on the evening of 30 March, her ignorance was surely remarkable. From her description it is clear that the sexual act was incomplete; it was not unusual that her cycle should have been disrupted, and the fainting fits so typical of endometriosis had happened before, for example in November 1921. It was almost as though she wanted Freddy to think that she was carrying a baby – *his* baby – or perhaps she did indeed believe it. If so, she seems also to have believed, with that odd inconsequence she could display, that the herbs would work as before. Later in the letter she told Freddy about the Bournemouth holiday being planned for 8 July, during which she presumably did not expect to be nearly four months pregnant.

> While Avis was over last night he asked her to come with us. The suggestion was nothing to do with me – it was his entirely and altho' I wouldn't have suggested such a thing for the world – I'm glad – because if things are still the same and we do go – a third party helps to make you forget that you always lead the existence we do.

But this letter was hopping with plans for things *not* to be the same.

> I don't think we're failures in other things and we mustn't be in this. We mustn't give up as we said. No, we shall have to wait if we fail again. Darlint, Fate can't always turn against us and if it is we must fight it – You and I are strong now   We must be stronger. We must learn to be patient.

It was the language of Lady Macbeth – we fail? – but she, after all, had only been urging her husband to do something he already wanted to do. And here? What had Freddy Bywaters written, to make Edith respond in this geeing-up, screw your courage to the sticking point manner?

'Why was it so emphatically said "She incited Bywaters"?' it is obvious her letters were answers to questions.' So wrote Avis Graydon to the prime minister, Andrew Bonar Law, on 30 December 1922.

This, on 1 May, was not exactly an answer to a question, but it was plain enough that it was a reply of sorts.

> You said it was enough for an elephant. Perhaps it was. But you don't allow for the taste making only a small quantity to be taken. It sounded like a reproach was it meant to be?
> Darlint I tried hard – you won't know how hard – because you weren't there to see and I can't tell you all – but I did – I do want you to believe I did for both of us.

The following day she received another letter, and resumed her own, again in part-reply.

> I was buoyed up with the hope of the "light bulb" and I used a lot – big pieces too – not powdered – and it has no effect – I quite expected to be able to send that cable – but no – nothing has happened from it and now your letter tells me about the bitter taste again. Oh darlint, I do feel so down and unhappy.
> Wouldn't the stuff make small pills coated together with soap and dipped in liquorice powder – like Beechams – try while you're away. Our Boy had to have his thumb operated on because he had a piece of glass in it that's what made me try that method again – but I suppose as you say he's not normal, I know I shall never get him to take a sufficient quantity of anything bitter…

'Have you,' the solicitor general asked Bywaters, 'any doubt that you understand that to mean the husband?'

To which he replied firmly: 'I did not understand that.'

'To whom did you understand it referred?'

'Perhaps she had made a mistake in the words.'

'And meant "me"?'

'Yes.'

'"I know I shall never get 'myself' to take a sufficient quantity of anything bitter". Is that how you read it?'

'Yes; she did not like the taste of quinine.'

It was a valiant defence, and it did neither of them any good. As much as anything, it was this very valour that helped to convince people that Freddy Bywaters was Edith's plaything, not a pet wolf but a bright-eyed retriever, following at her unworthy heels.

On 15 May Edith wrote again, a very different kind of letter. She told Freddy about her racing bets; about Percy being made a commission agent for the Sun Life insurance company by his friend Sidney Birnage; about trying on mourning hats at Carlton & Prior, breaking the cheval glass on her dressing table, the swinging pendulum of luck. She wrote, as usual, of the books that they had been reading, discussing the characters as if they were not merely real but she had entered their reality: 'I love Maria and I admired Deborah.' Then, in a delicious sisterly snap:

> I don't know whether Avis liked the books or not – but if you asked her why she did or did not she couldn't say, could she do you think – she couldn't discuss each character as we do – she wouldn't remember enough about them – she would only remember the general theme of the book – so why ask?

Edith would never feel herself inferior to Avis – she knew that she was not – but Avis had the one thing that she did not: freedom. It was her sister's sole card in the game that they still played over Freddy Bywaters, but it was a trump, and Edith could never quite forgive that she held it.

As an exhibit, this letter had little to offer the prosecution case. More useful was the one dated 18 May, which introduced the novel *Bella Donna* by Robert Hichens. Edith began by quoting a passage from the book about 'digitalin, a cumulative poison'. In a letter dated five days later she returned to the subject: having sent two novels to Freddy she wrote 'I'd like you to read "Bella Donna" first you may learn something from it to help us.'

The book had at its centre an eponymous heroine aged forty-two, older than her husband by six years, who falls beneath the spell of a seductive Greek-Egyptian ('she felt cruelty in him, and it attracted her, it lured her'). Although written by a respected author it belonged to the same genre as Edith Maude Hull's *The Sheikh*, which became the film that made Rudolph Valentino a star; it was a just-about acceptable form of fictional pornography, set in what would have been called 'far-off climes', despised by the literati and of course enormously popular. So what, asked the solicitor general, did Edith think that Bywaters would learn from *Bella Donna* that would help them?

She replied: 'The book was really about Egypt, and I thought he might learn something in it about Egypt.'

At this early point in the discussion Mr Justice Shearman, apparently unable to contain himself, intervened: 'I should like to clear this up. Is not the main point of it that the lady killed her husband with slow poisoning?'

Edith said: 'Do you ask me that question?'

'Yes,' the judge replied. 'It is plain to me – '

'I was going to deal with it in cross-examination,' said the solicitor general, but the judge was not to be stopped: 'Although I never like to take part in it you know it must come out... Possibly some of the jury might not know it, and I thought it ought to be cleared up.'

Later, as it were in his own time, the solicitor general would revert to this point. 'There is a plot,' he stated, 'which is really the plot of the story, to poison her husband, without anybody finding out what she was doing?' Edith, who despite her terror had not lost all her wits, answered:

'It is a matter of opinion whether that is absolutely the plot, is it not?'

'Anyway, that is an important incident in the book?'

'At the end, yes.'

The defence had earlier quoted Edith's critical opinion of Bella Donna – 'I hate her – hate to think of her... Yes she was clever – I admire the cleverness – but she was cunning, there is a difference darlint, I don't admire that' – and now, at the end of her evidence, Sir Henry Curtis-Bennett attempted to shore up at least this part of the wreckage. He reminded the court that Bella Donna resembled Edith in no way whatever, that she had loved money whereas Edith loved a man who had very little, that Edith had described the character as 'abnormal – a monster'. But the judge, who had a gift for timing his interpolations, had done his work. He had appeared to cut to the heart of the matter in a way that seemed helpful, that the jury would remember, for which they would be grateful.

★

'I'm counting the days now darlint,' Edith wrote on 18 May: there were eight of them left until she saw Freddy Bywaters again, wearing perhaps the new cream gabardine skirt that she described to him (not the new navy costume, he wouldn't like the longer coat). 'It doesnt matter where we meet... we mustn't think of other people being there we must just live for each other in that first minute   Dont forget darlint   Dont just say how are you "Chere". It so prosaic and were not are we?'

For sure, Freddy knew no other girl quite like that. And to have such a girl so deep in love with him... he had a good opinion of himself, especially when it came to attracting women, but this was something else altogether. He knew that other men would have envied him in ways that went beyond walking down the street with a stunner, a head-turner, a twenty-year-old typist with a clear young eye. Edith was in a different league; he knew that. She was under his skin, even if he didn't always want her there. And at the same time she was doing the rounds with that lumbering piece of pseudo-masculinity, Percy Thompson... Again the lovers saw little of each other until the end of the leave. Edith said that she would ask for the 31st as a holiday. This was Derby Day – the race was then run on a Wednesday – and she had backed the eventual third, each-way; a day with the crowds at Epsom would have been a delight to them both, in the magnificent weather that had suddenly taken a hold; yet this does not seem to have happened. She may not even have been given the time off. Then came the Whitsun weekend, which again was spent apart: Percy was at home. Freddy meanwhile was visiting his mother, the Graydons, Avis. But after this enforced and as it seemed fateful separation, with the knowledge pressing upon her that only three days were left before the *Morea* sailed for more than three months, Edith seized control. A couple of telegrams – Exhibits 66 and 67 – were sent to Tilbury. On Tuesday 6 June, the day after the Bank Holiday, she wrote 'Failed again perhaps 5 o'clock tonight' and on the following day 'Have already said not going 231 see you and talk six'.

On the 6th, therefore – having 'failed' to arrange a rendezvous at lunchtime (presumably) – the couple met at Fenchurch Street. Subsequently Percy would try to catch Edith out about this, claiming that a friend had seen her at the station with a man fitting Freddy's description: 'That's an awful lie darlint'. But Percy was alert as a fox that week. He had observed his wife's fractious boredom over Whitsun and known precisely what its source was. On Thursday the 8th he went to Shakespeare Crescent, where he was told that Freddy had gone out for his last night of leave with a 'pal' – naturally he had his own ideas as to who that pal might be. According to Edith – who was quoting Avis – Percy then remarked to the Graydons: 'I thought he was keen on you (Avis) – but now I can see it was a blind to cover his infatuation with Edie.'

'Darlint its not an infatuation is it? Tell me it isnt.'

A coda of sublime and childlike selfishness... Avis's unhappiness was a *bagatelle* at this time to Edith. That is the solipsism of romantic love. But it was dangerous to be so slighting of Avis, so trusting of her good nature.

The truth of what Edith wrote is always debatable; it does seem, however, that the other triangle in this story – the one between Freddy and the two sisters – was particularly evident in the first week of June 1922. On Wednesday the 7th a neighbour from Manor Park had seen Edith and Freddy together and reported the sighting back to Avis. What spies they all were in east London! Avis confronted Edith, in her passive way: 'of course I denied it – but she described my frock... Avis said she was upset because you had gone for good – she said she could hardly realise it.' These words sound true, dreadfully so. Avis had continued to hope, all through the year since the Isle of Wight holiday. She had surely known what Edith was like, but this was very hard to take. And still, she did not quite take it. Still she hoped, that in the end she would win the battle, which was as much about Edith as about Freddy.

Meanwhile Edith – the blithely dismissive holder of the spoils – hastened to reassure her boy. They had been seen on the Wednesday, she wrote, so that 'was all right'. Had they been seen the following day, goes the implication, it would not have been all right. Thursday 8 June was their last night, the one on which Freddy's leave – which could never quite fulfil what had been imagined of it – again acquired an urgent, clutching and clinging significance; they must have kissed, or something of that kind, in a place where they could have been overlooked. Madness, of course, but this was part of the thrill for Edith. She rather relished this sense of being spied upon – an audience – however much it was sometimes on her nerves.

They had sex that night of the 8th, when it was warm enough to do so outside, probably in Wanstead Park: the skies were light until late, but the gossips would have been in their beds by that time. 'Im so glad youre not sorry this time, no Im not a bit,' she wrote. Then she indulged in a piece of masochistic playacting, asking Freddy to leave on his ship the next day and forget all about her. She knew full well that at such a moment, when he was high on possession, he would refuse her 'request'. It was good advice, all the same.

What happened after *that* was described in a letter of 13 June:

Darlingest Boy,

I'm trying very hard – very very hard to B.B. [be brave]. I know my pal wants me to.

On Thursday – he was on the ottoman at the foot of the bed and said he was dying and wanted to – he had another heart attack – thro me.

Darlint I had to laugh because *I knew* it couldn't be a heart attack.

When he saw this had no effect he got up and stormed – I
said exactly what you told me to and he knew thats what I
wanted and he wasnt going to give it to me – it would make
things too easy for both of you (meaning you and me) especially
for you he said.

Yes: Percy could take out his anger on Edith, to a degree, but to Freddy
he could not, and his anger against the young man had become
immense by this time. He was not a fool, although he was behaving
like one; he surely recognized the glow on Edith as she drifted into the
bedroom, even if he had never been the cause of it.

And it was awful, just as it was for Avis, to know that one was the
less desirable option – people can rarely delude themselves about that
particular thing – and that there was really nothing to be done about
it. Having tried pleas, threats, violence, being nice, being foul, Percy
now reached for straightforward male dominance (which unfortunately Freddy did rather better): 'he told me he was going to break me
in somehow – I have always had too much of my own way and he was
a model husband – and in future on *Thursdays* the bedroom was to
be cleaned out.' Even in 1922, this was really not something to say to a
woman who earned more than he did.

Later in the letter, Edith described how Percy had gone to the
Graydons' house in a rage and 'told Dad everything': the episode
refuted at the Old Bailey as 'pure imagination'. Her letter claimed that
she had heard the story from Avis. So it is not completely impossible
that Avis – rather than Edith – invented the incident. She might have
done it, in an attempt to force Edith to give up Freddy – she knew that
Edith hated the idea of upsetting her parents – the fact that she never
worried about upsetting her sister must have been intensely annoy-
ing. So too was the fact that the Graydons remained as fond as ever
of their errant daughter, who turned up with presents every Friday
and created a starburst of glamour in their parlour. Psychologically,
therefore, it is convincing that Avis might have done this; although
it was a risk, because Edith might then have confronted Percy, who

would have denied it – and so on. Probably it did not happen that way. Nevertheless Avis's staunch, almost fanatical defence of her sister after the murder – when she said things that were not true, for instance that Edith was quiet and docile (!) – may have had its origins in a kind of guilt, that she had not understood Edith well enough at the time, that she had been one of those who worked against her. She had had grounds, of course. But her conscience would not have thought that good enough.

Assuming, however, that the episode was indeed *Edith's* invention; does that mean that the rest of the letter was imaginary also? No, because she testified openly to her defence counsel that Percy had claimed that night to be having a heart attack, and even at the Old Bailey she was unable to keep a note of contempt out of her reply: 'I knew when he had a heart attack; it was entirely different. The scene which took place on the night before Bywaters sailed was entirely due to the fact that I had been out that night and did not return till late.'

It sounded honest, decidedly so; although it may not have been the best way of putting things, when one was on trial for the man's murder.

★

Now began a separation of almost sixteen weeks and, in the letters, the pattern of yearning and urging gradually tightened, sharpened, as this absence – far longer than anything they had previously experienced – worked differently upon Edith Thompson and Freddy Bywaters.

On 14 June she wrote to Marseilles, reminding him of how, a year ago that day, they had taken a charabanc ride around the Isle of Wight: 'do you remember? Last night when I went to bed I kissed you good-night in my mind because that was the first time you kissed me.' The contrast was almost funny, almost hysterically so, between that lush memory and the previous evening spent at Richard Thompson's house in Seymour Gardens.

'Darlint,' she wrote *en passant*, 'how can you get ptomaine poisoning from a tin of salmon?'

On 20 June she wrote to Australia, again reminding him of the year before, the day on which he had said 'I love you'.

> From then onwards everything has gone wrong with our lives – I don't mean to say it was right before – at least mine wasn't right – but I was quite indifferent to it being either right or wrong and you darlint – you hadn't any of the troubles – or the worries you have now... darlint I am sorry I shouldn't mind if I could feel that some day I should be able to make up to you for all the unhappiness I have caused in your life – but I can't feel that darlint – I keep on saying to myself that "it will – it shall come right" – but there is no conviction behind it – why can't we see into the future?

Then she reminded him of the day, in 1921, when he took her to lunch at the King's Hall: 'do you remember?'

She wrote of a visit to the doctor. 'Are you enceinte?' he asked: 'to which I replied "No, I think not".' In truth she was not sure, such was her ignorance. She had not mentioned a period in May; but if she was pregnant in June it was by Percy, not Freddy. And why should she be, having almost certainly avoided this eventuality for more than six years? She had sex with Freddy on 8 June, but there were no means available in 1922 to know, a mere nine days later, whether *this* had resulted in conception. The constant talk about conception was more like another game, an intimate hold over her lover. As for the doctor: he clearly had a shrewd idea of what had gone on five months earlier, particularly when Edith refused to let him examine her. He diagnosed anaemia, asking pointedly if she had had 'an accident' and lost a lot of blood. 'I said "No" because it wasn't really an accident and I didn't want to tell him everything – he might have wanted to see my husband.' She was advised to drink Burgundy, that blood-like substance, with every meal – 'I hate the stuff' – and given pills to take until her next period. Doubtless these were the 'menstrual regulatives' advertised so coyly in the press, whose efficacy may well have been that of the placebo, inducing sufficient relief to restore the cycle.

'Darlint are you disappointed it is only that? tell me please?'

This was a ridiculous question, really – how could either of them want the complication of a pregnancy at that time? – and its silliness was underscored the following day, when she went to pick up her letters. Freddy had already put her off with a note sent from Dover, saying that he would write from Marseilles. Now she found another note, saying that he would write from Port Said.

At this point, she could have let the whole thing go and lived to be an old woman.

What an utterly absurd thing to say to me "Don't be too disappointed".

You can't possibly know what it feels like to want and want each day – every little hour – or something – something that means 'life' to you and then not to get it…

You force me to conclude that the life you lead away from England is all absorbing that you havn't time nor inclination to remember England or anything England holds…

If I am unjust – I am sorry – but I can't feel anything at present – only just as if I have had a blow on the head and I am stunned – the disappointment – no, more than that – the utter despair is too much to bear – I would sooner go under today than anything.

For the first time, Edith felt herself to be in the position that her husband inhabited every day: the one who is breezily left behind, without whom the other can live quite happily. And, like Percy, she was incapable of responding in kind. It seems never to have occurred to her to stop writing to Freddy, to give the arrogant wretch a jolt, to see how he fared without his glorious older woman. Such was her investment in the relationship – because love is about a person's own capacity to feel, not how much the recipient deserves it – that she literally could not cope with this sudden shutdown: it was not something to be ameliorated by tricks, such as flirting with another man. The very next day she would be doing exactly that, standing on the roof of a car (having been lifted up there by her admirer Mr Dunsford) to see the Prince of Wales lead a procession through London. Yet despite this life, the social round and the demanding job, she had poured everything that she valued in herself into the vessel of this affair.

So she tugged upon him: she exerted her submissive force.

> Ive been thinking & thinking such a lot & feeling so awful about it... I am sorry darlint – but I wrote how I felt & it was awful...
>
> Please forgive me & try to excuse your pal. She did feel so awfully down in the world when she found that or felt that the best pal a girl ever had had forgotten or neglected her.
>
> She'll try hard not to transgress again.

This letter was not put in evidence. Nor was the next, with its rather joyful tales of the garden party in Wanstead that ended at the fried fish shop, and the works party at Eastcote where Edith ran in the races and compèred the cricket. None of this was of use, or interest, to the Old Bailey, for all that it formed the greater part of what Edith wrote.

On 27 June, the day that their love affair had begun, and on which Freddy turned twenty, Edith sent a note to celebrate 'the birthday of the best pal a girl ever had'.

But on 4 July she was again knocked down. She wanted to hit Freddy's mother, who had cut her in the street; she had trouble again at the post office, with a man who refused to give her Freddy's letter from Port Said, saying that the GPO could not be used by anybody who had a London address. And when she finally got the letter: 'I didnt feel very satisfied darlint it didn't seem worth waiting all that time for – 24 days – however I wont talk about it'; which she proceeded to do. 'In one part of it you say you are still going to write to me because it will help, in another part you say – "Perhaps I shant write to you from some ports – because I want to help you" I don't understand...' Nor, it would seem, did Freddy himself. He was palpably torn as to what to do about this love affair, which gave him so much and so little.

Edith Thompson
(Keystone/Stringer/Getty Images)

Freddy Bywaters
(Popperfoto/Getty Images)

231 Shakespeare Crescent in Manor Park, the Graydon family home where Edith grew up, and where Freddy was apprehended on the day after the murder.

Edith and Percy in
September 1922, the
last photograph of
the couple together.
(Trinity Mirror/Mirrorpix/
Alamy Stock Photo)

Edith and Percy
Thompson, with
Freddy Bywaters, in the
garden of the house at
Ilford. The photograph
was taken in July 1921
by Edith's brother
Newenham. (Wikimedia
Commons)

Piccadilly Circus in the 1920s, where Edith Thompson spent her last evening of freedom. (Lionel Green/Getty Images)

Belgrave Road in Ilford, where murder took place among the rows of seemly Edwardian villas. (Topfoto.co.uk)

Freddy leaving Ilford police station after his arrest. (Topical Press Agency/Getty Images)

The two detective-inspectors who headed the investigation: Francis Hall (left) and Frederick Wensley, after the exhumation of Percy Thompson's body at the City of London cemetery. (Topfoto.co.uk)

Freddy at the inquest into Percy Thompson's death, held in October 1922 at Ilford Town Hall. (Topical Press Agency/Getty Images; *opposite* Illustrated London News/Mary Evans Picture Library)

THE ILFORD MURDER TRIAL: PERSONALITIES IN THE CASE.

PHOTOGRAPHS BY BARRATT'S, TOPICAL, G.P.U., AND PHOTOPRESS.

THE SOLICITOR-GENERAL, WHO PROSECUTED FOR THE CROWN: MR. T. W. H. INSKIP, K.C.

COUNSEL FOR MRS. THOMPSON: SIR HENRY CURTIS BENNETT, K.C.

COUNSEL FOR FREDERICK BYWATERS: MR. CECIL WHITELEY, K.C.

TAKEN AT ILFRACOMBE TWO YEARS BEFORE THEIR MARRIAGE: MRS. THOMPSON AND HER LATE HUSBAND.

INCLUDING THE ONLY WOMAN JUROR (SECOND FROM LEFT) WITH A WARDRESS (EXTREME LEFT): THE JURY ON THEIR WAY TO ST. PAUL'S FOR SUNDAY MORNING SERVICE THE DAY BEFORE THE TRIAL ENDED.

THE JUDGE, WHO SENTENCED THE PRISONERS TO DEATH: MR. JUSTICE SHEARMAN.

SENTENCED TO DEATH FOR THE MURDER OF PERCY THOMPSON: FREDERICK BYWATERS; AGED TWENTY.

SENTENCED TO DEATH FOR THE MURDER OF HER HUSBAND: MRS. EDITH JESSIE THOMPSON; NOW AGED TWENTY-EIGHT.

The dramatic trial of Mrs. Edith Thompson and Frederick Bywaters, for the murder of the former's husband, Percy Thompson, ended on December 11, when the prisoners were found guilty and sentenced to death. The victim of the crime, it may be recalled, was stabbed in a street at Ilford on the early morning of October 4. The case, which was heard at the Central Criminal Court (the Old Bailey) before Mr. Justice Shearman and a jury which included one woman, began on December 6 and lasted for five days. The prosecution for the Crown was conducted by the Solicitor-General, Mr. T. W. H. Inskip, K.C., assisted by Mr. Travers Humphreys and Mr. Roland Oliver. Mrs. Thompson was defended by Sir Henry Curtis Bennett, K.C., with whom were Mr. Walter Frampton and Mr. Ivan Snell. On behalf of Frederick Bywaters appeared Mr. Cecil Whiteley, K.C., Mr. Huntley Jenkins, and Mr. Myles Elliott. An extraordinary feature of the case was the amazing series of letters written by Mrs. Thompson to Bywaters. As shown in our other illustrations, the trial aroused unprecedented public interest.

The Old Bailey at the time of the Thompson-Bywaters trial. (Arcaid Ltd/ Corbis/Getty Images)

Edith leaving court during the trial. (Trinity Mirror/Mirrorpix/Alamy Stock Photo)

HM Prison Pentonville, on London's Caledonian Road, where Freddy Bywaters was executed and buried in an unmarked grave. (Hulton Archive/ Getty Images)

The Daily Mirror

24 PAGES

NET SALE MUCH THE LARGEST OF ANY DAILY PICTURE NEWSPAPER

No. 5,963. | Registered at the G.P.O. as a Newspaper. | TUESDAY, DECEMBER 12, 1922 | One Penny.

DEATH SENTENCE ON BOTH ILFORD PRISONERS

Mrs. Thompson on holiday with her husband, Mr. Percy Thompson, victim of the tragedy.

Studio portraits of Mrs. Edith Thompson and (inset) Frederick Bywaters.

Mr. Justice Shearman delivered a remarkable summing-up.

Places in the Old Bailey queue offered for sale.

The prison van entering the Old Bailey.

Bywaters arriving at court during the proceedings.

"Edith Thompson is not guilty—I am no murderer! I am not an assassin!" were the words with which Frederick Bywaters received the verdict of Guilty returned by the jury yesterday against both Mrs. Thompson and Bywaters at the close of their trial at the Old Bailey for the murder of the woman's husband at Ilford. "I am not guilty!

"Oh, God! I am not guilty!" was the cry of Mrs. Thompson, who had to be supported by wardresses. Sentence of death was passed by Mr. Justice Shearman, who in his summing-up made trenchant observations on the references to love and marriage contained in letters which figured in the case.

The front page of *The Daily Mirror* on Tuesday 12 December, 1922.

(Topfoto.co.uk)

John Ellis, who hanged Edith
Thompson. (Trinity Mirror/
Mirrorpix/Alamy Stock Photo)

The crowds gathered outside HM Prison Holloway on the morning
of Edith Thompson's execution. (Popperfoto/Getty Images)

Mr Carlton, wrote Edith, was the only person 'in this world' who was nice to her; and one wonders just what the boss thought about it all, when he was drinking a late morning brandy and soda with the enchanting Mrs Thompson; probably he thought that she was managing her lover just as capably as she did his business.

But in the letter, that other world, it was back to conjuring the past within the calendar of the present, here by reference to a film they had seen together: 'Last Friday last year – we went to see "Romance" – *then* we were pals.'

And, rather desperately, it was back to this: 'Why arent you sending me something… If I don't mind the risk why should you?'

'Will you tell me,' she ended, 'if youd rather I didn't write?' Then the postscript: 'Have you studied "Bichloride of Mercury".'

'Does a laundry steward in a ship,' asked the solicitor general in his closing speech, 'even one interested in chemistry, study bichloride of mercury?'

On 12 July, in a letter not put in evidence, Edith strove for intimacy again, telling Freddy that her period had come – thanks to the doctor's pills, as she believed – but that she had 'felt terribly bad & could not have gone to business had I had to do so… It wasnt the same sort of ill feeling that it was that time before tho.' By that, presumably, she meant that she had not miscarried; as indeed had never been very likely.

Then she began to plead, with the dignity of the abject, singing her lover's refrain – 'only you see me as I really am' – and pulling again on the ties that bound them.

Darlingest Boy – I cant bear to think of you being in England and not seeing me – must we be so very strict and stern – cant you imagine what your only pal – (no, not pal – Im talking to you darlint as the girl that loves you, Im talking to my veriest own lover not as & to a pal) will feel like knowing youre in London… Must you be so cruel darlint? See me once… I cant bear it if you go away without seeing me again – nearly 4 months after September – that makes it January 1923 its too long to wait...

So Freddy had not just said that he would write to her less often, but that he would not see her when he returned to England at the end of September. It is hard to understand, therefore, why she believed that he would see her the following January; and again the fact that she did not leave it, let him go, ensured a very different outcome for that month.

What had changed *him* is impossible to know. Avis Graydon may have said something, if – as is likely – he stayed at Shakespeare Crescent on his last night in England. Naturally it would be nothing direct. She need only have said, for instance, that she knew her parents to be 'worried about Edie'. Again this makes psychological sense, although it is mere speculation. Alternatively one might say that Freddy had become interested in another girl, although that does not fit the immediacy with which he stopped writing. Unless that girl was Avis... Was he, perhaps, trying to persuade himself that he should shift allegiance back to her? Easier said than done, however; for he had not lost his attachment to Edith. It was more that he was trying to do so. And in this attempt he was wise. He may indeed have realized that giving her up was for the best; that they could never be happy together, despite the power of their dreams, in a society that would be ranged so completely and lethally against them. He may have wanted to rid himself of the frustration and sheer oddity of the whole business, the pathetic husband with whom she went about so placidly, even as she wrote about leaving him, asking him for a divorce, poisoning him... It was a year since the addiction first caught Freddy Bywaters in its hot grasp, and over the next few weeks he sought to cure himself. It was a great pity that he did not succeed.

★

'When Bywaters was away from 9 June until 23 September this year,' said Sir Henry Curtis-Bennett to Edith, 'were you getting as many letters from him as previously?'

'No.'

'What did you think from that?'

'I thought he was gradually drifting away from me.'

'Did you still love him very much?'

'Yes.'

On 14 July Edith wrote to reproach Freddy for something that she called silly, which was in fact very sensible. He had written: 'Try a little bit every day not to think about me.' She was overriding him, wearing him down, trying to win the power struggle between them. At the same time she wrote about the age difference – '8 years is such a long time' – but her willingness to display vulnerability was always at the heart of Edith's strength.

He was in Australia when she went for her holiday to Bournemouth with Percy and Avis – for two weeks from Saturday 15th – and Australia always frightened her because of the mysterious girl there; did he ever discuss Edith with *her*? It is possible, although he would not have been ungallant. Edith had worried in the past when Freddy and her brother Bill met up abroad, what they might say to each other; but Bill – who himself eventually got out and moved to Australia – never showed any signs of knowing anything he should not. So she went to Bournemouth, which she described with much of her old spirit although she fairly hated it: 'the Boarding house was terrible – "Ladies are requested not to smoke in the house" – no drink allowed indoors and not too much grub... I think Avis & I managed to liven them up a bit.' The other guests, she wrote, could not believe that she was twenty-eight: 'they said I only seemed a child I felt glad they thought this pour vous – altho I really felt very old & miserable & lonely all the time I was away.'

But she showed off and climbed trees, surging with the sheer animal life that should have been powering her, while instead she languished in a life trapped by men. With Avis she took a boat and sailed around the sacred idyll of the Isle of Wight; when they landed at Ventnor they were told '"you can walk around naked if you like" Thats the place for us we said...' This was the ordinary Edith in full flight, taking Avis with her as it seemed, having girl fun as she loved to do. And yet, in the middle of it all, off she scuttled to send a postcard to Freddy in Sri Lanka, telling him that they must holiday together in Ventnor in 1923: *'please* take me'.

And on 15 August she was back in London, haunting the GPO again, where she found a letter from India and a note from Sri Lanka: 'I wonder if you have written to me since...' Now she pulled the favoured old trick of reminding Freddy just how many other men fancied her, telling the story of the lonely heart at the Waldorf who asked 'Are you Romance?' She described another row with Percy: before going on holiday she had asked for 'Rosie's' private address (also Mr Dunsford's, which was the real issue) '& he made ever such a fuss about it – said I was too familiar & deceitful – because I couldnt say what I wanted to on a post card to him (Mr D) at 168. We had a right royal battle about it & I was told I was impudent & all sorts of things bad & that I must have had a good tutor – that is quite a favourite phrase and is often used.

'Anyway he sulked for 2 days...' At which point Avis came to the rescue. Relations between the sisters were very good on their holiday, which may be another reason to suspect that Avis had said something pertinent to Freddy before he left. Certainly she was feeling more like Edith's equal. Now she informed Percy that he, the wronged husband and amateur spy, had himself 'been seen' in Bishopsgate with a girl. Oh yes, he said, Miss Tucknott, I took her for dinner because I wouldn't be at work for the next two weeks.

This letter did not form part of the evidence; although, in the climate of sanctimony that sheltered Percy, it is highly doubtful that anything would have been made of it.

Then Edith, who had become aware that Freddy had 'already started home' and would be in Aden by the time he received her letter, wrote a passage in which she seemed to feel the forces of destiny, or what she would call fate, moving towards her with the gigantic indifference of the SS *Morea*.

Ever since I've been back in Ilford Ive had most awful nights rest, I havent been able to sleep for more than an hour together & even when I do that I dream – sometimes theyre not very nice dreams. They are nearly always about you   One night I dreamed that you had married Avis… another night I dreamed I had been to a theatre with a man I know – I had told you about him & you came home unexpectedly & when you found me you just threw me over a very deep precipice & I was killed.

And again one thinks: leave it now, Edith.

★

On 18 August she wrote to Freddy a whole letter about the book that they had both been reading, *The Fruitful Vine* by Robert Hichens. She used the heroine, Dolores, as a means to explain herself, in a way that would both flatter and lure.

You ask if it is sufficient reason that a good woman knows she is wanted, that she sins… a good woman who had a husband or a lover who really loved him & whom she really loved – would never sin with another man
      … she makes the supreme sacrifice – (darlint it is the supreme sacrifice to give yourself to someone you dont love).
      I can feel with her & live with her darlint & I did.

This was not part of the trial evidence, although Mr Justice Shearman managed to allude to it in his summing-up, comparing it with Edith's analysis of Hichens' *Bella Donna*. 'No doubt the letter about "The Fruitful Vine" was something similar; they write chiefly about so-called heroes and heroines, probably wicked people, which no doubt accounts for a great many of these tragedies.'
      The next letter, dated 23 August, was also not put in as evidence, although after the tales of bets and books Edith wrote this:

Its rather funny sometimes at 41 [Kensington Gardens]: The
attacks continue so I am told of course I know differently – but I
say nothing & laugh all to myself right deep down inside. They
always happen after 'words' or 'unpleasantness'.

A Phrenologist at Boscome told him he would live to be quite
an old man.

It was the first time since early July that Edith had written anything of
this kind. Five days later, in a short letter that became exhibit 63 and
that was sent to commemorate the 'birthday' of the 27th, she returned
to another theme, that of the suicide pact:

'Fourteen whole months have gone by now, darlint, its so terribly
long. Neither you nor I thought we should have to wait all that long
time did we? although I said I would wait 5 years – and I will darlint –
its only 3 years and ten months now.'

On 29 August she wrote in reply to a letter from Freddy, which by
inference was so ambivalent as to make clear his raging confusion.
'You say you are longing for that letter from me,' followed by 'You
say I shant see you, just to know you are in London will be good.' He
also suggested that he might not even come to England but would
stay in India.

Then, on 7 September, Edith received a short note addressed to
'Miss P Graydon':

'If you wish to remain the friend of F Bywaters, be careful. Do not
attempt to see him or communicate with him, when he is in England.

'Believe this to be a genuine warning from

'A WELLWISHER.'

Here, indeed, was a conundrum. 'I had rather a shock this morning,'
she wrote, in a letter dated 11 September that enclosed the anonymous
note.

Do you know anything about it? I dont suppose you do darlint,
but Im just asking   Im sure if you had reasons for not wanting to
see me, you'd tell me and tell me the reasons – you couldnt resort

to letters of this description. I dont think it will be from anybody
I know – or from any relations of mine, because I am addressed as
"P" you will notice – & no one knows you call me anything but
"Edie". Also darlint I cant help noticing that it is posted in the *West
End on a Wednesday*. Write and tell me what you think about it…

By her last remark, Edith meant that the letter had been posted by
Lilian Bywaters, who went 'up west' once a week. And she was suggesting that Lilian, by some means, had discovered that her son called his
lover 'Peidi' and had written the note herself.

There was another possibility, of course, which was that Freddy had
written it, and sent the note to his mother to post. If so, the deliberate use of the letter 'P' was designed to let Edith know exactly that: to
underline his guilt, to make sure that she could not avoid it.

Yet she did. And the explanation for her apparent astonishing willingness to ignore, to overlook, to forgive her lover for this expression
of crudity, may lie elsewhere.

Around a month later, Edith's boss Herbert Carlton made a statement in which he said: 'The paper of the anonymous letter shown to
me by the Police appears identical with the paper which is known as
"Manifold Paper" which we have in use. I do not recognize the envelope.' Mr Carlton had been shown some of Edith's letters in order to
identify the handwriting; the 'wellwisher' letter was not put in evidence, so there is no particular reason why he would have seen that.
Therefore this reference in his statement to an 'anonymous letter' is
not entirely clear. However: if it *was* the one that Edith received on 7
September, then the inference – that she herself wrote it – is intrigu-
ing; and, bizarre as it sounds, not unconvincing. It is reminiscent of
the remark made by Mr Carlton's son, that she sent telegrams to herself
at the office. It also has a flavour of the 'Miss P. Fisher' episode, in
which Edith gleefully invented for herself an *alter ego*. It was drama;
but drama with a purpose. This note – sent to herself, then to Freddy
– would have been a way to implicate Lilian Bywaters as chief suspect,
to maintain the breach between mother and son that Edith pretended

to lament. It would also, more importantly, have been a means of provoking her lover: his temperament was such that he would defy any warning to leave Edith alone.

This is speculation. The letter may well have been written by Freddy. If she suspected as much and chose to pretend that it had not happened, more fool Edith. The rest of her letter chatted away as usual. Avis had visited and was displaying her superior knowledge of Freddy's movements, informing Edith that he was not staying in India, he was indeed coming to London (more fool Freddy): 'she said "Oh that was a lot of rot he was talking. I expect he has thought better of it."' Mrs Lester was resenting the attempts to evict her. 'Its awfully awkward – I have to rush home on Friday nights & do all my own shopping, carry potatoes etc – because if I ordered them & had them sent she wouldnt open the door when they came… She's done some very petty things this last fortnight…' Edith was trying again to employ Ethel, the maid, who arrived the day after Percy's murder. 'I shant be able to stand this state of things much longer Darlint. I hope I havent bored you with all this – I have just thought perhaps I have… Forgive me if I have, I didnt intend to – I just tried to make you live in my life.'

'Now you are nearing England,' she wrote in a letter dated 12 September –

I keep contrasting this home coming with the previous ones. I have been buoyed up with hope, bubbling with excitement   Just existing with an intense strung up feeling of seeing you and feeling you holding me in your two arms so tightly but this time everything seems different. I don't hear from you much you don't talk to me by letter and help me and I don't even know if I am going to see you.

… if you say "No I won't see you" then it shall be so, I'm quite reconciled to whatever verdict you bring forth and shall say to myself "It is for the best and it must be so."

Darlint you do love me still tho' don't you? and you will go on loving me even if we don't meet. Things are going smoothly with me – I am giving all – and accepting everything and I think am looked up as "The Dutiful Wife" whose spirit is at last bent to the will of her husband.

This was a new line, presenting an image of herself as not fighting with Percy but acquiescing to him, sleeping with him. It was a good trick, for it would have aroused Freddy's jealousy, the emotion that demanded satisfaction and made indifference impossible.

Nevertheless two letters, written at around the same time – 20 September, three days before the *Morea* arrived at Tilbury – begin in the same way: 'I'm fearfully disappointed'. In the first letter, not given in evidence, the disappointment was because no mail had arrived for her from Marseilles. Then at the end came an uplifted coda: she had just received a long letter from the post office, not without some difficulty as the question of her permanent address had again been raised. That particular outlet had had its day – another obstacle was raising itself in front of her – although at that moment Edith could not have cared less. She skimmed the letter briefly (it was 'statement day' at Carlton & Prior, which meant 'tons of work') before writing: 'Darlint darlint pal – Im so happy Ive heard from you… Must it be pals only darlint? If you say "Yes" it shall be.'

But she was not going to accept pals. She was going to drive on until Freddy Bywaters accepted what she knew to be the truth, that he loved her. She was going to throw everything that she had at him.

The next letter, Exhibit 28, was clearly written in response to his from Marseilles. The disappointment was because Freddy was not arriving in London on Friday 22 September, as she had thought. This disrupted her arrangements – she would not go to the hairdresser as planned on Saturday, but would spend the time with him instead – 'do you mind me having a dirty head for a week darlint – its very very dirty.' Extraordinary: most women would have planned their appearance down to the last detail before encountering a man they had not seen for some sixteen weeks, and they would certainly be sure to have their hair clean – but Edith's allure was of a different order – as was her female confidence; although at the same time she could write: 'Why are you so late this time – oh I hate this journey, I hate Australia...'

And Freddy's next journey, she had been told by Avis, would be longer still: to China and Japan. There was absolutely no sense, at this point, of anything changing. She would endure the separation, as she had before, and eventually her darlingest boy would come back to her.

Avis – the woman in the know – had told her something else: that Freddy had missed the ship at Sydney – 'she said "Oh I suppose he was drunk". Darlint, thats a lie isn't it – you promised me once that it would never be "too much"' (the same promise that she had once extracted from Percy). It is, indeed, very unlikely that he had been drunk. The incident was overlooked by the *Morea*, which he must have re-embarked at another Australian port, but it was reminiscent of when he had jumped ship altogether at the start of 1921. That time had possibly been connected with Edith. This time may have been to do with his Australian girl. Both times, really, were to do with his latent wildness.

'Im worrying about it – 231 have made me worry – by putting things into my head.'

She was also worried because Avis knew so damn much of what was going on – how did she, and why did she not give up the fight for Freddy Bywaters? In her way she was as tenacious as Percy. Furthermore she had become so cocky of late, as if this new shore leave had dealt her a new hand to play.

Did Freddy want Avis instead? Or did he, at least, realize that choosing her made more sense? Edith's fear – that her sister would win the game because she was free to do so – had never quite left her; and now, as her lover neared his journey's end, he was again writing that they should be 'pals' when they saw each other in London. 'Darlingest boy – I don't quite understand about "Pals". You say "Can we be Pals only, Peidi, it will make it easier".'

Do you mean for always? because if you do, No, no, a thousand times. We can't be "pals" *only* for always darlint – its impossible physically and mentally.

Last time we had a long talk – I said, "Go away this time and forget all about me, forget you ever knew me, it will be easier – and better for you."

Do you remember – and you refused, as I'm refusing darlint – it must be still "the hope of all" or "the finish of all"…

Please don't let what I have written deter you from any decision darlint – I don't want to do that – truly I'd like to do what you think best.

Nevertheless hope was glimmering inside her, because she was still able to make him jealous. 'No, I dont think the man who mistook me for "Romance" was decent darlint, but I do think he was quite genuine in mistaking me, I dont think it was a ruse on his part.'

That was in reply to a remark about the man who had chanced his luck at the Waldorf. This, however, was nearer the heart of the matter.

'Yes, darlint you are jealous of *him* – but I want you to be – he has the right by law to all that you have the right to by nature and love – yes darlint be jealous, so much that you will do something desperate.'

Then she sent a newspaper cutting – something that she had not done for a while – headlined: 'Chicken Broth Death'. A last throw of the dice.

★

'Never trust the teller, trust the tale,' wrote D. H. Lawrence, and as the story of Thompson and Bywaters reached its last chapters it became clear that it had acquired its own momentum, a logic that existed apart from the volition of its narrator-in-chief, Edith. In cases of murder it is natural to look for motivation – 'motive' – and here, in this classic example of a triangular relationship, it seemed simple enough; except that it was nothing of the kind. The perpetrator himself had no real explanation for what he had done. It was what he wanted to do at that moment, and it was the culmination of what had gone before. It was both irrational and inevitable. If his co-defendant could be loosely

compared with Madame Bovary then he, at the moment of the murderous confrontation, bore a certain resemblance to Julien Sorel in
Stendhal's *Le Rouge et Le Noir*, whose attack upon the woman that he
loved was similarly defiant of analysis: rather it was as if the story itself
had compelled the event.

So the *Morea* sailed into dock at Tilbury, and the lovers – soon to be
lovers once more, as Edith had intended, as had always been going to
happen – moved towards their endgame.

She was still unsure, although for the last time, when he did
not turn up to the meeting on Saturday 23 September that she had
arranged by telegram: 'Can you meet Peidi Broadway 4 pm'. She had
come back from work as usual and cooked lunch for her husband and
father. Then she went out at about 3.00, while the men were working
in the garden, raking leaves that had begun to turn a poignant flaring
red, taking in the very last of the heatless sun. She left them, giving
who knows what explanation, and she did not return until after 8.00.
According to Mrs Lester, Percy 'had words with her over being out
so long'.

The husband was on his guard again, despite the Stepford Wife
guise that Edith had been wearing. He had never bought the story –
which no doubt Edith had casually offered up – that Freddy might
remain in India rather than come home for his leave. Mr Graydon
may, on that penultimate Saturday in Ilford, have mentioned the
young man's imminent return, doing so in a hesitant, *faux*-normal
way that could only arouse suspicion. And Edith's mood would have
been odd, distracted, when she returned. Freddy's ship had arrived late
at Tilbury, but would she have known that? Would she have thought,
instead, that her darlingest boy had stood her up? It seems that she
wandered for hours around the 'Broadway', through the old familiar
area of East Ham and Manor Park, returning to Kensington Gardens
only when the sky had finally closed its curtains. Perhaps she had her
hair done, after all.

The next day was Avis's twenty-sixth birthday, so would have been
spent at Shakespeare Crescent. Again the ghost of Freddy danced

between the sisters. Again Edith's mood was probably somewhat febrile, although she seems always to have put on a show for her parents. On Monday morning she sent another telegram to Tilbury: 'Must catch 5.49 Fenchurch Reply if can manage.' So Percy was laying down the law about train times, making sure that there was no time for dalliance after work.

Nevertheless Freddy was outside Carlton & Prior by around 4.30 on the afternoon of 25 September.

Lily Vellender, in her statement to the police, recalled that Edith suggested she might have a cup of coffee with him in the Fullers tearoom across the road. Lily knew Freddy, from the Isle of Wight holiday; she also knew all about him, but nothing of this would have been mentioned at tea. Meanwhile Edith finished her work, in a state that may be imagined. Then she entered the café in her hat and coat, at which point Lily left. The waitress at Fullers, Edith Brown, gave a statement to this effect, and made identifications from a line of photographs.

Edith caught the 5.49 train as instructed, but so did Freddy.

'I had no intention of doing that,' he wrote –

it just happened thats all – I'm glad now chere – darlint when you suggested the occupied carriage, I didn't want to go in it – did you think that perhaps I did – so that there would have been an opportunity for me, to break the conditions that I had stipulated – darlint I felt quite confident that I would be able to keep my feelings down – I was wrong Peidi…

Peidi you are my magnet – I cannot resist darlint…

Darlint Peidi Mia Idol mine – I love you – always – always Ma Chere…

In the blink of an eye they were back as they had been; except that so much more, in the interim, had been added to the fire. Freddy wrote this letter when he was alone, back in his old bedroom at his mother's house, trying to calm his flesh; at the end he referred to Edith's long anxious letter of a few days earlier, which now belonged to an irrelevant past: 'Last night when I read your questions I didn't know how to answer them – I have now Peidi?'

He must have given her the letter the next day, Tuesday, when they met again.

'Darlint,' she replied the following morning, 'I didnt think you wanted to go into the other carriage – but I suggested it because I felt there would be less temptation there – not only for you but for me too – do you think it is less pleasure to me, for you to kiss me & hold me, than it is for you to do so?... I was strong enough in spirit, until I was tempted in the flesh & the result – a mutual tumble from the pedestal of "Pals only"...

> Please please lover of mine, dont use that word [idol] I dont like
> it – I feel that Im on a pedestal & that I shall always have to strive
> to remain there & I dont ever want to strive to do anything any-
> thing with or for you – thats not being natural...
>
> Darlingest – what would have happened had I refused – when
> you asked me to kiss you? I want to know.

They had met at Fullers on Tuesday 26 September. Another journey from Fenchurch Street, hoping for an empty carriage, bumping against each other and experiencing the peculiar pleasure of being together within a heedless crowd. For the time being they were contented, enthralled with their reunion, but it could not possibly stay that way: frustration would cease to be delirious and become merely unbearable.

Edith's letter, written on Wednesday, would have reached Freddy on Thursday. They met in the same way, at around quarter to six, on both those days. On Friday they met for lunch and then Freddy, having mooched around the City for a couple of hours, went again to Fuller's. At around 4.30 Edith wrote a note telling him to call for her in half an hour, and asked Rose Jacobs to take it to him. It is unlikely that Rose reacted any differently from most women to Freddy Bywaters. And if she found him attractive, as so many did, then that is surely one of the reasons why she resented Edith – for the carelessness (as she thought) with which she kept him waiting, and despatched other women to tell him to wait. Lily went next, at about ten to five. Edith was not worried about Lily, she was not worried about any girl. She held her darlingest boy in her hand once more, and the semi-secret knowledge was flooding her with bliss.

First, however, she finished her work; never once did she slacken at her job on account of Freddy Bywaters.

She sent Lily to him because he had come back to Carlton & Prior ahead of the hour, straining on the bit, in search of her.

'I saw him,' Herbert Carlton told the police, 'on 29th September in the porchway of my premises about 4.45. A few minutes later prisoner Thompson asked if she might leave and she left. I cannot say whether she joined Bywaters.'

They had a little more time that day. Edith went to Shakespeare Crescent as usual in the evening, where she met Percy; but before that the two figures of Thompson and Bywaters, enmeshed within an eroticized haze, moved free and futureless through the streets of the City, as the bells of St Botolph-without-Aldersgate and St Mary Woolnoth tolled six, then seven.

> Darlingest lover of mine, thank you, thank you, oh thank you a thousand times for Friday – it was lovely – its always lovely to go out with you.
>
> And then Saturday – yes I did feel happy – I didn't think a teeny bit about anything in this world, except being with you – and all Saturday evening I was thinking about you – I was just with you in a big arm chair in front of a great big fire feeling all the time how much I had won…

She had won, yes. On Saturday 30 September they had been together again, in the new autumn air, among the rich crisp falling leaves of Wanstead Park.

'Prisoner Thompson was away from business on 30th with my permission,' Herbert Carlton told the police. 'She gave no reason for being absent.' That was the closest that Edith ever came to jumping ship, a half-day off agreed by her boss.

Mrs Lester, in her statement, said:

> she left the house as usual to go to business with Mr Thompson. She returned however about 10.30, she had some shopping with her. She brought this into the house and left immediately afterwards, returning about 1.30 and cooked the dinner. Mr Thompson arrived home about 2pm. After dinner they dressed and went out together and returned home together, it was past midnight.

So Edith spent the morning with her lover and the evening with her husband. Freddy had left home at 8am, according to his mother, and made the long journey from Norwood to the Essex border. If Lilian suspected where he was going, she knew better than to try and stop him. She was simply relieved to have him at home again. For her part, Edith had been surprised when Freddy told her where he was spending his leave: 'You ask me if Im glad or sorry – darlint I dont know how I feel about it – Im glad for you darlint – because you know I always felt responsible for the break, I dont think Im glad for myself tho', I think I'm harbouring just a small petty feeling of resentment against them – I've tried so hard not to...'

But that was written some ten days earlier, as it were in another life. By Saturday 30th all was different; and they were having sex with each other, for the first time in three months; also, as it happened, for the last time.

> Darlint we've said we'll always be Pals haven't we, shall we say we'll always be lovers – even tho' secret ones, or is it (this great big love) a thing we can't control – dare we say that – I think I will dare   Yes I will 'I'll always love you' – if you are dead – if you have left me even if you don't still love me, I always shall you
>
> Your love to me is now, it is something different, it is my life and if things should go badly with us, I shall always have this past

year to look back upon and feel that "Then I lived" I never did before and I never shall again.

In the evening she was out with Percy at the Birnages'.

'My wife and I have visited them [the Thompsons] about six times,' Sidney Birnage told the police,

> sometimes by invitation, sometimes casually. The last time I saw them together was on Saturday evening 30th September. They came with Mr and Mr Graydon and Avis... they came about 5pm. My wife had written to Mrs Thompson a day or two previously asking her to fix a date...
>
> I have heard no quarrels or cross words between Mr and Mrs Thompson. They have appeared most affectionate towards each other and I have described them as such. I have never met Bywaters or heard his name mentioned.

Amid all these anodyne statements Mr Birnage mentioned something that interested the police a little more: Percy had asked him to 'effect an insurance on his life. I did so, the account being for £250 at death.'

On Sunday 1 October Edith and Freddy did not meet. 'He was at home all day,' Mrs Bywaters told the police. Edith and Percy went out in the evening. Mrs Lester stated: 'they both left home together about 7pm, returning home together about 10.30pm and went straight to bed.' Where they went is not known. It was not to the Graydons, the Birnages, or the Chamberses, because these people all gave evidence; it may have been to Percy's mother, or to Edith's friends the Akams. While they were there, Freddy wrote the letter that began: 'Peidi Darlint, Sunday evening...

'Darlint in the park – our Park on Saturday, you were my "little devil" – I was happy then Peidi – were you?'

He referred back to her long letter of 20 September, in which she wrote that she had kept hold of his watch – having had it mended – because reclaiming it would be a reason for him to come and see her.

I cant understand you thinking that the watch would draw me to you – where you yourself wouldnt... The way you have written looks to me as though you think that I think more of the watch than I do of you darlint – Tell me Peidi Mia that I misunderstood your meaning...

What have I found darlint? The darlingest little sweetheart girl in the whole world and "The Only Pal"   Now darlint pal – Im anxious about Avis – I hope you have found out all there is to know of the other night – I want you to tell me. Supposing she did stay with some fellow and she tells you and asks you not to tell anybody – are you going to tell me Peidi?

The meaning of this is obscure (sometimes only Freddy and Edith knew their own meaning). Was he asking if Edith would be prepared to keep a secret for her sister, as a way of asking if Avis would do the same for Edith? Was he showing interest, concern? Was he teasing out a small strand of jealousy, for old times' sake? Given the rest of the letter, which swoons and sickens with passion, it is frankly impossible to think that he was wavering in any meaningful way towards the younger sister.

'Good night now darlingest – dearest little sweetheart and big pal.'

In her reply, produced in fits and starts on Monday 2 October, Edith completely ignored the reference to Avis. Instead she wrote about the happiness of the meetings on Friday and Saturday, about being pals and lovers.

Saturday, it may be inferred, was something different for her: it was the first and only time that she truly understood how sex could be with this man; she gave herself to him, lost her perpetual aware-ness, and either climaxed or came very close. Even now, it is possible to feel, through words written on a breath of self-expression almost one hundred years ago, Edith Thompson's last shuddering sensations of pleasure.

I only know how I felt – no not really how I felt but how I could feel – if time and circumstances were different.

It seems like a great welling up of love – of feeling – of inertia, just as if I am wax in your hands – to do with as you will and I feel that if you do as you wish I shall be happy, its physical purely and I can't really describe it – but you will understand darlint wont you? You said you knew it would be like this one day – if it hadn't would you have been disappointed. Darlingest when you are rough, I go dead – try not to be please.

To read this on Monday, after a day away from her with his nerves alight – this intimate womanly voice, schooling him yet willing to learn – the promise that it held, of what had only just been achieved and was soon to be snatched out of reach again – for the *Morea* sailed again on Thursday... No, not easy.

'I tried so hard to find a way out of tonight darlingest boy but he was suspicious and still is' – Edith had to spend the evening with, of all people, her brother-in-law Richard –

I suppose we must make a study of this deceit for some time longer. I hate it. I hate every lie I have to tell to see you – because lies seem such small mean things to attain such an object as ours... I'd love to be able to say "I'm going to see my lover tonight." If I did he would prevent me – there would be scenes and he would come to 168 and interfere and I couldn't bear that – I could be beaten all over at home and still be defiant – but at 168 it's different. It's my living – you wouldn't let me live on him would you and I shouldn't want to – darlint its funds that are our stumbling block – until we have those we can do nothing. Darlingest find me a job abroad   I'll go tomorrow and not say I was going to a soul and not have one little regret. I said I wouldn't think – that I'd try to forget – circumstances – Pal, help me to forget again – I have succeeded up to now – but its thinking of tonight and tomorrow when I can't see you and feel you holding me

Darlint – do something tomorrow night will you? something to make you forget. I'll be hurt I know, but I want you to hurt me

– I do really – the bargain now, seems so one sided – so unfair –
but how can I alter it?

Then she wrote about the recently-mended watch that she had
given him.

'How I thought you would feel about the watch, I would feel about
something I have.'

Freddy had given her presents also, including some exotic beads (much
admired; she joked of offering to leave them to various people in her will)
and the bronze monkey that sat on her office desk. Of this she wrote:

'He's still well* – he's going to gaze all day long at you in your temporary home – after Wednesday.'

The 'temporary home' referred to a sketch of the *Morea,* which was
being framed in readiness for its collection on 4 October, when Edith
intended to hang it in her office.

'Don't forget what we talked in the Tea Room, I'll still risk and try
if you will – we only have 3¾ years left darlingest.

'Try & help

'PEIDI.'

This was Exhibit 60, the last letter that Edith wrote before the murder.

★

'On the 2nd Oct at 8.30am I answered a telephone call,' Lilian Bywaters
told the police. 'It was a woman's voice and I called my son and he
answered it. My son left the house shortly before 11am.'

So Edith was willing to ring Freddy at the Norwood house, despite
the *froideur* between her and his mother. The rendezvous was for
lunch that day. A simple enough arrangement; until Percy, yet again
on a spying mission, turned up at Carlton & Prior at around 12.30.

---

* At the trial, Mr Justice Shearman would suggest that this phrase referred to
Percy Thompson; the implication being that 'he' would not be 'well' for much
longer.

Charles Higgins, the warehouse boy at the firm, who had previously seen Edith with Freddy in the spring of 1922, told the police: 'Miss Graydon called me into her office which is on the ground floor, she was alone, she was in the act of wrapping up an order form with some writing on it, I could see there were only a few words, I should think about five or six. After she had wrapped it up she placed it in a white envelope, sealed it and said "Take this… to Aldersgate Street Station and give it to the gentleman who is wearing a blue overcoat and a trilby hat."' Higgins recognized Freddy as 'the young man who I had seen with Mrs Thompson. I gave him the letter and ran back to the shop. He did not speak to me or I to him. There were two words I noticed… it was "come" and "Peidi".'

The message was: 'Wait till one he's come PEIDI.'

In another statement Higgins said: 'I delivered two notes to the same man at the same place within five minutes of each other the same day between 12.30 and 12.45. They were both in envelopes, no address being written. The second letter I delivered ten yards from Osman's shop.'

Osman's stood at 165–6 Aldersgate Street, the other side of the alley in which Edith and Freddy must surely have embraced in part-privacy; it was a shop that sold knives.

Edith's second note was slightly panicked, what with Percy's sudden arrival and all. 'Mr Carlton has gone out to lunch now & I must wait until he comes back – Miss P. is not back yet – do you mind waiting there – I am sorry to ask you to wait such a lot but its awkward today – I had a terrible half hour.'

He waited. They had lunch. Later they had tea at Fullers. Then they separated: Edith went to 49 Seymour Gardens, where she hugged her secret knowledge in the respectable chill of Richard Thompson's drawing-room, and Freddy went to 231 Shakespeare Crescent, where he was greeted with pleasure by the Graydons and stayed until around 10.30pm. 'I was on very friendly terms with that family,' he told the Old Bailey. 'I asked Mr Graydon if he would get me some tobacco, and he said that he would.'

That day, as promised, Edith had bought him a new tobacco pouch.

Two days later, Richard Thompson told the police that he had seen his brother 'at my house on Monday evening the 2nd about 9pm. His health and spirits were then quite normal.'

★

On the morning of 3 October, stated Lilian Bywaters, 'the 'phone went and my son answered it. He did not tell me what the message was. He left the house somewhere before 12 o'clock but did not say where he was going.'

In fact he had gone as usual to the City, and took Edith to lunch in Cheapside. Later, once more, they met at Fullers. The waitress Edith Brown told the police: 'I again saw Bywaters in the shop about 4pm. He came in alone and sat there until 5.10pm when he was joined by the female prisoner... Bywaters asked her to have some coffee, and she refused. They left together about 5.15pm.'

To the Old Bailey, in reply to a question about what they had talked about in the couple of minutes spent at the tea room, Freddy said:

'The conversation I had with her was making arrangements for the following day. She asked me if I would be in town the following day as usual.'

They parted at Aldersgate station at around 5.30. Did they touch? Did they kiss? Surely yes. They looked like any young couple, parting with reluctance in a way that was commonplace for lovers; although their looks, their physical glamour, the intensity of their absorption in each other did set them apart: people noticed them. They remembered them.

Edith went down into the underground, on her way to Piccadilly station, where she would meet Percy, together with her aunt Lily and uncle John, for an evening at the Criterion Theatre. Freddy travelled in the opposite direction to the Graydons' house, where he would again spend the evening. The knife was in his inside coat pocket. Later he would say that he always carried a knife.

These evenings in the little parlour at Shakespeare Crescent would seem strange today, when the time would almost certainly be eased by the blessed company of the television. In 1922 evenings were long: this one in particular, perhaps, to Freddy Bywaters, although Mr Graydon testified that there was 'nothing unusual whatever' about his behaviour. They might have played whist, they would have had some supper and a couple of drinks, but mainly they talked. Well-meaning, sometimes slightly effortful, good-natured talk – a bit of chaff, a bit of a joke – a different conversational universe from the highly-charged whisperings with Edith about you, me, us, what we did before and what we must, will, *shall* do after. The men might discuss sport: the Cesarewitch at Newmarket, the recent defeat of the light-heavyweight champion Georges Carpentier, who had once paid a celebrity visit to the sports shop on Aldersgate Street. The women would smile indulgently and 'let them get on with it', then would bring the chat round to something more personal, such as the new pouch that Freddy was now filling with the tobacco supplied by Mr Graydon (a clerk with Imperial Tobacco).

'Both Mrs and Miss Graydon noticed it,' he testified to his counsel at the trial. 'Mrs Graydon said to me, "You have got a new pouch, Freddy. Was it a present?" and I said "Yes". She said, "From a girl, I expect?" and I said "Yes". She said, "I expect the same girl gave you that as gave you the watch?" I said, "Yes, the same girl gave it me," and she said, "I know who it is, but I am not going to say. Never mind, we won't argue about it. She is one of the best." I said, "There is none better."'

So here was acquiescence from Ethel Graydon. It was a head-in-the-sand attitude – foolish, perhaps, but what was the alternative? Ethel was not a weak woman, but nor was she combative like Lilian Bywaters. She took the view that there was nothing to be done, and it is impossible to say whether this was right or wrong. Might she have been able to stop Edith? It is hard to think that anything could, not least because there was no real solution to Edith's situation. Percy would not divorce her, she would not leave him; in a way that defies analysis she was addicted to having it both ways and neither way. As for trying to stop Freddy: that moment had passed.

Avis had given it her best shot, over the past few months; and what she thought now, about the provenance of the tobacco pouch and her mother's gentle affectionate teasing, can only be imagined. She may have been accepting, she may have been angry. It was certainly quite something to hear Mrs Graydon effectively giving her benediction to this 'flirtation' – as everybody still prayed that it was – between her married daughter and the man that her other daughter had hoped to marry.

Later Avis would claim that she had been invited to the Criterion Theatre that evening, and cancelled only on the day itself. In her letter to Andrew Bonar Law she wrote:

> I can assure you Sir that my sister had no idea that her husband was going to be murdered, as it had been arranged a fortnight before that, I should accompany them to the Theatre, & spend the night with her in Kensington Gardens, & she had no idea until she met her husband in the evening that I was not going to be of the party. Her husband telephoned me late in the afternoon & I told him that I had already made arrangements to go out for mother.

She did not, of course, 'go out' for her mother, she stayed in for Freddy Bywaters; it might well have been that she changed her mind about trekking into the West End when she heard that he was spending the evening at Shakespeare Crescent. It is by no means sure, however, that she was ever a member of the theatre party. Freddy's evidence on the subject is also contradictory. In his statement to the police, some of which he later refuted, he said:

'I remember Mrs Graydon's daughter Avis saying that Percy had phoned her up, and I gathered from the observations she made that he was taking his wife to a theatre that night and that there were other members of the family going.'

This was confirmed by Mr Graydon, who told the police:

'A short time after he arrived my daughter Avis came home from business, and whilst we were having tea (Bywaters included) said that she had received a telephone message from Percy informing her that he and his wife were going to the Criterion Theatre that night. I am sure Bywaters heard her saying it.'

The implication is that Freddy only found out at the last minute that Edith was out with her husband – she herself had not told him she would be gallivanting round Piccadilly Circus with the despised cuckold Percy – and that the shock of hearing this, the realization that Edith had lied, was the lethal drop of petrol upon the carefully laid fire. Against this, however, is the evidence that he gave at the trial. Asked about the remark quoted above, which suggested that he had not already known about the theatre visit, he replied: 'I did not say that.'

'Do you agree with me,' said the solicitor general, 'that the meaning of that paragraph is that you gathered it for the first time from conversation?'

'No.'

By the time of the trial Freddy would have realized, or been advised, that he should disengage himself from what he said at the police station. He told the Old Bailey that he had not wanted the police to think that he knew Edith's movements, which was fair enough. But if he *really* hadn't known, that raises two more questions: firstly, had Edith deliberately kept it from him? Secondly, did Avis tell him about it – oh yes, they're out on the town together, didn't you know – in order to make trouble? There is a story, not corroborated, that Freddy and Avis left the Graydon house on the night of the 3rd and went for a drink at the nearby Avenue Hotel. Such an interlude would have given Avis time to say any number of things. These need not have been about the theatre trip in particular, but about the Thompsons' marriage in general: that it was nothing like as unbearable as Edith sometimes made out, that Edith moaned about Percy but was fond enough of him really, that she had been looking forward to tonight even if she said she was dreading it… Avis, after all, had a motive for doing this, and it was sitting right opposite her.

A pub outing would also bring the rogue factor of alcohol into the mix, although Mr Graydon told the police that Freddy had no more than two glasses of ale at the house. But four drinks – say – is enough, when the blood is already up.

Against this theory, that the decision to attack was made on impulse during the evening of the 3rd: he had the knife with him already. Soon the police would take a statement from a director of Osman's, the shop across the alleyway from Carlton & Prior, who in September 1922 had sold a six-shilling hunting knife, the same make as the murder weapon, to a man resembling Freddy Bywaters (with 'the appearance of a young scout master'). This was not clear evidence – the salesman failed to identify the right photograph from a line-up – but then, no more so was Freddy's own statement that he had bought the knife a year earlier, and carried it much of the time because 'it was handy'.

'A knife of that size and character?' asked the solicitor general. The blade, which was double-edged, measured five and a half inches. Despite the sheath it was not an easy thing to carry, even in an inside overcoat pocket. One would be aware of its presence. Its appearance was said to have shocked the jury.

'Yes, handy at sea.'

'Handy at sea, but was it handy at home?'

'Yes.'

Also against this theory is that Edith would, almost beyond a doubt, have told Freddy that she was going to the theatre with Percy. After the trial, in a letter to the home secretary, he said that she had told him at lunchtime that day. Her last letter, written during Monday 2 October, referred to 'tonight and tomorrow when I can't see you and feel you holding me…': in other words, she was going out with Percy on both the 2nd and the 3rd. She did not want to do these things, she wrote, but 'we must make a study of this deceit for some time longer'.

Some time longer? That does not suggest that she was expecting Freddy to kill Percy the very next night. Nor does: 'Darlingest find me a job abroad   I'll go tomorrow and not say I was going to a soul and not have one little regret.'

But then there was this:

'Darlint – do something tomorrow night will you? something to make you forget. I'll be hurt I know, but I want you to hurt me – I do really – the bargain now, seems so one sided – so unfair – but how can I alter it?'

The lines resonated, reverberated: they were beautiful, and they were perceived to be an incitement to evil.

'What had Bywaters to forget?' The solicitor general again.

'That I was going somewhere with my husband.'

'What was he to do to make him forget that?'

'I wanted him to take my sister Avis out.'

'You say "I will be hurt, I know." What did that mean?'

'I should have been hurt by Bywaters being with a lady other than myself.'

Well, that was the truth all right; and what Edith suggested was indeed a way to make the bargain less one-sided. Its masochism was characteristic, as was the kindly cruelty that it inflicted upon Avis. It was, moreover, an unlikely thing to have invented.

Yet Edith's testimony was noted by the Home Office civil servant who made neat, sceptical comments upon her sister's letter to the prime minister, in which Avis wrote that she herself had been expected at the theatre that night. This was 'quite inconsistent with Mrs Thompson's explanation of a passage in her letter of 2nd October. "Do something tomorrow night." She said this meant "Take my sister Avis out"!'

Which was also true. Although Freddy did ask Avis out that night; as she told the Old Bailey.

'As I was letting him out of the door he said to me, "I will be down to take you to the pictures tomorrow evening." That arrangement was made by him just as I was letting him out the front door.'

She watched him walk down the dark crescent, at about 11pm, and probably went to sleep very happy.

★

Edith and Percy Thompson had met up with the Laxtons at 6.45. Her aunt Lily had written to Edith a couple of weeks earlier, suggesting an outing to the Ben Travers farce, *The Dippers*. It was a romp, a hoot, it had an Ivor Novello song in the middle; there is no reason to think but that all four of them had a very jolly time watching it, that they laughed merrily and exchanged glances with each other in the affirming little human way that says, yes, we're all enjoying ourselves, we're all sharing our moment of fun, God bless us all. 'During the whole of the evening we had a most enjoyable time,' John Laxton told the police.

And Edith had always loved being part of the London evening, emerging into streets as the electric gleam took custody of the sky, feeling her elegant silhouette trace itself against the backcloth of the city. She was in love with Freddy Bywaters, but she still wanted that quick hard glance of admiration from other men, even her husband, and no doubt she got it that night. She wore grey crêpe de chine under her musquash coat, and she carried a red cloth bag, large enough to contain her opera glasses, gloves and her husband's gloves. Percy, doing her perfectly proud, was dressed in a three-piece blue suit, which within six hours would be criss-crossed with slashes and cuts, his tie severed close to the knot he had remade in the gents' before leaving work.

After a pre-theatre supper, the couples went in to the show. 'On one occasion during the interval,' stated John Laxton, 'we Percy and I went into the buffett and had one Bass each.' The women probably had a cigarette and a chat: how was work, how was family? They were fond of each other; they saw each other quite often; a part of Edith was very much like this sensible, good-looking, apparently contented aunt. A part of her enjoyed this evening out with Percy.

At 10.45, around the time that Freddy Bywaters was thinking about leaving the Graydons, the Thompsons climbed the staircase up from the pit. Well, that was grand! Wasn't it now? The Criterion foyer, with its walls lined in rich tiles, was the last London interior that Edith saw in her free life, and Percy in his life. Out into the air. No, not too cold! The taxis hovered by Eros as the crowds were disgorged from the theatres, putting on their hats and coats, lighting fags, moving off into the mellow autumn night. The lights of Piccadilly Circus blinked on-off, on-off, the very essence of vitality, of liberty, of the shiny world of the New Aspirant. Neither Edith nor Percy would have looked at them much. They were Londoners, they had seen it all before. This was just one evening out of others, no different from others.

'They appeared a most affectionate couple,' said John Laxton. 'When leaving they appeared in the best of good health and spirits.'

They descended into the underground. The men bought the tickets while Edith and Lily waited in their furs and little hats. Lily described their leave-taking to the police: 'When they came up with the tickets Mrs Thompson said "You go that way" meaning towards Finsbury Park, "we go this way," pointing towards the lift down to the trains for Liverpool Street. I kissed her goodbye and shook hands with Mr Thompson and we parted.'

It was that journey once more into the suburbs, not long, somewhat tedious – change at Holborn, 11.30 from Liverpool Street, the quarter-hour or so walk from Ilford station – but they were used to it; probably they hardly noticed it. They arrived at Ilford just before midnight, crossed the railway bridge and stepped out for the last time into the cloudy grey air. It was mild: Percy was not even wearing a coat. Neither put on their gloves. Edith carried her husband's bowler hat. Ahead of them was the long straight Belgrave Road, with its regularly spaced intersections and its lamps on alternating corners, stretching into a distance whose end was not visible. They crossed York Road and began to walk down Belgrave. They may have talked of the play, although that would have been done on the train: easily, stiltedly, who knows. They may have discussed the maid, Ethel Vernon, who was arriving the next day at Paddington station. Edith said that she was trying to persuade Percy to take her to a dance a fortnight hence. There is no knowing what they talked about.

As it happened, another party of playgoers was on its way home from the station. They were Mr and Mrs Percy Cleveley of Mayfair Avenue, Mrs Jessie Secretan of Courtland Avenue and Miss Dora Pittard of Endsleigh Gardens: three of the near-identical streets that crossed Belgrave Road. From the stories told by these and other people it is clear enough what happened, although some of the timings conflict. This may just have been a matter of inaccurate memories. Anyway, not everything is explained.

Had somebody been able to hover and watch from above, it would have looked like another piece of theatre, open-air this time, as the various actors moved steadily through their roles. They walked, they stopped, they somehow avoided each other: it was a giant pavane, danced in the dark through this seemly grid of streets, with an ending – sprung by a character who emerged from the wings like a phantom – that would have left the audience stunned, almost disbelieving, atavistically thrilled.

The party of four must have walked behind the Thompsons along Belgrave Road, and at some remove. Even so their proximity makes what happened an act of still greater recklessness.

At around 12.10am the foursome separated at Mayfair Avenue, and Mr and Mrs Cleveley went into their home. Jessie Secretan said: 'Miss Pittard and I proceeded along Belgrave Road to the corner of Courtland Avenue.' This was the next street. The women were walking on the right-hand side of the road, given their direction of travel, and stood talking for a couple of minutes on the corner – outside a surgery, that of Dr Noel Maudsley – until about 12.12. Then Mrs Secretan saw a man, lurking inexplicably, on the same side of Belgrave Road as herself.

Dora Pittard told the police that she could not see this individual, as her eyesight was not good enough, but like Mrs Secretan she was unnerved. A man who did not seek to reassure ladies of his harmlessness was unusual in Ilford. The women returned to the Cleveleys' house and, as Miss Pittard stated: 'Mr Cleveley offered to escort us to our homes. We went to Courtland Avenue and saw Mrs Secretan enter her front gate. Then Mr Cleveley and I walked along Belgrave Road towards my home.'

Thus their movement through the streets was delayed by a few minutes. More separation was made between them and the Thompsons; and the events that would at any moment take place.

The unknown man passed Miss Pittard and Mr Cleveley on Belgrave Road. 'He was walking towards us slowly,' she said: 'a short man about 5 feet 5, age about 40 perhaps a little younger, medium build, dressed dark suit soft hat, carrying an overcoat over his arm.'

This man, who (allowing for Miss Pittard's short sight) resembled Frederick Bywaters, and who was behaving so oddly, was not in fact him. Nevertheless he was in the area. He had walked from Shakespeare Crescent to Ilford, a journey that took about half an hour. Mr Graydon told the police that he had stayed later at the house than usual: 'His practice being to leave at about 10.30, to enable him to catch the proper connection of trains to Norwood.' This, in itself, suggests intent.

Assuming that he arrived in Ilford at around 11.30, what he then did is unknown. But he had time to spare, which was dangerous: his thoughts could become less manageable. According to his own evidence he was at the station, then made his way as if towards Kensington Gardens. 'I knew that Mr and Mrs Thompson would be together, and I thought perhaps if I were to see them it would make things a bit better.'

He continued: 'When I got into Belgrave Road I walked for some time, and some distance ahead I saw Mr and Mrs Thompson, their backs turned to me.' Given the number of other people around that night – a surprising number, one might say – it is unlikely that it happened quite that way. Indeed it is well-nigh impossible. Freddy's evidence gave the impression that he had seen the Thompsons almost unexpectedly, as if they had suddenly materialized on a straight road. This was of a piece with his explanation as to why he walked to Ilford: 'It kind of came across me all of a sudden.' Nothing was planned, nothing foreseen. Nevertheless it is certain as can be that he took a different, less obvious route on his way to Kensington Gardens; probably up Cranbrook Road then on to The Drive, which runs essentially parallel to Belgrave Road. Also near-certain is that he did not follow the Thompsons, he was waiting for them.

He admitted this in his second statement to the police. Later he said that the words had been suggested to him: he was not a fool. But the houses on the corners of Belgrave Road have front gardens with small internal pathways, accessible from the pavement, shrouded by trees, within which a person could hide themselves, yet still see who was passing by. Most probable, therefore, is that he walked up The Drive, turned left into Endsleigh Gardens, walked along to the junction with Belgrave Road, and waited in the front garden of the house at the north corner, opposite Miss Pittard's.

The man whom she had thought so suspicious was in fact a harmless accountant named Joseph Row, who had spent the evening in De

Vere Gardens. To judge from his amblings and meanderings he was slightly drunk, although there is no reason to think him wholly unreliable. He had begun walking home at around 12.10am.

> I reached Belgrave Road in about a minute; when I had turned from De Vere and had proceeded along Belgrave Road for a few paces in the direction of Ilford station I heard a voice as though from an excited female. This voice came from the back of me and from across Belgrave Road. I stopped, looked round. I believe I saw the form of a person (I think a woman) under a lamppost on the other side of Belgrave Road. I paused and heard noises as though someone was vomiting, in fact I am nearly certain that someone was vomiting and retching but I could not see that person. I lit a cigarette and thinking that a drunken man was being seen home by his wife, I walked away towards home.

The vomiting and retching was from Percy Thompson; the wife was Edith Thompson.

Mr Row then passed Mr Cleveley, escorting Miss Pittard back to her home in Endsleigh Gardens, which was the street beyond De Vere. As he walked on, he heard a woman's voice behind him. She was saying: 'For God's sake help me. My husband has been taken ill and is lying on the pavement bleeding.'

Out of the darkness, Edith had run into Mr Cleveley and Miss Pittard; she threw herself at Miss Pittard and begged for a doctor to be brought. She said: 'His blood is all over me.' The three of them went back to Courtland Avenue, where they called for Dr Maudsley. Mr Row, who now stayed to watch, described Edith as sobbing and being supported by Miss Pittard. Then she ran back towards her husband. Percy was on the right side of the road; according to information supplied at the trial he was 154 yards from his home.

'Mr Cleveley and I followed,' said Miss Pittard. 'Between Endsleigh Gardens and Kensington Gardens, I saw a man lying on the pavement with his head against the wall.'

This mid-point between the two intersecting streets, with their dim streetlamps on alternate corners, was the darkest part of the road. It was thirty-seven yards from the nearest light.

'I struck a match,' said Mr Cleveley, 'and saw that he was saturated in blood.'

Observing this was a man named John Webber, who lived on the corner of De Vere Gardens. At about 12.30, by his own account, Mr Webber heard a woman screaming in what he described as a piteous voice: 'Don't, oh don't.' He came down from his bedroom to find out what was happening, and saw three people moving away from Courtland Avenue towards 'the scene of the occurrence. The woman in grey was running.' Mr Webber followed them.

> I saw a man propped against the wall; the woman in grey was standing against him. The other two stood a short distance away. I went over and said to the woman in grey, 'What's the matter, has the man fallen down?' She said 'I don't know.' I said 'Can I do anything' and she said 'No don't touch him, a lady and gentleman have gone for the doctor.'

According to his police statement, Mr Cleveley asked Edith how it had happened: ' "Did anyone strike him?" She replied: "Don't ask me, I cannot say; somebody flew (or brushed) passed me and he had fallen down on his head." She seemed anxious for the Doctor to come, so Miss Pittard and I walked towards Courtland Avenue and met Dr Maudsley coming.'

The doctor told the police that he found 'a man lying transversely across the pavement, and leaning against the wall with his head on his chest. His hands were cold and blood was welling out of his mouth. I formed the opinion the man had been dead about ten minutes.'

Edith, he said, 'was in a hysterical condition, markedly so, and standing quite close to the body.' Miss Pittard had similarly described her as 'incoherent and hysterical'; as did Mr Cleveley, who also said that the whole time she was holding a bowler hat in

her hand. To Dr Maudsley she said: 'Why didn't you come sooner
and save him?'

At the scene, the doctor suggested that Percy had died from a
natural haemorrhage. Nevertheless he straightaway informed Ilford
police. The call for an ambulance came into the station at 12.40am.
The doctor may have used the nearest telephone to hand – people by
this time were starting to come out of their houses, to see what was
going on – but still the timeframe is odd. Mr Row heard a woman's
'excited' voice at around 12.15. Mr Webber claimed to have heard
a scream at around 12.30. One assumes that the scream was followed, quite quickly, by the meeting in the street between Edith, Mr
Cleveley and Miss Pittard; and that Mr Webber came downstairs in
time to see Edith running back to Percy from Dr Maudsley's surgery.
The doctor's estimate that Percy had been dead for ten minutes,
and the logging of his call at 12.40, mean that Mr Row's evidence
is probably correct and Mr Webber's timing slightly wrong. Indeed
there were those, including the trial judge, who thought that Mr
Webber's entire evidence was wrong, and that it made no sense for
him alone to have heard a scream. It is unsurprising, perhaps, that
details are disputable. What is certain is that these events tumbled
over each other in the most rapid succession: that all of this was
happening as Freddy Bywaters ran at speed up Belgrave Road, past
Kensington Gardens and into Seymour Gardens, where he dropped
the knife down a drain; that he would have barely been absorbed
into the darkness of Wanstead Park by the time – 12.50 – that the
police ambulance arrived to take Percy Thompson to the mortuary
in Ilford High Road.

His blue suit was found to be a zigzag of cuts. There were four on
his waistcoat, three through his white linen collar, two on the neck
of his shirt and three on his tie, which was severed below the knot.
The suit jacket was sheared: fifteen cuts in all. When the clothes were
stripped from his body, the following injuries were discovered and
later detailed by the police surgeon: four slight cuts on the left of the
torso; two slight cuts on the front of the chin; two slight cuts on the

right of the jaw. These were the superficial wounds. There were also three deep cuts: on the inner side of the right forearm was a slash measuring 3¼ inches long, which had cut the sleeve of the jacket into two pieces. At the back of the neck was a stab wound, two inches deep, 1¼ inches wide, passing upward towards the right ear. On the right side of the throat was another stab, one inch long and about 2½ inches deep. It penetrated the carotid artery and the jugular vein, thus opening the gullet, through which blood flowed into the stomach, later found to contain about a half-pint of blood. 'This,' wrote the surgeon, 'was the wound that proved fatal.'

At around 3am Sergeant Walter Mew, one of the officers who had been at the mortuary when these injuries were revealed, returned to Belgrave Road with a colleague, Sergeant Walter Grimes. It was Grimes who had taken the original message from Dr Maudsley, and directed two constables to what he believed was a case of natural death. Now – remarkably, for the first time – the officers saw the extent of the blood: on the pavement, the road, the high wall that stretched between Endsleigh and Kensington Gardens. The blood trailed north, forming a stop-start pattern along the pavement, pooling every two or three steps. At one point it spread into the middle of the road. It was there that the fatal stab had been given: a six-foot jet of blood sprayed towards the kerb. The place where Percy died, sitting on the pavement with his back to the wall, was stained with blood from the wounds and from vomiting. It was some forty-four feet from the site of the first injury.

In terms of actual minutes, it would not have taken long. Yet it was a prolonged attack: a struggle between the two men, like the one that had taken place around the corner at Kensington Gardens in August 1921. This time the outcome was different, but it easily might not have been. If Mr Row had not been hanging around that night, unwittingly alarming two women who had intended to walk directly to their homes, Dora Pittard would most likely have reached Endsleigh Gardens in time to frighten off Frederick Bywaters before he became a murderer. So contingent was this story, in the end.

A couple of hours before he returned to Belgrave Road, Sergeant Mew had escorted Edith to 41 Kensington Gardens. 'Will he come back?' she asked, to which the officer replied, soothingly and perhaps uncomprehendingly: 'Yes.' Then she said: 'They will blame me for this.'

REX

'Hangman, hangman, upon your face a smile
And tell me that I'm free to ride
Ride for many a mile.'

From 'Gallows Pole', traditional folk song

I

"'And then," whispered Magda Leonides, her eyes suddenly widening, her face stiffening, "just *terror…*"

"Don't you think that would be the way to play Edith Thompson?"'

From *Crooked House* by Agatha Christie

F ROM THAT POINT, the story was written by other people.

This, for instance, was *The Times* on the morning of 5 October. 'A murder which presents several puzzling features occurred in the early hours of yesterday in Ilford. The victim is a shipping clerk named Percy Thompson… He was walking home with his wife between midnight and 1 a.m., when, within a hundred yards or so of his home, he was stabbed several times by someone unknown.' The report was inaccurate in several respects, but it made the following salient point.

'How he received his wounds is a mystery, and much may depend on any statement his wife can make.'

The police, who had taken Edith home with such care after Percy was taken to the mortuary, were back at her house a couple of hours later, their mood somewhat altered. In the interim she was placed, at first, in the care of her sitting tenant.

Mrs Lester had expected the Thompsons home late, as before leaving home on the 3rd Edith had told her that they were going to the theatre. 'The following morning,' she stated, 'about 1.15 the police brought Mrs Thompson home. She appeared hysterical and almost in a state of collapse. She said, "They have taken him away from me, if they would only let me go to him I am sure I could make him better."'

Sergeant Mew and Constable Pearcey took Edith through to the morning-room, where Percy and Freddy had had their altercation some fourteen months earlier. She could, the constable later said, walk unassisted. There she was settled on a sofa. Mrs Lester asked her for the addresses of Mrs Graydon and Richard Thompson, then gave these to the police; Sergeant Mew went straight round to Mr Thompson's house at Seymour Gardens and informed him that his brother had had a fatal seizure. Mrs Lester was told that Percy had suffered a haemorrhage and heart attack. Edith, she said, seemed unable to grasp that he had died.

'As far as you could form an opinion,' Sir Henry Curtis-Bennett asked at the Old Bailey, 'did you come to the conclusion that she did not realize her husband was dead?'

'Yes,' said Mrs Lester, 'she said so.'

'It looked clearly as if she thought that he was still alive?'

'Yes.'

Edith was saturated with blood. It was on her face, and particularly on her hands and clothes. She did not wash or remove her coat, and the furniture must have been similarly stained. She sat, prostrate.

Then Richard Thompson arrived. He had never got along with Edith but now, for a time, he comforted her. He told the police: 'I saw my sister in law was overcome. I said to her "What has happened?" She replied, "Percy has been taken away." I asked the cause. She said, "Percy has had a seizure, coming from the station. He complained of neuritis in his leg and he was rubbing it as he walked along and before I knew what had happened he fell against me with a cry of 'Oh'. That was the last he ever spoke."'

At the police court in Stratford, he gave more details as to the conversation with Edith.

'She said "Percy came over very bad with one of his attacks." I said, "Did he complain of feeling queer on the way down." She said, "He only complained of pains in his leg and when we came to Endsleigh Gardens he fell forward with the expression 'oh' and I noticed blood coming from his mouth"… I said "Did you see anyone else." She said "No".'

At the Old Bailey, questioned by Travers Humphreys for the prosecution, Richard Thompson said a little more; or made as if to do so.

'You understood her to say that the doctor said he had died from haemorrhage?'

'Yes.'

'Did you ask her any other question?'

'Well, it was a most difficult question to ask her, I mean to say – '

'What I want to know is did you ask her any other question?'

'No, I do not think I did.'

Throughout the early hours of Wednesday 4 October, Edith was in the house with Mrs and Miss Lester and Richard Thompson. So she was not alone, but she was without a protector – a husband – when Sergeants Mew and Grimes came to sit with her in the morning-room some time after 3am. They were quite kindly. Nevertheless they had that way of speech favoured by policemen: polite, weighty, circuitous and terrifying.

'Are you in the habit of carrying a knife?' said Grimes. 'Can you account for the cuts in your husband's neck?' said Mew. 'Did you or your husband see or speak to any person in Belgrave Road?' said Grimes. 'May I have a look at your handbag, Mrs Thompson?' said Mew.

The police were in search of a weapon, although the idea that such a thing would have still been in Edith's cloth bag – if it had ever been in there – was somewhat risible. Mew duly reported that he had 'found nothing with which the injuries could have been inflicted'. Nevertheless the contents – the gloves, the opera glasses, the bowler hat that she had been carrying – were marked with blood. Percy's pockets had also been searched for any sharp implement with which he might have hurt himself: another ludicrous premise. They contained a ten-shilling note, nine shillings in silver, a shilling in coppers, a pair of cufflinks and his white metal cigarette case.

Under the yellowish electric light, with the blood stiffening on her crêpe de chine dress and Richard Thompson possibly listening to her every word, Edith again told her story.

'We were just coming home from the theatre and walking along – my husband said "Oh", and fell against me. I said "Bear up", thinking he had one of his attacks. We walked on a little further, and he fell up against the wall and slid to the ground.'

There is no knowing at that point what the officers thought. They formed no particular conclusions. In a special report submitted a couple of months later to the assistant chief commissioner at Scotland Yard, it was stated: 'This was a most difficult case in its initial stages, as there was no clue upon which Police could work.' Mew was not unsympathetic to Edith: among the policemen he was the closest to her in age, and he told the Old Bailey that she had been 'very distressed'. He also repeated her remark, 'Will he come back' – at which the judge intervened in his querulous way. 'Who is *he*?' 'At the time, my lord,' said Mew, 'I thought she referred to her husband... I do not think she realized at the time that he was dead.'

After half an hour or so the officers left Edith to sleep, which she may have feared to do.

★

Meanwhile the other man, the one whose name she was not mentioning, had reached Norwood around the time that Mew and Grimes arrived at Kensington Gardens. It was a long, long journey from Ilford, and in the circumstances must have been made as in a dream, the body streaming with dirty adrenalin yet desperate for oblivion, moving through a London that was familiar, the landscape of the last twenty years, whose shapes now shifted with menace; except that the menace was him, he had become the thing that people feared, that his mother and sisters would have cowered from; like Macbeth he had crossed the small fathomless chasm that is marked by a couple of inches of blade. Later he said that he did not know at the time whether or not Percy was dead. It may have been true, but it was not really an excuse. He walked – ran – through Wanstead Flats, where he had played as a boy, south towards Stratford, where he managed to find a taxi that took him down the Mile End Road to Aldgate. Then he walked the short distance to Fenchurch Street – Fenchurch Street! – where another taxi, miraculously, took him close to home. It was comfort to put the key in the door, although really there was no comfort. There was no way back, although he may still have believed he could get away. The *Morea* sailed the following day: all he had to do was get through the hours, count them off one by one. If he only managed to do it, then Edith too would be safe – if he thought about that.

His mother heard him come in to the house; an alarm bell rang whenever the front door was opened. She got out of bed and called: 'Is that you, Mick?' He replied: 'Yes Mum.' His sister Florence may have heard him too. He had told his mother that he was spending the day at Chatham dockyard in Kent. Lilian was accustomed by now to Freddy staying out, keeping secrets. If she still worried about him as before, and guessed what he was really up to, she had learned to stay silent.

He was up at around 9.00; owing either to fatigue or indifference he had not washed the blood from his dark blue serge coat. Indeed he was wearing all the same clothes as the day before – a blue suit – including his undergarments, in which he had probably slept, although he had changed his collar. 'You were late last night, weren't you,' his mother said. 'I suppose you went to sleep in the train.' He said: 'Yes, I went to Norwood Junction and walked.' He spent the morning at home, with his mother and Florence; later they were visited by his older sister Lilian, who had recently married.

Then, at around midday, he went with his mother into London, where she was doing her usual Wednesday buying for her costumier business. Around twelve hours later, she gave a police statement to this effect. 'He said "Shall I come with you" and I said, "Yes."' They took the bus to Charing Cross, arriving at about 1pm. It was a limbo day, 4 October, strange and hollow and alert. He did not know, still, if these were his last hours of shore leave or his last of freedom. He was a hunted wolf taking refuge in a zoo, among other animals, looking for camouflage in plain sight. Again he went through the streets in a dream, expecting at any moment to be apprehended, but remaining courteous to Lilian; all right there mum, I'll get the lunch mum, thank you son. He visited a chemist, for reasons that may have been connected to the struggle in the early morning. As the day moved on, and London seemed to remain coolly unaware of his guilt, he perhaps grew more hopeful that all would be well. What was known, what could be proved? He had taken Edith out a few times, what of that? People were aware of it – they had not been as discreet as they might have been – but most of those people were on their side: his family, her family. Her letters were in his bedroom and his ship's cabin, but if the link between them were not discovered before he left England, what did it matter? The fact that he did not destroy the letters that day – which he could have done – suggests optimism, or possibly fatalism: it was a gamble, a final *danse macabre* with destiny. He did not know what was happening in Ilford, and he may have shut his mind to it. In fact by 3.00, the time that he parted from Lilian at the corner of Cheapside – the territory that had been his with Edith – the national press was already converging upon Belgrave Road to gaze at the blood that flowed through suburbia, and ponder the sublime mystery of respectability caught with a knife in its jugular. That was what it was by now, that private passion of theirs. Even as Freddy was pacing out his last afternoon beneath the open London skies, hands in the pocket of his bloodstained coat, it was becoming The Ilford Murder.

He had three hours left; that was how long it took the police to find him out.

But not through Edith. She said nothing. It was at 11.00 on the morning of the 4th that officialdom began to close itself around her in earnest, when into the house at Kensington Gardens – the house that she had earned but never really loved, except during the brief span when Freddy Bywaters was her paying guest – came Detective Inspector Francis Hall, bringing with him an authority that his colleagues had only hinted at. He had joined the force thirty years ago; there was nothing he had not seen.

Mrs Thompson, the wife of the murdered man, from whom one could reasonably expect every assistance, used her utmost endeavours to deceive, by deliberately lying to Police as to the identity of the assassin. She is a consummate actress, and it was only after searching enquiry that her secret lover was disclosed.

So ran the special report written for Scotland Yard, when the case was over.

Despite her terror, Edith kept herself pressed hard against the door that would, once opened, lead to chaos. She stuck to her story. Her mother was with her by then, probably also her sister, and that helped the world to right itself a little: it was a tremulously domestic scene, the Graydon women making tea and thinking to themselves God alone knows what. Mrs Graydon's father had been a police constable, and had imbued in her a belief that the law was benevolent. But this big moustachioed cold-eyed detective was something else altogether from the amiable Alfred Liles.

Meanwhile Edith's words had become a 'statement'.

We were coming along Belgrave Road, and just past the corner of Endsleigh-gardens, when I heard him call out 'Oo-er', and he fell up against me. I put my arm out to save him, and found blood which I thought was coming from his mouth. I tried to hold him up, he staggered several yards towards Kensington Gardens, and then fell against the wall and slid down. He did not speak to me. I cannot say if I spoke to him. I felt him and found his clothing wet with blood. He never moved after he fell. We had no quarrel on the way, we were quite happy together... My husband and I were talking about going to a dance.

Under cross-examination at the Old Bailey, she stated that it was DI Hall who told her that Percy had been killed. 'Did you not know that your husband had been assaulted and murdered?' asked the solicitor general.

'The inspector told me, but I did not realize even at that time that he was dead.'

'Inspector Hall had told you that your husband was dead?'

'He had.'

Mrs Lester and Sergeant Mew both testified that Edith did not understand that Percy had died; Edith's replies at the trial were true and not true, like so much of what she said.

Ten years later, after Hall's death, his superior officer at Scotland Yard, Arthur Neil, wrote an account of the case. Hall, he wrote, was not at first wholly suspicious of Edith, but nor was he entirely convinced by her. 'He could understand her natural distress, but her surprise when he told her of the knife wounds was more than he could understand. Some sixth sense told him that the woman was not clever enough to hide her natural cleverness. To put it briefly, in Hall's words, she was "swanking".'

She had not struck Mrs Lester in that way, nor Dora Pittard nor John Webber. They had all believed utterly in Edith's lack of control, her shock, her desperate pleas for Percy to be saved. They were like Dr Maudsley, who described her to the Old Bailey as 'confused, hysterical, and agitated'. Percy Cleveley, however, conveyed a certain reserve in his evidence. 'She seemed to come out of the darkness... I asked her how it had happened, and she said she could not say.' Sir Henry Curtis-Bennett referred to how Edith had run ahead from the doctor's surgery, then said:

'And when you and Miss Pittard got back you found her attending to her husband?'

'Yes – well, I do not know what she was doing, but she was kneeling down with him.' That was how apparently her clothing had become drenched in blood; although there was, of course, another possible explanation.

Mr Cleveley was one of those who was not sure about Edith, who did not care for her and therefore did not care to believe in her, and his tone sought to make that clear. DI Hall was the same kind. Her femininity, her vulnerability, her allure that was no less palpable for being bruised and pallid, induced in him that reaction which did so much harm, in which her attraction was perceived and resented to the point that it worked against her. *I* won't be taken in: one can almost hear Hall priding himself on it.

At one point, while the detective was at the house, Edith turned to her mother and said: 'Oh Mum, I did love him, and he loved me.' It was a remarkable statement, an ineffable composite of rue, grief, realization and half-truth. It did not appear in evidence, although Hall reported it to the authorities; a Home Office memorandum described it as 'playacting'.

According to Arthur Neil's account, Hall had not considered Edith to be a pretty woman.

> She was of a type, which was all that could be said about her. She had rather nicely-shaped eyebrows and eyelids, which had long, thick lashes. This physical asset accentuated the colour of her eyes, which in certain lights or shades added to her charm. Beyond this she was not a woman a man would turn round and look at a second time.
>
> Her personality was a matter of opinion. His sensible way of describing it was that if a dozen men were intimate were her, three might be influenced, but the other nine would remain impartial.

Which in its graceless way acknowledged her appeal, while insisting upon its limitations.

Edith had always been judged; she had always aroused strong opinions. But in the space of eleven hours these had ceased to be the stuff of gossip on the platform of Ilford station, and become a matter that would decide the course of her life. She sat facing DI Hall in her morning-room, she told him that she did not know what had happened, and he was not convinced by her. 'In view of this extraordinary and improbable statement, I asked her to come to Ilford Police Station,' wrote Hall in his report. There he rang his superior officer at Scotland Yard. By chance this was not Arthur Neil, who was on leave, but

Frederick Porter Wensley, a man with the aspect of a music-hall Satan and a member of what became known as the CID's 'Big Four'. Wensley was vastly experienced – a detective since 1895, soon to be a chief constable – and something of a moralist. One criminal said of him that he should have been a parson. He was also shrewd, although his memoirs of the case strayed into the ponderousness of the policeman: he was unable to resist portraying this really very straightforward investigation as a masterpiece of detection.

He met Edith at the police station on Ilford Hill, to which she was taken with her mother in a taxi at around 11.30. For a moment she had thought that she was going to hospital, to be treated for hysteria; then she realized the truth. Mrs Lester would have watched her leave. For a brief period, the sitting tenant was back in sole possession of the house. If Edith thought that she would ever see it again, she was wrong. Shrouded in her musquash coat, which no doubt Mrs Graydon had cleaned of blood, she walked down the little front path, with the tiny lawns to each side that had been trimmed by Percy, she went through the gate and it was over.

Shame, that emotion felt so deeply by the anxious, kindly, respectful class into which she had been born – but never much by Edith – had come at last to claim her. She was shown into the 'matron's room' at the police station, and placed under the care of a woman named Kate Keel. The room had barred windows – looking through clear glass was another thing that was over – and a couch. At this point she may, still, have thought that it would be all right. It is just possible that it would have been, had she been advised sooner by her solicitor Mr Stern. Later he would fight for her with a remarkable tenacity; Stern was one of the very few who believed in her. By 11 October he would be representing her at Stratford Petty Sessions. But at the crucial beginning she had no advice, simply the support of her mother, who as an innocent believer in the law felt that her daughter could not be harmed if she had done nothing wrong. Nothing *really* wrong.

'At this time, I should make it clear, she was not under any restraint.' So wrote Wensley nine years later.

Indeed, there was no reason why she should be. We had no idea that she had anything to do with the murder. She had been asked to go to the police station with a relative because it was convenient to have her at hand while we were looking for something that might give us a line.

Wensley met her for the first time after a preliminary word with DI Hall. 'No real suspicion of Mrs Thompson crossed my mind. There was no doubt that her distress was genuine.'

Then, more ambivalently, he added: 'Even seeing her as I did at this original interview, when she was under great stress of mind, she impressed me as being normally a woman above the average in intelligence.'

Despite the sleeplessness, the fear, the surroundings, the images of violence slashing through the darkness, Edith continued to hold out.

I managed to get her to explain in fair detail what had happened up to the moment just prior to the murder. There we stuck. She was either unable or unwilling to go further... For some hours, while we were straining every nerve to pick up some tangible line of inquiry, the matter remained thus. Whether deliberately or not, we were led to suppose that this crime had been committed by a total stranger... of course, it was not many years since the war, and during that time there had been a few cases of people doing extraordinarily motiveless things.

Wensley's analysis may have been intended to emphasize the mysteriousness of the crime, and thus the acuity with which it was solved. With hindsight it appears to be one of the least subtle murders ever committed, in which a human dynamic of extreme complexity was resolved – or obliterated – by an act of absolute simplicity. Nevertheless it is true that for a few hours, throughout half of Wednesday 4 October, the death of Percy Thompson was potentially classed as a random homicide. And if Edith said nothing, if the *Morea* sailed with Freddy (newly promoted to linen storekeeper) safely aboard, who could have argued otherwise? One of the big questions about Percy's murder was what was supposed to happen afterwards. How were the lovers intending to benefit from such a clueless crime? The authorities answered it with no trouble at all, thus: by the time Freddy returned from his long voyage to China and Japan, the murder would have been filed unsolved. After what was known as a 'decent interval' Edith would take off her widow's hat (supplied by Carlton & Prior, where she had naturally remained) and move with her new husband into a tumbledown nook, where they would live happy ever after; as long as guilt did not consume them as it did Thérèse Raquin and Laurent LeClaire, visions of a blood-drenched Percy keeping them apart as he had done when alive.

So the view of the police, then the court, was that Edith's behaviour on 4 October was essentially an act. They suspected as much, then they became sure of it. 'Whatever her state of mind and body she had control enough over herself not to betray Bywaters,' wrote Wensley, implying comfortably that she was protecting her lover because she had foreknowledge of his guilt, and because she was giving him time to get away. That there were other reasons why she dared not say his name was not countenanced; or acknowledged. Of course she was protecting him. She was also protecting herself. She knew that once Freddy was brought into this new story it might go in any direction, and that none of these led to safety. For the space of those few hours, she held to the belief that she could stall and stonewall until it went away. That did not make her guilty: there are worse crimes than lying, although it is one that the law is always especially unhappy about, as if a person who does not tell the truth to its agents is frankly capable of anything. Such leaps of reasoning would characterize the prosecution of this case. Edith's failure to be honest at the start of the investigation was held against her, like a flaming badge of dishonour, until its conclusion.

'Why did you tell the officer you had not seen anyone in Belgrave Road?' asked her junior counsel Walter Frampton.

'I was very agitated, and I did not want to say anything against Mr Bywaters; I wanted to shield him.'

And then the solicitor general, who read to Edith the statement that she made to DI Hall and said:

'Now, did you intend to tell an untruth about the incident?'

'Yes.'

'Was that to shield Bywaters?'

'It was.'

The solicitor general repeated part of the statement, the sentence in which Edith described Percy saying the word 'oo-er', which sounded more ridiculous, therefore more sinister, with every hearing; although more sinister still was the word 'untruth'.

'Did you intend, when you said that, to tell an untruth?'

'It was an untruth.'

'And you intended it to be an untruth?'

'I did, but I do not mean it was an untruth that he said "oo-er" and fell up against me.'

'It is an untruth in so far as it suggests that this was the first thing that happened?'

'That is so.'

'Was that again to shield Bywaters?'

'It was.'

But if she had said: yes, of course it was: because I didn't want the police to know that we were having an affair, I didn't want the disgrace of it nor the suspicion that would inevitably fall upon me (even though she believed that Freddy had destroyed her letters) – wouldn't you have done the same thing in the circumstances…? The law, however, would not have permitted such a reply, however true it was. Answer the question, Mrs Thompson. Was it or was it not an untruth? Yes. Speak up, the court cannot hear you. Yes.

★

The breakthrough came quickly and easily, like the snapping of a taut necklace and the spilling of its beads; notwithstanding the insistence within the report sent to Scotland Yard that the police work had been so very tricky, so outstanding.

The assistant chief commissioner, quite rightly, was not having any of it. In his reply to the report he wrote: 'The really difficult part, from the Police point of view, was finding out that the man Bywaters existed at all, as none of the relations either could or would give him away.

'I fully realize that all the Officers mentioned worked exceedingly hard for long hours, but I do not feel that this is a case for a <u>high</u> commendation' (although Hall, Mew and two others received bonuses of £2).

The suggestion that 'the relations' – which at this stage meant the Graydons – had not been completely open with the police is surely true. They all knew that Edith was seeing Freddy, although not the full nature of the relationship, and they said nothing about it. So at that stage of the inquiry, about twelve hours after the murder, the police had no actual evidence to suggest that Edith was implicated. Her marriage to Percy was described as happy. She was not in financial need. Nevertheless there was this strange sense of an *impasse*: of Edith, frozen in her emotions and her obduracy, facing the police and repeating the same half-story.

Then Wensley spoke to Richard Thompson.

Oddly enough Ethel Graydon heard some of this conversation, which implies that it happened at 41 Kensington Gardens. There was probably a lot of coming and going at the house, watched by the neighbours with the intensity that would now be given to an on-screen drama. Mrs Graydon may have returned to get some items for Edith, perhaps when Mr Graydon was with his daughter at the police station. Richard Thompson may have gone back to look through his brother's affairs. The shock to Ethel Graydon when she finally heard the name 'Bywaters' spoken aloud, must have been terrible; but that was not the end of it. 'I never could understand how Percy tolerated the situation,' Richard Thompson said to Wensley, with an air both severe and confiding, before going on to say that Bywaters was away at sea and could not have actually committed the crime. Effectively, therefore, he was supplying a motive for Edith herself to have murdered Percy. This was not a theory ever considered by the police, but Richard may not have known the strength required to make at least two of the wounds. It is understandable that he should have felt bitterly towards his sister-in-law – he was surely the one who had to tell his mother that Percy was dead; nevertheless her erstwhile comforter would now become increasingly savage. At a remand hearing on 17 October he gave evidence that the Thompsons had not lived 'on happy terms', which contradicted his earlier statement, but that his brother was 'too honourable' to complain about Edith. Asked if he had ever met Bywaters, he replied: 'I have. I saw him once, and that was quite sufficient for me'; an answer that caused Freddy to laugh out loud. A couple of months later Richard reached his peak of vindictiveness, in the interviews given to *Lloyd's Sunday News*. When these caused a friend of the Graydons to send him two anonymous letters, he wrote to the police on black-lined paper, asking for the help owing to an informant.

'May I appeal to you for some protective measure to be taken in regard to the enclosed… As you will doubtless remember Mrs Graydon was present when I suggested to you Bywaters' name, thereby being of some assistance to you in clearing up the case.'*

In fact he was not the only person who gave valuable intelligence to the police; and it might be said that the other, Rose Jacobs, had far less cause and justification.

On the morning of 4 October Avis Graydon had done a peculiar thing. She went to the premises of Carlton & Prior and spoke to Rose, saying: 'Will you take Miss Graydon's box and "Where is it" book home, and keep it till I ask for it. You'll find it in the desk.' The obvious assumption is that Edith had asked her to do this, some time before the arrival of DI Hall. That does not mean that she told her sister all that had happened the night before, although the inference was clear enough, and after all Avis had been the last person to speak to Freddy

---

* In 1948 Richard Thompson, who remained immovably bitter towards his late sister-in-law, complained to the Lord Chamberlain about a prospective dramatization of F. Tennyson Jesse's *A Pin to See the Peepshow*, which was sympathetic to Edith. The production was refused a licence, but three years later was staged in a theatre club, where the Lord Chamberlain did not have jurisdiction.

before he walked to Ilford; she knew better than anybody his state of mind at that time.

The knowledge that there were, at Edith's place of work, two wildly passionate love letters inside this box – plus a photograph kept within the pages of the book – would have been tormenting her. Unlike Freddy she was acutely aware of their evidential value, and could only pray with all her being that they might be removed before the police went to the firm (the fear that Freddy might not have destroyed her own letters was, presumably, one that she dared not confront. Anyway it was still a question of keeping ahead of the police. As long as they were unaware of the relationship, both he and she were basically safe). Possibly the strongest practical argument against Edith's foreknowledge of her husband's murder is that those two letters – written during Freddy's last leave – were not destroyed beforehand. But this point was never raised, and would not have made any difference.

Edith was not so stupid as to have left the letters in her desk before the murder; yet she was stupid enough now to leave them with Rose Jacobs. Unless it was Avis's decision to do that? Did Avis think that it was a risk to take the letters away herself? The tin box was locked, and perhaps Edith had the key, but both the box and the book could have been thrown into the Thames with nobody any the wiser. Avis had displayed some petty malice the night before; from now on, however, she would be fighting her sister's corner, and it is impossible to imagine that she was up to any mischief. No: the likelihood is that Edith had complete trust in her little friend Rosie, whom she had favoured and used so unheedingly. The girl lived in West Ham, not far from the Graydons, and Edith may have thought that Avis could get the box at a calmer moment. Nevertheless it was a desperately foolish thing to do, when what mattered above all else was that nobody should know anything. Nobody must talk.

Yet this was Rose, in her police statement:

On Wednesday or Thursday 4th or 5th October, when I heard of the Ilford murder, I went to Mrs Thompson's desk and took possession of a small tin box – locked, a book, and inside the book

was a photo of Bywaters and also in the desk was the letter which
I had addressed to Miss Fisher [the one used as fake identification at the post office]. Mr Carlton asked me about it. I told him
what I knew and he gave me the letter which I later burnt, together
with the photograph. I kept the box.

So Herbert Carlton had been brought into this also. He may have
seen Avis that morning and been given the news: an appalling shock;
perhaps not altogether a surprise. A man of his kind knew that women
like Edith generated hot blood, hot thoughts and hot deeds. To the
police he gave no details of this incident with Rose, beyond a suavely
dismissive: 'I had a conversation with her two or three days after the
tragedy.' Nevertheless he must have advised her to get rid of Freddy's
photograph – meanwhile busily putting two and two together – not
that he hadn't realized what was going on, of course he had. But he was
entirely loyal to Edith. And Rose, for her part, appeared to be. She took
the locked box back to her home, as requested by Avis. Her evidence
seems to suggest that Mr Carlton did not know about this; he might
have stopped it, but in the end it would not have signified, not with
Freddy's letters waiting to be found. Soon, probably on the evening of
the 4th, Rose would be handing the box to Detective-Sergeant John
Hancock. It contained the letter beginning 'Darling Peidi Mia', the one
beginning 'Peidi Darlint' and the 'blind' beginning 'Dear Edie', sent
at Christmas 1921 and deliberately kept for its friendly, anodyne tone:
Exhibits 14, 30 and 31.

★

Now that Wensley had the name of Frederick Bywaters, it was just a
matter of time before he had Edith within his grasp. If the letters had
not existed, this would not have been the case. He could have suspected
her as much as he chose, but he would not have been able to charge her.

Back at the station he asked both Edith and her mother when they
had last seen this young Bywaters fellow. He recalled 'some fencing

on this point', whereas Hall had said that Edith 'was quite natural in her replies': making their choice, no doubt, as to which was the most injurious description. Then Ethel Graydon said that Bywaters had spent the previous evening at Shakespeare Crescent, leaving the house at around 11pm, and the relative proximity of Ilford became immediately apparent. Also significant, according to Wensley, was the fact that Edith had never mentioned Bywaters' name until that time: 'why had she from the first so sedulously avoided all reference to this man? Why had she been so reluctant to speak about him, even when directly asked? At last some hint of a motive was apparent.'

Edith was held in custody, in the little matron's room, not a cell but a precursor. All her life she had sought freedom and autonomy. Now she was scarcely able to move: because of fear and because she was no longer allowed to do so. Today she would have known more about her rights. She had not been arrested or charged. Even then, a different class of woman might have challenged the police and their lack of evidence; but the Graydons had a respect for authority that was now paralyzing Edith, however much she had flouted it in the past. Her stubbornness against questioning was born of fear, not defiance. She was petrified, turned to metaphorical stone. All that made her Edith, the zest and light and prancing imagination, had fallen away and left a white figure huddled in fur, clutching a cliff edge, feeling it crumble and fray. As the afternoon moved slowly onwards, and the meagre October light turned deep grey between the window bars, the matron Kate Keel shifted in her seat and perhaps offered tea. Being alone in a room was also over. In her statement Mrs Keel said:

I saw Mrs Thompson rubbing her head just over the right forehead. I think she said to her mother 'Have I a bump there?' Her mother looked and said 'I don't think so dear.' I casually looked and saw nothing other than a slight redness on her forehead, which at the time I thought was caused by her rubbing it. I passed no comment. This is the only remark she passed during her detention with respect to her head, other than that she had a slight headache.

It was something else that the prosecution would call a lie; that she had been pushed against the wall along Belgrave Road at the start of the attack. To her defence counsel at the trial, she would say that both her mother and the matron noticed the bruise.

Outside, unbearably outside, was the great world of London, which she had walked through only yesterday as she chose – a worker, a commuter, an illicit lover, a wife, a niece, a theatregoer – not exactly happily, she had thought, but it turned out that she *had* been happy, if she had only known it: and in that world they were looking for Frederick Bywaters. The squads were out, in their long coats and hats: 'had he eluded us for twenty-four hours,' wrote Wensley, 'he might have got away to sea.' Wensley's description of the CID operation makes it sound like Marlborough at Blenheim, but there was nothing strategic about it; it was merely about numbers of men. There were officers outside Lilian Bywaters' house, at the *Morea* and the P&O offices, at various railway stations, at Kensington Gardens where the maid, Ethel Vernon, was due to turn up at around 5pm, to start her new job for the Thompsons. Bywaters did not deserve to evade the law. He was predator as well as prey. Yet his capture brought so much down with him that one cannot help but wish he had escaped: human nature favours the fugitive. Could he have done it, in fact? It was asking a lot. He would have had to be aware of the direct threat to his liberty, and then achieve two things: firstly, ensure that the letters in his bedroom at Westow Street were destroyed, perhaps by his sister; secondly, either find his way on to the *Morea* and get rid of the five bundles of letters kept in a locked box, or find somebody sufficiently trustworthy to throw the box into the sea. Once the letters were gone, it would be hard to prove anything (although this plan also required Avis not to have put her trust in Rose Jacobs). The forensics of 1922 were rudimentary in the extreme. He could have cleaned his coat sleeves in a public con- venience and probably got away with it. But he did not. He did nothing to save himself. He wandered through the City all afternoon, at 5pm he took the tube at Mark Lane (now defunct, close to Monument) and read in the *Evening News* that Percy Thompson was dead. Then he rode the eleven stops along the District Line to East Ham and the Graydon house, which the police were watching. The old lag who had shared an observation ward with him at Brixton said: 'He was in a trance.' It was true, although at the same time he maintained his physical confidence, his natural arrogance: he remained himself in a way that Edith did not.

He was, in a way, more of a mystery than she. Her complexities are susceptible to disentanglement. Because they manifest themselves so much through her writing, they can be subjected to a kind of literary criticism, which leaves certain things unexplained but nonetheless exists within a comprehensible sphere. Her life was so evidently in the mind, and the mind can be analysed. But he, as a killer – and that *kind* of killer, whose sudden snap into violence is so disproportionate – is instantly rendered opaque. He did something that very few people do. He himself was apparently not that kind of person, although in part he must have been. Yet he had refined sensibilities. His feelings for Edith had an integrity that the rest of his life perhaps did not, but that he knew how to value. He was defiant and courageous: had he been born just five years earlier he would no doubt have been a brave soldier. Had he been killed, his death might have been just as pointless, but it would not have seemed so to his family. As it was, his nephew would later say that the name of Frederick Bywaters could never be mentioned. That was shame, again.

It is unsurprising that Edith's influence was blamed for what he did. It was, at least, an explanation.

So he arrived at 231 Shakespeare Crescent at around 6pm on 4 October. 'I went to visit Mr and Miss Graydon at Manor Park, as there had been an arrangement made on the Tuesday that she should come out with me that night.' If he really intended to take the girl to a cinema, as had been suggested by Edith, the night after killing Edith's husband, then he was either a psychopath or – again – in a trance; and he was not a psychopath. He seems to have been wandering through the hours in a parallel consciousness, in which the reality of what had happened remained at a distance. Perhaps he honestly did not know, until he read the newspaper, that Percy had died. To be more accurate he may not have acknowledged it.

'Was that the first knowledge you had that Mr Thompson was dead?' he was asked by his counsel Cecil Whiteley.

'It was. I could hardly believe it.'

When he walked into the kitchen at Shakespeare Crescent he pointed to the *Evening News* and said: 'Is this true?' William Graydon replied: 'I'm afraid it is all too true.' How much *he* knew at that point can only be guessed; he had seen Edith at the police station, but with the matron in attendance it would have been impossible to say anything to the point. At the trial Travers Humphreys asked him: 'Did you know at that time that Mr Thompson had been killed by somebody?'

'I knew that Mr Thompson was dead,' said Mr Graydon. It was an obfuscation, but he was not pressed on it.

He sat with Freddy and his son Newenham, having cups of tea, explaining that Mrs Graydon was not there to pour as usual because she was sitting with her daughter in a not-quite-cell. The men waited for Avis: in such a situation one is always waiting. She was on her way back from Kensington Gardens, where she had gone to meet the maid Ethel Vernon, who – still all unawares – had travelled to the house from Paddington. She was not alone, however. She was in a car with two police sergeants, who had been outside the house on the lookout for Freddy, and had instead found Avis, who told them about her date that night with their chief suspect. Which was off, she then knew: the whole thing.

At about 6.30pm, according to a statement made by Detective Sergeant Ernest Foster, he arrived at Shakespeare Crescent with Avis and Police Sergeant Williams.

Miss Graydon knocked at the door, which was opened by her brother 'Nooney' Graydon. We entered the house and there saw the prisoner Frederick Bywaters sitting at tea in the kitchen with Mr Graydon, Senior. Upon entering the kitchen, Bywaters immediately rose and walked to the fireplace. Miss Graydon said to him 'Good evening Freddie.' He replied 'Good evening Avis.' I then said to Bywaters, 'Is your name Frederick Bywaters?' He said 'Yes!' I said 'We are Police officers and wish you to accompany us… in connection with the Ilford murder.' He made no reply. He finished his tea and together with Mr Graydon and his son we accompanied him to Ilford police station.

★

Wensley did not like him. The detective got the picture at once, that Freddy was not a man to be dominated by a woman; although that did not mean he intended to exonerate the woman. He also saw the dark spots on Freddy's coat and sent it to be tested by the police surgeon, Percy Drought. The test was hardly sophisticated. A corner of the evening paper was soaked in water and applied to the coat, whereupon it turned red. Eventually eighteen areas of blood-spotting would be found. When Drought reported back, Wensley told Freddy that he would be detained at the station.

'Why?' he said. 'I know nothing about it.'

'As he started to say something more,' Wensley later wrote, 'Hall interposed with a warning that he need say nothing, but if he wished to, it would be better to have it in writing. Bywaters assented.' To the Old Bailey, Freddy testified that he had spoken under a degree of duress. 'I was asked to oblige Superintendent [sic] Wensley.' He also said that the statement was taken in the form of questions and answers, a fact that Wensley glided over somewhat in his own account. 'I objected to a lot of his questions – I resented his questions,' Freddy told the Old Bailey, in part-explanation for the mendacity of some of the answers.

Rather as Edith had done, Freddy offered the police a pack of quite clever evasions and lies. He said that he 'had always been exceedingly good friends with Mrs Thompson,' that he met her regularly, that Percy did not always know about this. He described the row that had led to him leaving 41 Kensington Gardens, in which Percy threw his wife across the room: 'I thought it a very unmanly thing to do… I have known for a very long time past that she has led a very unhappy life

with him. This is also known to members of Mrs Thompson's family.'
He also said that he had written to her twice, addressing her as 'Dear
Edie': he was sufficiently self-possessed to realize that the police would
find the letter couched in those terms.

He denied any meeting with Edith on 3 October. That was stupid,
as it could easily be checked; and indeed Rose Jacobs would soon be
pointing the police in the direction of Fullers tea room. 'I went up West
and remained there until the evening,' he said. 'I then went to Mrs
Graydon's.' At around 11pm – or, he suggested, slightly later – he left
the house, took the tube at East Ham to Victoria and discovered he had
missed the last train to his station of Gipsy Hill. So for three hours he
walked: through Vauxhall, Brixton, Dulwich and on down to Norwood.

'I am never in the habit of carrying a knife,' he said. 'Mrs Thompson
has written to me two or three times... I have destroyed these letters.'

And so on, talking away until 9pm in the CID office at Ilford police
station, while at the house in Westow Street another detective inspector waited for the return of Lilian Bywaters.

What did Freddy think? He knew that Edith was at the station: the
Graydons would have told him. He had shielded her in the statement.
Did he believe, even now, that if she could hold her nerve as he was
doing, all might still be well? There was no proof of anything. The
knife was in a drain (it would be found five days later). No test then
existed to say that the blood on the coat was Percy Thompson's. It
would have been better to have destroyed the letters – far better – but
perhaps the police would not look for them, and anyway they did not
constitute actual evidence; so he might have thought.

He went to sleep in the room known as the library, a few yards from
Edith in the matron's room. By the end of 4 October the link between
the two had become a great deal stronger in the minds of the police.
The following day, the case was effectively over.

It was around 11.20pm when Lilian Bywaters returned from a night
out at a pub in Hammersmith to find Detective Inspector Frank Page
sitting with her daughter Florence. He told her that Percy Thompson
had been murdered, and that her son was helping the police with their

inquiries. Of course she understood the situation immediately. In his statement, DI Page reported that he searched Freddy's bedroom *at his mother's request*: as she herself put it, 'in consequence of what he said I took him to my son's bedroom where I saw him take some letters.' One cannot be certain, but the implication is pretty clear. Mrs Bywaters, who had always feared where her son's association with Edith might lead, who had had her blackest nightmares roundly realized, was going to make sure of one thing: that if Freddy was going down, he was taking the monstrous Mrs Thompson with him. She had tried to stop it all six months earlier. She had learned not to interfere – unless it was indeed she who had sent that anonymous letter in September – but she had known perfectly well what had been going on: the woman rang the house, after all. If she did not know for sure that Edith wrote to Freddy, it would not have been difficult to guess. So she took DI Page upstairs and let him do his worst.

In a writing case inside a suitcase, not locked, the detective found Exhibits 28, 47, 54, 55, 58, 60: the letters received while Freddy was in England. In a coat pocket were what became Exhibits 9 and 10: the notes scribbled hurriedly on Friday 29 September and Monday 1 October.

These letters were evidence of an affair. They referred to the interlude in Wanstead Park, which could hardly be construed otherwise than as a sexual encounter. With Exhibit 55, a short addendum in which Edith told Freddy that she would buy him a tobacco pouch ('je vais pour vous' she wrote, a perfectly understandable phrase that the Old Bailey barristers pretended to find puzzling; their own French being straight from Racine), she had included the cutting headed 'Chicken Broth Death'. This was the only such extract in the collection found at Westow Street. Edith's last letter contained the sentence that would become infamous – 'do something tomorrow night will you?' – but at this stage it floated free of the anchor that the prosecution would later attach to it: the numerous references to poisoning contained within the five bundles of letters stashed on the *Morea*.

So by the morning of 5 October the police had plenty, but still not enough. Later that day they would have the evidence from Rose Jacobs:

proof that Freddy was writing to Edith, and moreover in a tone of the most extreme passion. Rose would also state that the couple had met on 3 October, which Freddy had denied. His lies were almost always demonstrable, yet he told them with a proud, nonchalant conviction that was oddly impressive. It put Wensley's back up – the fact that he had lost two sons within the last five years was not irrelevant here – but others found it admirable: many of them interpreted it as a courtly shield held against Edith Thompson.

In fact they were still both shielding each other – which at this stage was the same thing as protecting themselves – as the stalemate continued, throughout the first half of Thursday the 5th.

The police left Edith alone until about 3.00, in itself a tactic. Then they presented her with their new intelligence: literally, by placing her letters on the desk in the CID office.

So Freddy did not destroy them... she could grasp that this was not all of them, only the most recent – she may have thought that he had got rid of the earlier letters, although this would have meant nothing to her, because she did not know what the prosecution intended to infer from them – to her they were all the same, and the shock of seeing them there would have been very great. Her schoolgirlish slanted handwriting, the medium through which she had transmitted her most precious private self, laid out on a wooden desk in a police station, handled by authority: it was the first chapter of the new story, in which words on a page could shift dimension, and become real objects, black as spiders, scuttling towards a gallows.

Nevertheless she gave a statement not unlike Freddy's. What, in that situation, would a person do? To lie was dangerous – every single untruth would have lit a flame of terror inside her – but to say what had actually happened was to take a leap of faith in the police, and neither Wensley nor Hall looked like the kind in whom she could put her faith. She had dealt with difficult men all her life – the tougher buyers at Carlton & Prior, her brother-in-law, her husband – but these detectives were of a different order, because they had real power over her, and they appeared to find enjoyment in the fact.

Wensley wrote that when Edith gave her first statement she was 'more composed'. She repeated her story about how Percy had been taken ill – including yet again the word 'oo-er' – and said, obviously in answer to a question: 'I cannot remember whether I saw anyone there or not, I know there was no one there when he staggered up against me.'

Then she described the relationship with Freddy.

'I know Freddie Bywaters, I have known him for several years; we were at school together, at least I wasn't but my two brothers were.' She recalled the row that led to him leaving Kensington Gardens, then said: 'We have been in the habit of corresponding with each other. His letters to me and mine to him were couched in affectionate terms' (this, again, was police language). So that was very much in accord with Freddy's description. But Edith too had told one lie that could be instantly uncovered, when she said that she had not kept any of Freddy's letters. Her statement did not mention the last time she had seen him – perhaps the detectives deliberately did not ask the question, as they knew the answer from Rose, and were interested to hear if Edith would admit to the meeting on the 3rd. 'There was not a word about seeing him on the day of the murder,' Wensley later wrote.

Stalemate still, therefore? Suspicion, to the point of knowledge, but no proof? Well: not for much longer.

*

Edith finished making her statement at around 4.30. What she thought would then happen is impossible to say. The circumscription of her life had been instant – rather as if she had been kidnapped – but she probably believed that it would be all right in the end, because how could it not be? How could there not be a way out of this life of grey rooms and stone corridors and no air and men bursting in on her with the aspect of torturers? What had her silly phrase been, when she had conjured notions of suicide with the self-absorbed delight of a romantic poet – 'the end of all', she had written. Was this, in fact, the end of all? No, it hardly seemed possible, there would obviously be somebody who would understand and put it right.

Then the police took her out of the CID room, back to the matron's room, and for the first time since the murder she encountered the figure of Frederick Bywaters.

She screamed: 'Why did he do it? I didn't want him to do it! Oh God, oh God, what can I do!'

The police had pulled a stunt. Almost certainly it was DI Hall's idea – 'dear old Frank Hall', as his friend Arthur Neil described him – and it had worked to a marvel. It was the kind of thing that they did all the time, trying to force a confession, although in their defence it must be said that Edith's confession was not fake. It was the absolute truth. Yet the actual words in which she made it, which clearly suggested no foreknowledge whatsoever of the crime, would become an irrelevance. They were the words of somebody who had lied for twenty-eight hours, so their sense could be safely ignored. What mattered to the authorities was that they had broken her down.

Wensley and Hall were highly sensitive to any possible accusation that they had, in fact, tricked her. In Neil's memoir of Hall's account, Edith had glimpsed Freddy through the window of the library as she was being taken back to her own room by the matron. 'It must have galvanised her heart's action to see him there; she thought that he was miles away, safe and out to sea.' That was nonsense. The *Morea* did indeed sail that day, but Edith's father and brother had accompanied Freddy to the station, and it is almost impossible that none of the Graydons should have told her this. She had seen the letters; she knew that the police were on to him. It was the sight of the man, the reconstituted shock that she had always felt at his physical presence, which caused her to collapse. 'Frank Hall was staggered at this outburst. The awful significance of what her words conveyed, for a few seconds overwhelmed him.'

In other words: Edith had seen Freddy by mere chance, and her reaction was scarcely stronger than that felt by DI Hall. Wensley described the event similarly.

> The CID office at Ilford, in which she had been interviewed, adjoins the main police station, and passage between them is through a yard which she had to pass on her way back to the matron's room. The way back led by the library... through the window she caught a glimpse of him. In an instant her nerve had deserted her.

Today, a defence counsel could have no end of fun with this kind of thing: the 'coincidence' whereby a woman charged with no crime was brought face-to-face with a man who was also not yet charged, and implicated him while in a condition of extreme sudden trauma. Her sudden outburst would probably be ruled inadmissible, although in a sense that too would be wrong, because what she said was true. Nevertheless DI Hall was obliged to admit at the Old Bailey that 'no steps were taken by the police to prevent Mrs Thompson and Bywaters from seeing each other.' It was Freddy's counsel Cecil Whiteley who gave the officer this moment of discomfiture. Sir Henry Curtis-Bennett fudged it, suggesting that Edith had been shocked into speech because she had not known that Freddy was at the station; a statement that Hall could plausibly refute.

In his closing speech, however, Curtis-Bennett returned to the issue of how Edith was broken down by the police, remarking upon the discrepancy between Hall's version of events and that of both defendants:

> by an extraordinary chance, if the story of the prosecution is to be believed, when Mrs Thompson was being taken back to the CID room she happened to pass the very room where Bywaters was standing, and she saw him. That is one story. The other story is that Mrs Thompson was actually taken into the room where Bywaters was, and they were confronted with one another.

In fact Curtis-Bennett had got it the wrong way round. Freddy, in evidence, said that he had been 'taken to Mrs Thompson. I was taken from the library to the CID office.'

Edith said the same thing. 'He was brought into the CID room where I was.'

What actually happened is that, after she signed her statement and made to leave the room, the door to the library was opened and Freddy emerged from it like an apparition. Not chance: orchestration. However quickly he was hustled back into the library, he heard Edith's screams and saw her rag-doll collapse. He would have known then that the game was up, that her nerve was gone. Eventually, out of her prolonged spasms of hysteria, she said 'I must tell the truth.' Hall quickly cautioned her – rules had to be followed – although then, according to her evidence, another outrage was perpetrated upon her. Her junior counsel Walter Frampton asked:

'Was it when you saw him [Bywaters] at the police station that you detailed the full story?'

'No,' she answered.

> I made my second statement, which is the true statement, after Inspector Wensley had said to me, 'It is no use your saying that he did not do it: he has already told us that he has.' The inspector then said to me, 'Go back to the CID room and think about it, and I will come for you in half an hour.'

It is a particular kind of torment, being forced to sit in a room that one had thought to be free of and inhale its peculiarly stagnant air – and then to sit there alone, trying to encompass the great lie about Freddy's confession, which naturally she believed... She was housed in a place dedicated to the pursuit of justice and there seemed, frankly, something almost lawless about her treatment, as if they could have done anything with her and nobody would have been the wiser. Already the quality of cruelty, of sadism, that characterized the treatment of Edith Thompson was becoming apparent; had she really deserved this, because of a few lies and a few letters? What, at this point, was the justification? In his memoir Wensley referred to 'a sinister undercurrent' in some of what she had written – he may very well have thought that, but was it evidence? No matter. It would soon be made clear that she *did* deserve this treatment. The strange pleasure in the prospect of her destruction – a pleasure both puritanical and orgiastic, which had taken sneaking possession of the men at Ilford police station, and was about to spread to the larger part of the nation – would be rationalized. Reasons would be found, *a posteriori*. Whether people believed in them or not, they would be consoled by the narrative of the dire things that she had done, and more than happy to believe that yes, never fear, she deserved all that she got. It was only when she was gone that they began to wonder, about both her and themselves.

Was she beginning to realize this: that they were using her to get Freddy Bywaters, but they wanted her at least as much?

She told DI Hall:

> When we got near Endsleigh Gardens, a man rushed out from the Gardens and knocked me and pushed me away from my husband. I was dazed for a moment. When I recovered I saw my husband scuffling with a man. The man who I know as Freddy Bywaters was running away. He was wearing a blue overcoat and a grey hat. I knew it was him although I did not see his face.

Then she went back to her mother in the matron's room. It was now around 5pm, and growing dark. In four hours' time Mrs Graydon would be required to leave. While the mother and daughter were sitting together, for the last time in technical freedom, Freddy was informed by DI Hall that both he and Edith were to be charged with murder. He replied: 'Why her?'

Then, despite the fact that he – like Edith – had no solicitor present, and according to his own account was given no caution, he agreed to make a second statement. He was, he told the Old Bailey, tricked into doing so. Naturally this remark was ignored, although a statement from DS Foster, one of the officers who had apprehended him at Shakespeare Crescent, tends to confirm it. Foster said:

At 5.30 pm, 5th October, I was directed by DI Hall to accompany him to the library... where Bywaters was detained. Before entering I was delayed a few moments. I then entered the Library and DI Hall was saying to Bywaters "I will take it down in writing and what you say may be given in evidence." He replied "All right". DI Hall then sent me for pen and writing material and when I returned with them DI Hall said to Bywaters: "Remember this is a case of murder."

At the trial, the solicitor general asked Freddy why he had revoked his first statement and changed his story. He said:

'I was told Mrs Thompson would be released if I made that statement.'

This was not the sort of thing that was supposed to happen in British police stations, but the convenient to and fro-ing of DS Foster had most certainly given Hall the opportunity to do it. The solicitor general hastened to remind the court that he was interrogating a liar.

'Was your second statement any more true than your first?'

'Yes.'

'Why did you not put into your statement of 5th October anything about the incident of the attack which you have told us today? Had you forgotten that?'

'No. When I saw Mrs Thompson she was so ill I thought she was going to die, and I thought that the sooner I got it down the sooner she would be released and could go home with her mother.'

Which made sense, whether the solicitor general liked it or not. The second statement was short, but it was a confession, and it was more than enough for the police. It contained sentences that he would later repudiate as having been forced upon him – by no means unlikely, although that did not of itself make the passages untrue; as for example when he stated: 'I waited for Mrs Thompson and her husband.' His account of the actual attack also changed somewhat in court, as suggested by the prosecution above. Again it is possible that this terse, fiery statement of 5 October was the more accurate record. It read:

I pushed her to one side, also pushing him further up the street. I said to him "You have got to separate from your wife." He said "No". I said "You will have to." We struggled. I took my knife from my pocket and we fought and he got the worst of it. Mrs Thompson must have been spellbound for I saw nothing of her during the attack...

The reason I fought with Thompson was because he never acted like a man to his wife. He always seemed several degrees lower than a snake. I loved her and I couldn't go on seeing her leading that life. I did not intend to kill him. I only meant to injure him. I gave him the opportunity of standing up to me as a man but he wouldn't. I have had the knife for some time...

Despite the pressure under which this statement was made, it is assuredly characteristic. It holds the authentic accent of Freddy Bywaters: a murderous Corinthian, an East End Lensky who won the duel (and much good it did him), high on notions of masculinity and honour that were once deemed worth dying for. There is no remorse. Indeed his blood still seems to run alive with contempt and anger for Percy Thompson. What he said that late afternoon is only a partial explanation – there was more to it than this, although nothing that could be said in a police station – but it surely contains something of the truth.

And the first words that he spoke were: 'Mrs Edith Thompson was not aware of my movements on Tuesday night 3rd October.'

Which made no difference; nor was the promise kept that if Freddy implicated himself then Edith would be released. At 8pm, two hours after the second statement was completed, the police charged them both anyway.

A week later they found the letters on the *Morea*.

II

JUDGE: 'If you just wanted to be free, why didn't you divorce him?'

YOUNG WOMAN: 'I couldn't do that!! I couldn't hurt him like that!'

From *Machinal* by Sophie Treadwell

THERE WAS NO evidence against Edith Thompson to speak of, but the machinery of authority clanked obediently nonetheless, and on Friday 6 October she and Frederick Bywaters were taken from Ilford to appear before Stratford Police Court. While there Freddy informed an officer of where he had dropped the knife: 'It should easily be found,' he said, although in fact it took three more days.

The report in *The Times* made it clear the Edith was already a figure of interest, of melodrama, whose suffering had the capacity to mesmerize readers. She was helped into the court by a female attendant and

> on entering the dock covered her face with the deep fur collar of her coat. She was requested to put the collar down, and on doing so disclosed a pale face. She was provided with a chair, and during the hearing sat with her limbs trembling and hands clutching at her garments. Neither of the prisoners was legally represented.

It was also reported that when Edith left the court she 'had practically to be carried out'. The process of her disintegration was continuing at speed; the shame, the sense of displacement, the disbelief that she was not making the journey to Fenchurch Street but was instead being watched by these strangers, among whose blank but avid faces were those of her mother, sister and brother Newenham, striving for dignity and composure as a means of transmitting it to her – yet why was this *happening*? Even from *The Times*, whose account was naturally devoid of sensation, there was the sense that a great deal was known about Edith that was not being said. Almost any reader with a modicum of shrewdness would have thought: 'Well, it's obvious – the woman was behind it all.' And yet there was nothing, really, to support that inference; except implication. DI Hall read out Edith's first statement, the one that denied all knowledge of what had happened to Percy. The Magistrates' Clerk asked the officer:

'Was she very agitated when she made this statement?'

'She appeared to be.'

Mr Graydon was not present at the court, because he was attending the opening of the inquest at Ilford's splendid town hall. There he identified the body as that of his son-in-law. The inquest was adjourned until 19 October and, remarkably, Percy was taken from the mortuary to 231 Shakespeare Crescent, where his body remained until the funeral on Tuesday 10th at the City of London cemetery near Wanstead Park. Edith sent a wreath of lilies and white chrysanthemums. The card on Mr and Mrs Graydon's wreath read 'From your mother and dad'. Percy's mother, Margaret, whose cross of flowers was 'to my boy', was not well enough to attend the ceremony. The Graydons and the Thompsons did not speak.

At the end of the hearing at Stratford, Freddy requested 'legal assistance', and on Monday the 9th he had his first meeting with a solicitor, Mr J. Barrington Matthews, who took his part with the same fervour as Mr Stern would take Edith's. For there were opposing sides within the defence as well; that was beginning to be clear. Then he was taken to Brixton jail – later he would move to Pentonville – and Edith to Holloway. Medical reports were made upon both, to show that they were fit to stand trial. Edith's ran as follows:

She was received on 6-10-1922 since when she has been under
observation in Hospital...

On reception she was somewhat agitated but did not show any
undue depression. Whilst under observation she has been rational in conversation, has conducted herself normally and shown
no signs or indication of insanity. Physically, she is anaemic, but
otherwise is of sound constitution and in fair general health.

Holloway, on Parkhurst Road not far from where Edith was born, was –
before its reconstruction in the early 1970s – an alien structure set upon
the everyday north London streets. To walk past it was to feel a fleeting
clench of the heart, then the quickening of animal relief that one was
among the free. As a symbol of the state, the workings of the law, it was
designed to terrorize and appal. Its façade, so deep in grime as to appear
half-charred, was castellated. Vast pillars stood either side of the entrance
gate, surmounted by dragons; beneath one of their claws, gripped tight
and mockingly untouchable, was a large stone key. Inside the prison, the
sound of female voices – despairing, defiant, jeering, joking – jostled like
coppers in a giant tin against the rattle of iron staircases and the jangle of
keys. There were six wings, all converging upon the centre of the building. The walls were high and deadly smooth, the windows barred and
freckled thickly with soot. Outside, beneath a strip of London sky, was
a paved exercise yard. Within, a woman was not Miss or Mrs, her first
name was lost to her, she was the Prisoner X. Once convicted she wore
clothes of coarse sacking. She was no longer quite a woman.

Eventually Edith would be taken to E wing, which contained the
condemned cell. But at the time of her reception she was in the observation ward of the remand hospital, where a prison officer named Jane
Ackrall later claimed to have had the new arrival in her care. 'In this
time,' wrote Mrs Ackrall, 'she was very quiet and kept to herself. She
received masses of flowers.' Along with much of her correspondence,
the flowers never reached her.

Freddy's report contained a little more information – it referred, for
instance, to his father's suicide attempt – and concluded:

He was quiet and rational in conduct and conversation on reception, and has been so since. He has fully realized his position. He has shewn no evidence of delusions or hallucinations or other indications of insanity. He has been somewhat depressed, but not more so than is usually found in accused persons similarly situated.

Later that month, by which time the case had become a *cause célèbre* of the most flagrant kind, Lilian Bywaters was approached at her house by a man purporting to be a night duty officer at Brixton. He told her that her son was being starved and neglected, and demanded £25 for the prison governor, in return for which Freddy would get a good defence counsel on the cheap. Mrs Bywaters did not hand over this money – she would not have had it anyway – but she did give the man £1, a bottle of port and a letter for her son. Afterwards, in an interview with the governor, she admitted that she should not have been taken in. The fact that a woman of her innate good sense could have succumbed to this impostor was a sign of her state of mind.

In fact Freddy had made no complaints to his mother about his treatment at Brixton, where prisoners on the observation ward were allowed a certain amount of licence. They talked through the night, like schoolboys in a dormitory. The old lag who later described his time in jail with Freddy said that he was 'tight as a clam the first fortnight'. Then he opened up a little.

I liked him at the finish. At first he was very dogmatic and self-opinionated – but he was in a trance. He didn't know what it was all about. He said to me, Do you think I'll get any more than a five-year? I said, get any more than a five-year, you chump... Me and the screw, we told him to prepare for the worst. We said, you ain't got no chance old chap, you're going to get topped.

On 11 October, Edith Thompson and Frederick Bywaters appeared again, on remand, at Stratford Police Court. 'Although the hearing was not expected to begin until 10 o'clock,' ran the report in *The Times*, 'a large number of persons thronged the entrance to the Court soon after 8.'

Curtain up.

> When the two prisoners stepped into the dock Mrs Thompson was at once given a chair. She was wearing a large velour hat, a brown coat with a deep fur collar, beneath which was apparently a black gown. Bywaters was wearing a dark blue suit, and from the breast pocket of his coat protruded a blue handkerchief of a lighter shade. He wore a black tie.

In front of thirteen magistrates, one of them a woman, the case was outlined by the Director of Public Prosecutions, Mr William Lewis. At one point he alluded to the sudden encounter between Edith and Freddy at Ilford police station, in terms suggesting that it had happened by accident: 'As Mr Lewis made this statement, Mrs Thompson showed signs of dissent, and her solicitor went across to her and conversed with her for some seconds.' This was Mr Stern, no doubt telling Edith to calm down, not to worry; because at this point he must have been confident. The publicity already accruing to the case was an occlusion, nothing more, and could be dispersed. The prisoners were remanded until the 17th, and at the end of the hearing Edith was allowed to see her mother for a few minutes.

But if Edith and Mrs Graydon had sought to cheer each other – of course it will be all right, of course it will get sorted out – then by the end of the following day the cliff edge to which they clung had become perilously friable. On Thursday 12 October Detective Inspector Scholes, of the Port of London police, made a search of Freddy Bywaters' cabin on the *Morea* at Tilbury. There he found the locked box that contained the rest of Edith's correspondence. As requested by DI Hall, Freddy handed over the key; and all changed.

As Hall went through the letters at the police station in Limehouse, the case against Edith – hitherto as frustrating and elusive as a phantom – began to fill out, to take on colour in the most glorious, satisfying and lurid manner. Good God, the things that the woman had written. The sex stuff – well, they had had a pretty fair idea about that, they had known what sort of a creature she was, man-mad, getting up to all sorts with the lodger while the poor bloody husband paid the bills, well no he didn't pay them all, and that was bloody odd come to think of it – what sort of woman pranced round the City, lunching out and putting herself about, instead of having kids and behaving herself… *This* sort. My word, my goodness, the things that she had written. They had been right about her, she was in it up to her neck, her poor old neck… Oh, it was gold. It was treasure.

21 November 1921: Yesterday I met a woman who had lost 3 husbands… and some people I know cant lose one.

December: I had the wrong Porridge today, but I dont suppose it will matter, I dont seem to care much either way. You'll probably say I'm careless and I admit I am, but I don't care – do you?

3 January 1922: Darlint, I've surrendered to him unconditionally now – do you understand me? I think it is the best way to disarm any suspicion…

10 February: About 2 am. he woke me up and asked for water as he felt ill… I told Avis about the incident only I told her as if it frightened and worried me as I thought perhaps it might be useful at some future time that I had told somebody.

22 February: Darlingest boy, the thing I am going to do for both of us will it ever – at all, make any difference between us, darlint, do you understand what I mean.

1 April:
   … he puts great stress on the fact of the tea tasting bitter "as if something had been put in it" he says.

24 April: I used the "light bulb" three times but the third time – he found a piece – so I've given up – until you come home.

1 May: I don't think we're failures in other things and we mustn't be in this. We mustn't give up as we said. No, we shall have to wait if we fail again…

You said it was enough for an elephant. Perhaps it was. But you don't allow for the taste making only a small quantity to be taken…

I was buoyed up with the hope of the "light bulb" and I used a lot…

I suppose as you say he's not normal, I know I shall never get him to take a sufficient quantity of anything bitter… You tell me not to leave finger marks on the box – do you know I did not think of the box but I did think of the glass or cup or whatever was used. I wish I wish oh I wish I could do something.

18 May: It must be remembered that digitalis is a cumulative poison…

I'd like you to read "Bella Donna" first you may learn something from it to help us.'

13 June: … he was on the ottoman at the foot of the bed and said he was dying and wanted to – he had another heart attack – thro me.

Darlint I had to laugh because *I knew* it couldn't be a heart attack.

14 June: …how can you get ptomaine poisoning from a tin of salmon?

4 July: Why arent you sending me something… If I don't mind the risk why should you?…

Have you studied "Bichloride of Mercury".

23 August: The attacks continue so I am told of course I know differently – but I say nothing & laugh all to myself right deep down inside….

And then there were the letters already in their possession, some of whose passages now seemed to have caught fire on the thin pages, like the illuminated words of a medieval manuscript.

20 September: Yes, darlint you are jealous of *him* – but I want you to be – he has the right by law to all that you have the right to by nature and love – yes darlint be jealous, so much that you will do something desperate.

2 October: Darlint – do something tomorrow night will you?
Don't forget what we talked in the Tea Room, I'll still risk and try if you will…
Try & help
PEIDI.

*

The letters found on the *Morea*, wrote Wensley in his memoir, demonstrated unequivocally that 'the project of murdering the husband had long been in the mind of the pair – indeed a literal interpretation of some passages suggested that previous abortive attempts had been made.' He went on to say that 'these grim hints were buried in a mass of vivacious personal gossip and endearments': what Mr Justice Shearman at the trial called 'gush'. In other words, although the letters contained a great deal more than the quotes selected above – which might have been put forward as an argument in Edith's defence – to Wensley there was something additionally wicked about that fact. The woman could not even concentrate upon the matter of murder. It was as if feeding a 50-watt light bulb to Percy Thompson was of similar note to buying a pair of lace-up shoes and waving from an open car to the Prince of Wales.

The alternative interpretation, meanwhile, was put some forty years later. 'If Edith Thompson was really plotting to kill her husband, she seems to have been incapable of keeping her mind on this not unimportant design for more than a few lines together.'* The sensible interpretation, one might say. But not, in 1922, the prevalent view.

The letters, the letters: they were the heart of the case, these little piles of paper that would be copied, made into evidence, read aloud like audition speeches by incompetent actors, wrenched from their priest's hole of intimacy and pushed into the unforgiving daylight. They were read by the jury in groups of three, leaning into each other like churchgoers sharing a hymnbook (except there was nothing holy about *this* content). They were scattered across the solid wood of the Old Bailey like pale leaves, their soft feathery crackle interspersing the sound of voices. 'What effect would letters of this sort have upon the young man whose affections she was engaging?' asked the solicitor general in his opening speech. 'The crime is one where one hand struck the blow, and we want to show by the letters that her mind conceived and incited it.'

*

On 19 October, the inquest was reopened at Ilford Town Hall before the coroner, Dr Alexander Ambrose. Copies of all the letters were handed to Dr Ambrose for his perusal, and the inquest was again adjourned for another four days. Freddy was there, having asked permission to attend; for him it alleviated the boredom. Edith did not go.

On 23 October both were present when the coroner called for the letters to be read, whereupon Edith's solicitor Mr Stern immediately objected to their admissibility. His client, he said, was charged with the wilful murder of her husband, but until a *prima facie* case had been made out, the letters could not be put in.

This was the argument that mattered: the one that could have saved her. Later it would be made by Sir Henry Curtis-Bennett. Before the trial opened, he said to Mr Justice Shearman:

---

* From *Sir Travers Humphreys: A Biography* by Douglas G. Browne (George G. Harrap 1960).

Now, the letters that I am objecting to contain certain passages, which make it appear that Mrs Thompson was writing to Bywaters suggesting to him that he should send her certain material for the purpose of giving it to her husband to cause his death, and also suggestions that she was herself administering certain things to her husband. I submit that the admissibility of letters such as those cannot be acceded to until the prosecution have, first of all, showed that Mrs Thompson took some active part in the murder, if it was murder, of her husband.

The argument was perfectly cogent (although how it would have spoiled everybody's fun, had it succeeded) and Curtis-Bennett believed in it. Mr Stern believed in Edith, which was not quite the same thing. Both men, however, understood that the letters existed in a different sphere from the murder. This was true in a practical sense, because the timeframe and frames of reference were utterly unlike; and – still more importantly – true in a metaphysical sense, because imagination and reality are still more unlike. The men also grasped the crucial point, that the letters had been seized upon as proof of something that had somehow already been decided: that Edith Thompson was guilty. The decision – irrational, irresistible – was apparent in her treatment at Ilford police station, it even permeated the sober reportage of *The Times*. Where her guilt actually lay had not been specified, because it couldn't be. She had lied, committed adultery, lied… whatever. It all added up, sort of. But the discovery of the letters meant that it *did* all add up. It might not have done, if there had not been the presumption of guilt in the first place.

So Mr Stern made his objection. The letters were obviously written some time before the crime, he said, and possibly they did express feelings against her husband, but the idea that this proved her to be an active participant in the murder was 'stretching the law altogether'. Indeed: another vital point. Furthermore, the evidence given by those who saw her that night – Miss Pittard, Mr Webster, Dr Maudsley *et al* – was rather in her favour than otherwise. Bywaters had shouldered the blame for the crime, therefore what point was there in putting the letters forward as evidence?

For a moment the thing wavered in the balance: the coroner was not going to be a pushover. 'I have gone through these letters,' he said, 'and I confess that there is grave suspicion in my mind.' Mr Stern was not having it. On this occasion he was the stronger. He replied firmly that his client had not yet been allowed to give her explanation for the letters; and at that point Dr Ambrose acquiesced. He was careful to say that the police had done right in arresting the woman, but that there was no definite evidence 'beyond the letters' to show that she had instigated the crime. There was something worthy of Lewis Carroll about this argument: that the letters would prove something that they were not allowed to prove until it had otherwise been proved. But then the whole case against Edith Thompson was of that nature, so elusive that neither side could catch it and trap it, although in the end the prosecution was deemed to have done so, simply because more people were *on* their side.

After a short adjournment, the inquest jury brought in a verdict of wilful murder against Frederick Bywaters.

That day, when the jury did not even mention her name and Mr Stern fenced so skilfully with the coroner, Edith may have thought that she was about to awaken from the nightmare of sitting in taxis next to the rough coats of police officers and returning to smooth prison walls. Beyond a doubt, Freddy was going to stand trial at the Old Bailey – he had been named by the jury, he was in the deepest danger – but how much would that have mattered to her, at that moment, when it seemed that she might soon be free? Whatever she still felt about him, the man sitting so close to her in the police court, hope and fear can suffocate all other emotions. And that was how she was living, hope and fear, hope and fear, quick breaths of each.

Back at Stratford Police Court the very next day, 24 October, the presiding magistrate Mr Eliot Howard ruled that the letters were admissible as evidence.

Mr Howard did not believe in Edith; he was in the opposite camp. He later wrote to the home secretary asking for mercy for Freddy Bywaters, citing the woman's influence over him, describing her as 'clever and unscrupulous'. How sure these people were! Their judgements were so preordained: there was really nothing to be done about it. It would still be that way today, except that it would not be a matter of life and death.

No question, said Mr Howard, there was a *prima facie* case against Edith Thompson. 'She must have known perfectly well who did it, and again and again in the course of that night's detention she told different stories.' This last is quite untrue – she did not repeatedly change her story – and the knowledge of who had committed the crime surely did not constitute a *prima facie* case. Nevertheless it facilitated what Mr Howard appeared to want, which was the admission of the letters into evidence. On 24 October, extracts were read for the first time in public, by DS Hancock, who doubtless would have wished the task upon anybody else.

Not long after the readings began Edith was removed from the court in a condition of collapse. Then she was brought back. When she again began to swoon Stern asked if she might be removed once more, but no, the law required her to stay. The law would require more and more from her that she could not bear, that she would in some way have to bear; she would be propped up, pushed, pulled, supported; smelling salts would be waved in front of her nose and a bowl of water supplied for her hands; the police matron would fan her face; eventually she would be stuffed and stunned with drugs – anything to get her through, to ensure that the procedures were observed, that the cool workings of authority were not interrupted as she shrank within her outer covering of fur.

By the end of the hearing, at which Rose Jacobs gave her Judas evidence and Herbert Carlton spoke briefly about his former favourite employee, it was reported that 'Bywaters appeared distressed, and held his head as if dazed. Mrs Thompson sat as though in a trance.' The horror of what had happened – was just beginning to happen

– was a highly wrought kind of torture, a violation that caused the body both to flood red and to blanch; the public reading of Edith's letters was comparable with the criminal conversation hearings of the eighteenth century, in which graphic evidence of adultery was given in open court and related hysterically in the press; it could also be likened to some of the worst kind of contemporary hacking crimes. But it was more serious and dreadful than either of those. However great the shame, as DS Hancock's London voice squirmed its way around phrases such as 'I have surrendered to him uncon-ditionally now,' it was not as great as the fear when he read, for instance, 'I was buoyed up with the hope of the light bulb.' These words were far more than sharp little tools inflicting humiliation and disgrace. They had acquired a dense significance: they were texts to be interpreted: the way in which their new readers did this would decide their writer's fate.

When the director of Public Prosecutions requested another adjournment, even Eliot Howard protested. 'You have seen,' he said, 'the effect upon this poor woman to have this hanging over her week after week.' The court reconvened the next day to hear evidence from Mrs Bywaters, Mrs Lester and Mr Graydon. The sight of her quiet little father caused Edith not to collapse, simply to cry. Then the DPP asked yet again for more time to prepare the case, and now the request was granted. When the proceedings resumed again on Wednesday 1 November, it was a month exactly since Edith had awoken to her new life, which would now be the rest of her life, sixty-nine more days of it. The following evening at around 9pm, beneath a moon so bright that the gravediggers did not need their lanterns, Percy's body was exhumed.

★

This was why the DPP, William Lewis, wanted more time. He was hoping to prove that Edith's reiterations about poison and glass were not fantastical (still a possibility, as he grudgingly acknowledged) but based upon fact. On 30 October he had written to Sir Ernley Blackwell, *Measure for Measure*'s Angelo transported to the Home Office. In his letter Mr Lewis referred to the correspondence discovered on the *Morea*:

> a good deal of time was occupied in endeavouring to fix their approximate date from internal evidence and from the dates of certain newspaper cuttings which in some cases accompanied the letters. The burial of the body took place some time before the letters were discovered.
>
> On the resumption of the inquest on the 24th instant the Coroner refused to admit any of the letters in evidence, on what ground is not clearly known, but on the next day the 25th instant, the Justices before whom the prosecution was proceeding admitted all the letters in evidence.
>
> In addition to indicating that the writer, Mrs Thompson who is some years older than Bywaters, was passionately in love with him (and from certain of Bywaters' letters to her which have also been discovered it is clear that he was as much in love with her) there are numerous indications that she loathed her husband, regarded him as an obstacle to her feelings towards Bywaters and communicated to Bywaters various attempts on her part to take her husband's life.

The DPP then cited several of the letters in which such references occurred.

> I had yesterday a long interview with Dr Spilsbury [the Home Office pathologist], I pointed out to him that the references to glass disappeared from the correspondence after the letter of May 1st and pointed out also the above quoted passages from the letters. He expressed the definite opinion that, as there is no evidence of any symptoms pointing to the administration of digitalin or bichloride of mercury [as per references in Edith's

letters], no trace of either of such poisons would now be found in the body, but there was a possibility, in view of what would appear from the letters to be a long continued effort to administer some poison to her husband, continuing up to a period shortly before his death, of discovering on analysis of the organs of the body some poison of a character of which the letters give no indication. He further said that there was a chance, although a remote chance, of finding in the appendix some particle of glass which had lodged there... If a fairly large fragment of glass with a sharp point or edge had been swallowed and this might have occurred unconsciously it is possible that some scar, on the gullet or elsewhere, caused by its passage down might be found.

With the exception of one day, the date of which cannot be fixed, the evidence is that Thompson was quite regular in his attendance to his duties as a clerk in the City and that even on that day he went out of his house for a walk. There are not any symptoms pointing to the administration of an irritant or an irritant poison, although from time to time Mr Thompson, whose heart was not in a satisfactory state, had fainting attacks.

On the one hand it may be that this woman was pretending to her lover that she was resorting to all kinds of expedients for removing her husband so as to thereby enable him, Bywaters, to indulge his passion without interruption and thus to attempt to stimulate, as it were, Bywaters' affection towards herself without any real attempt having been made upon her husband's life. On the other hand the letters are specific in places and somewhat mysterious in their allusions in others and the newspaper cuttings, which accompanied some of them, refer to poisoning cases.

In these circumstances it would appear to be right that an opportunity should be given for a complete analytical examination of the organs of the body which no doubt would have been done if these letters had been discovered before the burial took place...

The Home Office immediately granted permission for the exhumation.

A senior official analyst, John Webster, had already made a report dated 11 October, whose only comment of interest was that there may have been residual tincture of opium in Percy's liver and kidneys. A large bottle of this substance was said to have been poured away at Easter by Avis Graydon, but a smaller one was discovered by the police in the Thompsons' bedroom. The overwhelming likelihood was that Percy had bought it for self-medication. As Webster put it, 'If a person suffered with the heart chlorodyne or tincture of opium would produce relief. It is quite possible this is what I traced in the deceased's body. I detected no other poisonous substance.'

This was not much use to the prosecution. Fingers were crossed, therefore, for Spilsbury's report, which began with a description of the deal coffin, the brass fittings and the nameplate on the top. The three stab wounds were detailed, and the 'superficial cuts on the front of the abdomen and on the right arm.'

Internally, most of the organs were described as normal and healthy, including the arteries and the smoker's lungs. Percy's heart, of which he had frequently complained, 'was slightly enlarged the cavities were slightly dilated and the muscle was pale. The mitral valve was slightly thickened.'

Spilsbury had looked minutely for any scarring that might have resulted from glass in the food, and for any signs of poisoning. He reported:

> The tongue was uninjured. The oesophagus was normal apart from the wound… no scars were visible in its wall.
>
> The stomach had been opened and was empty: its wall was stained red with patches of green… there were no signs of poisoning and no scars were visible in the wall.
>
> The small and large intestines were normal and no scars were found in their walls… I also examined microscopically the contents of the vermiform appendix but I found no fragments of glass.

In conclusion, he wrote:

> I found no indications of poisoning and no changes suggestive of previous attempts at poisoning.
>
> I detected no glass in the contents of the intestine.
>
> On subsequent microscopic exam I found slight fatty degeneration of the heart muscle, liver and kidney.
>
> The fatty disease of the heart muscle, liver and kidney may have resulted from disease, but no disease was found in the body which would account for these changes.

Spilsbury then returned the digestive organs to John Webster for further chemical analysis.

★

On 1 November Edith and Freddy were remanded once more, and again on the 8th. On that day a short item in *The Times* reported that the list of trials for the November session at the Old Bailey included that of Frederick Bywaters. 'The Judges on the rota are Mr Justice Avory, Mr Justice Sankey and Mr Justice McCardle, but it is not yet known which of them will sit.'

So at that stage, following the inquest verdict at Ilford, it was Freddy alone who was to stand trial, and before a judge who would almost certainly have been more helpful to his cause than Mr Justice Shearman (none could have been less so than that peevish old puritan, whose mind wandered – 'what is Shakespeare Crescent?' – and fixated – 'we do not want this strewn with odd letters' – in wayward turn). A week later, however, it was reported that the case was 'still being investigated at the Police Court'. In other words they remained hopeful of charging the woman also.

This happened on 23 November, at the end of the hearing at Stratford.

Edith had arrived at the court in a different mood: more spirited. She had adjusted somewhat to the new circumstances – one can, as she herself would later say, get used to anything – and she had hope. Mr Stern gave her confidence. She had not been charged, and why should she be? Visions of the warm parlour at Shakespeare Crescent, which before would have been merely a torment, may have crept tentatively into her mind. As she entered the dock she shouted to Freddy – an act of defiance that cut clean through the lines of procedure – asking if he had received two letters she had sent this week. He replied that he had not. She had wanted to be heard saying this, to let the authorities know that she was no longer entirely quiescent in their hands, that the person she had once been was re-forming inside her and that those around her were intercepting her post. Which was, after all, the post of an innocent woman.

It was the first time that she and Freddy were reported to have spoken to each other; yet they were writing again. Quite astonishing, given what this had brought them to. It is impossible to know when the first letter was sent, or from whom. It was almost certainly after the correspondence began to be read out in court, but that did not stop them. Was this love, surviving the great rupture of their lives? For Edith, writing those letters had been her most significant act in the fourteen months leading up to the murder. To resume was therefore preferable to stopping. It had always taken her into another existence – as writing can; once it had been a removal from the fraught bustle of work or the leaden tramp-tramp of Percy's footsteps; now it was from the grey attenuation of the hours at Holloway. It had always been a declaration of autonomy, and now it was that in tremulous earnest.

Nevertheless it could have gone the opposite way between these two, when reality crashed their party. But their feelings had not evaporated into the lustreless air. If either believed that the other had brought them to this pass, as yet there was no resentment. They still craved communion, although that would change. Whether they would have done so if Freddy had got away with the murder – if it had been filed unsolved, and he had returned in 1923 to a free and widowed Edith – is a great imponderable.

So too is what she wrote in those unknown letters. Were they brave, despairing, hopeful, fearful? The only one that survives from this period is from Freddy, and *that* is remarkable for its ordinariness, although the spelling and grammar are unusually bad: possibly a sign of stress. It contains the only clue as to Edith's previous letter, when he replies to an enquiry as to how he spent his days. For the rest, he was seeking to bolster her courage, and at the same time his own. He was trying to return to their old ways, to 'talk' to her. He was a killer, but still there is something wholly pitiable about this little document, which exists in its original form: a thin folded sheet of closely spaced lines, covered in tidy slanted script, the handwriting of the boy that he was, and with the printed heading:

In replying to this letter, please write on the envelope:-

Number 8606   Name F. Bywaters

                        Brixton Prison

                        Nov: 18th 1922.

'G.M.M.C.', the letter began: his familiar greeting of old, meaning Good Morning Ma Chère.

Today I want to finish the conversation of yesterday. It was rotten – wasn't it – when I was feeling in a mood to talk for a long time I had to desist owing to lack of material. Now P.m. [Peidi Mia] comment ca vas –

Why haven't you written to me so that I rcd. letter first post this morning? Answer – A change for me to be in this position? – I'm going to take full advantage of the opportunity. The enclosed cutting – Is the part I have underlined quite correct? [there is no clue as to what this cutting was]. If it is – I shall have to use spectacles. Now suppose we have a convasation about the book. My opinion now – yours when you answer. In the first place, I don't think I liked it as much as I did "Atonement". The best parts I see you noticed. I think Coict made quite an unnecessary sacrifice

– though – she was prompted by the highest motives. If she had told Grier she would never had those times of torment – which – you can understand – but I cannot. (It was explained very well by A.M. Askew in "The Shulamite"). Did you like Grier? or Bentley?

Funny – I dreamed last night that you wrote to me & told me that you had been able to finish "His Daughter". I would talk about "Sam's Kid" more, only I have no particular wish to explain my feelings to an audience – you alone yes – it is different. You understand fully don't you Pal? You asked me what I do all day – I suppose practically the same as you. Sit on a chair – think or read, eat at specified times & then sleep; One day is over. I look forward to the day at the Court – it breaks the monotony. Do I sound a bit morbid & down – I don't feel over exhilarated – One of those 'One little hours' would be good now. But this I suppose is only a passing phase – not the longing for 'One Little Hour' – the other part. I'm going to finish now p.m. Carrissima mia goodbye Freddy.

From this letter several others can be inferred, but on 21 November a man named J. H. Wall, from the Prison Commission department within the Home Office, wrote severely to the Governor of Holloway:

Please note that letters written by the woman Thompson to the man Bywaters will not be posted. She will not, however, be told of this. If she writes any, they will be sent up to this Office, where they will be retained.

If she has written to him, or if she has received letters from him, why were they not submitted to the Commissioners. None appear to have been sent up.

The reply from the Governor, Dr Morton – a not unkindly man – was written on a Home Office memorandum:

Noted. Only 2 letters have been sent out by the woman Thompson, and 3 have been received from Bywaters, none of which appear to have any bearing upon the trial. Two of the letters received from Bywaters were destroyed by Thompson, but I attach the third letter [as above] for the Commissioners' perusal.

This was not remotely good enough for the bureaucrat Wall, whose blood ran reptilian-cold and whose reply was also minuted in the Home Office files:

The letter should not have been passed & two prisoners connected in the same case & such a grave case should not have been allowed to correspond without first obtaining the Commissioners' instructions.

Edith had still not been charged, she was on remand only, yet she was again treated as a convicted felon. Well: the authorities did not have long to wait.

After her outburst at the hearing on 23 November she settled back, no doubt with a kind of agitated impatience for it all to be over, as John Webster gave evidence on the results of his chemical analysis.

It had taken him no further than his conclusions of the previous month. He had, he said, found no trace of any poisonous substance and no suggestion that glass had been taken. From two of Percy's organs he had extracted a trace of an alkaloid giving a reaction for morphine. The magistrate Eliot Howard made something of this by producing the bottle of aromatic tincture of opium found at Kensington Gardens. 'Does that contain enough to be a poisonous dose?' Mr Webster answered that it did: it was a one-ounce bottle, and between a quarter and half an ounce could be fatal. This was, of course, true of a great many medicines kept in the home. To Mr Stern he agreed that anybody could buy such a bottle of opium, and that it was the kind of medicine taken by people looking to ease heart pain. 'And probably,' said Mr Stern, 'it was some compound such as that which produced the trace of morphine you found in Thompson's body?'

'It is quite possible,' said Mr Webster.

Then DS Hancock read again from Edith's letters. The evidence included the final passage of the last letter written before the murder: 'Don't forget what we talked in the Tea Room.'

Implication – inference… Yet the actual evidence remained ludicrously scant. The analyst's report amounted to nothing that could not be naturally explained away. Although Spilsbury's report was still a week away from submission, the authorities surely knew by then that he was not going to be much help to them. Yet the fat cloud of innuendo sailed on regardless. Something more was happening behind the scenes, something more was known – it had to be.

And so, at the end of the hearing, as if the authorities could wait no longer before bursting forth with the words, Edith Thompson and Frederick Bywaters were formally charged with murder and conspiracy to murder. In addition, Edith Thompson was charged with administering poison with intent to murder Percy Thompson; with soliciting and proposing to Frederick Bywaters to murder Percy Thompson; and with soliciting and inciting Bywaters to conspire with her and agree to murder Percy Thompson.

'The relevant sentences of the Offences against the Person Act of 1861 were ransacked to make sure of Edith Thompson,' wrote a commentator, many years after the event; 'one is left with the feeling that if barratry and arson could have been dragged in, they would have been.'*

Mrs Graydon, sitting in the court at which she had doubtless arrived in a state of hope – daring to think that the authority in which she trusted would at last call a halt – was heard to cry: 'My child, my child.' She rose from her seat and tried to clutch at Edith, who was half-dragged from the room and carted back to Holloway.

★

Eight days later Spilsbury's report was submitted, and when its contents were known a detective on the investigation said flatly: 'The

---

* Douglas G. Browne in *Sir Travers Humphreys: A Biography*.

case against Mrs Thompson has failed.' Yet the prosecution was not
deterred by the apparent blank wall into which it had run.

The trial was set to open on Wednesday 6 December, in Court One
at the Old Bailey.

In the interim the two prisoners continued to write to each other.
On 30 November the governor of Brixton handed over an unspecified
number of letters to the Prison Commission: 'Submitted – This sort
of correspondence has been going on between this prisoner and his
fellow prisoner in Holloway. The letters are not clear – Gov.'

The reply from Mr Wall was minuted in the Home Office file,
thus:

Spoke.

a) This letter will not be allowed to go. Please leave it with this
paper. He should not be told. No letters from this man to the
woman Thompson will be posted. He will not be told of this. He
may continue to write to her, but the letters will be forwarded to
this Officer. A similar instruction is being sent to Holloway
regarding the woman's letters.

b) What do you mean by 'this sort of correspondence'? No letters
to or from the woman Thompson have been submitted to you to
the Commissioners. If letters have passed why were they not
submitted.

It was reasonable that the Home Office should want to know what
the two suspects might be saying to each other; they might, after all,
have been gleefully recounting the events of the murder; but again,
given that they were still technically innocent, it was hard to see why
the letters – once vetted – could not be sent. What difference would it
have made? But no. A telegram written by Freddy – 'Have you received
letter are you ill let me know' – was actually shown to Sir Ernley
Blackwell. 'The telegram is not to go.'

Meanwhile Edith, who probably had no idea that her letters were disappearing into the black hole of the Home Office, made a last grand attempt to take her story back under her own control. She informed her newly appointed defence counsel, Sir Henry Curtis-Bennett, that she intended to go into the witness box and testify in her own defence. It was the action of a person who believed themselves to be innocent of whatever was being thrown at them, and Curtis-Bennett afterwards expressed the view that it had ensured the guilty verdict against her. The solicitor general, Sir Thomas Inskip, was deemed to have handled the prosecution case ineptly (which is odd, really, given that he won) yet the fact is that when he questioned Edith about certain passages in her letters she was lost: finished. Not testifying also carried a certain risk – what was she hiding and so on – but Curtis-Bennett had viewed it as essential, and told her so. 'Her determination in this respect was unswerving,' wrote one of his biographers. 'It is very hard indeed to decide why Mrs Thompson followed this course. She refused to listen to any legal advice to the contrary.'*

With regard to Curtis-Bennett's failure to defend the case more cleverly, it was later said that 'Mrs Thompson herself having done much to ruin it, the explanation may be that he lost heart. He was a man of temperament, and perhaps not best fitted for a cause in which temperament played an extravagant part.'†

She had had, her counsel said, some idea that she could carry the jury. She had always been able to persuade men. In fact the jury contained two women – their presence was still something of a novelty, having been legalized only three years previously, and it doubtless affected the rest: embarrassing them more than they might otherwise have been, obliging them to express more outraged shock than they actually felt – that was the way of things in 1922, but it was also not the point. There were plenty of men who were *not* susceptible to Edith, who were mysteriously enraged by the unconscious eroticism that palpated

---

* Edward Grice in *Great Cases of Sir Henry Curtis-Bennett* (Hutchinson 1937).
† Douglas G. Browne in *Sir Travers Humphreys: A Biography.*

beneath her more obvious attractions. Then there was the fact that the case against her rested upon her ability to incite and solicit. Aha – so *that's* how she hoodwinked young Bywaters, might well have been the reaction when she exercised her powerful female charm.

Filson Young, who edited 'The Trial of Frederick Bywaters and Edith Thompson' for the *Notable British Trials* series, wrote in his introduction about this fatal business of Edith giving evidence: 'For counsel to give actual advice on such a subject in a matter of life or death is to take a greater responsibility than is, perhaps, right; but I think if I had been in Sir Henry's place... I would have asked her to brief another counsel.' Young, who was very much in Edith's camp, courteously expressed his dismay with the conduct of her defence, saying:

> It seems to me that Sir Henry Curtis-Bennett lost one of the opportunities of his lifetime when, after the confused and uncertain opening of the Solicitor General, he did not for once do what counsel are so often telling juries they are doing, but, in fact, so seldom do – leave the prosecution to prove its case and attempt no positive defence.

How right Young was. His analysis went to the heart of this appalling business, this case against Edith Thompson. It was shrouded in mists of surmise so thick as to appear impossibly sinister, yet in truth they concealed almost nothing. It was only with Edith's own help, her willingness to position herself in the box like a target, that the mists could be wrapped around her like a winding sheet; had she kept out of their reach, it is quite likely that they would have dematerialized before they could touch her. Had she allowed her counsel to say that she knew nothing, that she was as shocked as everybody else by what had happened, and whoever says otherwise must go and find some actual evidence, then – Young again – 'I do not think you could have found a British jury to convict her.'

Curtis-Bennett reputedly thought Edith vain and obstinate. Later he himself was accused of vanity: he had not wanted to chuck the brief because he liked the kudos of appearing in such a high-profile case. It may have been, however, that no barrister could have kept her out of the witness box. Curtis-Bennett's biographer (a rather romantic soul) suggested that she had seen herself in the role of Bywaters' saviour, as well as her own, but that is unlikely. Nobility of that kind was not within Edith's compass. She might have wished it to be; it simply was not.

Almost thirteen years later a very similar case was heard at the Old Bailey, the trial of Alma Rattenbury and her much younger lover, George Stoner, for the murder of her husband. Stoner had unquestionably done the deed. Mrs Rattenbury was said to have conspired with him. The judge – a moralist as stern as Mr Justice Shearman, but capable of separating that from matters of law – was Travers Humphreys, part of the prosecution team in the Thompson-Bywaters trial. F. Tennyson Jesse, the author of *A Pin to See the Peepshow*, compared the two cases thus:

> Mrs Thompson, terrified and conscious of her own innocence of murder, never gave a thought to the safety of her lover, Bywaters. Mrs Rattenbury was willing and anxious to take the whole blame if by doing so she could save her lover... she would have hanged without a tremor if by doing so she could have saved Stoner.

In fact Alma Rattenbury was acquitted. She was saved, it was generally believed, by the ghost of Edith Thompson. Stoner was found guilty but later reprieved, by which time Mrs Rattenbury had killed herself, unable to bear the prospect of her lover's execution and a life blighted by infamy. Mr Justice Humphreys condemned her mercilessly in his summing-up, even as he directed the jury to acquit her. 'She was,' wrote Tennyson Jesse, 'innocent of the crime of which... she was accused, but, nevertheless, though her life was handed back to her, it was handed back to her in such a shape that it was of no use to her.'

Edith would not have reacted in that way. She was made of different stuff. There was something antique and dauntless about Alma

Rattenbury. Her love for Stoner was a less reciprocal passion than that of Edith for Freddy – he was an eighteen-year-old handyman, she a cultured woman of thirty-eight; it is impossible to imagine what they talked about or shared outside the bedroom – but it was also less solipsistic: perhaps more maternal and protective, which was not the dynamic between Edith and Freddy. Whether Alma Rattenbury would really have gone to the gallows with a martyr's eagerness, who knows. The fact that she killed herself suggests that she would, although that is not quite the same thing as being compelled by a bunch of bleak-faced people to march obediently to one's death. Nevertheless it is ironic – given her willingness to die – to think that she was saved, that her case was seen more clearly, because of what had happened to a woman who would have done anything – sacrificed anything except, perhaps, her beloved parents – simply to live.

On Monday 27 November Edith Thompson made her will. Everything, which in the end was just £600, was left to her mother.

III

'"People" – that dread judgment bar of daily life known as "people" – would always say: "Of course she told him to do it. And, anyway, she was a dreadful woman." For the world has progressed very little since Ezekiel wrote: "And I will judge thee as women that break wedlock and shed blood are judged, and I will give thee blood in fury and jealousy."'

From 'The Trial of Rattenbury and Stoner', part of the
Notable British Trials series, by F. Tennyson Jesse.

LET US BE honest. This is when these stories truly fascinate. The dock, the shadow of death.

We cannot pay our £5 to go and watch the woman poised above the trap, the *non plus ultra* of reality shows, in which despite the cloak of seemly legality the air is thick with pity and terror and excitation, and every misspoken word meets a hushed awareness that cataclysm has come closer. Some would still go to watch if they could; many would watch on a screen, where reality is mysteriously muted. Others would not watch at all, and might say that it would be far better if these trials had never happened. Nevertheless: what good stories they make. They are – or were – part of our collective consciousness: the capital trials of the century that spans the mid-nineteenth to the mid-twentieth, the there-but-for-the-grace-of-God murderers who belonged to the respectable classes, the not-quite-enough-money classes, the frustrated and dreamer classes. These people went through what we cannot know and what we most fear: the impersonal workings of authority, removing all agency from our lives. They are something like the biblical story of the scapegoat, in which one individual, whose fate quite often diverges only at a late stage from a wholly recognizable path, is caught out and required to suffer on our behalf, *pour encourager les autres*. And when that person is a woman – which happened very rarely – the story is more powerful still.

Our imaginations cannot help but respond. It is only human.

Nobody has been hanged in Britain since 1964, and the probability is that today a woman in Edith Thompson's position would not even be charged on such slight evidence. If she were unlucky enough to be tried, she might fare as did Ethel Le Neve, Dr Crippen's lover, who was both acquitted and pitied. More likely she would, as did Alma Rattenbury, suffer ordeal by public opinion. Either way the interest in her would be acute, but by comparison with 1922 it would be frivolous, because it would not lead to a gallows.

Nevertheless a trial such as Rex v Thompson and Bywaters would still generate extravagant comment. It would be covered over numerous sheets of newsprint and go viral on the internet: #oldbailey #cougar #sexyfelon #peidimia #teamedith #teamfreddy… and so on.

Not that it would happen in quite that same way today. The central characters are entirely knowable, but they would not coalesce as they did in 1922. An Edith would not have married a Percy, or if she had she would have got out of it with no harm done. Her imagination would have found a different outlet – perhaps as a romantic novelist – or perhaps she would not have needed one: she could have fulfilled her potential as a businesswoman, been truly independent and taken lovers as she chose. If a Freddy had crossed her path she would have known the proper way in which to view his attraction. Whether she would have been happy, in this modern incarnation, is impossible to know. Women today are not as happy as they should be, on the whole. And Edith, that Everywoman, was extremely complex, which makes contentment hard to find.

Still: in that telling of her story there would have been no deaths. Not much story, either. Stories are born out of friction, the lack of which does not necessarily bring happiness. The fact is that Edith, in a perverse and probably unacknowledged way, was rather enjoying the life that she had up to the murder: it gave her cause for much misery but it had interest and piquancy: it was hugely dramatic and she took the lead role in it. If she had wanted freedom enough, then she could have had it. Really, she could. What she wanted was more ambivalent than that, although she identified it simply with the figure of Frederick Bywaters. She wanted something other, something else, something not susceptible to definition: the many lives within one life. Perfectly normal, to want such a thing. What made her unusual was how close she came to expressing it, even at times to having it.

And then it came to the point where freedom was no longer a dream, to turn over in one's mind like the pages of a particularly delicious book, containing chapters about tumbledown nooks and return visits to the Isle of Wight. Freedom was a reality, and it was not to be had. Everything was reality, comfortless and graceless and without kindness: rooms; movements; authority; life; death; and words. Her own words in particular. Words that had been written on a moment of inspiration, in a breath of excitation; that might well have been forgotten within the space of a few hours, absorbed into the exquisite desire to write new and better words. Words that had meant she did not always know what, that had expressed something vitally important at the time but were essentially ephemeral, consumed as she thought to a fire or thrown into an ocean. And now such words – all those darlints and darlingest boys, that fervent joyful outpouring of a remarkable soul – were being pored over by learned men, products of public schools and Oxbridge, who took words no more seriously than she had done but who sought for meaning in a different way, a literal way. To them, each word equalled something real. They did not see that words were metaphors for the ineffable. It was as if a schoolgirl's diary, scrawled with the words I hate so-and-so I hope he dies, had been seized by the police and sent to the Crown Prosecution Service.

Except, of course, that Percy did die. And if the learned men worked backwards from that reality, Edith's words too became real.

As soon as the cross-examination began at the Old Bailey, Edith knew that this was what she confronted: the brandishing of her own words against her, and the absolute impossibility of dodging the bullets that they had become. She had known it already, in fact, during Freddy's cross-examination, when he himself was obliged to fence and obfuscate. But still she went ahead, even though Sir Henry Curtis-Bennett was trying to stop her until the last possible minute.

She insisted upon stepping into an arena that she knew to be as dangerous as a crocodile pit. It was an act of courage, and as such untypical. She did not lack bravery in the everyday sense – the ability to put on a show when she felt tired or ill, to battle gamely against a husband who could be brutish – but entering a witness box, confronting all those men, trying to control a body that insisted upon buckling and shaking: that was different altogether. Perhaps she did not realize the sheer lonely horror of it, the relentlessness and lack of courtesy. Or perhaps – it is possible – she was compelled by the idea of her moment in the spotlight, when she could show herself as the special person that she had always known herself to be. And she *did* do that, if not at all in the way that she had intended. Almost one hundred years later, the imagination still rises to see her there, white-faced beneath the drooping brim of her hat, her sweetly curved jaw trembling above her beautiful neck: there is a wretched sadism in conjuring her, because her terror is part of the fascination, so too is the knowledge of her fate: it is unbearable and it is irresistible, like the picture of Anne Boleyn before her judges; it is human to want to imagine it, just as it was to want to pay £5 for a ticket to the Old Bailey back in 1922, shameful and natural and entirely human.

So Edith did what she wanted, she made everybody listen and watch and remember her.

★

Number One Court at the Old Bailey is often described as calm, almost matter-of-fact, which only serves to emphasize that it is also nothing of the kind. 'There was nothing dramatic about it,' said the writer Beverley Nichols, who attended the Thompson-Bywaters trial. 'It was horribly antiseptic, but at the same time it was the atmosphere of a first night.' The court is built on the site of the old Newgate prison, where the last public hanging took place in 1868. It is wood-panelled, not large, and with imperfect acoustics. Edith was frequently asked to raise her voice ('we do not hear you, Mrs Thompson'). A dominant feature is the seventeenth-century Sword of Justice, suspended above the judge's chair, which stands on a dais level with the dock. The public gallery is also small, frustratingly so to those who wanted seats for this, the hottest of tickets even in an era of classic murder cases: in the past dozen years Dr Crippen and Ethel Le Neve had stood in the dock; so too the Seddons, who murdered their rich lodger; the 'Brides in the Bath' murderer George Joseph Smith; and the wife-killer Herbert Rowse Armstrong. These trials were the soap operas of the time, but none more so than that of Edith Thompson and Frederick Bywaters. The pair arrived at the Old Bailey on 6 December as prisoners and as celebrities. He looked like a young actor with his fine profile and his smouldering eye, she like a semi-exotic film star in the familiar musquash coat. They were what the national mood feasted upon, these products of the post-war decadence; and, in her case, what it resented and feared.

The journey to the court took Edith very close to Aldersgate Street, where the milliners in the workroom would have been discussing her with that mixture of compassion and *schadenfreude* that is again merely human. Cheapside, the shopping street of the City where she had walked so often with Freddy, led directly into Newgate Street; she would have passed the Old Bailey regularly during her thirteen years of working life. If she had done so on 6 December, early in the morning, she would have seen a gathering such as one might view today outside a cinema premiere, leaning on the ropes that line a red carpet. But they were there for her and Freddy; they had been there since four o'clock in the morning.

Among those with a place in the press gallery was James Douglas, editor of the *Sunday Express*, author of the 2d pamphlet entitled 'The Ilford Murder'.

> Let me analyse the unhealthy lure that drew a morbid mob to the guarded doors. The shivering women who stood in the street in the bitter wind all night were not a pretty sight…
>
> Three ordinary clerks! Nothing here to madden London with feverish emotion.
>
> Why, then, all the pother? The answer is – Mrs Thompson's letters. In them she revealed a neurotic pseudo-romantic personality, nourished on melodramatic novels and melodramatic plays like *Bella Donna* and *Romance*. She also displayed a mania for self-analysis in copious epistles to her lover that reeked of the theatre and of the novel. She stood forth as the creature and creation of a hectic and hysterical age…
>
> Mrs Thompson made all the melodramas I have ever seen look pale and colourless. She was pale and frail and pitiful. She drooped and collapsed like a lily. She vibrated like a violin, with every plaintive note in her beseeching voice. By turns she was weak and strong, vivid and colourless, alert and inert. Never was there a more elusive enigma of a woman, subtle and artless almost in the same breath, now like a broken reed and now like steel…

The Times, inevitably less lurid, nonetheless gave chapter and verse on proceedings in the 'Ilford Murder Trial'. Within the headline on 7 December was a phrase taken from the prosecution's opening speech: 'Hand that Conceived the Crime'. Again, the breakfast-table readership was not left in much doubt as to what had been going on.

And then there was Beverley Nichols, in attendance for the *Sunday Dispatch*, talking about Edith fifty years later with that catch in his voice, at having witnessed the destruction of something unusual and beautiful; describing 'her very immobility, her paleness, and her obvious terror…'.

The differences in the way in which Edith was viewed, the variety of reaction that she elicited, were astonishing from the first: yet all these views had this much in common, they were not indifferent. They were mesmerized by this ordinary woman, who held so much that was extraordinary, this creature of the suburbs who had been selected for a singular destiny. For some reason a sacrifice was being demanded by the post-war world, and she was supremely suited to the role. It could have happened to so many people, this sudden slip from the dreamscape into reality, but because of what she was like it was happening to her.

There was not much point in hope: that was made clear even before the thing started. Why, for instance, had Travers Humphreys, that able if moralistic barrister, been replaced as leading counsel for the prosecution by Sir Thomas Inskip, Solicitor General in the six-week-old administration of Andrew Bonar Law? Because the solicitor general represented heavier artillery. He had the right of reply to the closing speeches by the defence. These would usually fall at the end of the trial, to be left as it were echoing within the jury's ears; what instead concluded proceedings was the prosecution's summing-up (followed by that of a hostile judge). This circumstance formed part of the appeal. It was dismissed out of hand: 'at present, when the law officer of the Crown, whether he be the attorney-general or the solicitor general, appears in a Crown case – which is no mere accident – what it means is that those who have had to deliberate upon the matter have come to the conclusion that is a case in which, in the interests of justice, it is right that a law officer of the Crown should appear – when a law officer of the Crown does appear, then, according to the exercise of his discretion, he may exercise the right which at present he lawfully has...' Blah blah blah: in other words, the solicitor general had been appointed to lead the prosecution because it was right that he should do so, and if it was right that he should do so then whatever he did was right. *Why* it had been decided to wheel in this cannon of pomposity, who could fire last and leave the sound of his explosion in the air, was not explained, because that was the way it was. The circularity of the argument, the

Alice in Wonderland refutation, was wholly typical; so keen were the appeal judges to make their point that they described the solicitor general's closing speech as one of 'studious moderation'. Inskip could have said much more, much worse. The defence should think itself lucky.

This was how much the authorities wanted convictions for Edith Thompson and Frederick Bywaters. They were sure of him, but they needed to be sure of her also. It was utterly impossible that he should hang and she should not. Such was the national mood, the frenzy.

And then: before proceedings began the defence attempted to have the couple tried separately. That failed immediately. Afterwards came the more pressing matter of the letters, which was debated in the jury's absence. Sir Henry Curtis-Bennett set out an argument – perfectly clear, within its legalistic phrasing – that related to the separate indictments under which Edith was charged. The first of these, that of wilful murder, rendered the letters inadmissible because there was no *a priori* evidence showing her involvement in the crime (this had been Mr Stern's argument). The second indictment contained a number of counts of soliciting, conspiracy and incitement, in regard to which the letters would be admissible. However the prosecution intended to proceed only with the first indictment: the capital charge. Therefore, said Curtis-Bennett, the letters could not be used.

His unspoken implication was that if Edith were to be tried at all, it should be on the second indictment. Had this happened, she would have been found guilty and received a jail term; the death sentence that would still have been given to Freddy Bywaters could have been commuted without fuss. The logic of this course of action now seems overwhelming. It would have satisfied the belief in Edith's complicity and enabled the authorities to save Freddy's life. But it was not what the story was dictating at the time. Its course was bent elsewhere, towards that cathartic conclusion; to pull back from it had become implicitly impossible. Edith, said the solicitor general, was being charged as a principal in the second degree – a principal in the murder who did not strike the blows – and the letters were admissible, therefore, to show that she gave the incitement without which the crime would not have been committed.

Curtis-Bennett gave it one last shot; he knew that his only real hope of saving his client was by keeping the letters out of the case.

> In my submission, there must be some nexus between those let-
> ters and what they contain and the killing as it took place. The
> killing which is alleged to have been murder took place by a stab,
> as is alleged, by Bywaters on Mr Thompson. Now, where is the
> connection between that act of murder and these letters which
> are written months beforehand? In my submission, there is no
> nexus between them at all…

'I think,' said the judge, 'they are evidence of intention and motive. It is a very difficult question…' And then, as if it had ever been in doubt: 'I *shall* admit them.'

Only half the extant letters were put into evidence, which was a gamble by the defence and probably a mistake. Those that referred directly to Edith's procured miscarriage were removed, as were others deemed too obviously sexual or simply irrelevant; any that were susceptible to sinister interpretation were left in. Had everybody been able to behave in a more adult manner, the missing letters might well have helped Edith's cause, not least by showing that she was capable of writing at great length without ever mentioning poison or ground glass. But the jury, who knew that some letters had been withheld from them, were bound to speculate on their contents, and in a way that was not helpful at all.

Now the solicitor general made his opening speech, which was exactly what one would expect.

Parts of the newly admissible letters were read out.

> Some of the passages are indicative of nothing more than guilty
> passion between the parties, but the letters are important when
> you come to decide the question as to whether Mrs Thompson

had any reason to get rid of her husband…

Then, in full knowledge that Spilsbury would be giving evidence that did nothing for the prosecution case:

> You are not being asked to say whether she attempted to poison her husband; all you are asked to consider is whether Mrs Thompson incited Bywaters to kill her husband, and the letters are important from that point of view. They are important to show that she so worked and preyed on the mind of this young man by her suggestions that, although it was his hand that struck the blow, it was her mind that conceived the crime.

That brought the argument back to Curtis-Bennett's point about the lack of a 'nexus' – that writing about poisoning in May did not lead inevitably to a dagger in the neck in October – but not to worry, the nexus was there for those who wanted to find it badly enough.

> I suggest that through the correspondence it becomes clear that it was Mrs Thompson who was urging Bywaters on to commit the crime in some way or other in order to secure the happiness upon which her passion was set. He may have been reluctant or not, but can you, members of the jury, have any doubt after hearing these letters that she was not reluctant?

The solicitor general alluded to the 'cooling' on Freddy's side in the three months before the last leave; thus making Edith sound pathetic as well as domineering. 'Bywaters' ship arrives at Tilbury on 23rd September, and she sends him a telegram, "Can you meet Peidi Broadway 4 p.m." That she was not content even then to leave the man alone appears from another newspaper extract dated 20th September, headed "Chicken Broth death…"'

He quoted from the end of Edith's last letter: 'Don't forget what we talked in the Tea Room.' But this, which seemed to her accusers to offer up her guilt on a plate, did nothing of the kind. It always sounded – still does, in truth – as though Edith's reference was to a final breathless meeting at Fullers, in which the couple brought their heads together over the walnut cake and finessed their strategy. It even sounds as though that meeting took place on the day of the murder itself. But that could not have been so; although nobody ever made this clear, least of all the defence counsels. The letter was written on Monday 2 October, in the brief intervals of Edith's working day, then handed over to Freddy for him to read later (a familiar practice with these two): handed over, therefore, when they met at Fullers. This was the day before the murder. But unless Edith took out her pen and wrote the damning sentence there and then, scribbling amid the cups, her reference must have been to a conversation of *the previous week*, in which they met at the tea room three times. She was probably thinking of the most recent occasion, on Friday 29 September, and there is no knowing what they talked about that afternoon. Obviously they dreamed about their future – 'we only have 3 ¾ years left darlingest' alludes to Edith's reiterated desire for her life to change, before a shifting period of time had elapsed. There was no evidence to say that she meant change brought about by murder; although the solicitor general thought otherwise.

'I ask – what did they talk about in the tea room? I put it that there was a long course of suggestion resulting in a desire to escape from the position, and a fresh suggestion was made in the tea room...'

In conclusion, he ran around anxiously blocking all possible exit routes. It did not matter how the murder was committed, nor indeed when; it did not even matter if Freddy had decided to do it of his own free will.

'It is no answer that the whole of the incitement should come from Mrs Thompson. It may be that the passion of the young man may have led him in that direction. There is the undoubted evidence in the letters upon which you can find that there was a preconcerted meeting between Mrs Thompson and Bywaters at the place' – this outrageous statement referred, presumably, to what the solicitor general alleged had been discussed at Fullers –

> but supposing you were not wholly satisfied that there was a conspiracy made to effect the murder at this place and time, if you are satisfied that Mrs Thompson incited the murder and that, incited and directed by her controlling hand, Bywaters committed the murder, then it will be my duty to ask you, after hearing the evidence, to find her who incited and proposed the murder as guilty as Bywaters who committed it.

★

Confused and uncertain this speech may have been – as Filson Young would later say – but in its inelegant way it did its job rather well. For elegance would not really serve, in this instance. What had to be done was to keep throwing mud until enough of it had stuck: until the court was brought to the point of thinking, well, this or that may not be proved, there may or may not be a nexus, whatever that is; but taken for all in all, let's face it, she's guilty as hell. Which was quite some way to conduct a trial.

Young also wrote this, a beautiful puncturing of the righteous and self-important atmosphere within the Old Bailey:

> Criminal lawyers have an incorrigible instinct for melodrama; and they are apt to see, or rather to present, every one in the light of martyr, hero, or villain. Some of them seem to have a quaint theory that human nature is divided into two kinds of people: on the one hand, plain, decent people, the stuff of which judges and juries are made, who are shocked and horrified at any transgression of the moral law... on the other hand, blackguards and devils, degraded by such things as passion; guilty, outside the licensed degrees, of a thing called love; and generally and deservedly in trouble of some

kind until they are swept within the meshes of the law. The Ilford case was no exception to this rule. The three persons concerned were duly presented in this melodramatic way. The good, patient and unoffending husband; the manly young fellow, corrupted and debauched by the experienced woman of the world; and the black-hearted sorceress, weaving her spells, casting her nets, and bringing ruin upon everybody connected with her.

No doubt about it: the vast majority of observers, even the intelligent ones, were wholly influenced by this narrative. Only a handful of the more perceptive – including Beverley Nichols, the editor of the *Daily Express* Beverley Baxter, and Young himself – were able to pierce the fog of cliché. Because that narrative was how people *wanted* the story to be told; and there is no end to the determination within people to hold on to their preconceptions.

Almost all the witnesses in the case were for the prosecution. On the opening day these included Mrs Bywaters, Mr Graydon and Mrs Lester, who gave evidence favourable to the defendants; as well as various police officers and Richard Thompson, who did not. Also testifying were those who had seen Edith in Belgrave Road in the early hours of 4 October. Curtis-Bennett made the most of them: to Dora Pittard he put it that Edith was 'very agitated and it was very difficult for you to hear some of her replies, almost – incoherent, you say?' Again, Percy Cleveley did not quite play along. 'She was certainly very excited...' but the impression was successfully given that Edith had been in a desperate and bewildered state.

The police surgeon, Percy Drought, detailed the wounds inflicted during the attack. 'Show us,' 'just show us,' Mr Justice Shearman repeated, as Drought pointed obediently to the site of the injuries on his own body. Then the weapon was produced. 'Show it to the jury,' said the judge, and the long thick knife glinted dully in the court. If Freddy Bywaters had ever had any chance of evading execution, he probably lost it at that moment.

'The knife destroyed all my pity,' wrote James Douglas; 'a great dagger with a guard... The witness who heard the woman did not hear any cry from the murdered man. He was butchered like a sheep.'

Drought was questioned on whether Percy was first attacked from behind or confronted face-to-face. The more superficial wounds were inflicted to the front of the body, the major wounds towards the back. The likely scenario, therefore, was that the attack began face-to-face; that Percy then moved off into the road and received the fatal wound from behind; and that he finally staggered to the wall, against which he was found slumped. There was also a cut to the inner arm, which appeared to have been delivered when the arm was raised. Given that the trail of blood measured some forty-four feet, a struggle was most definitely implied, although Dr Maudsley testified that he saw no sign of one on Percy's body. But it was surely impossible that the men should have travelled so far along the pavement – out into the middle of the road – if they had not been scuffling and battling with each other? With a knife of those dimensions, Freddy could have killed his victim outright and instantly. Especially if Edith, armed with foreknowledge, had helped to hold the victim.

But how bad it all sounded, in that courtroom. The solicitor general asked:

'Was there anything to show the place at which he sank down, we are told, against the fence?'

'Merely the blood.'

The judge, as if to impress upon the jury that the wounds had been made with the utmost deliberation, said:

'You have left the impression on my mind that all these wounds were not slashes but stabs?'

Drought concurred: 'Stabs.'

Coming after this, Lilian Bywaters with her desolate defence of her 'boy' – his school reports, his record with P&O – was hard to encompass: how could she describe him as one of the best sons that a mother could have? Unless, of course, he had been incited to that terrible crime by the woman... So handsome he looked in the dock, smiling at his mother, while the creature next to him swooned and swayed.

But her father, next up, was a pitiable figure also. So polite, so decent. 'What day would that be, sir?' he replied to Travers Humphreys, when asked about Freddy's visit to the house on 2 October. By comparison, the judge was immensely rude. Irritably obsessed as he was with the letters and cuttings that were the main trial exhibits, he interrupted Sir Henry Curtis-Bennett in the middle of asking Mr Graydon about a couple of these – 'Now I just want to ask you about Exhibits 15a and b' – with the pettish query:

'Have you thought of having some copies of these extracts made for the Jury? If they are going to be read out it would be much more satisfactory... You understand how difficult it is' – while Mr Graydon stood in the witness box, in his black suit and laundered collar, waiting to give evidence in the trial for his daughter's life.

'He had better take them,' said the judge, meaning that the extracts should be given to Mr Graydon. 'Just show them to the Jury. You heard them read, gentlemen [sic]; they are scraps from newspapers.'

'Might the witness have them in his hand for a moment?' said Curtis-Bennett, with what one hopes was a note of reproof; not that the judge would have been confounded. 'Certainly,' he replied. He did not particularly like Curtis-Bennett, and sought regularly to disrupt his witnesses. Now his prolonged fussing about extracts and copies and passing things to the jury meant that Mr Graydon's next statement – that Edith had invented an entire episode in one of her letters: one of the most significant points made in the whole trial – was submerged in a tide of trivia.

The last witnesses on 6 December were Herbert Carlton and Lily Vellender, whose grave normality may have been still more difficult for Edith to bear; the life that they represented, the harmless flirtations, the businesslike camaraderie of Carlton & Prior: if only that had been enough.

★

The next day, after evidence from the waitresses at Fuller's, from Rose Jacobs and from the police officers who described the discovery of Edith's letters, Detective Inspector Hall took the stand. He was in some measure called to account for his stage-management at Ilford police station, although it did not seem to signify greatly. As with any point made by the defence, it disappeared into the vortex of its own careful phrasing: Hall's reading out of the statements made at the station became far more important. Even the findings of the analyst John Webster and the pathologist Bernard Spilsbury were deficient in force. Spilsbury, just a month away from receiving his knighthood, had a huge reputation. He had been the crucial witness at other great Old Bailey trials, notably those of Dr Crippen and George Joseph Smith; the fact that he had obtained nothing from Percy Thompson's exhumation should have been a show-stopping moment. Curtis-Bennett certainly made much of it in his summing-up. Yet in his actual evidence, Spilsbury was not quite as wonderfully adamant as he might have been.

'Did you find any indication of ground glass in the appendix?' asked the solicitor general.

'No.'

'Is the negative result of your examination consistent with glass having been administered?'

'Some time previously, yes.'

'Is it possible that a large piece would have passed through the system without injury to the organs, or without leaving any signs behind?'

'It is possible.'

Similarly with regard to poison, Spilsbury refused to be unequivocal. Edith's letters contained references to hyoscine, digitalin, bichloride of mercury and ptomaine: 'There are not many of those poisons... that would leave any permanent effect at all,' he said, unhelpfully, to Sir Henry Curtis-Bennett, who pressed him nonetheless to be clearer.

'At any rate, there was no trace, either post mortem or by analysis, of any poison having been given?'

'No.'

Despite the reservations this was, from Edith's point of view, by some measure the best evidence offered so far. It said that she had intended her husband no material harm, and that what she wrote in her letters was not necessarily literal truth. Yet again this crucial point seemed to leave no impression on the surface of the trial. The solicitor general had covered it in his opening speech, when he stated that the jury was 'not being asked to say whether she attempted to poison her husband; all you are asked to consider is whether Mrs Thompson incited Bywaters to kill her husband.' In fact the one point was dependent on the other. The greater part of Edith's 'incitement' came in the form of asking for poison, saying that she was trying to administer poison; which Spilsbury's evidence suggested she had not done. But this concept of incitement had become as fluid as the Thames. It meant whatever the prosecution decided that it should mean, from one minute to the next.

'We have not heard the late Mr Thompson's side of the case,' wrote James Douglas in his pamphlet, which was true enough, although what followed was not. 'How much did he know? Not very much. His wife and her lover were secretly plotting to poison him. She said he was suspicious. He seems to have been singularly unsuspicious... although he found glass in his food.'

If Mr Douglas actually believed that he had heard that statement given in evidence, then the trial of Thompson and Bywaters might just as well never have happened: they should have hanged the pair of them summarily and saved everybody's time.

Spilsbury was the last witness for the prosecution. As a case it had been pretty poor. There was no need for a case against Freddy, because there was nothing really to prove, while against Edith the prosecution had proved absolutely nothing. Never mind: the real case against her was about to begin.

In an act of excruciating and shambolic theatre, given in front of an audience that hissed and giggled and chattered like a mob in furs and pearls – and yes, Edith's lifelong craving for an audience had deserted her at this moment – the letters used in evidence were read aloud in court; at least until the procedure was halted as interminable. The duty was shared, in part, between the junior counsel Roland Oliver and Sir Henry Curtis-Bennett, but it was performed in the main by Travers Humphreys, who in the words of Filson Young

> had practically nothing to do except occasionally to read the long extracts from the letters which took so many hours. It was a curious occupation for him, thus to be reading aloud these passionate utterances in the presence of the woman who wrote them; and it is to his credit that, much as he disliked the task, his reading of those letters was by no means unsympathetic; and some of their haunting phrases which were heard so often in Court will be forever associated in my memory with the tones of Mr. Travers Humphreys.

At one point Curtis-Bennett cut Humphreys short, when he had nearly reached the end of the letter in which Edith told Freddy how 'grand' it had been to see him, 'how grand it was to feel you hold my shoulders': a lovely letter, fresh and alive with a young woman's passion. Curtis-Bennett said politely that he did not need the whole of it to be read. The judge agreed. 'I don't wish to say anything offensive,' he said, 'but it is gush, is it not?'

In the middle of the afternoon Freddy Bywaters took the stand.

James Douglas, who despite his lapses was genuinely compelled by the central figures in the case, was struck by his looks: 'a keen, finely carved profile, a trenchant, high forehead, brilliant eyes, and a great wave of thick brown hair brushed back high from his white brow. He is virile and vigorous in his gait, walking with a firm step and swinging arms.' Douglas was impressed by the boy's composure in the witness box, betrayed only by the clenched fist that tapped constantly on the ledge of the witness box. Edith, wrote Douglas, barely looked at her co-defendant. Perhaps she could not bear to do so. She had endured the reading of the letters 'with her head hanging on her breast', and now sat immobile within her heavy fur, the look on her face scarcely definable: it expressed a suffering so great as to have removed all expression.

There was nothing much that Freddy could do for himself, although he instructed his counsel that no question must be asked that would impugn or endanger his co-accused. He was vastly brave, and he sought at all times to protect Edith Thompson. In so doing he harmed her immeasurably. His shielding of the woman made it seem all the more likely that he was in her power; heroically disdainful of the police and prosecution, it also portrayed him as an entirely noble person, which he was not. Filson Young, another man who did not like him, described him as a 'virile degenerate'. Too harsh, perhaps, but an interesting counterbalance to those who romanticized him.

In fact both views contained something of the truth, as did the multifarious views of Edith. Where all these opinions were wrong, however, was in their certainty that they were right; nothing about these people was that simple. Freddy Bywaters was a man whose passions led directly to aggression, but nonetheless had a kind of purity about them. He was dishonourable in some respects, yet he had a sense of honour. Above anything else, he was very young. And one forgets, so easily, what that feels like. The extremity of it. How unstoppable one is; how lost in oneself; how proudly indifferent to consequences. It is quite true that Edith should have known all this, and handled it, rather than seeking – for her own sake; very little to do with him – to encourage it.

Freddy Bywaters was buzzed up to the hilt with great quantities of testosterone; he was alternately frustrated and sated; he was wayward, through circumstance and nature. In jealousy – that least controllable of emotions, which Edith aroused both deliberately and unconsciously – he was as unmanageable as a rampant stallion. Yet throughout the last three months of life he acquired a quite astonishing self-command, foreign to us today, not subdued or deferential but full of power. His ideas about masculinity – which he revered and in which he abounded – were those of a boy; but if he had decided to behave 'like a man' then he did not let himself down.

Very little in his testimony was true. It is impossible to know how much or how little. He lied from the first, saying that the affair – the 'attachment' – had begun in the autumn of 1921. He lied with conviction, although what he said was not convincing. He was unabashed about it, almost as if the court had no particular right to know about his private correspondence. To his counsel, Cecil Whiteley, he talked about divorce, separation, suicide – anything that might explain the letters without reference to poison, glass, murder. Whiteley's job was impossible, but he conducted it with a kind of sincerity. Of all the counsels he talked the least like a lawyer ('I ought to have asked you this before, Bywaters') and his obvious decency again helped Freddy (because he obviously liked his client) in a way that harmed Edith. Freddy could not be acquitted – even his poor barrister knew it – so why should she be?

The sole straw at which Whiteley clutched was an attempt to bring down the charge from one of wilful murder. This should have helped Edith as well as Freddy, as it meant no premeditation; but it did not.

The trouble, as always, was the difficulty in interpreting the letters. As Freddy wrote to the home secretary before his death: 'Sometimes, even I could not understand her.' It was clear enough that Edith had asked for a divorce or separation – for example, after the row in August 1921 – and that Freddy did the same thing when he went to see Percy later that year. It was demonstrable that Percy was not willing to agree. Thereafter, the letters harp repeatedly on her desire for freedom, but there is often no knowing what she meant by this: divorce, moving abroad, walking out on Percy, killing him – or nothing substantial at all.

Whiteley read this passage, for instance, from a letter dated 10 February:

'Darlint – You must do something this time – I'm not really impatient – but opportunities come and go by – they have to – because I'm helpless and I think and think and think – perhaps – it will never come again.'

In reply to his counsel, Freddy said: 'I hardly know what that refers to,' which was really the only possible answer. Whiteley continued:

'It is suggested by the prosecution that that means that you were going to do something in connection with her husband. Is there anything in that?'

'It is entirely wrong.'

'Did she ask you more than once to take her away?'

'Oh, yes.'

'Tell us about it. Was it a genuine demand by her or not?'

'Well, she appeared to want to go away, but she used to get very hysterical. She was of a highly strung nature.'

And again that has an air of truth; too subtle, however, for Mr Justice Shearman, who came crashing in with: 'Did she ask you to take her away or not?'

'Oh, yes.'

Another passage was read, more overtly problematical, from 4 July: 'Why arent you sending me something... If I don't mind the risk why should you?'

'What was it she asked you to send her?'

'More letters.'

'Where did the risk come with regard to these letters?'

'The risk was people seeing them; she did not want any one to see them; that was all. There was always the difficulty as to where the letters should be sent to.'

Again, quite true; or at any rate plausible. This was the first day of his evidence, and it ended thus:

'In these letters that have been read, was there anything which incited you to do any act of violence to Mr Thompson?'

'Nothing whatever.'

'Had it any effect on your mind at all, as far as Mr Thompson was concerned?'

'No, I never considered them much.'

Which even in her trance of agony may have struck at Edith's heart, and stayed with her on the rattling evil journey back to Holloway; although whether *that* remark was true was another imponderable; like so many others between these two, it was both true and not true.

★

In the world that Edith now inhabited, one in which feelings of shame and terror had become entirely normal, day two of the trial was a good one. Spilsbury, Webster, Whiteley: all positive. The cliff face to which Edith clung had regained some stability.

Day three, Friday 8 December, was not so good.

Freddy claimed to have attacked Percy in self-defence. He had not said this at Ilford, but now he put it forward.

Whiteley took him through the events of 3 October, from the time that he left the Graydons: 'Bywaters, I know it is difficult, but I want you to tell us in your own way what your feelings were towards Mrs Thompson?'

He replied that, as he walked away from the house at Shakespeare Crescent:

> I was naturally thinking of Mrs Thompson. I was thinking how unhappy she was, and I wished I could help her in some manner...
> When I arrived at East Ham station [very close to the Graydon home] I thought, 'I don't want to go home; I feel too miserable. I want to see Mrs Thompson; I want to see if I can help her'...

'What was your object in going to Ilford?'

'I went to see Thompson to come to an amicable understanding for a separation or divorce.'

'Until that moment had you any intention of going to Ilford at all that night?'

'Oh, no. It kind of came across me all of a sudden.'

He had, he said, overtaken the Thompsons on Belgrave Road – which could only have happened if he had been waiting for them on the darkened corner of Endsleigh Gardens, otherwise he would have been seen by any one of the numerous people walking home that night. This, he did not say. Then he described the confrontation. He pushed Edith to one side and held Percy with his left hand, 'caught him by the back of his coat [jacket] and pushed him along the street, swinging him round.

> I said to him, "Why don't you get a divorce or separation, you cad?" He said, "I know that is what you want, but I am not going to give it you, it would make it too pleasant for both of you." I said: "You take a delight in making Edie's life a hell." Then he said, "I've got her, I'll keep her, and I'll shoot you."

It had been quite believable, up until that point.

'As he said that he pushed me in the chest with his left fist, and I said, "Oh, will you?" and drew a knife and put it in his arm.' This was Percy's right arm, which had been raised; whether in attack or self-defence is unknown.

'Did he', asked Whiteley, 'do anything before you took the knife out?'

'Yes, he punched me with his left hand and said "I'll shoot you", going at the same time like that with his right hand': Freddy moved a hand towards his hip pocket. As James Douglas put it, 'he stood for a moment in a fixed, tense attitude, simulating the pose of the dead man.'

'Why did you draw your knife?'

'Because I thought I was going to be killed. After I put my knife into his arm there was a struggle. All the time struggling, I thought he was going to kill me.'

Then Whiteley asked about the deep stabs through Percy's neck, and Freddy answered: 'All I can say is I had the knife in my left hand, and they got there somehow.'

'At the time did you realize that he was dead?'

'No, he was standing up when I left him.'

The solicitor general, naturally enough, had a field day with all of this.

'Do you mean to suggest that he made the first assault upon you?'

'Yes, he did.'

'And that you then drew your knife?'

'I did.'

'Is it the fact that you never saw any revolver or any gun at that moment?'

'I never saw it, no.'

'Did you continue to stab him in the expectation of seeing one at any moment?'

'I did not know I was stabbing him. I tried to stop him from shooting me; that is all.'

Earlier in his questioning, the solicitor general had asked about Freddy's knowledge of where to find Percy Thompson. 'Did you not discuss in the tea room that afternoon the possibility of meeting them later that night?'

'We did not stay in the tea room. She did not come into the tea room; I left it to join her.'

Here Freddy had his facts right, and had no intention of having them falsified by the prosecution.

'Did you not discuss with her something desperate?'

'I did not.'

And at that point it seems quite astounding that Mr Whiteley did not stand up and object, because what the solicitor general was insinuating was beyond reason; also beyond what he had implied in his opening speech, which in itself had been mischievous. He was back with that infamous sentence – 'Don't forget what we talked in the Tea Room' – but now he was semi-suggesting that this talk had happened on the *very day* of the murder, despite the fact that the sentence appeared in a letter written the day before. The solicitor general must have known this. Yet he was airily conflating Edith's remark with the visit to Fuller's on the 3rd; which was not even a meeting, as the couple had left the tea room immediately. It was exactly the kind of vague allusive linking upon which the prosecution case relied, and it should have been ripped apart by the defence.

The cross-examination was an endurance test, as much as anything. One wanted it over, yet at the same time it was one's only chance, and its ending was a terrible prospect, because over really meant over. The final gamble had been struck; there was no calling it back. As well as the constant tapping on the witness box Freddy had begun to pass his handkerchief over his face. The court was hot, the air thick and fuzzy with accreted concentration upon the two men.

Edith pushed back the protective covering of the fur coat that now enveloped her diminished body. Beneath it she was wearing mourning, a black suit borrowed from her mother.

If she was capable of cogent thought she would have recognized the part-truth of what Freddy said to his questioner, when he came very close to admitting the fantastical basis upon which their feelings – real feelings – had rested.

The solicitor general asked him about the suicide pact theme that ran waveringly through the letters.

'I never really considered it seriously.'

Of course he did not. Then: 'Did you tell your learned counsel that you read her letters as melodrama?'

'Some.'

'What was it you understand as melodrama?'

'She had a vivid way of declaring herself; she would read a book and imagine herself as the character in the book.'

'Do you mean that you read her reference to poison as melodrama?'

'Some as melodrama; some as general knowledge.'

'I don't understand that. What did you understand when she mentioned a particular poison?'

'To what are you referring?'

'Are you aware, or do you remember, that she mentioned several times a poison in her letters?'

'Yes.'

'Did that suggest to you a dose of poison that might kill her husband?'

'No.'

'Did you not read those letters as meaning that the idea was in her mind?'

'No.'

Then, in reference to Edith's statement that she had 'used' pieces of a light bulb, which Freddy told the court he had connected with her suicidal urges:

'Did you understand that to mean that she had taken glass?'

'I understood that to be a lie from her to me.'

'Look at the next sentence: "I quite expected to be able to send that cable." Do you suggest that after she had taken the dose that would kill her she was expecting to send you that cable?'

'No, I do not suggest that.'

'What do you suggest?'

'That she would have sent me a cable if she had been successful in getting a divorce or an agreement of separation.'

And: 'Did you ever mean to do anything to make a divorce possible?'

'No.'

'You had no intention of taking any action?'

'No.'

At other points in his evidence he stated the opposite of this; but probably what he said then was closer to the truth, and they both knew it.

They knew that the director of Public Prosecutions had come close to the truth in his letter to the Home Office, before going on to semi-dismiss it: 'it may be that this woman was pretending to her lover that she was resorting to all kinds of expedients for removing her husband…' The DPP had seen that was a possibility, but he didn't want to accept it. Sir Henry Curtis-Bennett, who wanted the jury to accept it: 'The real truth about Mrs Thompson, as borne out by her letters, was that she was a woman who would go on telling any lies so long as she could keep her lover Bywaters.' They knew it because Freddy Bywaters wrote it himself to the home secretary:

I am asking you believe me, sir, because what I say is the truth, that Mrs Thompson never had any intention or the slightest inclination to poison her husband or to kill him in any way. The only way to treat those letters is the way in which I read them…

I was astounded when I heard the sinister translation the prosecution had put to certain phrases, which were written quite
innocently. Those letters were the outpourings of a hysterical
woman's mind, to relieve the tension & strain caused by the agony
she was suffering. If you like sir, merely melodrama.

But a deadly sexualized game could only be explained in a court of
law if people were permitted to speak more directly, slicing through
circumlocution; yet also allowing for nuance, ambivalence, the mysteries of human fallibility.

Instead there was Mr Justice Shearman, priding himself on his rectitude, taking the literary literally.

The author herself then took the stand, and the judge courteously
offered a chair.

★

Her short journey from the dock to the witness box was probably
the most intense piece of theatre that any of those present ever saw.
Sir Henry Irving, Ellen Terry, Donald Wolfit: their histrionics would
have been as nothing compared with the effortful walk of this pale,
tired woman in her black suit and fur coat, moving slowly through the
courtroom as time, briefly, held its breath.

Was she a disappointment to her audience? She was just a woman,
after all, like any other in the room; she was not Lady Macbeth or
Lucrezia Borgia. She had a soft, self-improved London voice, with
which she spoke hesitantly, not boldly; she did not declaim or solilo-
quize. She was holding on to herself, giving very little, even as she
tried to make something of her chance to tell her story. But she
had grace, and a kind of magic. And there she was, in her corporeal reality. Amid all the newsprint and gossip and rumour it was as
though she had a dual identity: not just 'Edith Thompson' but also
Edith Thompson, ribs rising still within the thin cloth of her blouse,
a person who existed outside the collective imagination of her judges,

whose destiny was not yet entirely in their hands; although there was not now long to go.

Walter Frampton, who led the questioning for the defence – perhaps to make it look as though she did not need the big gun of Sir Henry Curtis-Bennett to boom her innocence – took her gently through an account of her unhappy marriage. Like Freddy she cited the desire for a separation, or for a suicide pact, as means to explain certain passages in the letters; as for instance when she wrote 'you won't always be "the man with no right" will you?' This, she said, referred to her hopes of obtaining a divorce and marrying her lover.

But very quickly, even under the tender handling of her own counsel, she ran into difficulties. She was unable to use words in the way required in court, which anyway could not possibly explain the words she had written.

'It would be so easy darlint – if I had things – I do hope I shall,' she had written on 10 February. What, asked Frampton, did that mean?

'I wrote that to let Bywaters think I was willing to do anything to help him, to retain his affections.'

'Look at your letter of 22nd February, where you write – "I suppose it isn't possible for you to send it to me – not at all possible, I do so chafe at wasting time darlint." What were you referring to when you wrote that?'

'Mr Bywaters had told me he was bringing me something and I suggested to send it to me, to allow him to think I was eager for him to send me something to do what he suggested. I wanted him to think I was eager to help him, to bind him closer to me, to retain his affections.'

Not unreasonably, Mr Justice Shearman intervened at this point. With the telling simplicity of a child he asked: 'But what was "it"?'

Edith turned to the judge. 'I have no idea,' she said. 'It was something he suggested.'

Thus, almost from the first, she spent much of her time in the witness box implicating the man who had just tried to save her. Her performance on this little stage was not noble. Perhaps she had intended it to be. But instead it was all too human in its selfishness and panic; both of which were entirely justified.

She was thinking about herself. She had not committed any murder. She had not really done anything. She had no reason to be giving evidence in the first place. It would have been marvellous if she could have said as much – rather than pretending that these idiotic questions had any meaning – but that would never have done. So she tried to explain herself, as she had obviously believed that she could, which proved impossible in that arena.

Of course what she did – showing that everyday quality of self-preservation, rather than the poetic one of self-sacrifice – was catastrophic. Nothing could have looked worse. Far better if she had said: I take responsibility for anything that Mr Bywaters may have inferred from what I wrote to him. *Then* she would have received some sort of approbation. But Edith did not have that in her. She was splendid and she was also small: this, too, was part of her fascination, what Margery Fry, with the cruelty of the impersonally kind, called her 'flimsy' personality. She was not one of those who could be casual and superb as her life fell around her. And why should she be? She had shielded Freddy after the murder, and that was why she was standing in the dock with him now. She had been shielding herself as well, and now she did so in earnest. Much of what she said was the truth, which was why it sounded so strange.

She *had* wanted Freddy to think that she was eager to help him, to bind him closer to her. That was exactly what she had been doing. Walter Frampton asked her about the novel *Bella Donna*, from which she had quoted a passage about digitalin: 'Did you know what digitalin was?' 'I had no idea', she replied.

'Why did you write and ask Bywaters "Is it any use?"'

'I wanted him to feel that I was willing to help him; to keep him to me.'

This, indeed, was how it had been. It was a lover's emotion, but it was also writerly: there was an unparalleled enslaving thrill in giving these things reality through the letters.

Towards the end of his questioning, Frampton took Edith through the events of 3 October. She described being pushed aside by her husband's assailant, hitting her head against the wall and coming to her senses as the attack was taking place. 'He seemed to be scuffling with someone, and he fell up against me and said "Oo-er".' That absurd word again. Was she trying to make her account accord with her police statements, or had Percy really said this? She became very distressed, her face contracting beneath the soft black hat. 'The doctor was a long time in coming, an awful long time.'

'You mean it seemed a long time to you.'

She said: 'When the doctor came I asked him if he could get my husband home, and he said, "He is dead". I could not believe it, and I still entreated him to let me take him home.'

At that point, as Edith began to pour with tears, the judge interrupted smartly.

'I hope that gentleman is not sketching over there, is he?' There was a rather long pause while one of the police officers in court went to check. 'No, my Lord, he is writing shorthand.' 'Ah'.

It was almost as if he had not really been listening; although clearly he had, because his timing could hardly have been better.

'Did you watch your husband and Bywaters scuffling together?' asked the solicitor general, at the start of his cross-examination.

'I did not watch them; I saw them. When I say "scuffling" I mean that I saw my husband swaying, moving about.'

'Was it all over in a moment?'

'As far as I can recollect.'

'Then it would not be right to say that you watched them?'

'Oh, I did not. I mean that I saw the two men together, and it was over.'

Then Edith said that she had recognized Freddy Bywaters as he was running away, not beforehand: 'by his back'.

'Do you really suggest that?'

'I do.'

'Did you not know at the beginning, as soon as something happened, that it was Bywaters?'

'I had no idea.'

'All you can say is that when you recovered your senses and saw someone in front of you you knew it was Bywaters?'

'I did when he started to move away.'

'Had you any doubt when you were asked by the police about it that it was Bywaters who was there and was the man?'

'No, I had not.'

'May I take it that when you made the long statement [the first at Ilford police station] you left out Bywaters' name in order to shield him?'

'I did so.'

And so it went on, pushing and hounding her into corners that she need never even have entered; what difference did it *really* make if she had recognized Freddy by his face or his hat? It did not make her guilty or innocent. But it made her look like a liar, a counterfeit. She became upset easily; well, women like her could do that, and to those who did not believe in her these shows of vulnerability brought out a smiling desire to bruise and break. Then it got far, far worse. It was horrible. The public gallery, with its scented rows of 'society women', were certainly getting their money's worth if they had wanted to see one of their own poised above the trap: in this particular episode of the reality show, the trap was opening a little wider with every reply, and met every time with a corresponding outrush of air from the watching crowd. 'Men and women held their breath during a tragic answer,' wrote James Douglas, 'and then came the sudden rustle of amazement and dismay.' The solicitor general may not have been the world's greatest lawyer but he was an accomplished bully, deploying the repetition that is a favoured weapon of his kind. What Sir Henry Curtis-Bennett must have thought, listening to his client's attempts to reinterpret her own words in a way that would close the trap again, God only knows: he certainly knew that the game was up for the poor silly creature.

This was a typical exchange. The solicitor general read out the passage from the 4 July letter – 'why arent you sending me something... if I don't mind the risk why should you?' Then he said: 'you

were asking Bywaters to send something which he had said, according
to you, he was going to bring?'

'That is so.'

'What was it?'

'I have no idea.'

'Have you no idea?'

'Except what he told me.'

'What did he tell you?'

'He would bring me something.'

'Did he not say what the something was?'

'No, he did not mention anything.'

'What did he lead you to think it was?'

'That it was something for me to give my husband.'

'With a view to poisoning your husband?'

'That was not the idea, that was not what I expected.'

'Something to give your husband that would hurt him?'

'To make him ill.'

Then: 'He suggested giving your husband something to hurt him?'

'He had given me something.'

'Given you something to give your husband?'

'That is so.'

'Did the suggestion then come from Bywaters?'

'It did.'

'Did you welcome it when it came?'

'I read it.'

'What?'

'I read it and studied it.'

'Did you welcome the suggestion that something should be given to
your husband to make him ill?'

'I did not.'

'Did you object to it?'

'I was astonished about it.'

'Did you object to it?'

'I did, at the time.'

'And although you objected to it you urged Bywaters to send it more quickly than he intended?'

'I objected at the time. Afterwards I acquiesced.'

Mr Justice Shearman was not a fair-minded man, and his summing-up was generally vicious, but he had a point when he made the following remark:

> You have noticed, I daresay, in the course of the case that where the woman made statements they are mostly something excusing her and implicating the man, but in some of them, when the man is making statements, they are always exculpating the woman. It is said that is chivalry and that is why he is doing it.

What nobody ever considered was whether she might have been speaking the truth: that the idea of murder did perhaps come from her lover, rather than herself. After all, he was the one who was capable of putting a knife through layers of muscle. He was the wild one; for all her non-conformity she was far less daring. That might be thought to accord with ideas of secret poisoning. But when Edith wrote a sentence such as this – 'You tell me not to leave finger marks on the box – do you know I did not think of the box but I did think of the glass or cup or whatever was used' – it implies, indeed it positively states, that Freddy had written: Peidi, don't leave finger marks on the box.

The whole point was that they were inciting each other, feeding off each other. They were Thérèse Raquin and Laurent LeClaire, high on erotic yearning for a future they did not even really want. When Freddy tried to stop writing to Edith – between June and September – she stopped writing very much about poison. Her letters became straightforward pleas for his attention. If he was not playing the incitement game, nor did she. It had reached a peak in the spring of 1922, and it was only when Freddy turned the full force of his passion back to her that she began again to write in this manner: 'yes darlint be jealous, so much that you will do something desperate... do something tomorrow night will you?'

Words that he may, indeed, have misinterpreted. He asked Avis out on a date, as Edith claimed she had suggested. But he also did the other thing.

'Can you understand the feeling I have?' Thus began a letter written by Freddy Bywaters in the week after the trial, to an unknown recipient – described only as 'a friend' – and reproduced in 1930.

> Gradually, bit by bit, the trust and faith that I have put in somebody seemed to be dragged out and thrown in my face, and it hurts. When I have said that, I have said all. Put yourself in the position I occupy and just think. I tried to think after last Friday week, but really I could not muster one clear thought. Everything seemed topsy-turvy, but things seem clearer now. I suppose it is one of the hardest things in this world for a person to recognize and admit that he or she has misplaced their trust.

In the end he abandoned this attitude, this sense of betrayal by Edith's testimony. He realized, eventually, three things: that she had spoken as she did out of an irrepressible terror, that she had spoken something of the truth, and that she had been sitting there giving evidence because of what he himself had done.

★

Her last words on 8 December were in response to cross-examination:

'You were acting to Bywaters that you wished to destroy your husband's life?'

'I was.'

'One moment,' said the judge. 'I do not want to be mistaken. Did I take you down rightly as saying, "I wanted him to think I was willing to take my husband's life?"'

'I – I wanted him to think I was willing to do what he suggested.'

'That is to take your husband's life?'

'Not necessarily.'

The solicitor general resumed: 'To injure your husband at any rate?'

'To make him ill.'

'What was the object in making him ill?'

'I had not discussed the special object.'

'What was in your heart the object of making him ill? So that he should not recover from his heart attacks?'

'Yes, that was certainly the impression, yes.'

At that point the court was adjourned. Edith had been in the witness box for four hours. Her head was falling forwards, she looked near-dead already. Exhaustion, of course. Yet how could she have slept that night, with the wardresses' eye upon her and her mind going round and round that grotesque entanglement of words? Then the next day, Saturday – the half-day at work, a brandy and soda with Mr Carlton, a bit of life, dear sweet normal life – but no – back into that terrible wooden box, gripping the edges, trying to make herself heard so as not to annoy the judge, trying not to say, I can't go on any longer, just get on with it and do your worst... The solicitor general was off again with his sharp yet pointless questions, stabbing everywhere except to the heart, but causing sufficient damage all the same.

'Were you going to undeceive Bywaters?'

'I never studied it – I never thought about it.'

'Did you deceive Bywaters right up to his last visit to England?'

'I had never any intention whatever of poisoning my husband.'

'I will take that from you at the moment. What I was asking you was this: you told me that you deceived Bywaters because you wanted to keep his love?'

'That is so.'

It *was* so; but it had become inexplicable; nothing that she said made sense any longer, and the re-examination by Sir Henry Curtis-Bennett – stepping in to protect her like a kindly father – could only do so much, which was not very much at all.

Edith was still shaking in the dock as Avis gave brief evidence about two episodes: the one in which the opium was poured away, and the one that her sister had invented. Mrs Graydon testified that there had been a bump on her daughter's head when they were together at Ilford police station. That was it. The trial of the year, for which the queues had now begun to form during the afternoon of the previous day, was almost over.

Cecil Whiteley gave his closing speech. He made extremely important points about the police conduct of the case ('I ask you to put aside altogether the statements, having regard to the circumstances in which they were made') and about the solicitor general's right to the last word: 'It is a curious position.' His sense of decency was affronted, and in his moderate way he made that clear.

He then said:

You may have noticed that I asked no question of Mrs Thompson, although I was entitled to do so. Why did I not? For this simple reason: my instructions... were that neither by word nor deed, in conducting this case on behalf of this man, should a word be said by us... which would in any way hamper the defence of Mrs Thompson.

Mrs Thompson: the woman whose conduct in the witness box had been so undeserving of this sacrifice. How chivalric Freddy seemed by comparison, and how Percy Thompson would have been laughing in his grave. He, who had liked his killer at the start, had seen the other side of him; he would have told the court a thing or two.

Whiteley argued against any sort of criminal conspiracy – 'I ask you to distinguish in the letters fact from fiction' – and for a reduced charge of justifiable homicide or manslaughter. He suggested that there was nothing unusual about a sailor (in fact a clerk-cum-steward) carrying a knife, and disputed that Freddy had gone to Ilford with the intent to kill. That was credible enough; although he was obliged to take on Freddy's testimony, that he had acted as he did in the belief that Percy might have a gun. Yet absurd though this sounded it received a degree of backing from Edith's aunt Lily, who wrote to the government on the last day of 1922:

My husband & I were the aunt & uncle with whom Mr and Mrs
Thompson spent the evening at the theatre, & I assure you
Gentlemen, that from Mrs Thompson's manner, conversation &
also arrangements we all made to go to dances, dinners, & other
theatres, during the season, it was absolutely impossible for Mrs
Thompson to have entered into any arrangement with Bywaters
to commit the crime.

Moreover, knowing the late Mr Thompson very well, I say the
lad's story is true & undoubtedly he acted as he thought in self-
defence, Mr Thompson being just the kind of man who would
bluff having a weapon.

It was an interesting opinion from a sensible woman. Nevertheless one
is bound to say that the official comment upon it was equally clear-
headed:

the story of self defence was an <u>afterthought</u> and is quite incredible. If it had been true he must have said so at once: but even if
true it wd still have been necessary to explain away the carrying
of that dagger. He clearly took it there for the purpose of killing
Thompson.

Freddy's old lag companion at Brixton had said much the same thing:

he told me he didn't mean to stab him, see, he meant to talk to
him. I said, well, what was you tooled up for? You must have
meant something if you had a tool on you. He said, I only had
nail scissors. I said, you're a liar... I used to say, what did you want
to torture the poor bleeder for? You didn't have to torture him,
kill him. 'Cos he nearly died once, you know, with that broken
glass, that powdered glass.

Thus deeply – through the thick walls of Brixton jail – had belief
permeated in Edith's guilt. The Home Office, of course, had never

doubted it. With regard to the first part of Lily Laxton's letter, the comment was: 'Mrs Thompson is shewn by her own letters to be quite capable of talking of these arrangements for the future as a "blind" so that she wd be able to refer to them as proving that the attack upon her husband was a surprise to her.'

Her counsel, Sir Henry Curtis-Bennett, presented a very different view. In his closing speech he came into his own. He was at last suited to what he was doing, offering up an interpretation of his enigmatic client that came very close to the truth, presenting her through the artistic prism of his own intelligence. He sought to make the jury see her from that point of view, to accept his reading of the story. How far he carried them, before the solicitor general and the judge repossessed the case, is unknowable: his judgement was certainly ahead of its time, out of tune with the contemporary mood, although he tried to flatter his audience into believing themselves better than that.

> You have got to get into the atmosphere of this case. This is no ordinary case that you are trying… Am I right or wrong in saying that this woman is one of the most extraordinary personalities that you or I have ever met? Bywaters truly described her, did he not, as a woman who lived a sort of life I don't suppose any of you live in – an extraordinary life of make-believe… You have read her letters. Have you ever read, mixed up with criticisms of books, mixed up with all sorts of references with which I shall have to deal, more beautiful language of love? Such things have been very seldom put by pen upon paper. This is the woman you have to deal with, not some ordinary woman. She is one of those striking personalities met with from time to time who stand out for some reason or another.

He then offered his theory about the letters, the romantic's view as it might be called; but then Edith *was* romantic. 'It was an extraordinary way of showing, "I am prepared to go to any extreme to keep your love." '

The prosecution, dogged Roundheads at the battle, had tried to prove their own theory by having Percy Thompson exhumed. 'What did they find?' Spilsbury was his trump card, evidentially, and he played it brilliantly. 'I do complain,' he said, 'that the prosecution are not generous enough to say, "We will let you have the whole benefit of that. It is true that there is no sort of corroboration that you ever gave poison or glass to your husband."'

Unanswerable, one might think? But as the Saturday session came to its end, Mr Justice Shearman cut off Curtis-Bennett's speech in his prim, discourteous way, and said:

> Before the Court rises for the day I wish to offer you, members of the jury, this advice. Of course, you will not make up your minds until you have heard the whole case. The only other thing is, having regard to the surroundings for so many days, by all means look at the atmosphere and try to understand what the letters mean, but you should not forget that you are in a Court of justice trying a vulgar and common crime. You are not listening to a play from the stalls of a theatre. When you are thinking it over, you should think it over in that way.

Thank you and goodnight.

★

Part of the appeal against sentence was that there had been misdirection by the judge. This was dismissed: the learned judge had said what he said and it was all correctly said.

> The case was clearly put before the jury. There was simple evidence, partly direct evidence, partly evidence from which inference might properly be drawn; and upon that evidence, in a case which from beginning to end exhibits no redeeming feature, the members of the jury have convicted the appellant[s].

When this immovable weight of preconceived belief was taken into account, Mr Justice Shearman's summing-up was indeed perfectly fair. Travers Humphreys later said that it was, but then he became the judge whose words to the jury about Alma Rattenbury – 'you cannot have any feeling except disgust for her' – helped push her to suicide. Shearman was impartial, if one accepted that the balance of the trial was already askew. 'Having regard to the way in which the case was conducted and to the very definite trend of the judge's summing up, it became increasingly likely that the jury would find both the prisoners guilty of murder.' So wrote Filson Young. 'So much prejudice had been created, the jury had so evidently been allowed to take for granted that Mrs Thompson was the real originator and inspirer of this crime...' It *was* taken for granted. It was a given. Young's edition of the Thompson-Bywaters trial was reviewed on its publication in December 1923, and it was clear that his more broad-minded views were still officially unacceptable. This, from *The Times*, could have been written by Mr Justice Shearman himself:

> The rather flamboyant introduction, with its attempt to throw a romantic glamour over the murderous futilities of the woman, and the quite unnecessary textual reproduction of her letters, tend to pander to the same class of morbidly emotional people who hung around the Old Bailey and the gaol gates to stir their little souls with second hand terror.
>
> When all is said and done, nourishing hate in the heart in an evil process, and unfaithfulness in marriage is a grossly antisocial act... The woman sought to live in a dream world of freedom from all moral rules, where she dallied with the thought of murder, and sunk herself in passion. Reality broke rudely in, and the end of that matter was the rope.

In such a context, it was quite true to say that the solicitor general was 'studiously moderate' in his closing speech, which ended thus:

The case for the Crown is that there was an agreement between these two persons to get rid of Mr Thompson, or that, if there was not actual agreement in terms, there was an instigation by Mrs Thompson to get rid of him, on which Bywaters acted so as to kill him.

That did, indeed, sound quite reasonable – it was so vague and large a proposition that it could hardly do otherwise – and it was the starting-point from which Mr Justice Shearman immediately jumped.

'It is inevitable,' he began,

that you should have been surrounded by a different atmosphere from that which prevails in the ordinary humdrum of the Courts, and you must throw that aside, try to escape from that, because this charge really is – I am not saying whether it is proved – a common or ordinary charge of a wife and an adulterer murdering the husband. That is the charge; I am not saying for a moment it is proved...

Now, I have only one other observation about Sir Henry Curtis-Bennett; he said, and, indeed, I am afraid it has become now a precedent in these Courts, that he 'thanked God that you to decide and he had not'. If that remark is intended to frighten you, I hope it will not. We are dealing with law and justice here and I do not like invocations to the Deity...

There is only one other observation I am going to make, and it has nothing whatever to do with counsel. You are told that this is a case of a "great love". I am only using it as a phrase. Take one of the letters as a test... "He has the right by law to all that you have the right to by nature and love." Gentlemen, if that nonsense means anything it means that the love of a husband for his wife is something improper because marriage is acknowledged by the law, and that the love of a woman for her lover, illicit and clandestine, is something great and noble. I am certain that you, like any other right-minded persons, will be filled with disgust at such a notion.

How did this man sleep at night, one wonders: the answer, undoubtedly, would have been very well indeed. The sleep of the just. He was, at that particular point in social history, the voice of the nation.

He began with Bywaters: the less interesting bit. Having picked apart the notion that the letters referred to constant demands for a divorce – which of course they did not – he then addressed the manner in which the attack was committed, which was of course brutish. He dismissed the suggestion that the police had pulled a stunt in order to break Edith down: 'there seems to be a conflict of evidence about that; it does not seem to me to make any difference.' He recalled Bywaters' description to the police of where to find the murder weapon. 'The importance of it is that he is admitting that his was the knife, and not the woman's, that did it.' This was putting ideas into people's heads with a vengeance: there had never been the slightest implication Edith had played any physical part in the crime, but that form of words – 'not the woman's' – could only have the effect of suggesting that she *had* held a knife.

With regard to a verdict of justifiable homicide, the judge dispensed quickly with the idea that Bywaters had acted in any kind of self-defence: 'if you believe that Thompson made an unprovoked attack upon him… you will acquit him altogether. If you think it is a fabrication from beginning to end you will reject it.' He then dealt with manslaughter – the question of whether Percy might have been killed in the course of the confrontation, after provoking Freddy to extreme violence – but this too was dismissed: 'it is inconceivable that it would be any provocation for a man to say, "I will not allow you to run away with my wife." Provocation means blows or violence. But then, in the middle of this story, he says, "he hit me on the chest and then he put his hand behind [sic]: he provoked me" …was there a blow at all? Is there any injury to this man or to his clothing?'

Before a short adjournment, the judge concluded thus:

> even if you really think him a young and honest person, and that he lost his head altogether, if you think that he was inflamed by sexual impulses and that the real truth of the matter is that he

went out with the knife, put it in his pocket in order to kill the man… if you are satisfied of it, then, however unpleasant your duty is, you must give effect to it.

Which was as good a way of any as beginning the summing-up against Edith Thompson.

Listening to every word, praying with every new sentence for a measure of understanding, or a removal of pressure from the accelerator, she may, at the start, have felt a tiny flare of hope. 'She is just as much guilty of murder if she sets loose an assassin as if she fires an arrow… But I do not think that is quite the case you have got to consider here.' There was, he said, an absence of evidence that 'makes these letters of so much importance'. Then he was off.

Bywaters' letters were an irrelevance – they 'only breathe this insensate silly affection' – but Edith's letters were the whole of the matter.

It is said by the prosecution that from beginning to end of these letters she is seriously considering and inciting the man to assist her to poison her husband, and if she did that, and if you find that within a week or two after he came back the poisoning is considered no longer possible, he has no longer studied or has not studied bichloride of mercury, but has read "Bella Donna" without seeing how "Bella Donna" can be of any use to him, they would naturally turn to some other means of effecting their object, and it is said to you they naturally would, when you find them meeting day after day, parting at half-past five, meeting the husband at six, and she telling him where they were going, and he immediately, as soon as he gets an opportunity, if you believe he waited for them coming back, and knew they were there – gentlemen, you may say here are circumstances following the long-studied incitement for him to help her to poison.

Outrageous beyond belief: the leaps across logic from letters to meetings to particular meeting to murder, from a written phrase about poison to an actual stabbing, with nothing to link them together except surmise and supposition – nothing *on earth* to say what these two discussed at that wretched 'tea room', a reference anyway to a conversation that took place *days* before the murder – but this old monster got away with it. 'It is on that you are asked to draw the conclusion that she was a party to the act of Bywaters in killing her husband at that time and place. You will not draw it unless you are satisfied, and if you are satisfied you will draw it; and there is the whole matter.'

Along the way the judge chucked more opprobrium upon the letters – 'full of the outpourings of a silly but, at the same time, wicked affection': he was hell-bent upon ensuring that the jury did not succumb to Curtis-Bennett's appeal to them as mature, worldly, compassionate people. Indeed his speech was something of an insult to Curtis-Bennett, as well as to the defendants. His own life must have been remarkably upright. Lady Shearman doubtless had nothing to complain of. He was a former athlete, the author of a chapter in the 1887 *Badminton Library of Sports and Pastimes*, one of those healthy-mind-in-healthy-body types; but the narrowness of that mind made him a liability to any but the most clean-living of defendants, who by definition were few and far between.

Extracts were read from the letters, all the most damaging (and particularly so when removed from any context), for instance 'I used the light bulb three times, but the third time he found a piece.' That might have been a moment to mention the evidence of Spilsbury and Webster, but neither was referred to in the summing-up. Not once. Instead the judge said:

Of course, you know her explanation is that this was merely – I don't know what word to call it – swank – to show what a heroic person she was; that she was prepared to do all sorts of things which she was not in fact doing, and his explanation was always to exculpate her, and to say she was a melodramatic being. You will give what weight you think to it.

Then the argument turned to the novel *Bella Donna*, one of whose themes was the poisoning of a husband. Edith had said to Freddy that she would like him to read the book, followed by *The Fruitful Vine*. 'No doubt,' said the judge, 'the letter about *The Fruitful Vine* was something similar…' Some guesswork there from the learned judge, although not as much as in his analysis of Edith's last letter, with its fateful sentence 'Don't forget what we talked in the Tea Room.' Using the passive construction that served him so well, he offered this: 'It is said that this is what they talked about: "We have got many things to consider; shall we run away if we can get the money, or shall we try poison? We will talk it over."' It was almost as if he had been there, moonlighting as a waiter at Fullers.

Lastly, the judge considered the circumstances of the actual killing; in particular the evidence of John Webber, who heard the wrenching scream of 'don't, oh, don't'. This testimony seemed very favourable to Edith, one might say wholly consistent with shock and innocence. Yet it was regarded with scepticism not just by Shearman – who noted its divergence from her claim to have been stunned or dazed – but by the Home Office mandarins. Essentially, they did not believe Webber. One might say that they did not want to do so. It does seem strange that nobody else heard this scream, but if it came earlier than the given time of 12.30 – as indeed it must have done – then the other main witnesses may have been too far away (the drunken Mr Row, who was nearer, did claim to have heard 'an excited female'). Another issue was the distance of Mr Webber's own house from the murder scene, although on a calm Ilford night sound would travel easily into an open window. However:

'You know he is some way off,' said the judge; 'I am not saying it is true; it is for you to say whether it is accurate, or whether it is imaginary, or whether he has made a mistake; but there is the evidence.'

Sir Ernley Blackwell wrote similarly:

Undue importance was, I think, attached to the evidence of a witness, Webber, who lives at No. 59 De Vere Gdns on the corner of the turning <u>next but one</u> from the place where the attack was made… I do not think, therefore, that any importance at all can be attached to the expression 'Oh, don't; oh, don't!' which he is supposed to have heard, or that they were in fact uttered by Mrs Thompson and heard by him at the moment that Bywaters was stabbing Thompson. Fortunately the mistake was altogether in favour of the accused Mrs Thompson. I think it is quite clear that Mrs Thompson knew perfectly well at the moment that Bywaters was attacking and murdering her husband. Her subsequent conduct… and her expressions, 'If they would only let me go to him I could make him well', and 'oh, I did love him, mum, and he did love me', were simply play-acting.

Mr Justice Shearman made the same points, although with the careful disclaimers – 'you will weigh this'; 'it is entirely for you' – that enabled him to escape censure.

'It is always relevant,' he said,

to see what is done before and after the deed. It is said by the prosecution that it was arranged he should run away, and she should go to the doctor. It is said that their letters are suggesting they were arranging how to avoid suspicion when it was done, and the letters bear that out. Now were they; do they bear that out?

No interpretation of the letters could possibly 'bear out' this assertion, which is a fabrication to rank with any attributed to either Edith or Freddy; and how those two kept silent during this long, finicky, frankly rather wicked speech is a very great mystery.

Inevitably, as the police had done, the judge made much play with the fact that Edith had concealed knowledge of the assailant's identity until she was confronted by him at Ilford station.

As soon as she sees him at the window [sic] she said, "Oh, God! oh, God! what can I do? Why did he do it? I did not want him to do it." Now there, again, look at these statements... Again it is noticeable that she is throwing the blame on him, "Why did he do it?" and she is excusing herself.

He moved on to Mrs Lester's evidence, her recollection of Edith's words: 'They have taken him away from me. If they would allow me to go to him I could make him better' – 'quite incomprehensible, you know... Do you think that she did not know he was dead or what had happened?'

Before the end of the speech he managed one last lie. 'Her story is that she knew nothing about it; it was a surprise; in fact, she was pushed aside, and she immediately fainted.' Edith did not say that she fainted. She said that she hit her head and was dazed. Nevertheless the use of such language was clever; because it did not merely impugn her behaviour at the time of the murder. It suggested that here, now, in the courtroom – where she dropped her head and cried, where she staggered helplessly as she rose from her chair – she might conceivably be acting still; it suggested that any sympathy, aroused by her terror and her debilitation, should be weighed as carefully, as coldly, with the same righteous scruples as the evidence.

★

Of the judge's summing-up, James Douglas wrote, as if in awe: 'His logic marched step by step, and as the hours went by one felt the last lingering doubts fading away.'

The jury was sent out at 3.30 on the afternoon of Monday 12 December. They debated their verdict for something more than two hours. Then there was a stir in the courtroom. As the jurors returned, their demeanour allowed for no possible doubt as to the decision that they had reached.

There was a long delay before the defendants emerged at the top of the staircase leading from the cells. Freddy Bywaters came first, striding steadily. Edith Thompson was half-walking, half-carried by the wardresses. She clutched at the dock. When the verdicts were given

Freddy called out: 'The jury is wrong,' and turned to look at Edith for the last time. 'That woman is not guilty.' The square of black flopping on the judge's head was awry, and throughout the long pronouncement of the sentences of death the women continued to hold Edith up by her arms, like a puppet.

As she was taken down there was an inhuman wail, like that of an animal caught by prey in the night. For a moment nobody knew where it came from. Like everybody else Edith heard it; she was making the sound herself.

When her family went to see her in the cells, before she was removed to Holloway, she took hold of Mr Graydon's coat with both hands and said: 'Take me home, dad.'

IV

'"I'm in a terrible do about my bracelet of lucky charms – no value to anybody else – really – too too sick-making. Just when I managed to get a bit of hangman's rope, Mrs Thompson too, did I tell you?"'

From *Love in a Cold Climate* by Nancy Mitford

AMID HER SCREAMS Edith Thompson was heard to cry 'I am not guilty, oh God I am not guilty': but what is guilt, in this case? She was guilty, merely by the fact of her existence. Otherwise Frederick Bywaters would not have murdered Percy Thompson. Her strength of personality, her erotic hold over the man; these were indisputable. She was guilty because she had written things, and she should have known that words have consequences. On the night of the attack Freddy was inflamed as never before, and the fact is that the letters *did* play a part in this, they were the build-up, the paper stacked high on a smouldering fire. They were not literally responsible for what he did, but without them it would not have happened.

They taunted him, in their soft goading way. 'Supposing Fate has it written down that you & I are never to be happy, you'll fight against it, but you'll have to give in…' This was a challenge to a young man of his kind: it said 'what are you going to do about this? *Can* you do anything about it?' Meanwhile she herself, with her Scheherazade tales of poison and glass, seemed to mock the very idea of action.

He had been trying to pull away from Edith for the past fifteen weeks. Wanting to be 'pals only'. Dallying with his girl in Australia.

Sensing danger, in the quality of the relationship, which almost without her volition – because she was the kind of woman who generated such emotions – had acquired a tentacular aspect: it was more than merely an affair, it was something that wrapped around the whole of their lives. So he sought to disentangle himself, but she would not let him go; and it is perhaps in her sudden success – he returned to her without resistance, after the first short meeting on his final leave – that the reason for the murder lies.

She brought him back, her pet wolf, with her atavistic call. That didn't mean he was really tamed; the desire to be free was still there; it was a push-pull between them, as it had always been, and by September 1922 it had reached the endgame. She was married and it was clear that she always would be. If he too wanted to marry, then it would not be to her. They could go on and on with their letters, their plans for a future together, their reunions, but nothing would change. She had brought him back at an immense cost to her pride and with a remarkable expense of effort – had bent her will to tugging away the dam that he had tried to build around his feelings – now these rushed out again towards her, quick and torrential, and there was actually no point in any of it. All she had done by reclaiming him was prove that she could do it. He had trailed obediently back to her and her response was to go out with her husband: on Saturday, Sunday, Monday, Tuesday. All very well to say that she didn't want to do so, to shake her head at him across the tea table and say that it was awful and horrid and that Percy's touch, which she clearly accepted, was repellent and dreadful. All very well to have written about poisons and ground glass and to have sent little cuttings: to keep clinging on, like the stem of a flower tied to a stake, with the lovely black narcissus head wafting around his face. She had got him back, she had directed a tide of banked feeling in her direction, and when she wrote 'darlint you are jealous of *him* – but I want you to be,' he took it at face value because it was what he already felt. And jealousy is the most lethal emotion of the lot.

Then she wrote: 'Darlint – do something tomorrow night will you?' If he did indeed misinterpret those words, he may have done so deliberately, as a way of bringing to a close the game that they had played for so long, and that had become suddenly unbearably irksome.

He had the knife with him; it is hard to believe that he carried it around at all times. In Wanstead Park with Edith? To the Graydons for a game of whist? So that means intent ('what was you tooled up for'), although he may have been deliberating all day whether or not he would actually use it. It is possible that some words of Avis Graydon's pushed him finally over the edge – troublemaking, trying to get him back as her sister had done, but in a small petty way rather than with that great undertow of sensual force – and Avis perhaps suspected herself of this for the rest of her life. It is also near certain, although the prosecution sought to ridicule the idea, that he did have some sort of struggle with Percy Thompson. Why, otherwise, was the assault so prolonged? Why did Freddy overtake the Thompsons on the road – which he must have done, given that the minor wounds at the front were inflicted before those to the back – when he could have jumped his victim and put the knife clean in his neck? Cecil Whiteley may have felt that such a line of questioning threatened to impugn Edith – what on earth was she doing, while such a struggle took place – but she was asked that anyway. And indeed anything that helped Freddy also helped her; which was of course part of the reason why the court did not want to help Freddy.

'Her husband's death in service is not sufficient grounds on wh. to respite her son for such a cold blooded and deliberate murder' was the comment upon a letter from Lilian Bywaters, pleading for Freddy's life. Yet it was not really proved that the murder was cold-blooded and deliberate. It was sort of taken for granted. Freddy never had much chance – like Edith, he would have been far better served if they had been tried separately – their physical proximity in the dock had so much imagistic power; but the police had not followed proper procedure in taking his statements, and it was the repeated changes to his story that made his evidence seem so fatuous (Whiteley asked the jury to ignore the statements, which they would not have done).

Remarkably, in his letter to the home secretary, Freddy wrote that he had been advised, at the inquest, to seek a reduced charge. 'I mentioned this to my solicitor who said it would be best to say nothing until the trial at the Old Bailey': in fact nothing was ever said.

He and Percy had had a confrontation before, at Kensington Gardens. This was a re-enactment: a culmination. Percy was angry too, resentfully and grimly so. The sudden appearance that night of his wife's boyfriend would have enraged him. He was a man of 'violent temper', according to his sister-in-law, of 'peculiar character' according to his aunt by marriage; but even if he were not those things, why should he not have fought back? He was not frightened of Freddy. The dialogue between them, as retold, changed somewhat in detail but remained characteristic. Had the defence asked more about Percy – his assault on his wife, her fear of being 'knocked about', the drinking allegation, even Miss Tucknott – then it would not have seemed as though Freddy had knifed a latter-day saint. The suggestion that Percy might have had a gun sounded idiotic, but it was an attempt to make it clear that the man was not a pushover, that he too was capable of aggression. The scuffle began face-to-face, then – as Percy tried to run – there came the insane firecracker explosion that led to the double plunge of the knife in the back.

In the strangest way, it was as though the person being attacked was Edith: it was she that Freddy was bringing down, because she was the magical creator of a story that she did not really mean, but that had acquired its own life nonetheless.

So she was guilty of something, but nothing that was the business of the law.

*

Or did her guilt take another form? Was she guilty, in truth, in a way that went beyond the scattergun assertions of the trial?

At the time, almost everybody thought that she had been rightly convicted. Not all of these people were carried along on a wave of prurient puritan hysteria, which contemplated the execution of a beautiful woman with a kind of dark excitation. Margery Fry, the prison visitor who fought for the abolition of the death penalty, completely accepted the verdict and was baffled by Edith's own refusal to do so. James Douglas, who was deeply affected by events at the Old Bailey, nevertheless admitted that were he a jury member he would 'find both guilty and both equally guilty'. *The Times* commented succinctly upon a trial that 'for no very clear reason, has absorbed the public attention,' stating that there were 'no circumstances in the case to evoke the slightest public sympathy. The crime was premeditated and long contemplated... simple and sordid.' The *Daily Mirror*, playing to the gallery, applauded Mr Justice Shearman's summing-up: 'Very wisely the Judge set himself to dispel the irrelevancies of sentiment.'

The *Daily Mail*, striking a safe middle course, wrote:

> The jury were a long time coming to their decision, but it was the proper decision; and they are to be congratulated upon having done their duty in a case which afforded features of a pseudo-romantic type and an appeal to neurotic sympathy...
>
> Undoubtedly the woman dragged Bywaters down. He refused to have her cross-examined or to do anything that might have endangered her chances of getting off. All this might have influenced the jury, but they kept their heads, arguing very properly that Bywaters was a grown man and that he had killed the unfortunate husband. There was an atmosphere about the case of a kind which the judge declared 'we must get rid of', and the jury have taken the sound view that murder is murder and that society must be protected.

The *Daily Chronicle*, whose editorial on 12 December was the best of the lot, nevertheless concluded:

> It is a notable verdict, for a weak jury might have found an easy escape from it. It means that in the jury's opinion the crime was

concocted between the lovers in the teashop on the afternoon before the murder. There was no direct evidence on that point, and in the nature of things there rarely can be direct evidence in such cases. Nearly always there is some gap in the chain of proof, and in this case the gap was undoubtedly very wide. The jury must have hesitated before they decided that it was their duty to jump across it. The jury can hardly have been much tempted to believe the story of Bywaters that he killed the husband in self-defence. But it might, had it been indolent or sentimental, have decided to find that there was provocation, and so have reduced the crime to man-slaughter. The letters which were read had only this bearing on the charge, that they showed that the guilty pair had plotted the poisoning of the husband, and so established a probability that, if the plans for getting rid of the husband were changed and physical violence was preferred to poisoning, the woman not only knew all about it, but plotted beforehand to make the attempt possible. It would, we say, have been easy to shirk responsibility of finding this to be the fact. It is to the credit of the jury that it refused to shirk...

The *Daily News* wrote simply: 'The verdict is a just one, and if society is not to dissolve into atoms, the only one.'

All this was published on the day after the trial, when verdicts are regarded as synonymous with truth. Fifty years later, however, the radio programme about the case – sympathetic, intelligent and balanced – still seemed to come down, in the end, on the side of Rex rather than Edith. By then it was possible to separate the fact of Edith's execution, generally regarded as an outrage, from the facts that might indicate her guilt. And in this respect the programme did offer some new information.

It began with a man who had, he claimed, overheard a conversation between Edith and Freddy on a bus whose route led to Ilford.

I couldn't hear what they were saying in the general run, because they were speaking quietly. And then suddenly she says to him,

And you who profess to love me so much, you won't do such a simple, such a little thing for me. So he says, I'm not that kind of chap.

So then she sounded very annoyed, and she said, Well, if you're not that kind of a chap, I haven't got much interest for you, and if you want to hold my interest, you'd better change.

And how did he take that, asked the interviewer.

'Well, very forlorn, very sullenly. Just sort of – you know, hangdog face, never answered. And it was quite a few minutes before I heard any mumble of conversation again.'

This, he said, happened not long before reports of the murder began to appear in the newspapers, 'I said to one of the boys in the factory, I know these two people.' But he did not go to the police. A friend advised him that 'it's best you don't say anything because you don't know enough – let things ride.' It was certainly true that this man – just nineteen at the time – did not know enough, and one begs leave to think that he may have been romancing, although he had been sufficiently struck by Edith's appearance to be sure of what he said. In any event the radio programme thought the interview worthy of inclusion.

But the more noteworthy contribution came from the pathologist Professor Donald Teare. His interest had been aroused by the guarded performance of Bernard Spilsbury at the Old Bailey.

It had been clear, somehow, that all was not quite right with the evidence from the man who should have been Edith's star witness. Professor Teare located the source of doubt, finding it in the last sentence of Spilsbury's post-mortem report: 'The fatty degeneration of the heart muscle, liver and kidney may have resulted from disease, but no disease was found in the body which would account for these changes.' The wording was extremely precise. It was designed – suggested Teare – to imply that nothing was proved but something was possible.

A multitude of poisons, including chloroform or phosphorus, can cause such symptoms as were identified in Percy's body: 'And presumably,' said Teare, 'Spilsbury had this in mind, when he went to the

trouble of excluding natural disease as a cause of fatty degeneration.'
It was, he continued, 'quite possible that something was administered
to Thompson of a poisonous nature.' Against this was the chemical
analysis of the organs, with its negative findings. 'Even so there are
certain poisons, particularly I suppose the poisonous hydrocarbons,
which certainly fifty years ago might be difficult to identify after a
month's interment.'

There was the question of how such poisons, strong in taste and
smell, would have been administered. 'You might in alcohol. Certainly
not in tea or coffee.' But it was said by Avis Graydon that Percy was a
heavy drinker. 'He might well have put himself at risk if he was drinking heavily. There's no doubt about that.'

Within the second indictment against Edith, the lesser charges
on which Curtis-Bennett had implied that she should be tried, there
were two specific counts: that of 'administering poison with intent
to murder', and of 'administering a destructive thing with intent to
murder'. Apparently Travers Humphreys had asked for them to be
added. 'There must,' said Teare, 'have been some basis for including
these, even though they weren't proceeded with. And it is quite possible that these observations of Spilsbury at least started this off.'

More to the point, throughout the four weeks between the death
sentence being pronounced and carried out – a period in which the
Home Office was asked repeatedly, in the most persuasive manner, to
consider a reprieve for Edith Thompson – it is possible that Spilsbury
made representations to suggest that this should not be done. 'I haven't
any doubt that he would. He was a very conscientious man, in constant
touch with the judiciary – people who really mattered – and his words
would have had weight.'

Hydrocarbon poisoning, which today is most likely to result
from sniffing glue or ingesting cleaning products, does not directly
connect with Edith: she might perhaps have used some household
substance. Yet she never mentioned any such thing in her regularly
chanted litany of poisons (darlint what do you think about turps…?).
Nor is there any evidence that Percy's excess drinking, if indeed this

happened regularly, took place in the home. The picture of Edith hovering above a whisky bottle with a can is not merely incongruous; it seems to bear no connection with her own image of poisoning her husband, as given in her letters.

And yet. However strong one's belief that sending a person to their death on such grounds, on an interpretation of their words, is the action of a monstrous dystopia rather than of England in the 1920s, there are a couple of passages that do give one pause.

This, for instance, from 22 February:

> Darlingest boy, the thing I am going to do for both of us will it ever – at all, make any difference between us, darlint, do you understand what I mean   Will you ever think any the less of me – not now, I know darlint – but later on – perhaps some years hence – do you think you will feel any different – because of this thing that I shall do…
>
> Sorry that Ive got to remain inactive for more than another whole month, and I had thought by that time I should be seeing you for just as long and every time you wanted me   However, for that glorious state of existence I suppose we must wait for another three or four months   Darlint, I am glad you succeeded Oh so glad I cant explain, when your note came I didn't know how to work at all – all I kept thinking of was of your success – and my ultimate success I hope.
>
> I suppose it isnt possible for you to send it to me – not at all possible, I do so chafe at wasting time darlint…

From 1 April:

> Don't keep this piece.
>
> About the Marconigram, do you mean one saying Yes or No, because I shant send it darlint I'm not going to try any more until you come back
>
> I made up my mind about this last Thursday.

…he puts great stress on the fact of the tea tasting bitter "as if something had been put in it" he says. Now I think whatever else I try it in again will still taste bitter he will recognize it and be more suspicious still and if the quantity is still not successful it will injure any chance I have of trying when you come home

Do you understand?

I thought a lot about what you said of Dan.

Darlint, don't trust him. I don't mean don't *tell* him anything because I know you never would. What I mean is don't let him be suspicious of you regarding that – because if we were successful in the action – darlint circumstances may afterwards make us want many friends or helpers and we must have no enemies – or even people that know a little too much. Remember the saying, "A little knowledge is a dangerous thing".

And from 1 May:

You said it was enough for an elephant. Perhaps it was. But you don't allow for the taste making only a small quantity to be taken. It sounded like a reproach was it meant to be?

Darlint I tried hard – you won't know how hard – because you weren't there to see and I can't tell you all – but I did – I do want you to believe I did for both of us…

You tell me not to leave finger marks on the box – do you know I did not think of the box but I did think of the glass or cup or whatever was used. I wish I wish oh I wish I could do something.

It is easy to say oh, there is nothing here; anybody who thinks otherwise is unable to distinguish fact from overwrought fantasy. Probably that is right. Nevertheless these are extreme remarks, even allowing for Edith's unusual mind. The fear that Freddy might think of her differently, worse, after 'this thing that I shall do' – which cannot be another abortion – however much it might sound that way, the dates make it impossible: *that* has an air of reality. The phrase 'don't keep this piece', which at the trial she insisted referred to a scrap of paper pinned to the letter: that too seems real. Alert. Forward-thinking. Still more so the exhortation not to trust 'Dan', which implies an event capable of corroboration. As for the 'elephant' and the 'finger marks': these might be dismissed as invention, were it not for an incident recorded within the Home Office files, closed under the 100-year rule and viewed in the writing of this account.

A confidential file dated 23 December 1922 was headed: 'Interview with Mr Whiteley.'

Beneath this were the minutes, handwritten by a civil servant of some seniority.

> Bywaters' counsel Mr Whiteley would have liked to see Sir E. Blackwell. He was anxious to say something & not in writing. Finally he told me.

> Bywaters says that between 17–20th March, under pressure from Mrs Thompson, he gave her a large quantity of a white powder, calling it cocaine. She gave it to Thompson. This is the elephant dose. It was quinine.

> B. says he <u>never</u> procured <u>poison</u> for her (But he did stick a knife three times through her husband's neck).

> This helps B. very little & damns Mrs T.

> Mr W. also said B. is a good chap & that his father was killed in the war.

This, then, was Freddy Bywaters' revenge for Edith's betrayal in the dock. It was the reaction of a man who was, indeed, capable of deliberate action. He had offered this information to his counsel and told him to do something with it. He was twenty years old, he did not want to die, and the pride that he took in his manly demeanour had briefly cracked. It was understandable. Possibly his mother encouraged him to do it, and that too would have been perfectly reasonable behaviour.

He had danced and dodged about this 'quinine' business while in the witness box, giving nonsensical answers about humouring Edith in her desire to commit suicide; obviously he had been lying, and what he now said was probably true. Of course it could only be proved by his own letters to Edith – the missing part of the story – and they still could not prove what he actually gave to her. It may have been cocaine, obtained for him by the mysterious Dan. Whatever it was, Edith may have merely pretended to use it. The fact that in her 1 May letter she also wrote about putting a light bulb in Percy's food implies that she was, indeed, playacting: a bowl of porridge that contained oats, cocaine, a dash of turpentine and a garnish of ground glass? How mad it sounds.

Nevertheless people did do such things. Madeleine Smith and Adelaide Bartlett, attractive charming women of the Victorian era, had not seemed likely to poison a lover or a husband, and they both got away with doing so, but it is almost beyond doubt that they did exactly that. So why not Edith Thompson? Certainly there was, in the spring of 1922, a heightened quality to the relationship with Freddy, a kind of compulsive quickening, as if the dreams of murder had acquired an *element* of the factual – like people who fantasize about attending an orgy and go so far as to make a date: whether or not they actually keep that date is another leap altogether. There is no knowing whether Edith made her version of that leap, and dropped something – just once, perhaps – into her husband's food or drink. All that is known is that, if she did, it didn't kill him.

He was ill, however, in early June: 'Darlint I had to laugh because *I knew* it couldn't be a heart attack.' Does that sound suspicious? Perhaps. But as ever, she could have been simply saying it.

None of it amounted to anything that should have convicted her of wilful murder. There was no proof. There was, indeed, no nexus. Nor is the theory of Spilsbury's suspicions entirely convincing. First, what is suggested seems to relate to activities independent of anything in the letters. Second, F. Tennyson Jesse – who knew a great deal about the case – claimed to have been told by Spilsbury that he did not believe Edith ever administered poison or glass to her husband. Third, why was this not brought up properly at the trial, rather than left hanging in the air as something obviously unsaid? Fourth, was Percy's alcohol intake not a possible factor in the condition of his heart and liver? Last – and most importantly – there is no mention of this matter in the confidential Home Office files. Admittedly some of these were destroyed, although almost certainly none that related to Edith's possible guilt. If a representation from Spilsbury had helped to convince the authorities that the woman should hang then there should surely, somewhere, have been some record of this.

Yet the authorities were so adamant! Well: there was another circumstance, again brought up only obliquely, during the questioning of the police surgeon Percy Drought. The solicitor general was asking about the injuries to the body.

'Were the superficial cuts on the chin as far as you could judge the result of blows at the same time, or could they have been caused otherwise – were they fresh?'

Drought replied: 'I beg your pardon?' and the solicitor general had another go.

'What do you think as to the time at which the wound on the chin was struck, that is what I want to know?'

Again Drought did not quite catch the import of the question, and answered: 'I think they were just done by the point.'

'At the same time as the other wounds were struck?' *That* was the point.

'The same time as the other front wounds – not immediately the same time.'

'On the same occasion?'

'On the same occasion, yes.'

The solicitor general was asking, rather daintily, if there had been any possibility that the minor injuries – which were of a different nature from the deep stabs to the back – were inflicted not by Freddy but by Edith. She had been searched by the police to see if she was carrying a weapon. Clearly she had not wielded the big dagger, but a smaller knife (or the nail scissors that Freddy told his fellow prisoner he had been carrying) could have made the cuts to the face. In 1925, an article was published in *Thomson's Weekly News* by a private investigator, which began by asking why the authorities had been so determined to execute this woman and offered the familiar answer, 'that the authorities were fully of opinion that if Mrs Thompson did not actually commit the murder, hers was the brain that planned the affair.' That, beyond a doubt. But then:

> the authorities believed that not only was she the instigator of the murder, but that she took an active part in the crime… My own inquiries suggested to my mind that Mrs Thompson was responsible for two of the wounds in the body which she inflicted with an instrument which the police were never able to discover.

This, again, was without proof or substance. And it is wildly unlikely, although it was related in some measure to the doubts about John Webber, who claimed to have heard the cry of 'Don't!' How – asked the judge – was that claim consistent with Edith having been dazed throughout the attack? If she was not in fact dazed, then what was she doing while the attack was going on? Watching Bywaters in glee? *Helping* Bywaters?

The question remains unanswered; although this is perhaps the best explanation. When Freddy first overtook the Thompsons he did push Edith against the wall, rendering her not exactly dazed, but in a state of shock – as one would be – although not undue terror; because she did not anticipate murder. She saw the struggle between the two men, which had of course happened before. And she screamed when she saw, out of the near-total darkness, that Freddy had raised a knife.

One thing about the knife: it is odd to think of Edith and Freddy having lunch together, embracing in the shadow of Aldersgate Station, and her remaining in ignorance that this weapon was stashed in the inside pocket of his overcoat. Not that this is impossible, but it is an odd thought. Yet when all is said and done, her behaviour was overwhelmingly that of an innocent person. The prosecution said that she could have known Freddy was going to murder Percy, but still been shocked when it happened; that is true. They said that she acted her distress and hysteria; which could also be true. Any foreknowledge, however, would have caused her to destroy his last two love letters and his photograph. And why not have planned the murder for the following day, when Freddy could have sailed away within the next few hours? Why, above all, insist upon testifying at the trial? She was not guiltless. But the idea that what she had done required expiation on a scaffold was an insult to justice.

So the situation, after 11 December, was this. A woman was condemned on evidence that would not, as they say, hang a dog. That had been the desired end to the story. Now – immediately – there was uncertainty, disbelief of the kind that Edith herself would have recognized, that something so fervidly imagined might actually be going to happen. The authorities were unnaturally high on rectitude; keen to show women that equality meant equality and that if they wanted the vote they must also put up with the rope; trapped by the fact that if one defendant were reprieved then so must the other be, and how could *two people* get away with a crime so threatening to the nation's moral welfare? They were in a spin, frankly, and that made them all the more determined to stand firm. Which meant that these helpful little ideas – that the woman may have had some nail scissors that she somehow got rid of, that Spilsbury may have known something that he could not quite say – yes yes yes, oh there was so much more against the prisoner Thompson, oh good Lord yes: it was all rather consoling to that bunch of men, the Home Office Angelos, who at the end of 1922 had got themselves into one hell of a situation.

★

There was also a new home secretary, Sir William Bridgeman. By a matter of some seventy-five days Edith and Freddy missed the former incumbent, the compassionate Liberal Sir Edward Shortt. He had recently reprieved a female co-defendant who had, according to the judge, acted under the influence of her husband. The pair had murdered and robbed the woman's ex-boyfriend. The judge was Mr Justice Shearman.

Bridgeman wrote to his mother the day after the Thompson-Bywaters trial: 'I was surprised at Mrs Thompson being convicted' – not very astute of him –

and wish she had not been as I shall be flooded with petitions to let her off, I expect. There is a rumour that she is pregnant and if that is true she can't be hung and I may be saved from the anxiety of taking a decision about her – but if she gets off being hung, people will begin to say Bywaters being less guilty than she, ought not to suffer a more severe penalty.

Oh dear: in at the deep end.

This rumour as to Edith being pregnant was powerful, so much so that it still has some currency today. There is absolutely nothing in the Home Office files to support it; and indeed logic has always suggested that it made no sense. Clearly Bridgeman would have jumped at the chance to respite her on those grounds, as had happened before. The Governor at Holloway, Dr Morton, would have been acutely aware of the possibility, on the lookout for symptoms and, again, would have seen Edith's pregnancy as the happiest way out for everybody. So too would the female doctor, Dora Walker, who later had Edith in her care. As for Edith herself: well. She was ignorant about her body, but not to that extent. She had been pregnant in the past, a year ago now. She knew that to be so again would save her life. The idea that she would not have hoped for it – that she did not pray with all her being that she had not tried to avoid conception from the last sexual encounter with Freddy, on Saturday 30 September, with its promise of future ecstasy – is not to be credited.

She gained a lot of weight in the eight weeks between her condemnation and execution, which has partly contributed to the pregnancy rumour. Again, however, Dr Morton would have been alive to what that might mean. In his handwritten report on Edith for the Prison Commissioners, detailing her behaviour between 11 December and 9 January, he wrote: 'She has taken her food well consistently as is shown by the fact that her weight on reception was 118 lb and her weight on January 8th was 133 lbs' (the report of her execution the following day in fact recorded 130¼ pounds). There were probably two reasons for this: she had scarcely ate or slept during the trial, which lowered her weight to beneath its usual point, from which it recovered slightly; and she was drugged up to the eyeballs, full of substances that slowed and thickened her body.

She arrived back at Holloway after the trial and was 'received into the convicted portion' at about 6.15pm.

'On reception,' wrote Dr Morton,

she was depressed and obviously very tired after the strain of the trial. I visited her the following morning about 10am she was bright, cheerful and in reply to my question, how did you sleep, said, "I have had the best night I have had for a month in fact I slept almost all night", her statement was confirmed by the night report. At this visit I discussed the matter of her diet in which she took a lively interest and when offered cigarettes expressed a strong desire to be allowed to smoke which of course was granted.

I have had reports kept by each pair of officers who have been in charge of the prisoner. I may say that almost every report starts with either the word cheerful or bright; occasionally the report reads, was somewhat depressed but soon became bright again after she had had some tea or a cigarette.

On the 11th, when Freddy Bywaters was returned to Pentonville, he asked the Governor if he might send a message to Edith: 'B.B. and P.G.', meaning 'Be Brave' and 'Pray God'. The Governor put this request to

Mr Wall at the prison commissioners, saying 'I told him I would do what I could to pass the message. It was a last request & to him may be of deep sentiment. These 2 prisoners did not communicate in any way with each other throughout the trial.'

The reply, as noted in the Home Office file, was:

'This cannot be permitted. It is hoped that you did not lead him to think that it would be. Wall 12/12'

To which the Pentonville Governor obediently responded:

'Noted. I told him I would do what I could to pass the message. I did not say it would be. I had had in my mind it would be a matter for you to decide.'

On 12 December Edith was visited by her solicitor Mr Stern – who afterwards stated his intention to appeal against the conviction – and by her mother and Avis. At Pentonville Freddy was visited by his mother and sister Florence. He reportedly said: 'I never imagined she would have turned against me as she did in the witness box.' His feelings were conflicted between guilt and rage. He seemed still to be obsessed with Edith, whereas she had now left him behind. Her love had always been essentially solipsistic; perhaps that is the more typical female way, careful with itself despite all its proclamations to the contrary.

The following day, Mr J. Barrington Matthews announced that Freddy would also appeal. He attended the court hearing; Edith did not. To sit and wait for the decision in Holloway, to hear the lawyers debating her life or death in between lunch at the Garrick and dinner at Brooks's: both were unbearable although one of the two would have to be borne. But while the appeal was pending there was hope, and reality was not yet entirely real.

'When I informed her two days after her sentence that the execution would take place on Jan 3rd she was quite calm and collected,' wrote Dr Morton. That day, 13 December, he sent this to the Prison Commissioners:

Gentlemen,

I beg to report that the above-named Convict has been received into this Prison under sentence of death, and to request that I may be furnished with the List of Candidates reported to be competent for the Office of Executioner... I beg also to apply for a copy of the Memorandum of Instructions for carrying out the details of an Execution; also for a copy of the Table of Drops.

As an appeal prisoner Edith wore a grey serge dress and blue checked apron, with a white cap around her hair.

On Saturday 16 December her father and brother Newenham visited; she sent birthday wishes for the following day in a letter to her mother. She was still in control of herself, because of the appeal.

'Her spirits were always at the highest during a visit,' wrote Dr Morton, 'when she would laugh & discuss various frivolous subjects.'

On Monday, a week on from the final day of the trial, she wrote to her old school friend Bessie Akam: a letter utterly unlike the ones to Freddy, but no less remarkable.

Yes, it was awful last Monday. I can't explain what it felt like. I suppose no one knows unless their position is the same. It would be so much easier to bear if I knew or even felt that I deserved that verdict, but I'm hoping for such a lot on Thursday [the appeal]. Everybody seems so hopeful for me. I suppose it is catching.

The time here, on the whole, seems not so long as in remand – so many things are different. I can't tell you because it is against the rules, but it is a fact, and I sleep better here than I did there, really I have very good nights' rest.

There is plenty of time and opportunity to think all day long, so that by the time the night comes my brain is quite worn out and rests quite naturally.

This is something I am really pleased about, because I never – no, I think, not once – had a really good night's sleep. I have asked and obtained permission for you to visit me. Now, as you are going away on Friday, I wonder if you will have time, but if you don't come I shall quite understand, and hope that you will be having a real good rest over the holidays.

I remembered it was mother's birthday yesterday and wrote to her. I'm glad you went down to see them. I expect they want cheering a little.

You know, dear, it's really about them I worry far more than about myself. It must be painful for them – the publicity alone must be more than they can cope with. You see I am shut away here and know nothing of all that...'

Of course the Graydons were hounded and surrounded every time they left the little house at Shakespeare Crescent. They spoke to the press, as did Mrs Bywaters: partly out of naivety, partly because the money was welcome, mainly in the hope that it would rally public opinion to their cause. In contrast to this there was a certain peace within the prison hospital, where newspapers did not penetrate. Days were a loose chain made up of small events: smoking, reading, knitting, doing crochet-work, spending an hour outside alone in the yard. It was the first proper rest of Edith's life. The only problem was the appeal, which she wanted to come quickly and in another way never to come. In the same way, was it good that the days went faster now, or worse?

She sat in Holloway under the perpetual light, in the perpetual company of the wardresses, while the judges comfortably debated her fate.

The grounds of her appeal – as with Freddy's – were that the verdict was against the weight of evidence, that the defendants should have been tried separately and that the letters should not have been admitted. Then came the damning instances of misdirection to the jury by the 'learned Judge':

a) by directing them that there was evidence of a continuing conspiracy between the Appellant and F.E.F. Bywaters to murder Percy Thompson up to the 3rd day of Oct; b) by omitting to call their attention to phrases in the said letters relied upon by the Defence and limiting his direction to the phrases in the said letters relied upon by the Prosecution; c) by failing to direct them at all upon the evidence of Dr Spilsbury and Mr Webster as to the results of the post-mortem exam; d) by failing to direct them that the evidence of Dr Spilsbury and Mr Webster supported the evidence of the Appellant in that she swore that she had never administered poison or other dangerous thing to the said Percy Thompson; e) by directing them that they were entitled upon the evidence to consider that the said F.E.F. Bywaters came to the scene of the murder at the direction of and by arranging it with the Appellant; f) as to the incidents following the attack upon the said Percy Thompson; g) by failing to direct them at all upon the evidence of witnesses called for the Defence; h) by failing to direct them that there was no evidence that the Appellant was a party to or had knowledge of the attack upon Percy Thompson on the night of Oct 3rd 1922; i) by failing to direct the Jury on matters raised by the Defence.

Which pretty much covered it, one might say; but would three judges be willing to admit that one of their kind had got *quite* so much wrong? Furthermore, as Travers Humphreys wrote in his memoirs, 'In practice the Court of Appeal regards the finding by a Jury as sacrosanct.'

The appeals were heard on 21 December by the Lord Chief Justice, Mr Justice Darling and Mr Justice Salter.

Darling was known to be something of a joker. He described Edith with a nudge-wink levity, an ageing clubman's lasciviousness. When Curtis-Bennett read out the passage in which she expressed the fear that Bywaters might think less of her in the future, he said: 'Yes. Didn't she mean to say to him that one day they might be sitting by the fire and he might be thinking to himself, "That woman poisoned her husband and now I am in his place. What about me?"' It got a jolly good laugh from the public, present yet again *en masse*, although perhaps not from Mr Graydon and Mrs Bywaters, who also attended.

By the afternoon it was all over. Edith's father and Freddy's mother made the journey back to their homes, not to give the news – their families would have heard the cries of the paper boys – but to continue with the process of moving through lives that had become unrecogniz-able, seeking comfort in the warmth of a teacup, looking at each other dumbly as the clocks ticked. 'That this should happen to people like us,' as Mr Graydon said, with the meekness of acceptance, the terrible dignity of the well-behaved. 'The punishment of years of confinement is bourne by the offenders, but the punishment of hanging, is bourne by the parents & relations,' Lily Laxton reminded the government. 'Crimes of this sort must necessarily bring sorrow & disgrace upon parents and families,' was the handwritten comment upon her letter.

At about 5pm the Governor entered Edith's cell and told her that the appeal had been dismissed. He then told her that the date of her execution was fixed for 9 January, nineteen days away: 'she replied I understood you to say the date was Jan 3rd, and when I explained that that date was cancelled owing to the appeal, she thanked me.' Nineteen days was a long time when one had nothing to do. It was a yawning gap, containing Christmas – also Edith's birthday – and meals and cigarettes and books. And all those visits, ordeals in their way, with the bright brave eyes looking at her and the ridiculous conversations that had lost any meaning, except that they showed an immensity of love – and then it would be the last visit. The last time of looking at people, of turning a page, of putting on stockings, of looking at oneself: not yet possible to imagine, although the realization was getting closer.

She wrote to her parents. In her new, half-dead way she was doing what she had done before: writing to make sense of her life. She was still able to make use of her time to do this most important thing.

Dearest Mother and Dad –
Today seems the end of everything. I can't think – I just seem up against a black, thick wall, through which neither my eyes nor my thoughts can penetrate.
It's not within my powers of realisation that this sentence must stand for something which I have not done, something I did not know of, either previously or at the time. I know you both know this. I know you both have known and believed it all along.

However, I suppose it is only another landmark in my life – there have been so many when I look back, but somehow they are not landmarks until I look back upon the journey, and then I know that certain events were landmarks.

I've tried to unravel this tangle of my existence, this existence that we all call life. It is only at these times that we do think about it.

It has been an existence, that's all, just a 'passing through'; meeting trials, and shocks and surprises with a smiling face and an aching heart, and eventually being submerged and facing Death, that thing that there is no escaping – no hope of defeating.

You both must be feeling as bad and perhaps worse than I do today, and I do so hope that this will not make things harder to bear, but I really felt that I should like to talk to you both for just a little while, after I was told the result.

Even now I cannot realise all it means; but, dearest mother and dad, you both must bear up – just think that I am trying to do the same, and I am sure that thought will help you.

EDITH.

Dr Morton sent the letter to the Prison Commissioners.

In view of your instructions as to letters of prisoners under sentence of death I beg to submit the attached for your perusal. Although this woman has written a number of letters since she was condemned to death I may say they have all been couched in a more or less frivolous style.

This is the first letter she has written in which she shows that she has begun to realize what her sentence means.

Also I beg to draw your attention to para. commencing "However I suppose" and ending "I know that certain events were landmarks."

Reply: 'The letter may be posted.'

★

After the mockery of Christmas, lunch eaten with a fork and spoon, Edith wrote again to Bessie Akam.

> I wanted to write to you yesterday and yet I couldn't. I could do nothing but sit and think. Who was it said, "Some days we sits and thinks, and some we simply sits"? Well, yesterday was a "sitting and thinking day".
>
> I got your little letter on Saturday. Yes, the result of the appeal was a great shock – I had such hopes of it – not only hopes for mercy, but hopes for justice; but I realise how very difficult it is to fight prejudice.
>
> If you have facts to fight, and you fail, you seem more reconciled, but when it's only prejudice – oh, it's awful.
>
> You talk about not having to suffer the extreme penalty. Do you know that I don't dread that at all. I feel that it would be far easier than banishment – wrongful banishment for life. I feel no apprehension of what might be ahead after this life.
>
> Yesterday I was twenty-nine; it's not really very old, I suppose, and yet it seems so to me.
>
> I suppose when you're happy age doesn't count; it doesn't seem to matter; it's when you're not that the years seem so frightening.
>
> Yesterday I was thinking about everything that has ever happened, it seems to help in all sorts of ways when I do this. I realise what a mysterious thing life is. We all imagine we can mould our own lives – we seldom can, they are moulded for us – just by the laws and rules and conventions of this world, and if we break any of them, we only have to look forward to a formidable and unattractive wilderness.
>
> I've often thought how good it would be to talk, to pour out everything, it might have pained as well, but it would be pain that comes with sudden relief of intolerable hurt.
>
> However, I'm going to forget all that now. I'm going to hope

– because everybody tells me so. I'm going to live in those enor-
mous moments when the whole of life seems bound up in the
absolute necessity to win.

Extraordinary, again. It seems a great pity that she had not 'talked' this
way to Bessie Akam when her life was her own; she had only talked to
Freddy Bywaters, with whom everything was seen through the shim-
mering prism of sex: it had been magnificent, but it had not been wise.
It had been a young person's game. Now Edith, rushed prematurely
through years, still writing in order to discover herself, was finding
wisdom. She was able to make something of her new perceptions,
which were slowed by confinement, reshaped by suffering. The last
sentence of her letter is very beautiful, a statement of splendid rich
irony, made by somebody who knew that autonomy had been removed
– that winning was not within her control – but that there was a kind
of freedom, nonetheless, in her ability to express such a thought.

It was a letter similar in spirit to the one she had written to her aunt
Edith three days previously:

Auntie dear, I have learnt the lesson that it is not wise to meet and
try to overcome all your trials alone – when the end comes, as it
has to me, nobody understands.

If only I had been able to forfeit my pride, that pride that
resents pity, and talk to someone. I can see now how different
things might have been but it's too late now to rake over ashes in
the hope of finding some live coal.

She was in her cell, very near the end although she had still not quite
realized it, and inside her head were these lovely things; while a few
miles south in Whitehall free men tidied her away into files and did
everything in their power to justify killing her. One feels it now, so
strongly, that all they had to do was throw up their hands and say: all
right, let's just reprieve the bloody woman. And the boy – he'll have
to get off as well. What the hell, we've done it before. They could have

argued: if he was under her spell then he isn't really a cold-blooded
murderer, and her spell isn't really something we ought to hang her for.
Instead they turned their faces against all that was human and flawed
and forgiving, all kindness to the parents in their little gas-lit parlours
full of absence, and observed the due process of the law.

On 28 December Sir Ernley Blackwell, doing his inimitable stuff,
produced his resumé of the case for the consideration of a reprieve.
It was a masterclass in immutability, the definitive production of one
who was only obeying orders.

'The Appeals were dismissed in the most scathing terms,' he
wrote. 'The Lord Chief Justice said it was a squalid and rather inde-
cent case of lust and adultery in which the husband was murdered
in a cowardly fashion, partly because he was in the way and partly, it
would seem, because the money he possessed was desired.' This last
shows that Blackwell, like the 'convicts', was not above a bit of casual
lying; there was nothing whatever to suggest any financial motive.
The life insurance policy of £250 was really not something that Edith
needed. Kensington Gardens, which had been put into the hands
of the receivers and valued at £800, was joint-owned and many of
the contents belonged to her. She had earned more than Percy and
that too had been held against her ('perhaps because there were no
children, or for other reasons, she was carrying on her employment',
was an apparently nonchalant aside in the solicitor general's opening
speech).

But the reference to Percy's money helped Blackwell make his most
important point. It changed a *crime passionel* into a long-planned
strategy, which more than anything justified the death penalty.

> The Lord Chief Justice described the letters in effect as showing
> that continuously over a long period, beginning months before
> and <u>culminating at the time immediately antecedent to the com-
> mission of the crime,</u> Mrs Thompson was with every sort of
> ingenuity, by precept and by example, actual or simulated (it does
> not in the least matter which) endeavouring to incite Bywaters to

the commission of the crime. There was a continual entreaty and
hope that that which they both desired would be accomplished.

That 'does not in the last matter which' was a brilliant catch-all phrase:
if it meant anything, it meant that Sir Henry Curtis-Bennett's entire
defence had been a waste of time because, even if Edith had only
been pretending, she was still guilty. She should have known what her
reader might infer from her writing. What *she* might have inferred
from Freddy's writing was therefore also of significance, but never
mind that, on we go to the events of 3 October.

'Undoubtedly Bywaters knew their plans, and the Jury were certainly entitled to infer that at tea time, when they were together in the
teashop, they arranged for the attack.'

So now it was possible to hang somebody on what the jury inferred
from a conversation that did not even take place, because on 3 October
the couple did not stay in the tea room, they left it immediately. The
evidence of the Fullers waitresses would have told Blackwell exactly
that (because obviously he did not choose to believe Freddy).

> As regards the attack, it is impossible to say exactly what hap-
> pened because we have only the prisoners' obviously incomplete
> and untrue accounts of it. All the wounds in the neck appear to
> have been inflicted from behind and Bywaters says that he saw
> the pair in front of him and overtook them.

There were superficial wounds to the front of the body, which strongly
suggests a fight that escalated and became murderous at the end: the
fatal wound was the last inflicted.

> ... as regards Mrs Thompson's behaviour during the actual attack,
> we have only her own account, which cannot be accepted, namely
> that Bywaters seized hold of her and threw her against the wall
> and thereafter she was practically senseless and did not know
> what happened.

She did not say that she was 'senseless'. As to being knocked against the wall – rather than seized and thrown – this would happen quite naturally if she was walking on the inside of the pavement (which a woman would have been): her mother testified to the bruise on Edith's head, although the police matron denied its existence.

'I believe that a totally false view has been put forward by these two prisoners of the domestic relations that outwardly, at any rate subsisted between Mr and Mrs Thompson. Their relatives on both sides profess to know nothing of any serious disagreement between the pair.' Avis was never asked; Mrs Lester, the person most likely to know, testified as to constant arguments. However:

> I was shown a photograph yesterday by Inspector Hall. It was taken at Boscombe this summer and showed Mr Thompson lying on his back on the grass with his head in his wife's lap, with both her arms round his neck clasping his wrists and both smiling out of the picture. I am told that about this very date Mrs Thompson was writing to Bywaters asking him whether he had studied bi-chloride of mercury and was it any use!

This was a postscript to a letter of 4 July that was, in the main, about Edith's fear of losing Freddy; it was in fact her last reference to poison until she sent the 'Chicken Broth death' cutting in mid-September. The notion that she never let up, that she solicited continually, was untrue.

> On the very night of the murder Mrs Thompson had been to the theatre with her husband on perfectly friendly terms, although I think it must be taken for certain that she must have known, either that her husband would be attacked that night, or that at any rate in the near future one or other of the means which she had discussed with Bywaters would be taken to get rid of him.

Masterly, yet again.

The whole of the Press, so far as I am aware, with the exception of one or two papers of less importance, has been in favour of the law taking its course in both cases... I have never known a case in my experience where we have had so many letters from people strongly protesting against a reprieve being granted in either case.

That was very far from being the whole story, as Blackwell knew only too well, having been obliged to dismiss as a stunt a *Daily Sketch* petition for Freddy's reprieve bearing some 900,000 signatures. Nevertheless a large number of letters in favour of the law taking its course were, indeed, published in the newspapers, including the one written by T. S. Eliot.

The memorandum did go on to address the possible grounds for reprieve; firstly for Freddy Bywaters.

As regards the plea of youth: Bywaters was 20 years and 3 months old when he committed this murder. For many years the rule has been that for a prisoner over 18 years of age youth alone is not sufficient to entitle him to reprieve... The murder in this case was a planned and deliberate crime carried out in circumstances of the greatest treachery after months of consideration and discussion of means which might be adopted for getting rid of Percy Thompson.

As for the second plea, the familiar one, that Freddy had been under the influence of a manipulative older woman – 'Bywaters explained at the Trial that he regarded Mrs Thompson's discussion of poisons and ways and means of getting rid of her husband as so much melodramatic nonsense.' So, no incitement then.

Then came the more vexed question of Edith, soon to become the first woman to be hanged for fifteen years, a period of time in which reprieves had been given to women who had killed their children, to a woman who set her lover alight with paraffin, to a woman who lured

her ex-lover to a remote place where he could be robbed and murdered… It still, yes, confounds all reason, it still offends in a way that
can never be comfortably forgotten, that she, Edith Thompson, should
have been the one whose neck the law chose to break.

> The only possible argument that could be urged for the reprieve
> of this woman may be summed up in the expression "We don't
> hang women nowadays". This is an entirely fallacious idea… If
> the capital sentence in the case of women is to be abolished, this
> must be by legislation and not by the exercise of the Prerogative
> of mercy.

The following day, 29 December, Sir John Anderson wrote upon this
document, with its appended list of condemned, reprieved and executed female prisoners:

'I entirely agree with Sir E Blackwell's memo within.'

And yet: no decision was announced as to the commutation of the
sentences. On 30 December the newspapers reported that the home
secretary was debating the matter with his cabinet. What Edith had
described, without the first clue of what she was talking about, as 'the
end of all': it had not quite come.

★

That same day, 30 December, Mrs Graydon wrote to Queen Mary, who
forwarded the letter to the Home Office.

'Most Gracious Sovereign,' she began:

> as a mother, you well realize the torment through which I am
> passing knowing that my daughter is the victim of the most com-
> promising circumstances but yet being absolutely innocent of the
> awful charge upon which she has been convicted, and I now
> appeal to you as Mother of the Nation to be pleased to show your
> gracious mercy towards one who, up to the time of the terrible

catastrophe has always been a most dutiful and loving daughter and who has always been the first to help others in the hour of their distress...

The same day Avis wrote to Andrew Bonar Law, asking the real questions that nobody cared to answer:

How can they pass sentence of <u>Death</u> on her?

Mr Spilsbury gave evidence that there was no trace of poison in the deceased's body, how then can it be said, she poisoned him.

Why was all the evidence of defence put on one side, & only the black side – the foolish letters of an overwrought, unhappy woman – placed before the Jury...

Why was it so emphatically said "She incited Bywaters"? it is obvious her letters were answers to questions, where are Bywaters' letters to prove his statement that Mrs Thompson is innocent? Why has no benifit of the doubt been given in this case to the accused.

Can it be my sister is insane! Is this question having the prison doctor's attention.

If you had seen my sister at any time, there could not be any doubt in your mind that the verdict is wrong.

I beg you to shew mercy on her, for her parents sake, you are a father therefore understand their feelings. We are helpless & know she is <u>not Guilty.</u>

The sudden remark about Edith's sanity is very odd: whether it was an attempt to raise the issue of diminished responsibility, or whether her sister's behaviour really did strike Avis in that way – so profound was her shock about the correspondence with Freddy – is impossible to know. The civil servant who commented on Avis's letter did not address the issue, nor indeed any of the other, trickier points that she had made.

That same day, the 30th, Lilian Bywaters wrote to King George V asking him to spare her son. On the 31st Lily Laxton sent her letter to the government, addressed to 'The Gentlemen of the Cabinet'.

What all four of these women wrote was impossible to ignore, and therefore ignored.

The bells rang in 1923.

On 1 January Edith was visited by her mother and sister, accompanied by a girl named Ida Burton with whom she had attended Kensington Avenue School, and who had previously sent a letter of introduction from an Ilford priest named Palmer. This incident later formed part of another report by Dr Morton for the Prison Commissioners, in which he found himself wriggling uncomfortably like a fish on a hook. 'During the visit,' he wrote, 'Miss Burton said "I wish you would let Canon Palmer visit you just as a friend, he won't talk religion, he is very sweet I am sure you would like him." On Jan 2nd Thompson applied to me for permission to be visited by Canon Palmer'; a request to which Morton acceded.

Also that day, in Pentonville, Freddy Bywaters wrote a letter on small sheets of blue lined paper.

Edie – I want to ask you not to give up hope. I know & you know & some others know also, that you should not be in the position that you find yourself. I'm still hoping that the powers that be, will exercise some common sense & displace their suppositions with facts. I know this must be a terrible strain on you, but Peidi Mia, don't lose heart – B.B. I am keeping quite well & I've heard that you are a lot better. I'm glad.

I have seen Florrie today & she told me that she had written to you explaining the misunderstanding. I should dearly like to pull the snub nose of a certain person – do you know to whom I refer? [this reference is unclear]

I've read two books by Baroness Von Sutton 'Pam' & 'What became of Pam' – one of Hichens 'An Imaginative Man' & one of Rolf Wyllards 'There was a Crooked Man' since I've been here. If you are able, will you write? I want to say a lot, but cannot, you

understand. I can only hope & trust that some time in the future
we will be able to talk to one another.

 Goodbye Peidi Mia – B.B. –

Always

Freddy.

The letter was not delivered. Although Edith and Florence Bywaters
corresponded – the breach between them healed by circumstance -
and exchanged a couple of messages to and from Freddy, it does not
appear that Edith wrote to her former lover during their time under
sentence of death.

★

Yet on Wednesday 3 January her mother brought her the framed
sketch of the *Morea*, which she had intended to hang in her office at
Carlton & Prior, and it seemed to give her pleasure.

 Again she wrote to Bessie Akam: 'I know I ought to have written to
you yesterday – but I didn't feel I wanted to – that's my only excuse.' She
thanked her friend for sending a book, saying that she read one a day and
was now reading Dickens; she reminded Bessie of how they had done
this at school.

> Does it seem three whole months since I first came here to you?
> Some days it seems like three weeks and others like three days.
> Time is always our enemy, don't you think? It either goes too fast
> or too slow always...
> Today it is lovely; the sun is shining and everywhere looks
> bright and cheerful. I begin to feel quite cheerful myself – isn't the
> sun wonderful, it always raises your spirits. But I don't like it as
> cold as this. I'll be ever so glad when the summer comes.

She had hope still, she wrote. Not without reason. For instance on
the day that *The Times* reported the dismissal of Edith's and Freddy's

appeals it noted in a short article, printed adjacently but probably not with any particular intent, that four death sentences had been commuted. And it was on 3 January that Freddy Bywaters, the man who had brought Edith to destruction – who had tried to shield her, then to implicate her – now made his decision: he would try to save her, and incidentally himself, by writing to the home secretary.

> In the first instance I wish to speak to you of Edith Thompson. The case for the prosecution was based entirely upon a series of extracts from letters written by her to me… I wish to say that she never suggested to me that I should kill her husband. She is not only unjustly condemned, but it is wicked & vile to suggest that she incited me to murder. God knows that I speak the truth when I say that there was no plan or agreement between Mrs Thompson & I to murder her husband. I can do no more sir, than ask you to believe me – the truth – & then it is for you to proclaim to the whole world that Edith Thompson is 'Not Guilty' & so remove the stain that is on her name.

Honourable now for good and all, Freddy had addressed the woman's case before his own. Then he wrote of himself: of the failure to caution him at Ilford police station, and a little of the disgraceful trial, thus:

> Mr Justice Shearman suggested to the Jury, that my knife was in my pocket for one reason only – namely that I had agreed with Mrs Thompson to murder her husband on October 3rd. … My knife was in my pocket then & it had been there since 23rd September. I was in the habit of carrying either a knife or a revolver.

It still sounded unlikely. It *could* have been that way. This, on the other hand, was fact:

> At the inquest, Dr Drought in his evidence stated that the first blow had been delivered from the front. That is quite true, you

have my statement made in the witness box at the Old Bailey. If I could speak to you I could explain any point you might wish, more fully, but my space here is limited...

The Home Office minutes stated:

It has been conclusively shown that the construction which he sought to put upon the letters is an impossible one... As regards the facts relevant to the murder charge I do not think that either he or Mrs Thompson has told the truth within any single particular. They have lied consistently...

And so on.

That same day, 3 January, this handwritten addendum appeared on the file containing the resumé of the case: 'I have seen Mr Justice Shearman, and, after hearing what he has to say, find myself in complete agreement with Sir Ernley Blackwell's memorandum and recommendations. Bridgeman.'

Edith did not know that the home secretary had denied the reprieves when she wrote to her father on Thursday 4th, to say how much she looked forward to seeing him the next day, meaning Saturday. Mr Graydon had a job; his visits to Holloway were restricted to weekends. Nobody would be offering compassionate leave to the father of the girl who wrote the sexy letters. As shame and agony engulfed their hearts, the humdrum clerks and milliners caught their trains and did their work.

The letter to him was censored. The authorities did not like something in it. So these, Edith's last known written words, are not quite her own: that final freedom had been dismantled.

Dearest Dad –

Somehow today I feel I'd like to write to you. It seems such a long time since I saw you – and yet it isn't. It's only the same distance from Saturday as it was last week. I wonder why some days seem so long ago and others quite near?

Of course nothing different happens here, every day is the same. The best part of each day (and of course the quickest) is the half an hour's visit I have. It never seems to be longer than ten minutes.

Do you remember the book I told you I wanted? They tell me it is out of print, and I couldn't help thinking that even in little things my luck is entirely absent…

I've been reading Dickens's "Our Mutual Friend", but the print is so frightfully small and indistinct that I can't see anything if the light has to be on, and it is after dark always that I feel I would like to read the most.

Yesterday mother showed me the sketch of the Morea. It looks nice in its frame, don't you think? I was quite pleased about it.

I'm getting quite used to things here now. It's really astonishing what you can do without when it's 'Hobson's choice'.

You'll be coming to see me on Saturday, won't you? On that Saturday of last year, I wonder if you remember what we did?

I do, quite well. We were all at Highbury, and the huge dinner Harold [her youngest brother] ate I can see now if I close my eyes. And then there were the rattles and trumpets and whistles in the Tube and Avis getting out without her ticket and we throwing it out of the carriage on to the platform when it was too late. Oh, dear! What a lot can happen in a year!

I hope Saturday comes quickly, it's been such a terrible long week. Au revoir until then.

EDITH.

★

The following day, 5 January, the refusal of the reprieves was announced. A collection of near-identical typed letters were sent to the prisons, the police, and to Mr Justice Shearman: 'I have the honour, by direction of the Secretary of State, to inform your Lordship that he has given his careful consideration to all the circumstances in the case of Frederick Edward Francis Bywaters and Edith Jessie Thompson, convicted before you at the Central Criminal Court of murder and sentenced to death; and that he has failed to discover any sufficient ground to justify him in advising His Majesty to interfere with the due course of the law.' Letters were not, however, sent to the families, who learned the decision through the newspapers.

This was the day that Edith began to fall apart.

In his report, Dr Morton wrote:

Thompson continued to be quite calm and seemed in no way perturbed until the evening of Friday 5th. About 3 p.m. I read the letter I had received from the Under Secretary of State informing her that the Secretary of State could find no grounds etc etc. This had very little effect on her at the time but about an hour after she became very violent and had to be held in bed. I was sent for and when I saw her she was in a hysterical state, crying "I never did it". I gave her ¼ grain morphia hypodermically and within 10 minutes she was quite quiet and went to sleep. During Friday night she slept badly not more than an hour and complained of a bad headache in the morning. About 12 noon on Saturday she became brighter took 2 pieces of bread & butter, cheese, tomato & tea & smoked 2 cigarettes. She remained in bed & did not go to exercise.

Mr Graydon, braced hard against this new knowledge, striving to keep his daughter from the sight of his own desire to cease consciousness, visited that day along with his wife, daughter and son Newenham. They had issued a statement to the press, saying that their hopes had been 'buoyed up by the long delay of the authorities in making the announcement with regard to a repeal.' The home secretary's decision was 'inhuman'. It was the closest that the family came, before Edith died, to shaking off their innate deference towards officialdom.

Also on the 6th, a letter was written by Freddy's sister Florence.

Dear Mrs Thompson,

I received your letter this morning and read it out to Mick when I saw him. Oh God what <u>can</u> I say to you now? Words are such poor things. Mother is nearly mad today. I wonder if she will pull through?

But I daresay you are anxious to hear what Mick has to say, First of all re: the monkey [the bronze ornament that Edith had kept on her desk]. He says for you to keep that, but that he would like Frankie (my little brother) to have the watch. So you could perhaps have it sent on. He told me to tell you he understands the message and it is reciprocated. Also he sent his love and says to try and bear up. He has written to you but the letter was first sent to the Home Office. So I doubt whether you will get it now. Of course Mick poor dear didn't know when I saw him. Even then he didn't seem much concerned with himself – his one thought was for you. Oh what a great heart he must have. But then you must of course know that as well as I.

I'd be so glad if you would drop me a few lines – so that I could let him have any message – will you. I can't say any more now – my heart is too full. With our kind thoughts and wishes

Sincerely yours. Florrie Bywaters.

The note on the Home Office file read: 'This letter will not be passed.'

This strange, formal closeness between Edith and Florence – Florence who had seen her mother's raging anxiety about Edith, and moreover seen it justified – was a generous relationship. Edith had been a *femme aux hommes* all her life, she had not always been good to her own sister, yet her friendships with women, few though they were, had an absolute integrity. This one cut through the layers of blame and guilt that connected those entities, Thompson and Bywaters, it cut to the heart of things, and to refuse delivery of Florence's letter was simple sadism: no other description is possible.

For Lilian Bywaters, suffering the torments of the damned, sparing herself nothing in memories of her boy – his birth, his childhood, his wildness that had always worried her, and yet how attractive it had made him! – wishing only that it could be her who would die on Tuesday: for her, no reconciliation was possible with the woman who had wasted his life and traduced him in court. While the Graydons no doubt tormented themselves about Edith – should they have seen more of what was going on? Should they have said something? – Mrs Bywaters was in a situation that was slightly worse: she *had* seen, she *did* say something, and she had absolutely failed. And now her fine, handsome, clear-eyed son was filled once more with guilt at having brought Edith Thompson to this end, and was asking his mother to forgive, to think kindly of the creature, to write to her expressing belief in her innocence, and for his sake she would do it, as the last great gift she could offer.

Edith would not receive Mrs Bywaters' letter. She was a convict, she was Thompson, she was nothing except the regularly weighed parcel labelled for removal. There was a kind of logic in the determination to remove all succour (except the official appearance of the chaplain or the prison visitor), because she was no longer anything that merited it. Perhaps if she had behaved differently, showed some sign that she understood why she was there? The warders at Pentonville loved Freddy Bywaters, they discussed the football results and had endless games with the boy, the lad, the decent young fellow laid low by a rotten tart. But how was Edith to sit and play draughts with her pinched and anxious wardresses? That was not a woman's way. Not this woman's, certainly. Instead she tossed in her narrow bed and screamed the unanswerable question: 'Why am I here? *Why* am I *here*?' She moved restlessly and without control, flailing her limbs in the outrageous need to escape until once more a needle was pushed into her arm and she dropped for a time into a shallow pool of calm.

Nevertheless she received some consolation from Canon Palmer, who on the afternoon of 6 January spent half an hour with her, then returned to the office of Dr Morton.

He informed me that the prisoner wanted to have his ministrations, he proceeded to tell me how difficult it would be owing to all his engagements but that he would cancel everything & spend the whole of Monday with her except ½ hour which he would want for 'his office'.

I informed Canon Palmer that it would be necessary for me to speak to the Chaplain on the matter & having had his comments I would then have to present the facts to the Prison Commissioners. I promised to telephone if permission was given or not.

The Chaplain was not at home & I thereupon visited the prisoner and asked her if she had any remarks to make to me in connection with Canon Palmer's visit. She replied, Oh yes I want him to attend to me or words to that effect.

I then rang up the Commission & spoke to the Secretary Mr Wall who raised the point what religion Canon Palmer was & informed me that he knew there was a Canon Palmer of Ilford who was a Roman Catholic Priest.

Wall instructed me to find out the Chaplain's or Roman Catholic Priest's views in the matter as the case might be & if they objected Canon Palmer could not visit.

The canon was a Catholic, of course. Edith had known this perfectly well, but when asked by the prison chaplain if she wanted to convert to Catholicism, she said that she did not. She had two and a half days left to live; she did not have time for this. But Morton, a beleaguered placeman, who did not dare subvert the rules and was frankly terrified of Wall, telephoned the canon on Sunday 7th and informed him that he could not visit Edith again.

'He asked had the woman refused to see him & why would I not admit him, in reply I informed him I could give no reason on the telephone & referred him to the Home Office, which he said he would visit tomorrow (Monday).' Craven and fearful for his job – about such an episode, an attempt to cast a speck of light upon Edith's dwindling hours – Morton wrote in his report that he been wholly unaware of Canon Palmer's religion; he had instructed the man to visit Thompson as a *friend* only; and all in all he was terribly sorry and anyway it wasn't his fault. He was putting his story forward, gabbling it on to the official blue pages, before Canon Palmer should stride into the Home Office and ask what on earth was going on with you people: why a woman facing death had been capriciously deprived of his company.

The canon was his own man, not part of this tight-lipped system. He let the story be known of how he was turned away from Edith Thompson, and soon after her death reports began to spread that she had been denied the comfort of a priest. Slightly panicked, especially when the stories began to catch fire in the new Irish Free State, the Home Office prevailed upon Sir Ernley Blackwell to come up with one of his gruesome responses, minuted thus:

> We could say that Mrs Thompson was a member of the Church of E. & was receiving the ministrations of the Church of E. Chaplain. When asked whether she wished to become a member of the Roman Catholic Church she stated definitely that she did not. It was therefore impossible to allow Canon Palmer to visit her except as a friend & this he had been allowed to do upon Jan 6th. Mrs Thompson had not been acquainted with him previous to that visit and was then unaware of the fact that he was a Catholic Priest.

By February 1923, the matter had still not gone away. It was taken up by the Graydons' MP, who asked a question in the Commons. Afterwards Mrs Graydon wrote to him: 'The reply the Home Secretary gave you re the visit of Canon Palmer to my daughter is an absolute falsehood.' The mother became fiery as well as embittered after the execution. She wrote letter after letter to the Home Office demanding the return of the 'black costume' that she had lent Edith for the trial; the damn suit was an irrelevance, but why should *they* have it? They did not have it, in fact. Edith had been hanged wearing it, so the suit was destroyed. They were reluctant to say so, even though *they* had done the hanging. So Mrs Graydon simply kept writing – about the return of the suit, about the return of her daughter's body, about the burial site – she was having none of their nonsense. After fifty years of obedience and belief in the benevolence of the law, she was no longer content to know her place.

On the subject of Canon Palmer, she wrote that Edith was

> fully aware of the fact that he was Father, and his visit to her on the Saturday was one of the happiest half hours that she had had while there. If he was allowed as a visitor why was he not allowed to see her during the visiting hours of Monday. As to Spiritual Advisor he was much more capable of this than the Senior Chaplain of the Prison, who allways made his visits to her most objectionable, as he was very pressing for a confession, and many times she told him she had nothing to confess being quite inno- cent of the crime before and after.

Despite the priest's visit on 6 January, and the expectation that he would return on Monday, her last full day of life, Edith was deteriorat- ing fast. Dr Morton wrote:

> She did not sleep well on Saturday night & complained of bad headache on Sunday morning when I visited. I considered the headache was rendered worse by the fact that her bowels had not moved for 2 days & gave suitable treatment with satisfactory result. On Sunday night I decided to give her 1/6 grain of morphia. She slept very well and was cheerful & talkative in the morning.

The drugs, perhaps. But one begs leave to suggest that Morton was not telling the whole truth. That day, Sunday, she was seen by Margery Fry. After the trial she had refused a different prison visitor; now perhaps she thought it would at least fill an hour or two. She sat facing the woman with the kind, clever, unreachable eyes, and she refused to do the proper things such as admit guilt, show remorse, prepare to meet her maker. She was flimsy, all right, but she was also innocent. So she told Margery Fry, who was perplexed by the 'foolish girl'.

Also that day two 'reply paid' telegrams were handed in at East Ham. The text was identical: one was sent to Queen Mary at Sandringham, the other to George V at Buckingham Palace.

> May I humbly beseech Your Majesty as last resort to exercise your Royal prerogative of mercy towards my daughter Mrs Thompson now under sentence of death I am broken hearted at the terrible injustice of her sentence caused entirely by prejudice
> Mrs Graydon

★

But something else was happening on 7 January, more than the hopeless sending of telegrams to people who might feel a qualm, a moment of fellow feeling, then put it to one side and go into luncheon, more than Margery Fry and her impersonal goodness that consoled so little.

Freddy Bywaters, who had murdered crudely and pointlessly yet had in him much that was good, had determined to die nobly, seeking for the last time to save Edith Thompson. During a visit from his mother on Saturday 6th, he sobbed like a child as he said: 'I swear she is completely innocent. She never knew that I was going to meet them that night. She didn't commit the murder. I did. She never planned it. She never knew about it. She is innocent, innocent, absolutely innocent. I can't believe that they will hang her.'

So much misery; so easy to have stopped at least some of it.

Later Mrs Bywaters would vehemently deny that Freddy had said these things. But that day, out of love for her son, she allowed some of her last moments with him to be dominated by thoughts of the woman. To ease his mind, her own no longer being of any account, she deployed her old, capable skills and encouraged his cousin, Agnes Simmons, to go to the offices of the *Daily Express*. The editor Beverley Baxter – later an MP and ferocious campaigner against the death penalty – had continually urged Edith's reprieve. Now Baxter contacted the Home Office, where he was informed that Bridgeman was at his country house. Then he rang the solicitor Stern, with the news that in the presence of prison warders Bywaters had confessed and exonerated Edith Thompson; effectively, had made a new statement. Stern consulted with Sir Henry Curtis-Bennett. Both men were convinced of the innocence of their client (although Curtis-Bennett believed that she would have been rightly convicted under the second indictment at the Old Bailey). Both in their way had done their best for her. Now Stern, unable to shrug and look away, decided that he must speak to the home secretary in person. The telegram was sent:

> Mr Bridgeman Home Sec Leigh Manor Minsterley Salop
> Am coming down from London tonight in Hope of seeing you
> On matter of vital importance
> FAS Stern

Confronted by the prospect of travelling across the country on a freezing Sunday in winter, Stern tried to command a plane to fly to Shropshire. Having failed to find a pilot before darkness fell – in the middle of the afternoon, at that dire time of year – he took trains and finally hired a car. He had no reason to know whether Bridgeman would even see him as he bustled and motored towards the charming manor house, where the secretary of state was doubtless seated beside a fire in an armchair: the image of delight that Edith had conjured for Bessie Akam, in a letter written on 3 January, when she still had hope ('with a nice book – yes, and some nuts, I think'). Before Stern left he had given a brief interview to Baxter's *Daily Express*:

> There are several facts I wish to lay before the Home Secretary, the most important of these being a new confession from Bywaters. This confession makes it more than ever clear that Mrs Thompson had nothing whatever to do with the murder...
>   Then I want to direct the consideration of the Home Secretary to what I believe is a growing public feeling of disquiet... the

thoughts in the minds of so many people that there is a doubt. I cannot rest until I make this final effort.

The next day, Monday 8th, the *Express* published the story under the headline: 'Final Effort to save Mrs Thompson – New Facts', and reported that Bridgeman, who did indeed agree to see Stern when he arrived at 11pm, 'has promised to consider the postponement of the execution of Mrs Thompson and said that he would communicate with Mr Stern at London tomorrow.' Tomorrow, of course, was cutting it fine for postponements. What actually happened was recorded in a Home Office file; Bridgeman listened to Stern but told him that there was nothing new in what Freddy Bywaters said. It was not true that he ever considered postponing Edith's execution. At 6.35pm on 8 January a civil servant rang Stern's clerk, saying that a letter was in the post: 'but as it wd not reach Mr Stern till tomorrow he read to him the communication sent to the Press this evening to the effect that Secretary of State found no ground for departing from his decision in both cases.'

The home secretary was accorded police protection. A couple of months later an anonymous poem was sent to him, a poor but passionate relation of Shelley's 'The Mask of Anarchy', which began: 'Poor Edith Thompson shrieking in her death cell/ Bridgeman running howling down the endless corridors of Hell.'

Virginia Woolf had heard Edith screaming too, or so it seemed to her, in the early hours of Sunday. Her friend Margery Fry would later be at Holloway. The presence of the condemned woman was in the air like London smoke, and her soft blurred face was an image in the collective mind's eye. Now, unable to sleep at her house in Bloomsbury, Woolf heard a woman cry, 'as if in anguish, in the street, and I thought of Mrs Thompson waiting to be executed.'

Edith was under the nation's skin, more so than Freddy; although the sympathy for him was greater she had caused disquiet; in the hours before her death just as she had throughout her life.

★

'She remained cheerful during Monday took all her food & smoked several cigarettes.' So wrote Dr Morton, lying his head off to placate the Prison Commissioners. She stayed in bed through the morning, as had become her custom. Having been denied the presence of Canon Palmer she was visited instead by the Bishop of Stepney, who brought her a message from Freddy Bywaters. Be Brave, perhaps. Then she waited for her family, slumped in her cell with the four attendants, calmed with drugs, while in the execution shed the apparatus was tested for the last time, the gutta percha having been warmed and manipulated in accordance with correct procedure. The sandbag would be left in place overnight, the shed locked, the key kept by the Governor.

The final visit from her family – parents, sister, brother, aunt Lily – was lightened immeasurably, which may or may not have been a good thing, by an event that had taken place as Mr Graydon was entering Holloway. He was handed a message that apparently came from Lord Bethell, an Essex MP, which read: 'I have sent telegram to the Home Secretary and the king for pardon for your daughter. Good news coming.'

Well now! – they entered the cell all smiles, which wavered only momentarily at the sight of Edith no longer putting a face on things, scarcely able to rise to greet them. Who could have doubted it, Edie, eh? The last-minute reprieve: that was how these things worked. That was *how they did it*. In the eighteenth century it had been the horseman waving a piece of paper, galloping towards the hanging tree. In the twentieth century it was a chain of bureaucracy that slipped a link as somebody, for some reason, decided to break from procedure. As had always been going to happen. Whoever had thought that Edith – Edith! – would end her days in such a way? Not the golden girl of the Graydons. The one who had been a bit daft, sailed near to the wind, made a spectacle of herself, for sure; it wasn't going to be easy for her, but who cared about that as long as she was here. No, it had all been put right before the worst had happened. Eh, Edie.

She herself was too slow and bewildered to make sense of what they said. She was wearing her dressing gown, had not bothered to make much of this last day. Not your last day, Edie! It was always going to be all right, in the end! 'Don't you worry about it,' said Mr Graydon, 'you'll be home with us tomorrow night.' Yes, she said quietly, take me home. She had said it before, and it had broken his heart, but this time – well. It would be happening, because it had to.

So they left her in a muddle of cheerful laughter that suppressed sick twists of agony, of hands clutching hers in a despair that they told themselves was quite unnecessary, because they would soon be seeing her again, of eyes looking deep into hers as she blinked and tried to focus. They left her.

She was moved to a new cell, in E wing. It had a door leading to the execution shed. The walk was a matter of seven yards although she would not be able to do it. At that point – by which time the Graydons had realized what they had of course always known, that the message from Lord Bethell was nothing of the kind, it was a fake from a person evil in a way that Edith did not know how to be – the Governor entered the cell and told her, finally and definitively, that the law must take its course.

From then on it was a fight. Some of those around her had compassion, others did not. It was a job that had to be got through (although what would have happened if they had all said no, we can't do it?). Some of them were fitted for it, others less so. Morton felt, no doubt rightly, that the only thing to do was drug the woman into semi-consciousness, and then pray to get through the hours, the minutes, the tick-tock-tick. If only they could have let her slip away, drift into the dreamscape that she had always loved, but the law did not work like that.

'On Monday night I gave her another injection of morphia at 9.30pm.' She asked for her musquash coat, her wedding ring and the letters that she had received in jail to be given to her mother. 'I promised that I would forward her application to you for consideration,' Morton wrote the next day to the Prison Commissioners, who granted the request. The report continued:

'She did not go to sleep until 11 pm, by 12 midnight she was sleeping soundly and remained asleep until 3.15 am was awake for about half an hour and slept again till 5.15am.'

True? Well, perhaps. Her dreams, though; what if her dreams had been of freedom.

★

Freddy Bywaters was easier. He was physically brave, and exhorted his mother to be so too. He was actually guilty of something, which made the grotesque retribution more bearable, although what he struggled to bear was the thought of what he had done to the woman, with her body made for pleasure and her mind full of mysteries. He had tried, however, and right up to the end he continued to do so.

On the 8th, Freddy wrote to an unknown friend in his *Boys' Own* idiom:

> I want you now that you know Edith always to love and cherish her memory as a bravehearted, noble, and loyal woman. You can understand what she has suffered. Don't pity her, but love her. We will soon be together, and what was not to be on this sordid plane, the land of cowards and curs, will be in another world.

He spent some of the night talking to the Governor of Pentonville: 'he told me how beautiful were the colours of the Aurora Borealis, and the wonderful sunsets, and about the strange lands he had visited...

'I looked at this lad, and I thought, Is it necessary to take his life?'

A few minutes before his execution he was reported, in a Home Office file, to have said that he was 'sincerely sorry for what he had done'. Then he said: 'Edith Thompson had nothing to do with the crime.'

This, together with the statement that he had made on 6 January, led to a memorandum being produced immediately after his death. It hinted faintly at official discomfiture, and duly soothed the very remarkable conscience of authority.

Assuming, therefore, that he had abandoned his former attitude as regards himself that he admitted his guilt and wished at any cost to his own memory to exonerate Mrs Thompson, feeling that his words uttered at the last moment must be given the fullest possible credence, his statement nevertheless falls far short of proving Mrs Thompson innocent of murder.

That Mrs Thompson incited or persuaded Bywaters to remove or help to remove her husband by <u>poison</u> is proved by her letters as clearly as anything can be in a Court of Law.

Her expression 'be so jealous that you will do something desperate' suggests that she not merely intended that the method of effecting her husband's removal was not to be confined to poison but was indicating the means actually adopted by Bywaters.

Both morally and legally his statement does nothing to exonerate Mrs Thompson.

I think it is well to put this aspect of the case upon record...

★

What they took from her.

'My own very darlingest boy,' she wrote in a letter of 15 May,

I received the mail this morning but am not going to answer it yet. I've got several other things I want to tell you, and talk to you as well. I had no time to read your letter alone, so what do you think I did darlint. I got on the top of a bus – back seat by myself and went to Hyde Park Corner in my lunch hour and read it. I couldn't stop in in the lunch hour – it was such a glorious day in fact it has been a beautiful week end warm and sunny – quite warm enough to wear very thin clothes and not feel cold   I do love this weather – it's not too hot yet – but even it is I'm not going to grumble – this winter has been terribly long and cold...

She was awake at 5.15am on 9 January, and Dr Morton reported that 'she was given a mug of tea which she enjoyed and smoked 1 cigarette. When the night officers left her at 6.30 her condition was described as cheerful.' She dressed in her mother's black suit, fastening the hooks and eyes with fingers that refused to work properly, and tied back her hair. She was given, ridiculously, some toast and an apple.

By this time Holloway, the whole great castellated monstrosity, was alive with animal tension. The other prisoners were unable to sleep: they were with Edith, their imaginations pierced to the quick: what was it like to be her? To have lost even their thin shadow of freedom? The cold gracelessness of it all. The stone and brick, the rough hood and the rougher rope, the hands with their quick shoves and grips, all to push a breathing woman through a trapdoor. All these men now in the prison, the officers brought in from Pentonville – Woods and Young – assistant executioners in case she kicked up rough, and then the other man, down from Rochdale, the one with the hangman's hands: John Ellis.

The deputy governor Mrs Cronin was also there, as was Dr Dora Walker, a woman of about Edith's own age, who lived to be ninety. Her account of the event, given to the authorities in 1956 prior to a House of Lords debate on the subject, was convincing: it seemed that she had forgotten nothing of it.

Much of the country woke to the instant awareness of what was being done. It would have felt any number of things, a heaviness, a thrill, a guilt, a righteous refusal of guilt, perhaps above all a relief, that after so long and fraught a journey they had arrived at last at the sight of the words 'Ilford Executions Today' (although not at Shakespeare Crescent, the paper boy had been told not to deliver). It would be done, at least. The clock would move on to 9.01. 'Come on mate, it'll soon be over': that was what William Young said to Edith as he lifted her around the waist. What else could he say? There was no other consolation possible; but still, could he not have afforded her some courtesy, some respect, some last sound in her ears that she was a woman, no longer a convict at this moment.

There were people congregated outside Holloway, held back by the police horses, holding umbrellas against the thin cool drizzle – a crowd of some 4,000 according to the *Daily Mail,* and still more at Pentonville: the ones who were compelled by the great drama, and among them those who were not comfortable with what was happening. But there were many who felt otherwise, because they wrote to the home secretary to tell him so. They wrote to the newspapers about it. This, for example, was published in *The Times*:

Two years ago the Legislature, by an Act of the widest application, removed, as thoroughly as legislation could remove, all the disadvantages, or supposed disadvantages, which women suffered merely by reason of their sex. It must also have intended to remove – again as far as possible – the 'sex disqualifications' that tended in the other direction. If there was some plausibility before 1920 in the proposition that a woman's sex disqualified her from suffering capital punishment, there is none now.

And then there was the Thompson family, overlooked in the clamour – except when Richard gave his interviews to *Lloyd's Sunday News*, his attempt to ensure that Edith was not reprieved: presumably they felt that here was something for them, beyond the abstract acknowledgement of their loss? Although Percy, who in his way had loved his wife, would surely not have wanted this to happen. Poor Percy, who had also wanted to live, but had at least not walked down Belgrave Road in the certain knowledge that he was going to die.

As for the Graydons and the Bywaterses, about to become members of that strange sad-eyed fellowship – the families of the hanged – their pain was beyond encompassing, it stretched out towards unreachable places, as Edith's imagination had once done.

'I visited her between 8 & 8.30 she was calm and I think had been crying. I gave her a hypodermic injection of strychnine 1/32 grain.' This was a stimulant, because she could not be comatose. 'I injected her again at 8.40 and gave her scopalmine morphine (Purlight sleep)

1/100 grain & morphia 1/6 gr.' This was a sedative. The scopalmine contained hyoscine, one of the poisons she had been suspected of administering to Percy, because she had cut out a piece in a newspaper that mentioned it. During the evidence-gathering that preceded the 1956 Lords debate, this mixture of drugs was remarked upon by a Dr Snell (Morton was then dead): 'he says he has never known such a combination of stimulant and sedative to be given and cannot account for it. It may be that the Governor thought the earlier injection had had insufficient effect and thought it prudent to resort to sedation. In Dr Snell's view the sedative was strong enough to send a normal person to sleep but it would not have its full effect on a person in Mrs Thompson's position, particularly after the injection of the stimulant.' It seems that Morton was trying everything, anything, just to get it over.

The chaplain – who had made his petty protest against the visit of Canon Palmer, and later atoned for it with his description of hanging as 'judicial murder' – was now in the cell, speaking words that Edith had known all her life, since her visits to Sunday school in the little church where she married, but which meant nothing to her. Morton wrote that the chaplain 'informed me that very shortly after I gave her the second injection she became dazed and was in this condition when the executioners entered the cell.'

The assistants Woods and Young came in together through the main cell door. Ellis, who was in the shed, approached from the other direction and left the door open that led to the trap. In 1956 Mr Woods, whose memory was very good, gave a statement in which he said that he had been watching Edith for several minutes beforehand.

'At about 8.55am on the morning of the execution I looked through the observation hole in the condemned cell. Mrs Thompson was lying on the bed.'

At two minutes to nine, she was asleep.

AFTER

' "I do pity her. Who needs pity more than a woman who has sinned?"

' "You always forget that punishment is part of the scheme, an extremely necessary part of it... The Paradine woman will be hanged after three clear Sundays." '

Spoken in Alfred Hitchcock's *The Paradine Case*, 1947

THE STORIES ABOUT Edith Thompson's execution were beginning, even as the inquest was being held on her body. The *Daily Mail* report on 10 January, which the authorities later claimed to be accurate, was sanitized to an extent that implies a desire to quash such rumours at birth: the newspaper had always supported the upholding of the death sentence. It read:

If dazed, she appeared calm, but at the appearance of the executioner, who pinioned her in a few seconds, she gave way to distressful moaning.

Nevertheless, she was surprisingly calm on her way to the scaffold. She could have walked unaided, but gentle support was given her at either side, so that her weakness should not delay proceedings. She had but 7 yards to walk.

At 9 o'clock, as the clocks chimed the hour, she had paid the penalty which the law had decided was her just punishment.

The only intimation that the executions had taken place was the exhibition outside the prison gates in each case of a small black printed card with an official statement signed by the Sheriff of Essex and the Under-Sheriff and the governor.

In the large crowds assembled few questioned the justice of the sentences, but there was deep sympathy with the families of both Mrs Thompson and Bywaters.

The bodies were left hanging for an hour, again in accordance with due process, then were washed. The inquest on Edith took place in an office within the prison, some distance from the execution shed. Formal identification was made, yet another absurdity: in Freddy's case this was done by a detective, which implies that his mother was unable to face it, although Edith was identified by Mr Graydon, along with – of all people – Detective Inspector Hall. Both parents and Avis saw the body.

A couple of months later, when Mrs Graydon was engaged upon her fight with the authorities for the return of her black suit – displaying a toughness that reads almost repellently, as if all her old soft feelings had been surgically removed – she was told that Edith had been buried in the clothes. She wrote to Sir John Anderson:

> I was the last person to view my daughter's body at the inquest… when she was wearing what the Prison Officials told me were her burial clothes, namely, her silk under-clothes only! She was at this time already in her shell. How then could she possibly be buried in my blouse and costume?

The Home Office, somewhat at a loss, wrote on the file that contained this letter:

> MINUTES: She has read HO 241 as meaning that Thompson was <u>buried</u> in her clothes & suggests this cannot have been the case.
>   In fact these articles were destroyed.
>   ? Say that it was not suggested in the previous HO that her daughter was buried in the clothing in question. She was however, as was there stated, wearing them at the time of her execution, and they cannot therefore be given up.
>   Are these prisoners buried in 'shells'? Did Mrs G. see Mrs Thompson's body as she describes & were the outer clothes actually destroyed?
>
> Reply: Please see the Governor's reply herewith.
>   a) She was buried in an ordinary elm coffin.
>   b) Mr Graydon asked that he might with his wife and daughter be allowed to see the body. This request was made to me as I

was coming out of the mortuary with the Coroner. I said to the Coroner is it your wish that the relatives should see the body to which he replied 'Oh yes for the purpose of identification'. I therefore allowed the relatives to see the body.

    c) The outer clothes were burnt.

Mrs Graydon's cold anger was not to be contained. It probably kept her going. Meanwhile Avis, who had to live with this as well as so much else, wrote in a more naive spirit to the governor; her letter is missing but on 22 January Dr Morton forwarded it to Prison Commissioners, along with this covering note.

> I beg to submit a letter from the sister of the abovenamed, written at the request of her parents, expressing their thanks for kindness and consideration towards both the family and the abovenamed.
>
>   The attached letter may be useful to the Commissioners in case they should decide to take any action should statements of ill-treatment &c. towards the abovenamed whilst in custody here occur in the future.

Mrs Graydon had it right, really.

★

The inquest verdict stated 'That the said Edith Jessie Thompson died from fractured dislocation of the cervical vertebrae and so do further say that the deceased was duly executed by law.'

    The form detailing Particulars of the Execution read:

The length of the drop as determined before the execution.

6 feet 10 inches

The length of the drop, as measured after the execution, from the level of the floor of the scaffold to the heels of the suspended culprit.

7 feet ----- inches

Approximate statement of the character and amount of destruction to the soft and bony structures of the neck.

Bruising of neck from rope. Fracture of odontoid process and right half of arch of Axis

Height

5 feet 7 ¼ inches

Build

Spare but muscular

Weight in clothing (to be taken on the day preceding the execution) 130 ¼ lbs.

Character of the prisoner's neck

Well developed.

But the question was what lay within those neatly inked responses, and it would be asked, repeatedly, almost from the first. On 15 January an anonymous letter was sent to Dr Morton:

You must feel a very proud man after the splendid way you and your assistants murdered that woman on Tuesday last. Had you a spark of humanity in you it would have been an easy matter to phone the Home Office and told them it was impossible on humane grounds to carry out the sentence, instead you allow an unconscious woman to be carried out and hung – good God man didn't you ever have a Mother or some sisters. Had I been in your place I would rather beg bread or find it in the gutter than draw money for murdering women and what was in my estimation an innocent woman.

Your time will come to die some day and please God I hope

your dying agonies will be a thousand times more severe than those you helped to inflict on that woman. As a medical man you tried all night to rouse her instead had you been anything but a bloody inhuman brute you would have had the decency to leave her alone.

Its too late now for regrets but my God if I were in your place I should have some.

How pleased I would be to take you to the same scaffold together with those men that helped you, those old doddering judges and the Home Secretary and hang the lot of you – the world would be well rid of such a set of inhuman brutes.

Which implied that some facts had already emerged, as inevitably they would, given the number of people involved in the execution. This particular writer could be dismissed as a hysteric, but there would have been enough there to create unease (what else might be said, and by somebody more coolly persuasive?) and to treasure Avis Graydon's dignified letter as a possible means of rebuttal. Indeed the reaction to her letter was an admission in itself. So too was the police protection given to the home secretary and, subsequently, to Dr Morton.

Controversy about the Edith Thompson execution arose on three specific occasions: in 1930, when the Holloway chaplain gave evidence to the Select Committee on Capital Punishment; in 1948, when a Royal Commission was debating the abolition of the death penalty; and in 1956, when Arthur Koestler's book *Reflections on Hanging* was serialized in *The Observer,* and allegations about the event were debated in the Lords. But how it all began – what started the rumours – was a rumour in itself: Beverley Baxter claimed that on the afternoon of 9 January he was visited at his *Daily Express* office by two men who identified themselves as officials at the hanging. In 1948 he told the Commons – during a debate about abolition – that their faces were 'not human. I can assure you, Sir, they were like people out of another world. Edith Thompson had disintegrated as a human creature on her way to the gallows, and yet somehow they had to get her there.' Both Young and Woods strongly denied this visit to Baxter, regarding it as a breach of the Official Secrets Act and a slur upon their professionalism. When the story was repeated in 1956, a civil servant at the Home Office wrote:

> The Lord Chancellor of the day (Lord Jowitt) expressed the view in 1948 that the statement would have been actionable if it had been made outside Parliament and would in his view have entitled the two officers to heavy damages. Neither Beverley Baxter nor *The Observer*... appears to have made any apology to these two ill-used officers, one of whom has expressed to the Home Office his bitter resentment at the allegation. Beverley Baxter adheres to the story that two men who were undoubtedly 'prison officials' came to see him. He now appears to accept that they were not eye witnesses but adds 'things spread through a prison very quickly'.

A further story was that on the evening of 9 January, Dr Morton called on the editor of the *Daily Mail*, stating that he would never again take part in the hanging of a woman, and asking the newspaper to start a campaign against the death penalty. To this, the civil servant responded:

> Dr Morton and the editor in question are both dead. Miss Davies, who served under Dr Morton, and Dr Methven, a former Deputy Chairman of the Prison Commissioners, both flatly say that it would have been quite out of character for Dr Morton to have done this. Certainly his report on the affair gives no hint that he was upset. Dr Methven says he saw a good deal of Dr Morton at the time and he is sure that Dr Morton would have spoken to him frankly if he had felt strongly on the subject.

The officialdom of 1956 was not much different from that of 1922, of course, in its desire to protect itself. Nevertheless what it said in the files was true enough: in a factual sense. There is no real knowing how rumours start, only that they can never be stopped. The men who visited Baxter were not who they said they were, if indeed there ever was such a visit. The Governor of Holloway probably did not go to the *Daily Mail*; the newspaper's reporting suggested no such intelligence, and Morton remained in the prison service until his death in 1935. The chaplain, who expressed the view that 'the slaughter of women is peculiarly horrible, degrading and brutalizing' at the Select Committee on Capital Punishment, remained in his post until 1929. The hangman, John Ellis, who later wrote that 'Mrs Thompson was in a state of complete emotional collapse... She looked as though she were already dead,' and whose suicide has been connected with the execution, continued his duties for another year. During that time he hanged another woman, Susan Newell. In 1927 he took part in a sideshow act with a toy gallows.

So the authorities, defending themselves shakily, were able to display a certain defiant self-righteousness. They had their facts, as far as they went. However by 1956 – after the wrongful execution of Timothy Evans, the dubious one of Derek Bentley and the controversial one of Ruth Ellis – this was not, in fact, very far.

Then there was the most difficult rumour of all, that Edith Thompson had been pregnant at the time of her death, and that her 'insides had fallen out' when she disappeared through the trap.

This was said repeatedly, and continues to be so, but it was its proclamation in 1956 by Arthur Koestler – a man whose stature made him impossible to dismiss, damn him – that caused most concern. The Home Office file contained the observation:

> Since this sort of statement about the possible effect of execution on women has been made elsewhere, it should be known that nothing of the sort happened at the execution of Mrs Thompson or of any other woman, that there is no reason to expect it to happen, and that no special precautions are taken against its happening.

An additional comment read: 'This is anatomically impossible... the only possibility that bears any relation to this story is that a prolapse would occur. There is no evidence that it did occur.'

The story originated, almost certainly, with Margery Fry. In 1948, during the debate on abolition, it was reported to the home secretary that shortly after the execution she had told the then lord chancellor – Lord Jowitt – that Edith had had to be sewn into leather knickers to prevent the entrails dropping from the body, 'and that when the woman was told why this had to be done she was very much affected.' Unspeakable though this is, if it *had* been done then the still more unspeakable image of the 'insides falling out' could not have happened. Both allegations cannot be true. Nor is it true that Margery Fry was present at Holloway on 9 January. Accordingly a reply was given to the home secretary,

> that no special precautions or special garments were used at the execution of Mrs Thompson. The only special medical attention given to her was a dose of morphia. There does not appear to be any substance in Miss Fry's story of the leather garments.
>
> If a woman were to be hanged who had a tendency to a prolapse of the uterus this might take place, but this would not happen to a normal woman. In any case there would be no actual detachment such as has been suggested.

It is unclear, because nobody would have cared to admit to it, whether or not the women hanged after Edith – eight of them; because furthermore nobody was going to admit that hanging women should never happen again – were indeed obliged to wear protective garments. If they were, however, it was not because Edith's insides fell out. It has long been suspected that evidence as to her pregnancy would be found within the files closed under the 100-year-rule, but there is no such admission, nor was there ever likely to be. Somebody – not least herself – would have noticed three missed periods during her time at Holloway and viewed them as a gift from God. The more likely truth is that she lost an excess of menstrual blood during the drop; or that she simply lost control of her bodily functions.

★

There are three 'official' extant accounts of Edith's hanging, not entirely consistent with each other. The first was taken in 1948 by the assistant executioner William Young, who had contacted Sir John Anderson – by then Lord Waverley, formerly Under-Secretary of State in the Home Office – in order to protest against the account given by Beverley Baxter. Young was subsequently invited to London to tell his story. He did so briskly; neither his sleep nor his conscience was troubled by it.

> As soon as Ellis entered by the other door I went into the cell. I put my arm round Mrs Thompson's waist and lifted her up & said 'Come on mate – it'll soon be over.' The assistant strapped her hands. I kept my arm round her and we led her to the scaffold. I think the other officer had her arm on the other side to me. We got her on to the drop. Her head was on my shoulder and Ellis had to raise her head to place the cap on and then the noose. Ellis stepped off the drop and pushed the lever.
>
> It was as clean an execution as I've seen and when we brought her up there wasn't a mark on her.
>
> During my service I have attended seventeen other executions. There was nothing whatever to distinguish Mrs Thompson's case from the other executions.
>
> When she got on the drop one of the assistants placed a strap round her skirts and another placed a strap round her ankles.
>
> There is no truth in the suggestion that I and the other officer were extremely upset after the execution. We were the only two officers taking part and it is quite untrue that we went to Mr Beverley Baxter's office after the execution had taken place. Nor is it true that Mrs Thompson was in a state of collapse at the time.

According to Mr Young, therefore, Edith had walked with assistance to the scaffold. His account is clearly given with an agenda – all was well, good as gold – and against it in one particular was Dr Morton's testimony. In conversation with Sir Ernley Blackwell, he had explained the origin of the rumour that Edith was carried: her feet, as well as her wrists, were pinioned in the cell.

> The feet are usually not pinioned until the last moment on the drop. It was thought best in this case to do it in the cell. Prisoner was therefore unable to walk and had to be carried the few yards to the drop. Governor thought she could have walked with assistance but if she had collapsed on the way the necessary pinioning of the feet before the drop fell would have delayed matters and been awkward.

Alfred Woods, interviewed in 1956, is more believable – more observant – than his fellow assistant, and essentially gave an account that contained elements of both Young and Morton.

> With Mr Young I went into the condemned cell at about two minutes to nine. Mrs Thompson got up from the bed, the two woman officers helped her up, she appeared to have been asleep. She then realized her time had come and she gave a moan and collapsed. The other officer and I caught her and me on one side and the other on the other we held her up – still in the condemned cell – whilst the executioner Ellis put the strap round just below her knees and strapped her wrists behind her back. The other officer and I carried her to the scaffold making a seat of our hands for her. All this time she appeared to be under the influence of dope, the condemned cell smelt strongly of a hospital. We carried her to the scaffold and held her up on her feet while the executioner put the rope round her neck. We stepped back and it was all over in a matter of seconds. She did not use a chair nor did she collapse to the floor before the trap opened.

However: this story of how Edith was transported to the drop may have been concocted, as a 'humane' explanation for her apparent inability to move unaided after the event. Doubt as to its truth arises because it contradicts the recollection of Dr Dora Walker. Edith's near-contemporary, who outlived her by sixty years, was a very different sort of person from the two hardened prison officers, and undoubtedly the most convincing of the witnesses. In 1956 she was living in Exeter, where she was interviewed by the governor of the city prison. Afterwards he wrote to the Home Office:

> the doctor appears to have a very clear memory in spite of the fact that she had a breakdown some time ago & has been a voluntary patient. She came out of hospital almost 18 months ago.
>
> She was most cooperative & told me that she has been considering writing to the Commissioners on the subject. This questionnaire, she said, has helped her.
>
> I felt one could place reliance on what she said.

No connection was made between Dr Walker's breakdown and the event that she had been obliged to witness. Yet it was implicit, all the same. She was not melodramatic in her recollections, she sought rather for exactitude; but it was clear, perfectly so, that she had lived thereafter as one unable to scour certain images from their mind.

She stated that she was in the condemned cell with Edith and watched her go to the scaffold. 'She walked with assistance but appeared to hang back with some slight struggling.' The feet were pinioned on the drop; not in the cell. It had been suggested that Edith was unconscious at the time of her death but the doctor denied this. Seeking to explain, she said: 'She was a woman who had lived a life of unreality & it would appear that the sight of the scaffold brought reality close and knocked her back.' Then, as if still trying to express herself correctly, the doctor wrote in a subsequent letter:

> As far as I can remember, as soon as we had entered the condemned cell the doors into the execution shed were opened, and I saw Mrs Thompson raise herself on her right elbow on her bed and see the scaffold. She might be described as seeming dazed by what she saw. Events then moved very quickly.

Again in an attempt to be as honest as possible, the doctor suggested that the morphine – rather than removing the edge from what was happening – 'might have created an untoward awareness of the scaffold & leave Mrs Thompson without anything other than an animal fear of death.'

Edith did not scream, in the doctor's recollection. It was not quite that.

'She hung back and grunted as an animal going to be killed. It could not be described as a human shout or scream.'

How real it sounds, this account. As such it is far worse than any *grand guignol* rumours of a foetus on the drop. Dr Walker, who helped Dr Morton to wash Edith's body and attended the post-mortem, confirmed that there was no sign of prolapse. She also said, of the hangman Ellis: 'The executioner was most upset & completely broken down. He came out shouting "Oh Christ, oh Christ".' And that, too, sounds true.

★

Susan Newell was executed in Scotland, just months later, in October 1923. It was as if the authorities were saying: we did nothing wrong with the Thompson woman and look, here's the proof, we are doing the same thing again, almost immediately! This is the way things are, in this land of equal rights for women.

And they would prove it again, seven more times: with Louie Calvert in 1926; Ethel Major in 1934; Dorothea Waddingham in 1936; Margaret Allen in 1949; Louisa Merrifield in 1953; Styllou Christofi in 1954; and Ruth Ellis in 1955. It was this last woman – convicted of shooting her errant lover – who had most in common with Edith, being unusually attractive and, by the standards of the time, morally lax. The others, more obvious misfits, had aroused prejudice of a simpler kind, less troubling to the nation's conscience. Louie Calvert was a criminal type (one of her aliases was 'Edith Thompson') who strangled and robbed the woman with whom she lodged. Ethel Major, drab and middle-aged, poisoned her husband. Dorothea Waddingham, a geriatric nurse, poisoned a patient for a legacy. Margaret Allen, a transgender lesbian with mental health issues, battered a neighbour for no apparent motive. Louisa Merrifield – whose husband was acquitted of the same crime – was housekeeper to an elderly woman whom she poisoned for gain. Styllou Christofi, a Greek Cypriot with imperfect English, strangled her daughter-in-law, and eventually was buried in the same plot as Annie Walters, Amelia Sach and Edith Thompson.

To dismiss these women thus is, of course, to play the authorities' game. They were people. But they were also, at the time of their conviction, viewed as dispensable, as worthy scapegoats. In that respect they resembled Edith Thompson. Where they differed from her is that they were guilty of the crime for which they were executed.

What happened to her did not bring about an ending to the death penalty, nor to the miscarriage of justice that cannot be rectified. Nevertheless it was, as became gradually apparent, the beginning of the end. That was the sole but significant comfort: she was not forgotten. She is under our skin still. Her story could not, cannot, be dislodged from our collective memory. She would have liked that.

★

The Graydon parents continued to live at Shakespeare Crescent: Ethel died in 1938 and William in 1941. Their oldest son Newenham, who had supported them staunchly through the trial and aftermath, married and moved to Hertfordshire. The other two, Bill and Harold, who are not recorded as having visited their sister in Holloway (although of course they may have done so), got away: Bill to Australia, where Mr and Mrs Graydon visited in 1934, and Harold to Shrewsbury, where he died unmarried in 1978.

Lilian Bywaters sold up her business and died in Worthing in 1941. Her two daughters and younger son Frank all married, had children, lived their lives; according to Frank's own son, the name of the murderer in their midst was not mentioned.

Avis Graydon moved to Ilford in 1941, and died there in 1977. Fifty years after her sister's execution she said: 'I'm still very sad about

it, very sad, very sad. It's altered the course of my life completely.'
Impelled perhaps in the first instance by Edith's half-hour of consolation with Canon Palmer, Avis converted in 1923 and worshipped
in Stratford. There she became friendly with the sister of a fellow
Catholic and east Londoner, the Leytonstone-born Alfred Hitchcock.
Later, at a church event, she met Hitchcock himself; not for the first
time, as it happened, although neither party was willing to say so. For
Hitchcock had known Avis in her former guise. Her father had taught
him to dance. And Hitchcock remembered her, the game and dutiful
girl headed smilingly for the shelf; he remembered too the fleeting
appearances of her sexy, starry sister, who had disseminated so much
scented vitality and whose fate had naturally fascinated him. It was all
there for Hitchcock, almost every one of his obsessions. For instance
there is much of Edith in the character played by Alida Valli in his
film *The Paradine Case*: Mrs Paradine is a woman of imperishable
romance and allure, not one of his doll-like blondes but an enigmatic
exotic, in love with a handsome younger man and accused of the slow
poisoning of her husband. She arouses her defence counsel to a hopeless self-destructive passion, and excites in her judge an eroticized
desire to condemn her to death. Again, however, the difference is that
Mrs Paradine is guilty as charged, and hangs for something that she
actually did.

In the 1970s, Hitchcock told the story of his connection with the
Graydons to his biographer, John Russell Taylor. Then, when he considered the nice lady with whom he chatted in the church, and the
expression in her eyes, he asked that it be removed.

Released in 1947, *The Paradine Case* was based upon a novel by
Edith's favourite author, Robert Hichens, whose *Bella Donna* had
caused her so much trouble in court. Mrs Paradine, wrote Hichens,
ten years after the Thompson-Bywaters trial, 'had the secret inexplicable gift that here and there a woman possesses, and by its possession
makes men do what are called "mad" things.'

Edith's own words, and the interpretations that her readers may find
in them, are here still, although the letters themselves have vanished.

Sources

This is the first book about the Thompson-Bywaters case written with access to all the Home Office files, including those held under the 100-year rule that have been prematurely opened. The vast two-part file HO 144/2685 collects together a wealth and variety of material, some of which was previously available; some not. Of particular interest, given the many years of speculation on the subject, is the material relating to Edith Thompson's execution and the detailed accounts given by three of those present at the event. Other new information includes the fact that Frederick Bywaters attempted to implicate his lover after the verdicts, although he subsequently reverted to proclaiming her innocence.

Along with HO 144/2685 I read the following police and prison files at the Public Records Office:

MEPO 3/1582
CRIM 1/206/5
PCOM 8/22
PCOM 9/1983
PCOM 8/436

Also 4629/1/1923/15 and 4629/1/1922/371, relating to Sir William Bridgeman.

I should therefore like to thank the enormously kind and helpful staff at Kew, where I spent several weeks transcribing material. I also spent time at the British Library, reading books and newspapers; and I am especially grateful to Vedita Ramdoss, Sound and Vision Reference Specialist, who arranged for me to hear the BBC recording [T10391R C1] entitled *Hanged for Adultery?*

'The Trial of Frederick Bywaters and Edith Thompson' edited by Filson Young, part of the *Notable British Trials* series (William Hodge & Co. 1923), was of course a vital source, although the verbatim record of the trial – held within HO 144/2685 – was still more useful, with its fidelity to speech patterns and to the frequent interpolations by the judge. The 1923 book also carried the speeches given at the failed appeals; and, most valuable of all, transcripts of the extant letters between Edith Thompson and Frederick Bywaters.

I am deeply indebted to two superb books about the Thompson-Bywaters case: firstly, F. Tennyson Jesse's novel *A Pin to See the Peepshow* (Heinemann 1934), which I read as a teenager and which led me to the events upon which it is based; and René Weis's *Criminal Justice* (Hamish Hamilton 1988), a masterpiece of research that makes a passionate, moving and frankly unanswerable call for the guilty verdict upon Edith Thompson to be revoked.

The following were also of great interest and use to me:

Sir Travers Humphreys: A Biography by Douglas G. Browne (George G. Harrap 1960)

Great Cases of Sir Henry Curtis-Bennett by Edward Grice (Hutchinson 1937)

Criminal Days: Recollections and Reflections of Travers Humphreys (Hodder and Stoughton 1946)

Margery Fry by Enid Huws Jones (OUP 1966)

40 Years of Man Hunting by Arthur Fowler Neil (Jarrolds 1932)

We Danced All Night: A Social History of Britain Between the Wars by Martin Pugh (The Bodley Head 2008)

Road to Divorce: England 1530–1897 by Lawrence Stone (OUP 1990)

Detective Days by Frederick Porter Wensley (Cassell and Co. 1931)

Index

Note: Page numbers followed by an n indicate footnotes.

31   32   33

WANSTEAD

Elm Hall

Old Red Ho. P.H.

Red Br.

Stonehall Farm

Rectory

George Green

C C

St Mary's Ch.

The Warren

Lincoln I.

The Castle

Beehive F.

St Andrews

VAUGHAN

Rook I.

The Basin

Cricket Ground

Golf Course

The Grove

The Temple   Grotto

Wanstead Park

Recreation Ground

D

Heronry Pond

Perch Pond

WOODLANDS AV.

NORTHUMBERLAND AV.

Mornington Villas

Sch.

Ch.

Cottage Hosp.

Sewage Works

Rifle

Alderbrook E.

Ranges

Ilford Golf Co.

R. Roding

Alders Brook

E

Cricket Ground

Wanstead Flats

City of London Cemetery

Band Stand

GREAT EAST

Capel Road

Band Stand

F

Manor Park Cemetery

Ind. Sch.

FOREST VIEW ROAD

MANOR PARK STA.

WASHINGTON RD.

WANSTEAD PARK STA.

DURHAM RD.

CLARENCE RD.

Sch.

Ch.

Sch.

HAMPTON   ROAD

CLAREMONT RD.

WINDSOR RD.

Ch.

Wood Grange Pk Cemetery

WOOD GRANGE PK. STA.

SHERRARD ROAD

School

Ch.

G

Ch.

Sch.

HALLEY ROAD

Ruskin Ave.

COLERIDGE AV.

DURHAM RD.

WHYTEVILLE RD.

Jews Cemetery

ROSEBERY AVENUE

Continued on 17

Scale of   0   1   2   3   4   Furlongs

Half a Mile   0   200   400   600   800 Metres